HARVARD THEOLOGICAL STUDIES

HARVARD THEOLOGICAL STUDIES

EDITED FOR THE
FACULTY OF THEOLOGY
IN
HARVARD UNIVERSITY

BY

JAMES H. ROPES AND KIRSOPP LAKE

WIPF & STOCK · Eugene, Oregon

HARVARD THEOLOGICAL STUDIES
XVI

THE TWO TREATISES OF SERVETUS ON THE TRINITY

ON THE ERRORS OF THE TRINITY
SEVEN BOOKS · A.D. MDXXXI

DIALOGUES ON THE TRINITY
TWO BOOKS

ON THE RIGHTEOUSNESS OF CHRIST'S KINGDOM
FOUR CHAPTERS
A.D. MDXXXII

By MICHAEL SERVETO *alias* Reves
a Spaniard of Aragon

NOW FIRST TRANSLATED INTO ENGLISH BY
EARL MORSE WILBUR, D.D.

ISSUED AS AN EXTRA NUMBER OF THE
HARVARD THEOLOGICAL REVIEW

Wipf and Stock Publishers
199 W 8th Ave, Suite 3
Eugene, OR 97401

The Two Treatises of Servetus on the Trinity
On the Errors of the Trinity, Seven Books, MDXXXI,
Dialogues on the Trinity, Two Books, On the Righteousness
of Christ's Kingdom, Four Chapters, MDXXXII
By Serveto, Michael and Wilbur, Earl Morse, D. D.
ISBN 13: 978-1-62564-081-9
Publication date 5/15/2013
Previously published by Harvard University Press, 1932

CONTENTS

INTRODUCTION	vii
LIFE OF SERVETUS	xix
BIBLIOGRAPHY	xxix
TRANSLATOR'S NOTE	xxxvii
ON THE ERRORS OF THE TRINITY, SEVEN BOOKS	1
DIALOGUES ON THE TRINITY, TWO BOOKS	189
ON THE RIGHTEOUSNESS OF CHRIST'S KINGDOM, FOUR CHAPTERS	225

INTRODUCTION

THE little works here for the first time presented in English dress, although they were famous in their time and had significant influence on the development of religious thought in the first two centuries of the Reformation, are now among the world's very rare books. While no census is known to have been taken, it is doubtful whether more than a score of copies are extant in Europe, for the most part jealously guarded in public libraries, while in America there are perhaps no more than two or three copies, even less accessible. The *Dialogues* is considerably rarer than the *Errors*. The original editions can not have been large, and as they soon fell under the ban on account of their heretical character, doubtless many copies were soon destroyed, so that at the trial of Servetus in 1553 none could be discovered to introduce in evidence. The rarity of the originals led to the making of manuscript copies, which are to be found in libraries almost as frequently as the originals.

Nearly two centuries after their first publication these books were still so highly prized and so eagerly sought after that about 1721 the enterprising Lutheran superintendent, Georg Serpilius, observing this, had a carefully simulated counterfeit reprint of both works made at Regensburg, and sought to pass copies off at a handsome price as originals, letting it be whispered that he knew of sources in Poland whence he could procure copies.[1] This reprint is to be found in various libraries, but is itself also very rare and is seldom offered for sale. The reprint of the *Errors* and that of the *Dialogues* were apparently first published separately, but in most extant copies they are bound up together. The counterfeit copies the original page for page and as a rule line for line, even to typographical errors and the table of *errata* at the end, so that it has often been taken for

[1] See his suspicious letter in J. H. Seelen, Selecta Literaria, Lübeck, 1726, p. 54.

the original; but the two are easily to be distinguished from each other by the following marks, among many.[1] The counterfeit uses single hyphens throughout, beginning with the title-page, while the original uses double ones, if any; it uniformly prints *est* with a long *s* (though not in the *Dialogues*); it prints the frequently capitalized CHRISTUS in italic capitals, etc. Bibliographers distinguish two different editions of the *Dialogues*, but the only difference seems to be that in the course of the printing fresh and slightly different ornamental initials were substituted for worn ones on pp. A2a and C6b, and that an error in spelling on the title-page was corrected.

The only translation of the *Errors* hitherto published is one into Dutch by Regnier Telle (Regnerus Vitellius).[2] The author, though a professed Calvinist, favored the Arminian party; and his motive in publishing the translation was, as appears from his preface, to show that Servetus was not so bad as he had been painted. Episcopius, upon being shown the translation, eloquently warned Telle of the evils that might result from publication,[3] and it was withheld for six years until, after Telle's death, the Synod of Dort had made permanent the breach between Remonstrants and Calvinists. Even then the translation of the *Dialogues* promised on the title-page and in the table of contents was omitted. The translation is far from adequate. It often misunderstands, freely paraphrases or even omits difficult passages, and sometimes interpolates the translator's comments into the text, or gives them as marginal notes. It gives little if any help toward understanding the original.

---

[1] A careful collation of the two editions of the *Errors* shows over 2150 cases of typographical differences, which occur on every page but two. More than two-thirds of these are mere matters of punctuation, abbreviations, capitals, accents, spacing, and the like, apart from numerous variations in orthography; but 25 typographical errors in the original are corrected, nearly an equal number are allowed to stand, and half as many new errors are incurred. The most significant change is the substitution in three instances of *Tritheitae* for *Tritoitae*.

[2] Van den Dolinghen in de Drievvldigheyd . . . overgeset in onze Nederlandsche tale, door R. T., etc. (Amsterdam), 1620. 110 ll. 4°. Mosheim speaks also of a manuscript French translation known to him (Anderweitiger Versuch, 315).

[3] Praestantium ac eruditorum virorum epistolae, Amsterdam, 1660, p. 419; Allwoerden, Historia Michaelis Serveti, 167–175; Mosheim, Anderweitiger Versuch, 310–315.

INTRODUCTION ix

Servetus was doubtless impelled to print his work on the *Errors of the Trinity* by the fact that he had failed to make the desired impression upon the reformers at Basel and Strassburg in his oral discussions with them, and he may well have hoped that through the medium of the printed page he might both be more persuasive with them and reach a much wider public. Having been unable to find any printer at Basel or Strassburg who would undertake the risk, he got his books printed at the well-known press of Johann Setzer (Johannes Secerius) at Hagenau in Alsace, some twenty miles north of Strassburg. The rash young author did not scruple boldly to place his name on their title-pages, but the printer was more discreet, though his identity seems to have been soon discovered.

The intention of the work was, as its title implies, not so much to deny the doctrine of the Trinity as to call attention to the errors in the doctrine as it was commonly held and taught at the time, and to set forth a truer statement of it, more consistent with Scripture, more acceptable to reason, and more helpful to piety. The *ad hominem* style of its argument suggests to the reader that it is (especially in its earlier parts) based upon notes of oral discussions previously held with the reformers at Basel and Strassburg, or with fellow-students.[1] It shows evidence of a more or less carefully considered plan, with numerous cross-references; yet it also betrays frequent evidence of haste, is often ill-digested, and is written in rather crude Latin which would be by no means easy to understand, even did it abound less than it does in the terms of scholastic theology. In short, it is such a work as might be expected from a precocious, impetuous, fervent youth of twenty. It is suffused with passionate earnestness, warm piety, an ardent reverence for Scripture, and a love for Christ so mystical and overpowering that the author can hardly find words to express it;[2] while on the other hand he

---

[1] Tollin's view (Henri Tollin, Das Lehrsystem Michael Servet's genetisch dargestellt, Gütersloh, 1876–1878, 3 vols.), that in the work there can be traced five successive stages of the author's thought and experience, while ingeniously defended, seems not to be sufficiently well-founded.

[2] It is significant that throughout the *Errors* (save in Book V., for no clear reason), the names Christ and Jesus are habitually printed in capitals.

burns with anger or overflows with scorn toward those who by their artificial and barren teachings have served to keep men from the saving knowledge of Christ. Hence in the heat of his feeling he is often betrayed into the use of epithets and expressions which gave great and needless offence, and doubtless kept his discussion from being calmly considered on its merits.

Servetus's reasoning is throughout solidly based upon Scripture, and he shows a breadth and exactness of knowledge of it surprising in one of his years. He quotes from or alludes to no fewer than fifty-two of the sixty-six books of the Bible, and six books of the Apocrypha. He uses his citations with the independent freedom of a scholar who has studied them in their original tongues, discusses the proper meaning of the Hebrew or Greek words used, notes the differences between the different versions, and now adopts the Vulgate rendering, now that of Pagnini, and now gives a rendering of his own. Whatever the Bible may say he accepts as authority not to be questioned. In his interpretation of it he is a biblical literalist. While he occasionally adopts the allegorical or mystical interpretations in vogue in his time, his method is in the main well in advance of his age. Influenced perhaps by his legal studies, he makes habitual use of the now accepted hermeneutical principles of interpreting lexically, grammatically, contextually, and in accord with the general tenor of the writing, and he insists that Scripture clearly interprets itself if you rightly compare one passage with another.

He also shows wide acquaintance with the Fathers of the Church, of whom he cites nearly two score. Of these he owes most to Irenaeus and Tertullian, whose interpretation of the doctrine of the Trinity furnishes the key to his own, but their authority is nowhere placed on a level with that of the Bible. Finally, he is familiar with Aristotle and with the mediaeval theologians, Peter Lombard, Thomas Aquinas, Duns Scotus, William of Occam, Robert Holkot, Pierre d'Ailly, Henry of Ghent, and John Major, whom he cites chiefly to expose the absurdity and inconsistency of the views they sustain. From them he appeals to reason, but above all to Scripture; while his citations of the various writers, which are so very numerous in Book I., grow steadily less frequent as his work proceeds.

The contention of Servetus, as has been said above, was not against the doctrine of the Trinity as such, but against the unscriptural and unprofitable form in which it had been presented to him. The scholastics in applying to theology the metaphysics and dialectic of Aristotle had, as has been well said, run out into the discussion of useless and unprofitable questions, which could not be determined, and would be of no practical value if they could. Lombard's *Sentences* contain discussions of many useless and intricate questions — especially in regard to the Trinity, whose meaning it may be doubted whether he himself, or any other man, ever fully understood; and a large proportion of the writings of the schoolmen are just commentaries upon Lombard's four books, full of innumerable questions of the most intricate but most trifling sort.[1] Thus the doctrine which had once been esteemed the very heart of Christian faith, upon the acceptance of which one's eternal salvation depended, had degenerated, Servetus felt, into something wholly artificial, abstract, speculative, sterile, and fatal to vital piety. The scholastics themselves trifled with it and admitted its difficulties, and held that it was beyond all human reason, while the common man could only assent to it by a blind act of faith. Its three persons or hypostases were mere mathematical abstractions, having no relation to the living God, nor to the Christ of the New Testament, nor to the Holy Spirit of Christian experience. Its very terms — Trinity, hypostasis, person, essence, substance — were inventions of philosophers, and had not a shadow of support from Scripture. Its Christ was but a phantom. It was utterly confusing to thought, it led men astray from the correct knowledge of God and into what was in effect atheism, and it offered an insuperable obstacle to the universal acceptance of Christianity, especially by the Jews and the Mohammedans.

Now when Servetus, as a young law student at Toulouse, made his memorable discovery of the Bible, he seemed to see

[1] William Cunningham, Historical Theology, Edinburgh, 1862, i. 415.

the whole substance of the Christian faith in a new light, having as its centre not an artificial, incomprehensible, philosophical concept, but an actual historical person in Jesus of Nazareth; and, as he later testified, he felt moved as by a divine impulse to make this simple and vital object of faith known to the world, confident that it had only to be stated to be accepted on its obvious merits, and that when once proclaimed it would win the whole unbelieving world to Christianity. If the enthusiastic youth had not at once succeeded in commending his discovery to the reformers of Basel and Strassburg, already committed to the traditional view, he still believed that when men once had it carefully stated in print, and could reflect upon it calmly, they would without doubt embrace it. It was thus that these little books came to see the light.

While it would of course be possible out of Servetus's writings to piece together more or less of a system of doctrine, yet he was writing not to set forth a rounded system of Christian faith, but rather for an immediate controversial purpose. It will thus do his thought better justice if a brief review of it is given largely in the order in which he himself presented it. In investigating the doctrine of the Trinity Servetus begins at the near end, the person of Christ. Supporting his argument at every step by ample scriptural proof, he points out first that Christ, instead of being merely an abstract human quality assumed by God, was an actual historical man, as the early Fathers also taught. Yet he was more than merely a man, for he was also the Son of God, because miraculously begotten by the Word of God; not an hypostasis, but a real Son of God by nature. Finally, he was also God, sharing God's full divinity but none of man's imperfections, equal with God in power, though not identical in being, and God in the same sense in which the word is applied in the Old Testament to exalted beings. Likewise, as will be shown later, the Holy Spirit is not a separate being, for this would lead to a plurality of Gods, and belief in that would in effect be atheism. In fact, when speaking of the other two beings, the Bible often fails to mention the Holy Spirit. Scripture proves not the unity of the three persons, but rather their harmony in mind and will; and the current arguments for the Trinity rest upon misunderstanding of Scripture, or upon grounds merely fantastic. There is not one word in the whole Bible about a Trinity, nor about such things as persons, essence, substance, or hypostases. The scholastics have confused the matter by introducing such terms. They are imported from Greek philosophy, lead to countless difficulties, and hinder the spread of Christianity. But if one must use terms foreign to Scripture, let it be said that the three persons of Father, Son, and Holy Spirit are three wonderful *dispositions* of God in which his divinity variously appears, and this is the true Trinity; whereas if we held to one divine essence existing in three separate beings, we should have not a Trinity but a Quaternity.

Having thus canvassed the general field in Book I., Servetus goes on in the later books to take up certain aspects of the doctrine in detail, and with not a little repetition of thought. Thus in Book II. he treats of Christ as the Word of God, and of the Holy Spirit. Christ himself was with God in the beginning, in the form of the Word which God uttered in creating the world. This Word became incarnate in Jesus as God's firstborn, and his agent upon earth, who is proved by his resurrection to be the Son of God, both human and divine. God's spirit animates all men and all things, but when acting within us it is known, in a more intimate personal relation, as the Holy Spirit. It is sometimes an angel, but though distinct from Christ, and divine, it is not a separate being, but a power of God, sent to sanctify and teach us.

In Book III. discussion of the Word is continued. The Word existed before the world, but when once uttered by God, it became incarnated in Christ as God's Son. God's creative power acts through him, and he is given highest honors, but not as an abstract being, and no longer as the Word. To believe in him as Christ, the Son of God, is to be a Christian, and sure of salvation.

Book IV. discusses the three *dispositions* and how they operate, and gives Nature, Person, and Substance their proper definitions. Disposed as the Holy Spirit, God acts only within man. Only through the impersonation of the visible Christ is the invisible God to be seen, represented as by an image; and the Word has now ceased to be. The term Nature should be applied only to God; Person means the representative of another; and Substance means being. In Book V. study of the two Old Testament words for God shows that one refers to Christ as Saviour, the other as Creator. Faith that he is the Son of God is what brings us salvation. The incomprehensible God (Book VI.) is known to us not by our grasping philosophical conceptions, but through Christ, who manifests him. He is not a mere image of God, but an expression of God's very being; and only through faith in him can we know God and experience the Holy Spirit within us. The work concludes (Book VII.) by emphasizing both the deity and the reality of Christ and the Holy Spirit. The spoken Word of God was begotten as the actual Son of God, embodying his whole nature. He was a visible being, and not a mere hypostasis. The Holy Spirit also was an audible reality, and not a mere hypostasis. God has no bodily form but in Christ.

With all its lack of systematic arrangement of thought, its digressions, its inclusion of irrelevant matter, its repetitions, and its apparent inconsistencies, the central features of Servetus's criticism of the prevalent form of the doctrine of the Trinity stand out with tolerable distinctness: his objection to the use of non-scriptural philosophical terms in speaking of God, Christ, and the Holy Spirit; his special repugnance to the concept of an *hypostasis* as applied to a person of the Trinity; his conception of the Trinity as a series of *dispositions* of the divine being for different offices; his oft-repeated insistence upon the concrete reality of Christ as the centre of Christian faith, and of the Holy Spirit as the power of God working within man; his passionate attachment to Christ as the complete embodiment of God in human form; and his view that men are saved not by an attitude of personal faith in Christ, as the Lutherans taught, but by an intellectual belief that he was the Son of God.

Both in his criticisms and in the positive views which he put forth so confidently there was much to arrest attention, and the book met a various reception. It was approved so widely that the reformers became apprehensive of the harm it might do. Melanchthon himself confessed to reading the book a good

INTRODUCTION

deal, and both he and Oecolampadius admitted that it had some good points. But it had to be accepted or rejected as a whole, and it contained so many objectionable features that any early praise of it was soon drowned out by a general chorus of denunciation from the leaders of the Protestant movement. There were two causes for the violent feeling against it that soon became dominant: the manner of the work, and especially the offensive epithets the author had used against those whose views he criticized; and the objectionable doctrines he had put forth — in particular, that the Word no longer exists, and that the Holy Spirit is an angel. Servetus shrank from the attacks made upon his book, and to correct any mistaken views into which he might have fallen, and perhaps yet more to ward off a possible prosecution for heresy, he offered to publish a further book on the subject, by way of retraction. This book was *Dialogues on the Trinity*, in two Books, together with four chapters on Righteousness.

The book on the *Errors* had been a monologue, but the dialogue was at that time a favorite form for discussing serious subjects. In the *Dialogues* Servetus speaks in his own person, while he puts the objections to his views into the mouth of an interlocutor, Petrucius, who however plays but a minor rôle, and presently retires into the background, not to reappear save for a moment toward the end of the second Book: and he is used not only to present objections, but to give Servetus an excuse for restating more clearly or forcibly the views which he wishes to stress.

Even a cursory reading of the *Dialogues* at once discovers a marked change in tone from the *Errors*. The author is more guarded in statement, and restrains much of his former invective. In his prefatory statement he begins with an apparent retraction of all that he has previously written; but it at once transpires that by this he means not to disown anything that he has said, but simply to complete, improve, and restate it in a form less calculated to give offence. Nor does he in fact withdraw or even modify any of the main features of his thought as above stated. His emphasis is now indeed less on criticism than on the positive elements of his thought. He meets some of the objections that have been made, corrects some misunderstandings, and clears up some obscurities; but for the rest he contents himself with a restatement of his doctrine in its main features, though with a noticeable approximation to the current teaching and phraseology of the Church. He still objects to the *communicatio idiomatum*, while he reaffirms his doctrine of the *dispositions*, stresses anew the true sonship of Christ, and strongly renews his insistence on the visible reality of God in Christ as the centre of Christian faith and worship. The one outstanding instance of his squarely changing ground is at the very end, where he concedes that the Holy Spirit is not an angel.

The concluding tract in four chapters on the Righteousness of Christ's kingdom, which is appended to the *Dialogues*, bears no relation to Servetus's discussion of the Trinity, and is far less controversial in matter and spirit than that. It fulfils a promise made on p. 100a of the *Errors*, and is probably intended to justify the criticisms on the Lutheran doctrine made on pp. 82b, 99b, and 100a. It offers nothing of enough significance to arrest our attention for long. It occupies an intermediate position between the Catholic and the Lutheran view, and does not wholly agree, as it says in closing, with either party. It aims, in opposition to the Catholics (especially the monks), to show that good works in themselves (especially ceremonial works alone) are not sufficient to secure salvation; and in opposition to the Lutherans, that good works have a value in addition to faith; and it insists that love crowns them both.

The *Dialogues* in no wise neutralized the indignation which the *Errors* had stirred up. On the contrary, it was met with a fresh storm of disapproval, and the sale of both books was forbidden at Basel and Strassburg. The Catholics, indeed, paid little attention to them; but among the Protestants they had important consequences in two directions, the one tending to more carefully defined orthodoxy, and the other to bolder heresy. Until now it had not been quite clear what attitude the newly reformed part of Christendom would finally take toward the traditional trinitarian dogma. It had indeed been, as one may say, provisionally retained in the Augsburg Confession in

1530, but the leaders of Protestant thought were plainly wavering about it, in view of its lack of clear scriptural support. Not only had the scholastic theologians said much to bring the doctrine under criticism in esoteric circles, but Erasmus had expunged from the New Testament the chief proof-text. Luther disliked the terms in which the doctrine was stated, and left them out of his catechisms; Calvin had disapproved of the Athanasian Creed and spoken slightingly even of the Nicene, and had only lightly touched upon the doctrine in his Catechism; Melanchthon in his *Loci Theologici* in 1521 had hardly mentioned the doctrine except to pronounce it not essential to salvation; while Zwingli and Farel, Butzer and Oecolampadius, were far from being sound upon it. It thus seems possible enough that if the development of Protestant doctrine could have gone on without disturbance, the Athanasian doctrine might already in the sixteenth century have come to be as far ignored as it is in some evangelical circles to-day. The outbreak of Servetus interfered with all this; and in the face of the Catholic criticism which the reformers still feared might have such serious results for their movement, they made haste to assert their orthodoxy on this point. Melanchthon in his *Loci* of 1535 treats the doctrines in question as absolutely necessary to salvation; Calvin gives them full treatment in his *Institutes* in 1536; and all the Protestant confessions are henceforth unequivocal on this article. Protestant theology, indeed, does not retain the scholastic form of this doctrine — this much, perhaps, it owes to Servetus — but it is more than ever Athanasian.

On the other hand, there were leaders of thought in another direction with whom the views of Servetus found acceptance, and through whom they had an influence that did not die out. It is true that he founded no school of theology as Luther and Calvin and Zwingli did. He disappeared from the scene too early for that in any case, and his sytem, such as it was, was too immature, and too much open to criticism. Hardly one was his professed follower. But wherever his little books circulated, they seem to have opened the doctrine of the Trinity for independent discussion in circles where it had hitherto been regarded as sacrosanct. This was particularly the case in the liberal circles of Italian humanism. Servetus's influence had spread to such an extent in the Venetian republic as to give both Melanchthon and Calvin serious concern. It is thus that he seems to have given the impulse to those who a little later stirred up the ferment of antitrinitarian thought in the Italian church at Geneva, and who, when driven thence, promoted the movement in Poland and Transylvania which eventually developed into Unitarianism. It is this fact that gives Servetus his significance in the history of religious thought in Europe: that he was the fountain-head of the antitrinitarian tendencies that in a half-century after his time had become developed into a well-defined movement. They nearly all seem historically to derive more or less directly from him. Nevertheless, Servetus was not an antitrinitarian, for he held devoutly to belief in the Trinity, such as he defined it to be in accordance with Scripture. Nor can any one read his little books and for a moment call him a Unitarian, or even an Arian. His doctrine has closest affinities with that of Sabellius; but in fact he can not be classified, for he is *sui generis*. His particular teaching has not survived; but his indirect influence has worked like a leaven down to the present day.

A word should be said in closing upon Servetus's last work, *Christianismi Restitutio*, published in 1553, which brought him to the stake. It bears a certain resemblance to the little books treated of here, and in part treats of the same topics in the same order, but while reminiscent of them it is an entirely independent work, and represents a much maturer stage of the author's thought. Most writers upon the theology of Servetus have based their work upon this book. But while it is of high interest to any one wishing to trace the development of the author's thought, the whole edition was at once so nearly utterly destroyed that its historical influence may be considered negligible. In so far as Servetus had influence upon the course of religious thought in the reformation period or later, it was almost wholly due to the *Errors* and the *Dialogues*.

THE LIFE OF SERVETUS

ALTHOUGH one may not feel warranted in indorsing the enthusiastic judgment of Tollin [1] that Servetus was intellectually the equal of the greatest men of his great century, the greatest Spanish scholastic, a forerunner of modern biblical criticism, the founder of comparative geography, the discoverer of the pulmonary circulation of the blood, and an original and independent thinker in jurisprudence, philosophy, history, philology, mathematics, physics, astrology, and materia medica, yet for his adventurous life and tragic death, his extraordinary versatility of mind, his fervent piety, and his influence on the history of both theology and medicine, Michael Servetus, to use his name in its common latinized form,[2] may well be regarded as one of the outstanding figures of the early reformation period.

The data for the early life of Servetus, mainly found in the testimony elicited at his two trials at Vienne and Geneva, are scanty and in some respects contradictory to one another, but it seems likely that he was born in 1511 at Tudela in Navarre, and that while in early infancy he came to Villanueva de Sijena, a small town about sixty miles northeast of Saragossa, where

[1] Henri Tollin, 1833–1902, French Protestant pastor at Magdeburg, devoted nearly forty years of his life to unwearied research into every aspect of Servetus's life, and published nearly four score titles bearing upon it; but his judgments often rest upon slender foundation if any, even when positively stated, and his work needs to be used with watchful caution.

[2] The proper form of the name in Spanish is Miguel Serveto alias Reves; but the ending in -to, the alias, and the name Reves, all unusual in Spanish, long proved a stumbling-block to scholars. It has been assumed that the correct Spanish form must be Servede (so various scholars from Schlüsselburg to Harnack); that alias must have been intended as an equivalent for the Spanish y (so Tollin and Gordon); and that the real name was not Serveto but Reves (so Ceradini); or that this might be only an anagram for Serve; while typographical errors have given Renes, Rennes, or Revers. The correct name might have been observed even on the title page of Servetus's first two books, but the question was not finally set at rest until late in the nineteenth century by the discovery of a series of notarial documents attested by his father, in which the name invariably stands as above given; cf. Mariano de Pano, La familia de Miguel Servet, in Revista de Aragon, Zaragoza, ii., 119, 151, 1901.

the family residence, the casa de Reves, is still shown, the most pretentious house in the community. His father, Antonio Serveto *alias* Reves, was royal notary, his mother was Catalina Conesa, and a brother Juan entered the priesthood. The family lived handsomely. The local church contains an altarpiece dedicated by the mother and brother, perhaps as a sort of family expiation, five years after Miguel's death. It has been conjectured that Servetus may have pursued early studies at Saragossa with a view to the priesthood, but the first that is definitely known is that at the age of fourteen or fifteen he entered the service of a Franciscan friar, Juan Quintana, who a few years later became confessor to the Emperor Charles V. While in this service he went for two years to study law at the University of Toulouse, and while here he entered upon a revolutionary religious experience in the discovery of the Bible. So different was the religion which he found in it from that which he had been taught, and so much more simple and inspiring, that it seemed like a book fallen from heaven, containing the sum of all wisdom and all knowledge; and he felt divinely moved to make his new discovery known to the world.

Servetus was now called to accompany Quintana in the Emperor's train, and thus came to be present at the coronation in Bologna in 1530, where he was forced to contrast the outward ceremonial religion of the Church with the spiritual religion of the Bible. He saw the Pope almost adored as a god by princes and people, and at the same time he saw those in high station in the Church filled with worldliness, skepticism, and immorality. He appears next to have gone on with the Emperor's party to Augsburg, where the reformers were to present their views for imperial approval at the famous Diet. One may conjecture that what he saw and heard of the reformers here led him to believe that there was more hope for doctrinal reform among them than in the Church. At all events, in the autumn we find him at Basel in repeated conferences with Oecolampadius, leader of the reformation there, to whom he hoped to commend his views as to Christ and the Trinity. In this hope he was disappointed, for Oecolampadius found the youth intolerably conceited and obstinate, and at length lost all patience with him. He therefore proceeded to Strassburg, which already had a reputation for liberality in matters of religion, and there sought out the leaders, Butzer and Capito, who, though they had already been warned against Servetus, received him in friendly fashion, and at first gave him apparent sympathy. It was while here that his *Errors* was published. The effect of this work, and the acute fear of the reformers lest it do great harm to their cause, has been noted above in the Introduction. Servetus was forced to leave Strassburg, and returned to Basel, where he seems to have been tolerated until he should publish his recantation, in his *Dialogues*. But when the Rhine country became too hot to hold him, his life nowhere promised to be safe, so that he even thought of running away to sea, or of going to one of the "New Isles" (America). He finally solved his problem by changing not only his place but his name.

His acquaintances in the Rhine cities now lost all track of him, and after a few years the legend became current that he had starved to death in some castle dungeon. The fact was that he had turned up in Paris as Michel de Villeneuve (Michael Villanovanus) of the diocese of Saragossa, and under this name he continued to be known until twenty years later when his identity was exposed at his trial. Records of this period of his life are in confusion, but he seems first to have studied medicine at the College of Calvi, then to have turned his attention to mathematics at the College of the Lombards. Strangely enough, his future enemy, Calvin, was at this same time in Paris, living in secrecy, but already influential among the persecuted Protestants there. Whether they personally met is not clear, but at all events Servetus challenged Calvin to a discussion of religious questions, though for some reason not disclosed he failed to appear at the appointed time and place. Want of money now forced him for a time to interrupt his studies, and he replenished his purse by going to Lyon and securing employment as proofreader and literary editor with the celebrated publishing firm of the Trechsels. His first important work was a revised edition of Ptolemy's Geography, to which he made some original contributions, including some very pungent descriptions of the lands and people that he knew best. A slighting reference to Palestine as a very poor country for a "promised land," which was at his trial cited against him as a defamer of Moses, was not his own, but simply carried over from the earlier edition. A medical work which his employers were publishing, the proof of which he no doubt read, and with whose distinguished author, Dr. Symphorien Champier, he became acquainted, revived his interest in medicine, and after two years or so he returned to Paris for further study.

His medical studies occupied some four years, in the course of which he also lectured on geography and on astrology. He also published a controversial work against Dr. Fuchs of Heidelberg in defence of his friend Dr. Champier of Lyon, and a much more important work on the use of syrups in medicine, which was so much esteemed that it went to the fifth edition within a dozen years. It was in anatomy that Servetus most distinguished himself. Succeeding the celebrated anatomist Vesalius as prosector for Professor Günther, he won the latter's praise as a man very highly accomplished in every branch of literature, and as hardly inferior to any in knowledge of Galen.[1] In these studies it was that he is believed to have discovered the pulmonary circulation of the blood, through the lungs from the right to the left side of the heart, which he was the first to publish.[2] Servetus's career at Paris was brought to an end by an unfortunate incident. His lectures on astrology had been very popular, and had perhaps aroused some professional jealousy, and he had made sharp criticism of the medical profession for its ignorant

---

[1] Johannes Guinterius, Anatomicarum Institutionum ex Galeni sententia libri iiii. Basel, 1539, preface, pp. 7 f.

[2] There is no evidence that Servetus realized the importance of this discovery, or was particularly interested in it, for his only reference to it is the purely casual use of it as an illustration of a point in theology, in his Christianismi Restitutio, 1553, pp. 170, 171. This work was so throughly suppressed before it was published that very few copies were ever seen, and only three are now known to be extant. Servetus's discovery thus remained unknown to the world until 1694, when a London surgeon found and called attention to it; cf. William Wotton, Reflections upon ancient and modern learning, London, 1694, pp. 211–213. Meantime other anatomists had independently made the discovery, which at length was carried out in full by Harvey. Credit for the discovery has given rise to long and warm controversy between those who would ascribe it to Colombo (1559) or Caesalpinus (1569) and those who champion the claim of Servetus; but so far as first publication is concerned, there is no doubt that it was by Servetus.

neglect of the subject. He was remonstrated with, but his only reply was made by publishing a pamphlet containing a discussion in defence of astrology, marked by saucy and even insulting references to his critics. This proved too much for patience to bear. He was haled before the Inquisition charged with heresy, but acquitted; and was prosecuted before the *parlement* (judicial court) of Paris on behalf of the University. If convicted in either case he would have been subject to a sentence of death by fire, but the court contented itself with reprimanding him and requiring him to refrain from lecturing on the subject.

Servetus therefore left Paris. Where he won his doctor's degree is not known, but after a time he settled at Charlieu, near Lyon, where he practised his profession for two or three years. At length, having incurred enmity here, he accepted the invitation of the Archbishop of Vienne, who had known him in Paris, to become his personal physician and live in his palace. Here, from about 1540, he had ten or twelve happy years, not only in treating the sick, to whom he showed much devotion and who became devoted to him in turn, but also in further literary work for the firm of publishers, who had now removed from Lyon to Vienne. Thus he edited a new and revised edition of the Ptolemy, saw through the press two Latin Bibles, and edited a new edition of the celebrated Latin Bible of Pagnino, whose translation was designed to be an improvement upon the Vulgate. To this he contributed an important preface in which he showed himself an independent biblical critic, and marginal notes which show much originality and boldness by their anticipations of modern biblical criticism. He is also said to have seen through the press a Spanish translation of Thomas Aquinas, and to have translated into Spanish several works on grammar.

His interest in theology was thus kept alive, and he indulged it further by trying to draw Calvin into controversy through correspondence. The correspondence soon grew abusive, Calvin's patience gave out, and thus Servetus repeated his method of over twenty years before, and had recourse to print. He already had under way a theological work, the manuscript of a part of which he had sent to Calvin in order to draw him into argument. This was his magnum opus, the *Christianismi Restitutio*, an octavo book of over 700 pages, containing more than three times as much matter as his first two books together. The work begins with five books on the Trinity, and two Dialogues, covering in general the same ground as the two earlier works, and resembling them in plan, form, matter, method, and style, but it is in no sense a reprint of them; for Servetus had presumably dared keep no copy. To these parts much new matter on additional topics is appended, and the author's thirty letters to Calvin are thrown in for good measure. The whole work shows a thought much matured by twenty years of study and reflection, and it presents a view of God which many have regarded as pantheistic. A thousand copies of the work were printed in the greatest secrecy at Vienne early in 1553, but the edition was withheld from immediate sale and reserved for the Easter fairs at Lyon and Frankfurt. In the meantime, however, an acquaintance of Servetus at Lyon, who was in the secret, in a misguided moment sent a copy to Calvin, who acted without delay. Steps were taken by which the identity of Servetus should be betrayed to the Inquisitor at Lyon, and his arrest soon followed. In the examination which ensued, Servetus had poor success in his attempt to evade or explain away the evidence with which he was confronted, but before a conclusion was reached the court adjourned for the night, and Servetus was remanded to prison. That evening he sent his servant to collect a large sum of money due him, and early the next morning, perhaps through the connivance of influential friends, he made his escape. The trial continued without him during several weeks, the books were discovered and the printers identified, and Servetus was found guilty of heresy and condemned to death. In default of his person his effigy was burned, together with his books.[1] The trial had been in the civil court. One in the ecclesiastical court followed, and at the end of the year it too found Servetus guilty, but he had already perished at Geneva two months previously.

From early in April until the middle of August Servetus was a

---

[1] These comprised the half of the edition held at Lyon. The rest had been forwarded to Frankfurt, where Calvin later caused them also to be destroyed.

fugitive from justice uncertain which way to turn for safety. At length he determined to seek Naples, to practise his profession among the large Spanish colony there. Some sinister fate impelled him to go by way of Geneva, and even to spend the sabbath there, and to go to hear Calvin preach. He was at once recognized, and Calvin procured his arrest. After the due preliminary examination Servetus was brought to trial before the Little Council on a long series of charges of a theological nature, though the critical political situation at Geneva threatened also to enter into the case. The charges were judged sufficiently sustained to call for a state trial. The Attorney-General now took charge of the case, which dwelt less on details of doctrine than on the general grounds that Servetus had long been spreading dangerous heresies, had led an immoral life, and was a disturber of the public peace. As the Council did not think itself competent to pass upon the points involved, it was agreed that Servetus and Calvin should conduct a discussion of them in writing, and that the papers in the case should be submitted to the churches and councils of four of the other Swiss cities with a request for their advice. Calvin took the precaution to write in advance to the pastors in favor of his cause, while Servetus had no advocate. When the answers were received after a month, they all agreed upon the main point, that Servetus ought to be got rid of as one dangerous to their common reputation. The Council therefore had no recourse but to pronounce the prisoner guilty of obstinate and persistent heresy and to sentence him to death. Calvin made a vain effort to have beheading substituted for burning. Servetus remained stedfast to the end, and on the next day, October 27, 1553, he perished at the stake at Champel, in the outskirts of Geneva, dying with a prayer upon his lips.

While there were few enough to sympathize with Servetus on account of agreeing with his opinions, there was a strong suppressed feeling throughout Switzerland against the extreme penalty, and this was intensified by the fact that Calvin seemed in the prosecution to be moved by personal animosity. Soon after the tragedy a general revulsion of public feeling took place, and Calvin found himself so widely and cordially hated that he was almost driven to leave Geneva. He never expressed the least regret, however, and in the following year he published a defence of his own course and a bitter attack against Servetus.[1] The leading reformers with one accord expressed general approval of what had been done. On the other hand, some strong voices were now raised in favor of toleration, and against the capital punishment of heretics,[2] so that from this time on opposition to capital punishment of heretics in Protestant countries steadily increased.

Servetus's star had gone down in utter darkness, and however men may have written of toleration as an abstract principle, no one rose up in defence of Servetus as an individual. The judgment was generally accepted without question that he had been an obstinate and dangerous heretic, of whom there was nothing good to say, and it was a century and a half before even a timid voice was raised in his favor. In 1709 Gautier came to his defence in his *Histoire de Genève*, though his massive work was not published until 1896–1914; and in his annotations to the revised and enlarged edition of Spon's *Histoire de Genève* in 1730 he ventured to say that Servetus's views did not seem upon examination to be so detestable as they had been represented. At about the same time a copy of the *Restitutio* came to light in England and aroused fresh interest in its author. Some time before this, Michel de la Roche had made at Geneva a copy of the most important parts of the records of the trial and had published them in London, and in French at Amsterdam. The discovery of the passage on the circulation of the blood stirred up interest in other quarters. From this time on Servetus literature becomes more and more common. Allwoerden's *Historia Michaelis Serveti*, 1728, was the first well documented study; to

---

[1] Defensio orthodoxae fidei (often cited as Fidelis expositio); and in French translation, Déclaration pour maintenir la vraye foi. Answered by Sebastian Castellio, Contra libellum Calvini, 1562; reprinted with new title as Dissertatio qua disputatur, etc., 1612.

[2] Martinus Bellius (pseud. for Sebastian Castellio), De haereticis, an sint persequendi, 1554 and 1610; French trans., Traicté des hérétiques, 1554, 1913; Dutch trans., c. 1620. Answered by Theodore Beza, De haereticis a civili magistratu puniendis, 1554; French trans., Traité de l'authorité du magistrat, 1560. In behalf of toleration again, Minus Celsus, In haereticis coercendis quatenus progredi liceat, 1577; reprinted with new title, De haereticis capitali supplicio non afficiendis, 1584.

be supplanted in 1748 by Mosheim's *Anderweitiger Versuch* and its supplement, *Neue Nachrichten*, 1750. At the same time the Abbé d'Artigny published, 1749, in his *Nouveaux Mémoires* an account of Servetus which incorporated the records of the Vienne trial, now no longer extant. All these works had laid a steadily better foundation for accurate knowledge and a just appreciation, when in 1756 Voltaire published in his *Essai sur les Mœurs* two essays entitled *De Genève et de Calvin* and *De Calvin et de Servet*, which made a stinging attack upon the intolerance of Protestantism as illustrated in this case. It stirred up so much feeling at Geneva that the Syndics resolved that the whole story should so far as possible be buried in oblivion, and for many years no one was permitted to have access to the records of the trial in the city archives. It was well toward the middle of the nineteenth century before the official records were again opened to scholars. By that time the heat of the former controversy had subsided, and at length in 1870 all the documents in the matter, together with much other contemporary material bearing on it, were published in volume viii. of the *Corpus Reformatorum* edition of Calvin's *Opera*. In the meantime Henri Tollin, French pastor at Magdeburg, had become so deeply interested in Servetus that he devoted most of the rest of his life to Servetus studies. He did not live to produce a complete life of his hero, but he published half-a-dozen detailed studies and over sixty periodical articles touching upon every phase of his subject, personal, theological, and medical. Enthusiasm often carried him too far, and his statements must not be blindly accepted, but almost all subsequent writers have rested upon his authority.[1]

The interest which Tollin's incessant writings aroused has led to a steady stream of lives, studies, and articles since his time. The interest reached its culmination with the three hundred and fiftieth anniversary of Servetus's death, when (as the inscription relates) reverent and grateful sons of Calvin in both Europe and America united in erecting an expiatory monument to Servetus as nearly as possible on the exact spot where he had met

---

[1] His work is sharply criticized in detail in van der Linde's *Michael Servet*, 1891.

his fate. With this act the rehabilitation of Servetus may be said to have become complete. Three other monuments were erected not long afterwards, in which the motives seem to have been mixed between freethinkers' dislike of Calvin and all his works, and their desire to honor Servetus: in 1908 at Annemasse (in Savoy, just over the border from Geneva, where opposition was shown to the erection of the monument) and in the Place de Montrouge, Paris, and in 1911 in the Jardin Publique at Vienne. There are also unconfirmed rumors of a monument at Barcelona and one at Saragossa; while at Madrid there is a statue in front of the Anthropological Museum, and a medallion in the courtyard of the Medical Faculty. Streets bear the name of Servetus in Madrid, Vienne, and Geneva.

BIBLIOGRAPHY

OUT of the writer's comprehensive catalogue of more than 600 titles of Servetiana, the following are selected as including all those of most significance either on their own account or for the part they have played in the development of the subject. The arrangement is by titles, roughly in chronological order.

WORKS OF SERVETUS

De Trinitatis erroribus libri septem. (Hagenau), 1531.
> Counterfeit reprint (Regensburg, c. 1721). Dutch trans. by Regnier Telle, Van de dolinghen in de Drievuldigheyd, (Amsterdam), 1620.

Dialogorum de Trinitate libri duo. De justicia regni Christi, capitula quatuor. (Hagenau), 1532.
> Counterfeit reprint as above.

Christianismi restitutio. (Vienne), 1553.
> Page-for-page reprint (Nürnberg), 1791. Partial reprint, 252 pp. (London, 1723). Supposed copy of the first draft, in MS., Bibliothèque Nationale, Paris. German trans. by Bernhard Spiess, Wiederherstellung des Christentums, Wiesbaden, 1895–96. 2 v.

De regno Christi, liber primus. De Antichristo, liber secundus. Accessit tractatus de paedobaptismo, et circumcisione. Alba Julia, 1569.
> Reprint of some 166 pp. of Chr. Rest., with omissions, additions, and transpositions. Probably done by Giorgio Biandrata.

Rozdział Starego Testamentu od Nowego, żydowstwa od Chrześciaństwa, skąd łatwie obaczysz prawie wszystki roznice około wiary (The difference between the Old Testament and the New, from which you may easily see almost all the diversities in matters of faith). n.p., n.d.
> Trans. by Gregory Paulus, and published in Poland, perhaps at Pinczów, 1568. This and the following translate parts of Chr. Rest., as given in the preceding work.

Okazanie Antychrysta y iego krolestwa ze znaków jego własnych w słowie bożym opisanych, ktorych tu iest sześćdziesiąt (Description of the Antichrist and his kingdom with his true signs set forth in the word of God, of which here there are sixty). n.p., n.d.
> Trans. and published as in the preceding.

Ptolemaeus, Claudius. Geographicae enarrationis libri octo. Ex Bilibaldi Pirckeymheri tralatione, sed ad Graeca et prisca exem-

plaria a Michaele Villanovano iam primum recogniti, etc. Lyon, 1535.
> Preface and notes by Servetus. Second edition, revised and freely corrected. Vienne, 1541.

In Leonardum Fuchsium apologia defensio apologetica pro Symphoriano Campeggio. Lyon, 1536.

Syruporum universa ratio, ad Galeni censuram diligenter expolita; cui, post integram de concoctione disceptationem, praescripta est vera purgandi methodus, cum expositione aphorismi: Concocta medicari. Paris, 1537.
> Also Venice, 1545; Lyon, 1546, 1547; Venice, 1548.

In quendam medicum apologetica disceptatio pro astrologia. Paris, 1538.
> Reprinted from the unique Paris copy, with introduction and notes by Henri Tollin, Berlin, 1880.

Biblia sacra ex Santis Pagnini tralatione, sed ac Hebraicae linguae amussim novissime ita recognita, & scholiis illustrata, etc. Lyon, 1542.
> Preface and notes by Servetus.

Primary Authorities

Johannes Calvin. Opera (Corpus Reformatorum), edd. Baum, Cunitz & Reuss. Braunschweig, 1863–1900. 59 v.
> Vol. viii, 1870, has the records of the Geneva trial, and much other contemporary matter by Calvin and others.

Johannes Calvin. Defensio orthodoxae fidei de sacra Trinitate, contra prodigiosos errores Michaelis Serveti Hispani: ubi ostenditur haereticos jure gladii coercendos esse, et nominatim de homine hoc tam impio juste ac merito sumptum Genevae fuisse supplicium. Geneva, 1554.
> Also in Opera, vol. viii. Often cited as Fidelis expositio, the title of a part of the work. French trans., Déclaration pour maintenir la vraye foy que tiennent tous Chrestiens de la Trinité des personnes en un seul Dieu. Contre les erreurs détestables de Michel Servet Espaignol. Ou il est aussi monstré, qu'il est licite de punir les hérétiques: et qu' à bon droict ce meschant a esté exécuté par justice en la ville de Genève. Geneva, 1554.

L'abbé Antoine Gachet d'Artigny. Mémoires pour servir a l'histoire de Michel Servet. Paris, 1749.
> In his Nouveaux Mémoires d'histoire, de critique et de littérature, ii, 55–154. Contains the only extant records of the Vienne trial.

Biographical

Conrad Schlüsselburg. Haereticorum catalogus, etc. Frankfurt, 1597–99. 13 v. in 9.
> Tomus xi, Servetiani.

BIBLIOGRAPHY xxxi

Michel de la Roche. Historical account of the life and trial of Michael Servetus. London, 1712 ff.
> In his Memoirs of Literature, vol. iv. The first reports from the records of the Geneva trial. French trans. in his Bibliothèque Angloise, vol. ii, Amsterdam, 1717 f.

Henricus ab Allwoerden. Historia Michaelis Serveti. Helmstedt, 1727.
> Ed. 2 (1728). Dutch trans., Historie van Michael Servetus den Spanjaart, Rotterdam, 1729. The first attempt at a life of Servetus.

Armand de la Chapelle. Critique of the above in Bibliothèque Raisonnée des ouvrages des savans de l'Europe, vols. i, ii, Amsterdam, 1728.

Johann Lorenz von Mosheim. Anderweitiger Versuch einer vollständigen und unpartheyischen Ketzergeschichte. Geschichte des berühmten Spanischen Artztes Michaels Serveto. Helmstedt, 1748.
> Supersedes Allwoerden. Continued by the following.

Johann Lorenz von Mosheim. Neue Nachrichten von den berühmten Spanischen Artzte Michael Serveto, der zu Geneve ist verbrannt worden. Helmstedt, 1750.
> The above two works are still a rich mine of Servetus lore.

Friedrich Trechsel. Michael Servet und seine Vorgänger. Heidelberg, 1839.
> Vol. i of his Protestantischen Antitrinitarier vor Faustus Socin, nach Quellen und Urkunden geschichtlich dargestellt. Contains reprint of the Bern MS. copy of the records of the Geneva trial.

G. de Valayre. Légendes et chroniques Suisses précédées d'une introduction. Paris, 1842.
> Valayre rediscovered and used the records of the Geneva trial which had long been considered lost.

Albert Rilliet de Candolle. Relation du procès criminel intenté à Genève en 1553, contre Michel Servet, rédigée d'après les documents originaux. Genève, 1844.
> Reprinted from Mémoires de la Société d'histoire et d'archéologie de Genève, iii, 1844. Extracts from the Geneva records of the trial.

William Kirk Tweedie. Calvin and Servetus: the Reformer's share in the trial of Michael Servetus historically ascertained. From the French: with notes and additions. Edinburgh, 1846.
> Mostly merely a translation of the preceding.

William Hamilton Drummond. The life of Michael Servetus, the Spanish physician, who, for the alleged crime of heresy, was entrapped, imprisoned, and burned, by John Calvin the Reformer, in the city of Geneva, October 27, 1553. London, 1848.

John Scott Porter. Servetus and Calvin: three lectures on occasion of the three hundredth anniversary of the death of Michael Servetus, who, on the 27th of October, 1553, was burnt alive for heresy at the instigation of John Calvin. London, 1854.

Henri Tollin. Charakterbild Michael Servet's. Berlin, 1876.
> Sammlung gemeinverständlicher wissenschaftlicher Vorträge, Heft 254. English trans. by Miss F. A. Short, in Christian Life, London, Oct. 27–Dec. 1. 1876. French trans. by Mme. Picheral-Dardier, with important additions: Michel Servet: portrait-caractère, Paris, 1879. Hungarian trans. by Domokos Simén, Servet Mihály Jellemrajza, in Keresztény Magvetö, xiii., Kolozsvár, 1878.

Henri Tollin. Dr. M. Luther und Dr. M. Servet. Eine Quellenstudie. Berlin, 1875.

Henri Tollin. Ph. Melanchthon und M. Servet. Eine Quellenstudie. Berlin, 1876.

Henri Tollin. Michael Servet und Martin Butzer. Eine Quellenstudie. Berlin, 1880.

Robert Willis. Servetus and Calvin. A study of an important epoch in the early history of the Reformation. London, 1877.
> The best life in English hitherto, yet very inadequate. See the searching review by Gordon in Theological Review, below.

Marcelino Menendez y Pelayo. Historia de los heterodoxos Españoles. Madrid, 1877–80. 3 v.
> Vol. ii., 149–206, on Servetus. Edition 2, 7 v., Madrid, 1918 f., vol. iv, 209–387.

Antonius van der Linde. Michael Servet, een brandoffer der gereformeerde Inquisitie. Groningen, 1891.
> Extensive bibliography. Very critical of Tollin.

Grouwelen der voormaemste Hooft-Ketteren die haer in dese laetste tijden soo in Duytslandt, als oock in dese Nederlanden, opgeworpen hebben, haer Leven, Leere, Begin, ende Eynde... mitsgaders haere af-beeldingen nae 'tleven, etc. Leyden, 1607.
> Contains Christoffel van Sichem's engraving, the source of all Servetus portraits.

Mariano de Pano. La patria de Miguel Servet.
> Pp. xli.–xlv. of Juan Bautista Labaña, Itinerario del Reino de Aragón (Biblioteca de Escritores Aragonéses, Seccion Histórico-Doctrinal, tomo vii), Zaragoza, 1895.

Mariano de Pano. La familia de Miguel Servet.
> In Revista de Aragón, ii. 119, 151, Zaragoza, 1901.

Victor Oliva. La patria de Miguel Servet.
> In Joventut, iv. 789 f., Barcelona, 1903.

Benet Roura Barrios. Sobre M. Servet.
> In Joventut, v. 297, Barcelona, 1905. Trans., Quelques notes sur Michel Servet, in Chronique Médicale, xii. 556, Paris, 1905.

Marcel Bataillon. Honneur et Inquisition. Michel Servet poursuivi par l'Inquisition Espagnole. Bordeaux, 1925.
> Reprint from Bulletin Hispanique, xxvii. 5 ff. Cf. Alexander Gordon, Servetus and the Spanish Inquisition, in Christian Life, London, li. 414, Dec. 12, 1925.

Eloy Bullón y Fernández. Miguel Servet y la geográfia del Renacimiento. Madrid, 1929.

Émile Doumergue. Jean Calvin: les hommes et les choses de son temps. Lausanne, 1899–1927. 7 v.
> On Servetus in vol. vi.

Émile Doumergue. L'emplacement du bûcher de Michel Servet.
> In Bulletin de la Société d'histoire et d'archéologie de Genève, ii. 356–363, Genève, 1903.

Auguste Dide. Michel Servet et Calvin. Paris, 1907.

Pompeyo Gener. Servet. Reforma contra Renacimiento: Calvinismo contra Humanismo. Estudio histórico crítico sobre el descubridor de la circulation de la sangre y su tiempo. Barcelona, 1911.

Sigismundo Pey-Ordeix. Miguel Servet, el sabio víctima de la Universidad, el santo víctima de las iglesias. Su vida, su conciencia, su proceso, su vindicacion. Madrid, 1911.

David Cuthbertson. A tragedy of the Reformation, being the authentic narrative of the history and burning of the "Christianismi Restitutio," 1553, with a succinct account of the controversy between Michael Servetus, its author, and the Reformer, John Calvin. Edinburgh, 1912.

ESSAYS

Petrus Adolphus Boysen. Historia Michaelis Servati. Dissertation. Wittenberg, 1712.

François Marie Arouet de Voltaire. De Genève et de Calvin: De Calvin et de Servet.
> In Essai sur les mœurs et l'esprit des nations, ii, chaps. 133, 134, Stuttgart, 1756.

Charles Dardier. Servetus.
> Article in Lichtenberger's Encyclopédie des Sciences Religieuses, xi, 570 ff., Paris, 1879–82.

Charles Dardier. Michel Servet d'après ses plus récents biographes.
> In Revue Historique, x., Paris, 1879. Reviews Tollin's writings to date, Willis, etc. Spanish trans. in Anfiteatro Anatómico Español., June 30, 1879–March 31, 1880.

Édouard Schadé. Étude sur le procès de Servet. Thèse. Strasbourg, 1853.

William Osler. Michael Servetus. London, 1909.
: German trans. in Deutsche Revue, iv., 328 ff., 1909.

Alexander Gordon. Miguel Serveto-y-Reves.
: In Theological Review, London, 1878, xv. 281 ff., 408 ff. Reviewing Tollin's Charakterbild, and Willis.

Alexander Gordon. The personality of Michael Servetus, 1511–1553. Manchester, 1910.
: Reprinted in Addresses: Biographical and Historical. London, 1922.

Paul Louis Ladame. Michel Servet, sa réhabilitation historique. Genève, 1913.
: Reprinted from Bulletin de l'Institut National Génevois, xli.

Henri Tollin. Sixty-five articles in periodicals, as follows: (the number of articles in each journal is given in parenthesis).

(6) Archiv für die gesamte Physiologie, xxi–xxxv, 1880–84.
(10) Archiv für pathologische Anatomie und Physiologie, lxi–ci, 1874–85.
(1) Beweis des Glaubens, x, 1874.
(2) Biologisches Centralblatt, iii–v, 1883–85.
(2) Bulletin de la Société de l'Histoire du Protestantisme Français, xxviii–xxxii, 1879–83.
(1) Deutsche Klinik, xxvii, 1875.
(5) Deutsches Archiv für die Geschichte der Medicin, iii–viii, 1880–85.
(1) Evangelisch-reformirte Kirchenzeitung, xxvi, 1876.
(4) Historisches Taschenbuch, xliv–l, 1874–80.
(4) Jahrbücher für protestantische Theologie, ii–xvii, 1876–91.
(4) Magazin für Literatur des Auslandes, xliii–xlv, 1874–76.
(1) Protestantische Kirchenzeitung, xxii, 1875.
(2) Revue Scientifique, xviii–xxii, 1880–85.
(4) Theologische Studien und Kritiken, xlviii–liv, 1875–81.
(2) Zeitschrift der Gesellschaft für Erdkunde zu Berlin, x–xiv, 1875–79.
(1) Zeitschrift für die gesamte lutherische Theologie und Kirche, xxxviii, 1877.
(1) Zeitschrift für die historische Theologie, xlv, 1875.
(14) Zeitschrift für wissenschaftliche Theologie, xviii–xxxvii, 1875–94.

Histories

Abraham Ruchat. Histoire de la Réformation de la Suisse. Genève, 1727. 6 v.
: On Servetus in vol. vi. New ed., 1855. 7 v.

Timotheus Wilhelm Röhrich. Geschichte der Reformation im Elsass, und besonders in Strassburg, nach gleichzeitigen Quellen bearbeitet. Strassburg, 1830–32. 3 v. in 4.
On Servetus in vol. ii, 81 f.

Jean Gaberel. Histoire de l'Église de Genève. Genève, 1858–62. 4 v.
On Servetus in vol. ii.

Amedée Roget. Histoire du people de Genève depuis la Réforme jusqu'à l'escalade. Genève, 1877–1883. 7 v.
On Servetus in vol. iv.

Jean Antoine Gautier. Histoire de Genève des origines à l'année 1691. Genève, 1896–1914. 9 v.
On Servetus in vols. iii, iv.

THEOLOGICAL

Alexander Alesius. Contra horrendas Serveti blasphemias. Leipzig, 1554–55.

Wilhelm Heberle. Michael Servet's Trinitätslehre und Christologie.
In Tübinger Zeitschrift für Theologie, 1840.

Émile Edmond Saisset. Michel Servet.
In Revue des deux mondes, xviii., 1848. Emphasizes Servetus's pantheism.
Reprinted in his Mélanges d'histoire de monde et de critique, Paris, 1859.

Adolphe Chauvet. Étude sur le système théologique de Servet. Thèse. Strasbourg, 1867.

Henri Tollin. Das Lehrsystem M. Servets genetisch dargestellt. Gütersloh, 1876–78. 3 v.

Georg Christian Bernhard Pünjer. De Michaelis Serveti doctrina commentatio dogmatico-historica. Jena, 1876.

MEDICAL

George Sigmond. The unnoticed theories of Servetus, a dissertation addressed to the Medical Society of Stockholm. London, 1826.

Giulio Ceradini. Qualche appunto storico-critico intorno alla scoperta della circolazione del sangue. Genova, 1875.
Ed. 2, La scoperta della circolazione del sangue, Milano, 1876.

Giulio Ceradini. Difesa della mia memoria intorno alla scoperta della circolazione del sangue contra l'assalto dei signori H. Tollin teologo in Magdeburg e W. Preyer fisiologo in Jena. Genova, 1876.
Both the above reprinted in his Opera, 2 vols., Milano, 1906. Opposing Servetus's claim.

Henri Tollin. Die Entdeckung des Blutkreislaufs durch Michael Servet (1511–1553). Jena, 1876.
> Sammlung physiologischer Abhandlungen herausgegeben von W. Preyer, erste Reihe, sechstes Heft. Defending Servetus's claim.

Achille Chéreau. Histoire d'un livre. Michel Servet et la circulation pulmonaire. Paris, 1879.
> Opposing Servetus's claim. Reprinted from Bulletin de l'Académie de Médecine de Paris, 2ᵉ série, viii., 758 ff., 1879. Abridged in Revue Scientifique xvii, 63 ff., 1879. Spanish trans. in Independencia Médica, Barcelona, x, xi, 1878–80.

Édouard Turner. Remarques au sujet de la lecture faite à l'Académie de Médecine par M. Chéreau. Paris, 1879.
> Supporting Servetus's claim. In Progrès Médical, vii, 1879.

Emmanuel Orientin Douen. Une polémique récente. Michel Servet. Paris, 1880.
> Reviewing the above controversy. In Revue Politique et Littéraire, 2e série, xviii, 801 ff., 1880.

Toleration of Heretics

For works of Castellio, Beza, and Celsus, see page xxvi, notes 2 and 3.

Ferdinand Édouard Buisson. Sébastien Castellion, sa vie et son œuvre (1515–1563). Étude sur les origines de protestantisme libéral français. Paris, 1892. 2 v.

Étienne Giran. Sébastien Castellion et la Réforme Calviniste. Les deux Réformes. Haarlem, 1914.

Monuments to Servetus

Benet Roura Barrios. A proposit del monument expiatori de Geneva. Barcelona, 1903.
> In Joventut, iv., 776 ff., 1903.

Eugène Choisy. Le procès et le bûcher de Michel Servet. Paris, 1903.
> In Revue Chrétienne, i., 269 ff., 1903.

Monument expiatoire du supplice de Michel Servet. Souvenir de l'inauguration 1ᵉʳ Novembre, 1903. Genève, 1903.

E. J. Savigné. Le savant Michel Servet, victime de tous les fanatismes. Vienne, 1907.
> Account of Geneva and Vienne monuments.

Charles Achard. Michel Servet, brûlé vif par ordre de Calvin (1509–1553).
> Occasioned by the erection of the Paris monument.

A considerable number of poems, plays, and novels with Servetus as their central figure have also been published.

TRANSLATOR'S NOTE

THE text and the marginal notes are by Servetus, the latter being usually, it would seem, additions made to the original text as afterthoughts, while the work was going through the press. The author's careless punctuation and paragraphing have been much revised, and the paragraphs numbered for convenience of reference; but his use of capitals has been followed as far as it goes, and in some other cases significant words or phrases have been capitalized or italicized, to assist in the understanding of the text.

The numerous quotations from Scripture, which form so important a part of Servetus's argument, are often very loosely made, as if from memory; but when made with approximate exactness they have been put in italics, and have, when the text allowed, been rendered in the language of the American Standard edition of the Revised Version. The author's scripture references have been transferred to the footnotes, and many additional ones have been supplied to assist in identifying quotations or allusions; and since verse divisions had not yet been made when Servetus wrote, verse numbers have also been supplied. Chapter numbers, whenever (as in the Psalms) there is a variation, have been conformed to the English version, and some errors in references have been corrected. References to extrabiblical writers have been given wherever passages cited could be identified.

A transliteration and translation of Hebrew or Greek words occurring in the text has been added. The translator has endeavored to give as close a rendering as was consistent with idiomatic English, but has not hesitated to paraphrase when a literal version would have been blind. In a work involving many and peculiar difficulties, he can hardly suppose that he has in every case represented the author's meaning correctly; but he trusts that he has nowhere fallen into serious error.

The arguments and synopses at the head of the Books, the

foot-notes to the translation, and the paragraph numbers, have been supplied by the translator. The pages of the original are denoted by figures on the inner margin.

ABBREVIATIONS

R. V. ......Revised Version
Vulg. ......Vulgate version of the Latin Bible; noted when differing significantly from the English Version
Pagn. ......Pagnini's version of the Bible; noted when differing significantly from the Vulgate or the English
MPG ......Migne, Patrologia Graeca
MPL ......Migne, Patrologia Latina
ANCL ....Ante-Nicene Christian Library, Edinburgh, 1867–1872
ANF ......Ante-Nicene Fathers, New York, 1885–1887
NPNF.....Nicene and Post-Nicene Fathers, New York, 1886–1900
Dods .....Works of Aurelius Augustinus, tr. Marcus Dods, Edinburgh, 1872–1876

ON THE ERRORS OF THE TRINITY

SEVEN BOOKS

BY

MICHAEL SERVETO, *alias* REVES
A SPANIARD OF ARAGON

MDXXXI

BOOK I

Argument

ANY *discussion of the Trinity should start with the man. That Jesus, surnamed Christ, was not a* hypostasis *but a human being is taught both by the early Fathers and in the Scriptures, taken in their literal sense, and is indicated by the miracles that he wrought. He, and not the Word, is also the miraculously born Son of God in fleshly form, as the Scriptures teach — not a* hypostasis, *but an actual Son. He is God, sharing God's divinity in full; and the theory of a* communicatio idiomatum *is a confusing sophistical quibble. This does not imply two Gods, but only a double use of the term God, as is clear from the Hebrew use of the term. Christ, being one with God the Father, equal in power, came down from heaven and assumed flesh as a man. In short, all the Scriptures speak of Christ as a man.*

The doctrine of the Holy Spirit as a third separate being lands us in practical tritheism no better than atheism, even though the unity of God be insisted on. Careful interpretation of the usual prooftexts shows that they teach not a union of three beings in one, but a harmony between them. The Holy Spirit as a third person of the Godhead is unknown in Scripture. It is not a separate being, but an activity of God himself. The doctrine of the Trinity can be neither established by logic nor proved from Scripture, and is in fact inconceivable. There are many reasons against it. The Scriptures and the Fathers teach one God the Father, and Jesus Christ his Son; but scholastic philosophy has introduced terms which are not understood, and do not accord with Scripture. Jesus taught that he himself was the Son of God. Numerous heresies have sprung from this philosophy, and fruitless questions have arisen out of it. Worst of all, the doctrine of the Trinity incurs the ridicule of the Mohammedans and the Jews. It arose out of Greek philosophy rather than from the belief that Jesus Christ is the Son of God; and he will be with the Church only if it keeps his teaching.

Synopsis

1. This discussion of the Trinity will begin not with the Word, as is usually done, but with the man Christ. 2. Three points will be discussed. First point: *Christ was named Jesus, as is shown by* many texts from Scripture. 3. Early writers teach that Christ was a man, 4. as do various Scripture texts. 5. The nouns and pronouns referring to him imply this. 6. The language used of him is to be taken in its plain sense. 7. That he was a man is further shown by his relation to others; 8. while his miracles prove that Jesus was the Christ. 9. Second point: *Christ is the Son of God.* Many Scripture texts, referring to his supernatural birth, prove this. 10. Christ was begotten by the Word, and was an actual man in the flesh. 11. It can not be argued that there were two Sons. 12. Other passages of Scripture prove that Jesus himself was the Son of God, and that no hypostasis is implied. 13. Christ is a true Son of God by nature; others are sons only by adoption. He is Son, and God is Father, in a higher sense than that used of men. 14. Third point: *Christ is God,* as the Scriptures clearly prove. 15. The common doctrine of a communicatio idiomatum *is a sophistical invention, inconsistent with Scripture.* 16. God shares his full deity with Christ, but does not share any imperfections of man. 17. What has been said does not imply more than one God, but only a different use of the word, God; and Scripture plainly shows God and Christ as distinct beings. 18. The texts cited are not invalidated because heretics have misused them. 19. The word God must be interpreted in the light of its Hebrew equivalent. 20. The nature of Christ's deity is seen from the Old Testament use of the word Elohim *for beings less than the supreme God.* 21. Christ is one God with the Father, not a second God. 22. Christ came down from heaven as the Word of God, 23. sent as a man, who put on flesh. 24. Though humble in form, Christ was made equal to God. 25. This was equality in power, 26. not in Nature or Essence. 27. It was not robbery, for he bore the humble form of a man. 28. Psalms cx. 1 does not show the equality of Christ's Nature with God's. 29. In fine, all the Scriptures speak of Christ the man.

30. Philosophers make the Holy Spirit to be a third being, and this leads to a plurality of Gods. 31. Thus we become Tritoites and Atheists, though they affirm the unity of God. 32. The word spirit is variously used in Scripture. 33. Certain proof-texts for the Trinity refer not to oneness of Nature, but to harmony of mind and will. 34. It is oneness not of Nature but of power. 35. Christ's own words show that there is not a oneness of Nature. 36. The Father,

the Word, and the Spirit agree in bearing testimony to Christ. 37. The belief that Jesus was the Son of God is the foundation of the Church. 38. The text Romans xi. 36 does not refer to three Persons, 39. nor can they be inferred from numerals in a parable. 40. Many passages of Scripture emphasize God and Christ while ignoring the third Person. 41. The threefoldness in God sometimes inferred from Exodus iii. 6 is to be explained not as three separate beings, but as a distribution of functions. 42. In this passage God sought to keep the Jews from believing in more than one God. 43. The same passage properly explained, and many others, show that the Holy Spirit is not a distinct being, but an activity of God himself. 44. Current arguments of scholastic theologians are passed by as resting on grounds not mentioned in Scripture. 45. The beings are not even imaginable, but are pure phantasms. 46. What can not be understood should not be received. 47. The Old and New Testaments clearly teach one God, the Father, and one Christ, his Son, but nothing of beings. 48. The Fathers also teach that God is the Father of Christ. 49. The Old Testament repeatedly teaches but one God. 50. The Sophists, following tradition blindly, use terms they do not understand, disputing about mere words. 51. They use the term Persons in a wholly unscriptural sense. 52. The Jewish law teaches the strict unity of God. 53. Jesus taught that he himself, a man, was Son of God. 54. The same attributes are applied to the Messiah-king in the Old Testament as to Christ in the New. 55. The monstrous views of sundry heretics sufficiently shame the current view. 56. Also among teachers in the Church countless insoluble questions arise out of the doctrine of the Trinity, 57. and as to the relation of Mary, Christ, the Father, and the beings to one another. 58. Such subtleties are ridiculous, and wholly foreign to the Bible. 59. The Trinity excites the derision of Mohammedans and Jews, though Mohammed holds Christ and the Apostles in the highest honor. 60. This doctrine was due to Greek philosophy, whereas the Church should be founded on the belief that Jesus Christ is the Son of God. 61. Christ will be with the Church only on condition that its members keep his teaching.

ON THE ERRORS OF THE TRINITY
BOOK THE FIRST

1. In investigating the holy mysteries of the divine Triad, I have thought that one ought to start from the man; for I see most men approaching their lofty speculation about the Word without having any fundamental understanding of CHRIST, and they attach little or no importance to the man, and give the true CHRIST quite over to oblivion. But I shall endeavor to recall to their memories who the CHRIST is. However, what and how much importance is to be attached to CHRIST, the Church shall decide.

<small>These three things must be understood with regard to the man before we speak of the Word.</small>

2. Seeing that the pronoun [1] indicates a man, whom they call the human nature,[2] I shall admit [3] these three things: first, this man is JESUS CHRIST; second, he is the Son of God; third, he is God.

<small>The name and surname of the boy Jesus.</small>

That he was called JESUS at the beginning, who would deny? That is, in accordance with the angel's command, the boy was on the day of his circumcision given a name,[4] even as you were called John, and this man, Peter. JESUS, as Tertullian says,[5] is a man's proper name, and CHRIST is a surname. The Jews all admitted that he was JESUS, but denied that he was CHRIST, asking about JESUS *who is called* CHRIST,[6] and they put out of the synagogue those who confessed that he was CHRIST;[7] and the Apostles had frequent disputes with them about him, as to

<small>Note in what sense they took these things, before John wrote concerning the Word.</small>

whether JESUS were the CHRIST. But as to JESUS, there was never any doubt or question, nor did any one ever deny this name. See what the discourse is aiming at, and with what pur-

---

[1] *Ille Christus.*

[2] *Humanitas*, and so throughout the work.

[3] Throughout the discussion Servetus is addressing an imagined opponent, apparently using memoranda of oral debates had or planned with fellow students or others. He thus begins here with concessions.

[4] Luke i, 31; ii, 21.

[5] Adv. Praxean, xxviii, the argument of which Servetus follows here. (MPL. ii, 192 f.; ANF. iii, 624 f.; ANCL. xv, 399 f.)

[6] Matt. xxvii, 17, 22.

[7] John ix, 22; xii, 42.

pose Paul testifies to the Jews that JESUS is the CHRIST;[1] with what fervor of spirit Apollos of Alexandria publicly confuted the Jews, showing by the Scriptures that JESUS was the Messiah.[2] Of what JESUS do you suppose those things were said? Do you think they disputed there about a *hypostasis*? I am bound therefore to admit that he was CHRIST as well as JESUS, since I admit that he was anointed of God; for this is *thy holy Servant, whom thou didst anoint*.[3] This is *the most holy*, who, Daniel foretold, should be anointed.[4] And Peter spoke of it as an accomplished fact: Ye yourselves know, for the saying about JESUS is known to all men, namely, that God anointed JESUS of Nazareth with the Holy Spirit and with power, for God was with him;[5] and, *This is he who is ordained of God to be the Judge of the living and the dead;*[6] and, *Let all the house of Israel know assuredly, that this* JESUS *whom ye crucified God hath made both Lord and Christ*,[7] that is, anointed. Some, however, try to show that these pronouns mean another being. But John calls him a liar that denies that this JESUS is anointed of God;[8] and, He that admits that JESUS is the CHRIST is begotten of God.[9]

3. Tertullian also says that the term CHRIST is a word belonging to a human nature.[10] And although he makes careful inquiry concerning the word CHRIST,[11] he makes no mention of that being[12] which some make CHRIST out to be. Who, he also says, is the Son of man, if not himself a man, born of a man, a body born of a body?[13] For the Hebrew expression son of man, son of Adam, means nothing else than *man*. Again, the way the word is used implies this, for to be anointed can refer only to a human nature. If, then, being anointed, as he says,[14] is an affair of the

---

[1] Acts xviii, 5.   [2] Acts xviii, 28.   [3] Acts iv, 27.
[4] Dan. ix, 24.   [5] Acts x, 37, 38.   [6] Acts x, 42.
[7] Acts ii, 36.   [8] I. John ii, 22.   [9] I. John v, 1.
[10] Adv. Praxean, xxviii. (MPL. ii, 192 f.; ANF. iii, 624 f.; ANCL. xv, 399 f.).
[11] Adv. Marcionem III. xv, IV. x. (MPL. ii, 341 f., 377 ff.; ANF. iii, 333 f., 357 ff.; ANCL. vii, 148 ff., 205 ff.).
[12] *Res.* Servetus repeatedly uses this word in avoidance of the term Person (of the Trinity) to which he objects as unscriptural. This usage was very common among the scholastics. See par. 30.
[13] Adv. Marcionem IV. x. (MPL. ii, 380; ANF. iii, 360; ANCL. vii, 210).
[14] Tertullian, adv. Marcionem III. xv. (MPL. ii, 341 f.; ANF. iii, 334; ANCL. vii. 150).

body, who can deny that the one anointed is a man? Moreover, in the Clementine Recognitions,[1] Peter brings out the meaning of the word: because kings used to be called Christs,[2] therefore he, being distinguished above others by his anointing, is called Christ the king; because just as God made an angel chief over the angels, and a beast over the beasts, and a heavenly body over the heavenly bodies, so he made the man Christ chief over men.

4. Again, on the authority of Holy Scripture we are taught very plainly that Christ is called a man, since even an earthly king is called Christ.[3] Again, *Of whom was born* JESUS, *the one who is called* CHRIST.[4] Note the article, and note the surname; for these words and the pronouns are to be understood in the simplest sense: they denote something perceived by the senses. Again, *Thou shalt call his name* JESUS;[5] and he is very evidently writing of JESUS as a man, when he says, *And* JESUS *himself began to be thirty years of age, and was supposed to be the son of Joseph.*[6] And, *Of David's seed hath God according to promise brought* JESUS.[7] And John said, Think not that I am CHRIST.[8] How absurd John's disclaimer would be, if the word Christ can not refer to a man. Moreover, to what end does CHRIST warn us to shun those men that called themselves Christs?[9] CHRIST's question and Peter's answer would be silly, when CHRIST said, *Who do men say that I, the Son of man, am? And Peter answered, Thou art the Christ, thou art the Son of the living God.*[10] Nor would it mean the living Word of God, for in speaking to a man he ought to have said, CHRIST is in thee, the Son of God is in thee, and not, Thou art. And when he charged them there that they should tell no man that he was CHRIST,[11] tell me, what did he mean by that pronoun?[12] For it is clearer than day that he meant himself, and was speaking of himself. Do you not blush

---

[1] I. xlv. (MPG. i, 1233; ANF. viii, 89; ANCL. iii, 173).
[2] i. e., anointed.
[3] I. Sam. xii, 3; II. Sam. xxii, 51; Isa. xlv, 1.
[4] Matt. i, 16. *Jesus ille, qui.*
[5] Luke i, 31.   [6] Luke iii, 23.   [7] Acts xiii, 23.
[8] John i, 20; Acts xiii, 25.   [9] Matt. xxiv, 23, 24.
[10] Matt. xvi, 13, 16 (Pagn.).   [11] Matt. xvi, 20.
[12] *Quod ipse esset* CHRISTUS.

to say that he was without a name, and that the Apostles had preached him so long time without having called him by his own name; and do you on your own authority impose upon him a new and unfitting name, and one unheard of by the Apostles, calling him only the human nature?

5. Again, let not the Greek title χριστός [1] deceive you; but take the word מָשִׁיחַ,[2] or the Latin word *unctus*,[3] and see whether you, who admit that we have been anointed, will venture to admit that he was anointed. Nor should I so strongly insist upon proving this point, which is clear enough at the very outset, were it not that I see that the minds of some are misled. Again, CHRIST's testimony is very clear, when he calls himself a man: *Ye seek to kill me, a man that hath told you the truth*.[4] And, *A mediator between God and men, the man* CHRIST JESUS.[5] Again, pay no regard to the word *homo*,[6] which, if you hold to the *communicatio idiomatum*,[7] has been corrupted in meaning; but take the word *vir*,[8] and hear Peter when he says that CHRIST was *a man* [9] *approved*.[10] And, *Concerning* JESUS *the Nazarene, who was a man, a mighty prophet*.[11] And, *After me cometh a man*;[12] and, *Rejected of men, a man of sorrows*;[13] and, *Behold, the man whose name is the Branch*;[14] and, *God will judge by that man*,[15] namely, CHRIST.

Again, do not misrepresent the law of God by circumlocutions. Consider rather the nature of the demonstrative pronoun,[16] and you will see that this is the original meaning of the word; for when he is pointed out to the eye it is very often admitted, This is the CHRIST, Thou art JESUS; and that he speaks, asks, answers, eats, and that they saw him walking upon the

---

[1] *Christos*, anointed.   [2] *Mashiach*, anointed.
[3] Anointed.   [4] John viii, 40.
[5] I. Tim. ii, 5.   [6] Man, human being.
[7] Sharing of attributes: a doctrine as to the union of the divine and the human natures in the one person of Christ.
[8] Man.
[9] *Vir*, and so in the quotations immediately following.
[10] Acts ii, 22.
[11] Luke xxiv, 19, by a change of punctuation in the Latin.
[12] John i, 30.   [13] Isa. liii, 3.
[14] Zech. vi, 12.   [15] Acts xvii, 31.
[16] i. e., *ille Christus*, cf. par. 2.

water. Likewise, *I am he whom ye seek, Jesus of Nazareth;*[1] and, *Whomsoever I shall kiss, that is he: take him.*[2] And in another place, *It is I myself: handle me, and see;*[3] and, *This Jesus, whom ye slew, did God raise up, whereof we all are witnesses.*[4] Just what will you mean by such pronouns? As for an eye-witness, are we not in worse case than the Samaritan woman who said, *Come and see a man, who told me all things that ever I did: can this be the Christ?*[5] No wonder that a woman founded on Christ spoke thus, for when she was herself looking for a Messiah to come, who is called Christ, he replied, *I that speak unto thee am he*[6] — I, I, not the *being*, but, *I that speak*. 5a

6. Again, to what man do you understand that that word of the Apostle refers, *As by the trespass of one man, . . . so by the grace of one man, Jesus Christ;*[7] and, *As by a man came death, so by a man came the resurrection of the dead?*[8] For the Scripture does not take *man* connotatively;[9] it calls him not only man, but Adam.[10] Yet for our basis we would have a connotative man, and a speculative substance.[11] Away, I pray, with these sophistical tricks, and you shall see a great light. The foundation of the Church is the words of Christ, which are most simple and plain. Let us imitate the Apostles, who preached Christ not with words composed by art of man.[12] The words of the Lord are pure words,[13] they are to be received with simplicity. And witness the Apostle: *Not with excellency of speech* is the testimony of Christ to be proclaimed,[14] but plainly, and as if we had become babes,[15] and as if we knew nothing else *save Jesus Christ, and him crucified.*[16]

7. Again, what brotherhood shall you say that we have with Christ? Who is he that is exalted above his fellows?[17] What kind of comparison is it that the Apostle makes between Christ

---

[1] John xviii, 4–8.
[2] Matt. xxvi, 48.
[3] Luke xxiv, 39.
[4] Acts ii, 32; v, 30.
[5] John iv, 29.
[6] John iv, 26.
[7] Rom. v, 15–19.
[8] I. Cor. xv, 21.
[9] i. e., it is not speaking of man in general, but of a particular man.
[10] I. Cor. xv, 22.
[11] *Sophisticum suppositum.*
[12] I. Cor. ii, 1; II. Pet. i, 16.
[13] Ps. xii, 6.
[14] I. Cor. ii, 1; i, 17.
[15] I. Thess. ii, 7 (Vulg.).
[16] I. Cor. ii, 2.
[17] Heb. i, 9.

ON THE ERRORS OF THE TRINITY 11

and Moses, saying, *For he hath been counted worthy of more glory than Moses, . . . since Moses was as a servant, but* CHRIST *as a son?* ¹ To what end also does the Apostle in the same epistle ² so strongly insist upon showing that CHRIST was exalted even above the angels? For it would be silly enough to prove that the second Person of the Godhead is by nature more exalted than the angels. Nor can his meaning be thus construed; for the Apostle is speaking in accordance with the thought of the prophet, and David is marveling at the great glory of Christ because, though he is a man, all things have been subjected to him.³

5b

8. Again, he did miracles that we *may believe that* JESUS *is the* CHRIST, *the Son of God*.⁴ Note that he considers the matter settled as regards JESUS; but, that we may believe that this JESUS is he who was to be anointed, being begotten of the only God the Father. And how is the second unknown being recognized by miracles, unless it is understood of him whom they saw doing the miracles, as Nicodemus declares?⁵ For the outward miracles are no proof of the inward speculations. Likewise CHRIST himself bears witness that the works that he does sufficiently show that he has been sent by the Father.⁶ And Nathanael, from his saying, *I saw thee underneath the fig tree*, concludes that he is the Son of God who was to be sent as King of Israel.⁷ They draw a similar conclusion from his stilling the wind;⁸ and from the miracles that he did, Peter concludes, *We know that thou art the* CHRIST, *the Son of the living God.*⁹

6a

9. These conclusions also clearly prove what I said in the second place: namely, that he whom I call CHRIST is the Son of God; for from the miracles that he did they conclude that he is the Son of God. And it having been proved that he is JESUS CHRIST, this turns out as proved; for one who denies that he is the Son denies JESUS CHRIST, since Scripture proclaims nothing else than that JESUS CHRIST is the Son of God. Moreover, by

Second proposition.

---

¹ Heb. iii, 3–6.
² Heb. i, ii.
³ Ps. viii, 6.
⁴ John xx, 30, 31.
⁵ John iii, 2.
⁶ John v, 36.
⁷ John i, 48, 49.
⁸ Matt. xiv, 33.
⁹ John vi, 69 (Pagn.); Matt. xvi, 16.

many testimonies of the Scriptures he is shown to be especially the Son, and God is called Father with regard to him — really a Father, I say — because he was begotten by one filling the place of a human father. For he was not begotten of the seed of Joseph, as Carpocrates, Cerinthus, and Photinus [1] wickedly and falsely declared. But instead of the seed of a man, the almighty power of the Word of God overshadowed Mary, the Holy Spirit acting within her; and it continues, *Wherefore also that which is born shall be called holy, the Son of God.*[2] Weigh the word, *wherefore*, note the conclusion, note the reason why he is called the Son of God. The same kind of sonship [3] in the man JESUS CHRIST is disclosed to us by Daniel, who calls him *a stone cut out without hands.*[4] Again, the same kind of sonship is expressed when it says that she became with child of the Holy Spirit, and, That which hath been conceived in her has come from the Holy Spirit.[5] Tell me, pray, what is the offspring begotten and conceived in her, which comes from the Holy Spirit, from which he concludes that the son whom she brings forth will be the Saviour, Immanuel? Take note of what Luke says: This son whom thou shalt conceive and bring forth *shall be called the Son of the Most High.* He says furthermore, *He shall be great, and God shall give unto him the throne.*[6] Has the second Person, then, become great, and received from God the throne of his father David? Why did he not say, He shall be called the Son of the first Person, and the first Person shall give unto him the throne? But he said, *the Son of the most high God,* and, *God shall give unto him the throne.* Some, striving to pervert the words of the angel, misinterpret the word *holy* in this passage,[7] as though the first-born CHRIST were not worthy of it, although Luke also expressly shows in the chapter following why he had said holy; because every first-born thing shall be called holy to God.[8] In like man-

---

[1] Carpocrates, an Alexandrian Gnostic of the early second century; Cerinthus, a Gnostic of Asia Minor at the end of the first century; Photinus, Bishop of Sirmium in the fourth century. Servetus's statement as to Photinus is hardly accurate.

[2] Luke i, 35, cf. margin.   [3] *Filiatio.*
[4] Dan. ii, 34.   [5] Matt. i, 18, 20.
[6] Luke i, 32.   [7] Luke i, 35b.
[8] Luke ii, 23; cf. Ex. xiii, 2, 12; xxxiv, 19; Num. viii, 17.

ner the Apostles say, *Of thy holy Son* JESUS.¹ Moreover, they would call the power of God something merely speculative ² (but oh, that they knew what the Word of God is!). They neither show how that was instead of the seed of a man (for the angel answers the question asked by Mary as to the seed of a man); ³ nor do they explain what that is which, being begotten by the power which fills the place of the seed, will be called the Son of God. For Luke does not say that the *power* is called the Son; but, that which is begotten by the power.⁴ He shall be called the Son of God for the reason that the power of God is instead of the seed of a man.

10. Nor do they notice how wide and deep are the mysteries of this Word and of the seed, in illustration of which it says that the seed of the sower is the Word of God.⁵ For just as CHRIST was begotten and born by the Word of God, so we are born again by the Word of God; *born again,* says Peter, *through the Word of the living God.*⁶ And this seed he calls incorruptible; and, *He begat us by the word of truth.*⁷ They have speculated ill, therefore, in denying that the Son was a man, that they may make a Son of the Word; but the truth of the matter proves to be otherwise, and John thought it more fitting to say Word than Son. Indeed, in his discussion of the Word, the Son is said to be flesh.⁸ Of the Word, I shall speak later; ⁹ for the present let us keep his proper honor and glory for JESUS CHRIST, for even by this we shall understand the Word also. Again, the very nature of the word teaches us that the Son is called a man; for just as being anointed is an affair of the body, so being born is an affair of the flesh. The flesh, therefore, says Tertullian,¹⁰ was born, and the Son of God will be flesh. Again, who is the little boy of whom mention is so often made in Matt. ii., whom Joseph took [to Egypt] and back? Say, is boy the name of a *hypostasis*? See whether the boy there is the son called out of Egypt.¹¹ Again,

---

¹ Acts iv, 30.
² *Philosophicum.*
³ Luke i, 34.
⁴ Luke i, 35.
⁵ Luke viii, 11.
⁶ I. Pet. i, 23 (Vulg.).
⁷ James i, 18.
⁸ John i, 14.
⁹ Book III.
¹⁰ De carne Christi, vi. (MPL. ii, 763; ANF. iii, 526; ANCL. xv, 176).
¹¹ Matt. ii, 15.

tell me whether he whom you call the human nature was beast or man; for if man, he was both begotten and born, and if so, he had a parent. Say, then, of whom he was begotten and consequently he will be the son of him who begot him. Say whether he was begotten by Joseph as his father, or by some other father. Nor will you find any other father than God. Or will you say that he was a mere appearance,[1] and not flesh? For if he is flesh, he was born of some father, hence he is some one's son; nor do I believe that you can escape here, unless you make one son out of two, or conjure up imaginary sonships, unknown to CHRIST himself.

11. But what is there so strange, you will say (not to speak of *Substances*[2]), in acknowledging two Sons; for we admit that the two beings had two births, and very different ones, likewise that the two beings had two begettings; hence we can not deny that two were begotten and two were born. Speculate as much as ever you will on the kind of sonship, in order to make of the two one mass, one aggregate, or one connotative Substance;[3] for you are deceived if from this it seems to you that, taking Scripture in its plain sense, there was an only Son, when you nevertheless see before your eyes two begotten and born. Who would make any difference between *born* and *sons*?[4] Nor did the Scriptures ever contemplate such subtleties, but they speak in the simplest way of JESUS, the only Son of God. And Scripture mentions no other being, no other nature, nothing besides a man born or begotten. And so Ignatius, speaking of one and the same being, says, Concerning JESUS CHRIST, the Son of God, who was truly born of God and of the Virgin — of God before the world began, but afterwards of Mary, without the seed of a man;[5] but how — this will appear below.[6] For the present, I most sincerely would that little old women, half-blind men, and barbers might acknowledge that CHRIST is the Son of God, and that their root and foundation might be in him. We shall speak of the Word

---

[1] *Phantasma.* [2] *Suppositis.*
[3] *Connotativum suppositum.* [4] *Natos et filios.*
[5] Loosely quoted from Ep. ad Trallianos, x. (MPG. v, 791; ANF. i, 70 f.; ANCL. i, 202).
[6] Book III, paragraph 1.

more at large later on.¹ For CHRIST proclaimed even to women that he was the Messiah. Pray consider how a little old woman can understand the metaphysical Son, when most heresiarchs, and those the most subtle, have stumbled at it.

12. Again, in addition to what has been said before, God said to John, *Upon whomsoever thou shalt see the Spirit of God descending, and abiding upon him, the same is he. . . . And I have seen, and have borne witness that this is the Son of God.*² Pray note the words, very plain and without circumlocution. For in your opinion John would have been deceived in saying that the one whom he saw was the Son of God; nor is it credible that he himself had thought out anything about the separate being, nor had God given him any sign by which to recognize it. Or will you say that the voice from heaven was misleading in saying, *Upon whomsoever thou shalt see . . . the same is he?* It would also have been misleading when, descending, it said of a being present to all, *This is my Son*, or, *Thou art my Son.*³ If by the pronoun ⁴ he meant to indicate some other hidden being, then the witness would not have been clear; it would have led the people astray. Again, when JESUS, being asked, Who is this Son of God? answered, *Thou hast both seen him, and he it is that speaketh with thee,*⁵ what could have been said more clearly? This being plainly shown, the Centurion said, *Truly this man was the Son of God.*⁶ Observe now that the pronouns indicate a being perceived by the senses; nor do I believe that the Centurion would have played the Sophist, or have spoken of the *communicatio idiomatum*. Again, hear Paul, who, as soon as he received his sight, went into the synagogue and *proclaimed* JESUS, *that he is the Son of God.*⁷ Nor are we seeking here to make any discussion about a *hypostasis* of the Word. Indeed, he was afterwards proclaimed by John in order to establish this doctrine; for he is not opposed to our view, but joins us in proving it. See also whether the high priest had a second *hypostasis* in mind when he said, *Art thou the Son of God the blessed? And* JESUS *answered, I am.*⁸ *Ye say that I*

---

¹ Book III.
² John i, 33, 34.
³ Matt. iii, 17; Luke iii, 22.
⁴ i. e., *this*, or *thou*.
⁵ John ix, 36, 37.
⁶ Matt. xxvii, 54.
⁷ Acts ix, 20.
⁸ Mark xiv, 61 (Vulg.).

am the Son of God.[1] In like manner, *I have believed that thou art the* CHRIST, *the Son of God.*[2] But with what gross perversity these most transparent words have been misinterpreted in connection with the sophistical *communicatio idiomatum,* let them judge for themselves; for I understand the words of CHRIST in the very simplest sense, nor do I suffer any meaning to be imported into them. I would not have you press Scripture into service in order to construct fictions of your own. But because it attracts you when it is itself kept intact, I would not have you by your vain imaginings render uncertain such a manifest certainty of the Gospel.

13. If you say that nothing seems to be ascribed to CHRIST more than to other men, since we also are called sons of God; I reply that, on the contrary, from the fact that we are called sons of God, he himself is proved to be a real son. For men are called sons after the likeness of man; yet there is a wide difference, as will be evident when the mystery of the Word has been investigated.[3] And if we are called sons (that is, by the gift and grace given us through him), the author of this sonship is therefore called a Son in a far higher sense. And when mention is made of CHRIST, the article is used, and it says, This is *the* Son of God,[4] in order to indicate that he is called Son not by a general term, as we are, but in a certain special and unusual way. For he is a son by nature, while others are not sons originally: they become sons of God, they are not born sons of God. We are made sons of God, through faith, in JESUS CHRIST.[5] Hence we are called sons by adoption.[6] But to make CHRIST adopted in like manner is the heresy of the Bonosians.[7] For with regard to CHRIST no such adoption is read of, but a real begetting by God, his Father. And he is called not merely a son, but a real son;[8] not merely an ordinary son, but his own Son:[9] And God is called the Father of

---

[1] Luke xxii, 70.
[2] John (Servetus wrongly says Luke) xi, 27.
[3] Book III. [4] John i, 34.
[5] Gal. iii, 26; John i, 12.   [6] Rom. viii, 15; Eph. i, 5.
[7] The Bonosians in Spain and southern Gaul from the fifth to the seventh centuries held that Christ was the Son of God by adoption rather than by nature.
[8] Wisdom ii, 18 (Vulg.).
[9] Rom. viii, 32.

JESUS CHRIST¹ with just as good right as earthly fathers are called the fathers of their own sons. Else God could not be called an especially efficient cause, and one productive of any certain effect. For if he chooses to have some child for himself in particular, and of himself alone merely acts to beget him, just as an earthly father can act, why will he not with just as good right deserve to be called Father? *Shall I, that cause others to bring forth, myself be barren? saith the Lord.*² Nay, rather is he himself called Father, because *from him every fatherhood in heaven and on earth is named.*³ And that the more, because he not only begot him, but honored him with fulness of deity, that in this the Son may be made like the Father. Again, in another way God is said to be Father with better right than men, because he acts in the begettings of others. Others indeed do nothing in the begetting of their own sons; hence, if he is called Father with better right, CHRIST will with best right be said to be Son more than others.

14. In the third place, I said that this proposition is true: CHRIST is God, for he is said to be God in appearance, because, as the Apostle says, he was *in the form of God.*⁴ And, according to Tertullian, he was found to be God through his power, just as he was man through his flesh.⁵ For CHRIST after the inward man (to speak in the manner of Paul) means something divine, resulting from an inward anointing divinely done. According to the flesh, he is man; and in the spirit he is God, because *that which is born of the Spirit is spirit,*⁶ and, *God is a Spirit.*⁷ And, *Unto us a child is born ... his name shall be called ... Mighty God.*⁸ See clearly that both the name and the might of God are attributed to a child that is born, unto whom *hath been given all authority in heaven and on earth.*⁹ And Thomas calls him, *My God, my Lord.*¹⁰ And CHRIST is called, God in all things to be praised and blessed.¹¹ And in many other passages is his divinity

Third proposition.

---

[1] Rom. xv, 6.
[2] Isa. lxvi, 9 (Vulg.).
[3] Eph. iii, 15, margin.
[4] Phil. ii, 6.
[5] Adv. Marcionem IV. xviii. (MPL. ii, 402; ANF. iii, 375; ANCL. vii, 247).
[6] John iii, 6.
[7] John iv, 24.
[8] Isa. ix, 6.
[9] Matt. xxviii, 18.
[10] John xx, 28.
[11] Rom. ix, 5.

shown, because he was exalted that he might receive divinity, and the name above every name.[1] Let those therefore beware who endeavor to disparage him so much that they would have his human nature called only, as it were, a sort of inferior being, and make him out so much the more imperfect because they not only deny that he is their Lord, but deny that he was anointed by God King of the Jews, deny that he is a reconciler, a mediator, why, even rob him of what belongs to his nature, denying that he is the son of Mary, and finally deny that he is a man. Who can but weep at so great an injury to Christ, because the man Moses was called an earthly mediator between the people and God, while it is denied that the second man from heaven is a heavenly mediator. All these they would have as the names of a *hypostasis*.

<small>They deny that a man is a man, and admit that God is an ass.[2]</small>

15. For this reason the popular school of thought has devised the *communicatio idiomatum*, namely, that the human nature shares its properties with God. They invent some new application of the term, *man*, so that it may be equivalent to the phrase, bearing a human nature; and then, by this *communicatio idiomatum*, they admit that the man is God. This entire doctrine rests upon the passage in the first chapter of John, *The Word became flesh*;[3] but how far away they are from John's view, you shall learn hereafter.[4] Meanwhile ask yourself just this question: If CHRIST himself were to be questioned, could any such sophistical fancy be found in his mouth? For we ought so to speak, as Peter says, as if we spoke oracles of God.[5] After CHRIST commanded that he be called our Master, an answer was to be expected from his utterances. Ask yourself whether, if CHRIST, or his disciple Paul, were preaching to us again, he would be able to endure such inventions of men, and deliberate impositions of words, and that the universal and catholic faith should depend upon them. Are these things founded on the solid rock, or on the sand? How shall every tongue confess CHRIST, if these artificial and sophistical words are found in

---

[1] Phil. ii, 9.
[2] See below, paragraph 16, foot-note 8.
[3] John i, 14.   [4] Book III.
[5] I. Pet. iv, 11.

their tongue¹ alone? What view of faith would they deem that other nations held? If you would know whether these things are founded on the Scriptures, see whether the word, *man*, in the Bible has the meaning they put upon it; whether in the Greek or in the Hebrew, in place of the Latin word all this is used: *bearing a human nature*. Do they not make CHRIST a great sophist and master of sophists, when they say that the expression, CHRIST, was employed by the Prophets, Apostles, and Evangelists to signify the second Person, by connoting, *what bears a human nature*? But what would they say if, in place of the word, CHRIST, the word, *anointed*, were used throughout the Bible? Would they, speaking in the simplest way, say that the second Person was anointed, and that it had received the Holy Spirit, and power, as is said of the real CHRIST? ² Or could the second being say, *All things have been delivered unto me of my Father?*³ Would the Father also have spoken of it in a sophistical sense, saying, *Behold my servant, whom I have chosen, my beloved . . . I will put my spirit upon him?* ⁴ You will find that the reference is not to this, but to the man JESUS. Again, what is a "sharing of qualities," ⁵ and what is it like? For the quality, *bearing a human nature*, was formerly not appropriate to a man. How, then, does a man share his qualities with God, if they are not his own?

16. Rejecting these quibbles, then, we with a sincere heart acknowledge the real CHRIST, and him complete in divinity. But since this divinity of his depends upon the Mystery of the Word, let us for the present say roughly that God can share with a man the fulness of his deity, and give unto him the name which is above every name.⁶ For if we admit as touching Moses that he was made a God to Pharaoh,⁷ much more, and in a way far more exceptional, was CHRIST made the God, Lord, and Master of Thomas and of us all. And because God was in him in singular measure, and because through him we find God propitious, he is expressly called Emanuel, that is, God with us; ⁸ nay more,

---

¹ i. e., the Latin.   ² Acts x, 38.   ³ Matt. xi, 27.
⁴ Matt. xii, 18; cf. Isa. xlii, 1.
⁵ *Communicatio praedicatorum*, i. e., *idiomatum*.
⁶ Phil. ii, 9.   ⁷ Ex. vii, 1.   ⁸ Matt. i, 23.

he himself is called *El*.¹ Again, if we are given by God the privilege of being called sons of God,² with CHRIST the privilege will be the broader, not only of being the Son of God, but also of being called and of being our God; for, *Worthy is the Lamb that hath been slain* to receive divinity, that is, *to receive the power, riches, wisdom, might, honor, glory, and blessing*.³ And there is in him another and a manifold fulness of Deity, and other unsearchable riches of his, of which we shall speak below,⁴ which are all qualities that God shares with man. But man gives God no quality *de novo*, for what can man bestow upon God *de novo*? Either this quality is a thing trifling and indifferent; or it is perfection, and thus God would have lacked this perfection before; or it is imperfection, and thus you will say that a sort of imperfection is now suitable for God; and these are shocking things to say. Moreover, the fact that God gives something to man is not a detriment to God but an honor to man, nor is the change in God, but in man. For, if the pronoun indicates CHRIST, I admit this is our God, the blessed God, the mighty God. But if the pronoun indicates the invisible God, I have a great dread of admitting, this is something dead, this is a thirsting, eating man, this is an ass, this has long ears, as the Sophists with their uncircumcised lips admit without the slightest shame.⁵ Nor will it do you any good though you move heaven and earth in crying out against them; on the contrary, they will say, with brazen front, that these are the oracles of God, pure as fire. Nor is there any other stronger argument against such men than to recall to their

12a

---

¹ Hebr., God; Isa. ix, 6.   ² I. John iii, 1; cf. John i, 12.
³ Rev. v, 12.   ⁴ Book VII, paragraph 6.
⁵ Servetus follows Melanchthon's example (Loci Theologici, 1521, *saepe*) in calling his scholastic opponents Sophists, and Pharisees. Aquinas (Summa Theol., pars i, q. xxix, art. 4) in discussing the relations of the Persons of the Trinity, had argued that as a horse and an ass, though distinct, are one in being both of them animals, so with the Persons. This rather unhappy illustration was taken up by the later scholastic theologians (Duns Scotus, in lib. i. Sent., dist. 26, q. 1; dist. 2, q. 7; Pierre d'Ailly, in lib. i. Sent., q. 5; John Major, in lib. i. dist. 4; Robert Holkot, super quatuor libros Sent., lib. i, q. v., prop. 2). Such an illustration of the Godhead seemed to Servetus altogether shocking; and *personaliter* (as they defined Person) and *asinaliter* were associated in his mind as equivalent terms. He thus alludes, just below, to the Turks as calling Christians *asinarii*, ass-followers, or perhaps ass-worshipers. cf. marginal note, par. 14.

memories the precept of the Apostles Peter and Paul: *Hold the pattern of sound words as thou hast heard them from me;*[1] and, *If any man speaketh, let him speak as it were oracles of God;*[2] and, He that followeth a different doctrine from that which is according to godliness, the sound doctrine of CHRIST, he is puffed up, knowing nothing.[3] See now the "godliness" of the doctrine which they have learned from Paul, which admits that God has long ears, and is an ass. No wonder, if the Turks call us ass-worshipers, seeing that we do not blush to call God an ass. Let no corrupt speech proceed out of your mouth.[4]

17. In opposition to what has been said, you will insist, If CHRIST is God in that way, there will then be more than one God. Here I propose that CHRIST alone shall be my teacher, in order that he alone may defend me, for out of his words all your arguments can be refuted. To that argument of the Pharisees, the Master himself replies, *I said, Ye are Gods.*[5] CHRIST there makes it clear that he is God not in Nature but in appearance, not by nature but by grace. For when he was accused of making himself God, he spoke of God in his reply in the same way in which the prophet spoke of gods, ascribing that sort of deity to himself. Also, seeing that he adds, *If he called them gods unto whom the word of God came,*[6] how much more shall the Son of man, whom the Father sanctifies,[7] be called not merely Son, but even God. By way of privilege, therefore, it was given to him to be God, because the Father sanctifies him; he was anointed by grace, exalted because he humbled himself,[8] exalted above his fellows.[9] There was given unto him *the name which is above every name*;[10] and, as Peter says, *He received from God the Father honor and glory,*[11] which things are all according to grace. For that only the Father is called God by nature is plainly enough shown by Scripture, which says, God and CHRIST, CHRIST and God. It so joins them as though CHRIST were a being distinct from God. Likewise, when it says, God is the Father of JESUS CHRIST,[12] a

He refutes three arguments of the Pharisees. The words of Christ are to be especially heeded.

---

[1] II. Tim. i, 13.   [2] I. Pet. iv, 11.
[3] I. Tim. vi (Servetus says iv), 3, 4.
[4] Eph. iv, 29.   [5] John x, 34.
[6] John x, 35.   [7] John x, 36.
[8] Phil. ii, 8, 9.   [9] Heb. i, 9.
[10] Phil. ii, 9.   [11] II. Pet. i, 17.
[12] II. Cor. xi, 31; Rom. xv, 6.

difference is noted between God and CHRIST, just as between
father and son. And also when it says, *the* CHRIST *of God*,[1] *the
God of our Lord* JESUS CHRIST,[2] *the head of* CHRIST *is God*.[3] And
CHRIST cries to God, *My God, my God*.[4] And by common usage
of Scripture the Father is called God; and CHRIST, Lord and
Master. And Christ himself says, *That they should know thee, the
only true God, and him whom thou didst send, even* JESUS CHRIST.[5]
For although I say that CHRIST is very God, yet in the relation
which he holds to the Father this very passage notes a difference. In John it speaks of CHRIST in distinction from idols, and
from those whom they falsely named gods.[6] Likewise, only the
Father is called the invisible God.[7] CHRIST also, when he is
called good, transfers the matter of goodness to the Father.[8]

18. Nor let any one be surprised that I bring forward Scriptures that have been cited by heretics in their own behalf; for
although those have used them improperly, they have not for
all that lost their integrity so that one may never use them. For
I too, as well as you, understand them as referring to man. Nor
do I bring them forward for their [the heretics'] purpose. For
what if I say that JESUS CHRIST is the great God, and along
with this what he himself says in speaking most simply: *The
Father is greater than I*;[9] am I therefore an Arian? For when
Arius held the very foolish view that the Son was of different
Substance from the Father, having also no appreciation at all
of the glory of CHRIST, he introduced a new creature, more exalted than man; although he might nevertheless have excluded
this and every other distinction, and have admitted, *The Father
is greater than I*.[10] But preferring to speculate upon a plurality of
separate beings, he fell into most abominable error.

19. Again, let not the word, *God*, deceive you, for you do not
and can not understand its meaning until you know what
Elohim means, which, if you know Hebrew, I will make quite
clear to you below. For you must bear in mind that all things

---

[1] Luke ix, 20.
[2] Eph. i, 3.
[3] I. Cor. xi, 3.
[4] Matt. xxvii, 46.
[5] John xvii, 3.
[6] I. John v, 21.
[7] Col. i, 15; I. Tim. i, 17.
[8] Matt. xix, 17 (Pagn.).
[9] John xiv, 28.
[10] John xiv, 28.

that are written of CHRIST took place in Judaea, and in the Hebrew tongue; and in all other tongues but this there is a poverty of divine names. So we, not knowing how to distinguish between God [in one sense] and God [in another], fall into error. And that CHRIST became our God in the sense of the word, Elohim, is no more than to say that he became our Lord, our judge, and our king, after he was given by the Father a kingdom, all judgment, and all power. And Thomas shows this well enough when he says, *My Lord, my God*;[1] and Isaiah says, He shall be called Mighty God.[2] Hear also how Scripture calls Cyrus the King, who was a type of the real CHRIST, Elohim, the God of Israel: *I will give thee, it saith, hidden treasures . . . that thou mayest know that I am the Lord who call thy name the God of Israel*.[3] Likewise, if we admit that Moses was made Pharaoh's God,[4] why do we deny it concerning the real CHRIST? for CHRIST far surpasses Moses.[5] These are very poor comparisons by which to prove the exalted nature of CHRIST; but you force me to resort to them so long as you hold so unworthy a view of human nature, and do not keep in mind that God can exalt man more than can be declared, and place him at his right hand above every exalted being. But this is thus far but a slight thing, that you should hold a sound view about CHRIST, until you have learned the mysteries of the Word, and know that this CHRIST himself is, and from everlasting has been, God.

14a

God is not the name of a Nature.

20. Again, this kind of Deity in CHRIST you may learn from the Old Testament, if you observe carefully what Hebrew word is used when CHRIST is called God. And along with this, mark the difference between יהוה,[6] the proper name of God, and אל, אדני,אלהים,[7] and other similar names applied to God. And that Thomas spoke of CHRIST [8] not as *Jehovah*, but as *Elohim* and *Adonai*, I shall prove below.[9] Likewise the Apostle said *Elohim*.[10] But their ignorance of this matter strangely deceived the Greek philosophers. Indeed, as a matter of history, Solomon is here

---

[1] John xx, 28.
[2] Isa. ix, 6.
[3] Isa. xlv, 3 (Vulg.).
[4] Ex. vii, 1.
[5] Heb. iii, 3.
[6] Jehovah.
[7] El, Adonai, Elohim.
[8] John xx, 28.
[9] Book V, par. 2.
[10] Heb. i, 8; cf. Ps. xlv, 6.

called *Elohim*, for this passage is from the forty-fifth Psalm. Nor does the Apostle rest all the force of his proof on the word *Elohim*, but also on the fact that it says, His throne and kingdom are forever and ever.[1] For from the word *Elohim* alone he would not have proved CHRIST greater than the angels, nor greater than other princes who by the same prophet are called gods. On the contrary, by the same Apostle, and in the same passage, Angels are called *Elohim*, when he says, Worship him, all ye angels,[2] and, *Thou madest him a little lower than the angels*;[3] for in both passages *Elohim* is used. Nor shall I omit to mention here (although it seems to tell against me) that their idea is false who would have him said to be made lower than God, and not, than the angels; for they are far from the intention of the prophet, and from the Apostle's train of thought, which is wholly concerned with the angels. Nor do I care here to inquire concerning their Natures, but shall hold to this Hebrew expression; because with the Hebrews great beings are called by the name of Gods and of angels, and they use one common name when speaking of angels and of distinguished men. And Peter calls angels those who in Genesis are called *Elohim*, or, *sons of Elohim*.[4] And as of those, so of the angels in heaven, it says, *sons of Elohim*.[5] Likewise, it also says אלהים[6] of angels and mighty men.[7] This comparison serves to make the letter subordinate to the spirit. As I shall say below, does David, in his adversities, from which he was freed, bear the type of the passion and resurrection of CHRIST, and is he said to have been made lower than gods, because he suffers some calamities which gods and potentates are not wont to suffer? And just this is the meaning with regard to CHRIST, so far as concerns the time of his passion. For if you have with due care examined the saying of Paul, it contains nothing else than a translation of the Psalmist; so that this "making lower" is understood of the torment of death, and he was made lower than the angels when, being stripped of his angelic glory, he suffered a shameful death. And

---

[1] Heb. i, 8.
[2] Heb. i, 6; cf. Ps. xcvii, 7.
[3] Heb. ii, 7; Ps. viii, 5.
[4] Gen. vi, 2, 4.
[5] Job i, 6; xxxviii, 7.
[6] *Elohim*.
[7] Ps. lxxxix, 6; Job xli, 25.

these homely phrases the Apostles (following, as I suppose, the Greek version) ¹ are wont to indicate by the names of angels; as when, wishing to indicate some great thing, it says, *If I speak with the tongues of men and of angels;* ² *If we shall judge angels* ³ (that is, those things which are greater); and, *angels' food* ⁴ (that is, splendid food); *in the presence of the angels* ⁵ (that is, in the presence of princes). And the Chaldee version ⁶ also follows this in places. And in the Psalm quoted above,⁷ both in the Greek and in the Chaldee, *angels* is used to render *Elohim*. And it is the Greek version that was usually quoted by the Apostles, where there is no difference in the sense. And from this also Peter's saying about the angels is clear, for the Septuagint called them angels.⁸ And when a deed is related, reference should be had to the scripture narrative. And Peter, in the Clementine Recognitions,⁹ says that there were men who lived the life of angels. And the Epistle of Jude calls *angels* those notable beasts that had left their proper habitation and were roving about on the face of the earth.¹⁰ And it is these that are called pilgrims.¹¹ For Cain with his offspring (whom the Hebrews call great Demons) was a wanderer on the face of the earth.¹² But of these sayings of Peter I shall treat more at large in Book III.¹³ Let it suffice for the present to have explained the word *Elohim*, lest some one attempt to build some argument against me out of those passages in the Epistle to the Hebrews. For I not only do not reject those divine names, but I say that they apply to CHRIST *par excellence*. Thus, in order to mark a difference from other gods, it adds, the God of all the earth, a God great, terrible, mighty, wonderful, and over all blessed.¹⁴ But because of the poverty of the Greek in divine names, the Apostles could not ex-

15b

The Aldine edition is not that of the Septuagint.

---

¹ The Septuagint.
² I. Cor. xiii, 1.
³ I. Cor. vi, 3.
⁴ Ps. lxxviii, 25 (Vulg.).
⁵ Rev. xiv, 10; Ps. cxxxviii, 1 (Vulg.).
⁶ i. e., the Targums.
⁷ Ps. viii, 5, as quoted above from Heb. ii, 7.
⁸ Gen. vi, 2, 4; II. Pet. ii, 4.
⁹ I. xxix. (MPG. i, 1223; ANF. viii, 85; ANCL. iii, 163).
¹⁰ Jude 6.
¹¹ Ecclus. xvi, 15 (Vulg.).
¹² Gen. iv, 14.
¹³ Book III, par. 6.
¹⁴ Gen. xviii, 25; Deut. x, 17; Ps. lxviii, 35; Rom. ix, 5.

press this matter to the Greeks otherwise than by the word θεός;[1] although they rarely use it. All which things should be carefully weighed; nor would they have caused us so much trouble had the Greeks learned Hebrew.

All their arguments are turned the other way.

21. The argument made about a plurality of gods[2] can be turned the other way, for according to CHRIST's answer they are driven to admit that the three beings are Gods, and Gods by Nature. Either CHRIST is not God by Nature, or he did not reply to the point; for the question there was concerning his deity. Hence the argument runs against them, if they are gods in the sense in which the Son is God. And let them invent for themselves as many gods by Nature as ever they please; because to us, as to Paul, one God is enough, who is the Father, and one Lord JESUS CHRIST, who is the Son.[3] Add also to the refutation of their argument, that although CHRIST is God, yet he is one with the Father. Thus no plurality is shown as they suppose, for he is God, a kind of deity being shared by him with the Father.

The second argument of the Pharisees.

22. You will insist, moreover, upon asking how CHRIST is said to have come down from heaven, and to have been sent by the Father and come into the world. I have already said in the preceding argument[4] that those who rely upon arguments of this sort seem to be resorting to the weapons of the Pharisees, and to use the same carnal sense as they. For the Pharisees prated, *Is not this the son of Joseph, whose father and mother we know? how then doth he say, I am come down out of heaven?*[5] And the Master would not explain the truth to them; but afterwards, in explaining the matter to his disciples, he said, *What then if ye should behold the Son of man ascending where he was before? It is the spirit that giveth life; the flesh profiteth nothing: these words are spirit and life.*[6] Again, CHRIST, speaking not of the second being but of himself, says, *I am come down from heaven.*[7] Thus the reasoning turns out against you. I say, then, that that which came down from heaven, is the Word of God, as is said in Wisdom,

---

[1] *Theos*, God.
[2] In paragraph 16.
[3] I. Cor. viii, 6.
[4] Paragraph 16.
[5] John vi, 42.
[6] John vi, 62, 63.
[7] John vi, 38.

Thine all-powerful word, O Lord, leaped from heaven;[1] because God thundered from on high, and gave his voice from heaven, and this word on earth became the Son. And CHRIST, pausing to discourse on the bread out of heaven, explains himself. For what is *the bread which cometh down from heaven*[2] but the Word of God, by which man lives, rather than by material bread alone.[3] And this word, this bread, as he himself bears witness, is CHRIST his very self, the very flesh itself, the very body itself, of CHRIST.[4] But since these things presuppose the mystery of the Word, let them be postponed to the following Books.[5] Yet you might meanwhile have understood *down from heaven*, that is, down from above, because, as he himself bears witness, *ye are from beneath; I am from above.*[6] Also you might have understood the words of CHRIST thus spiritually; for CHRIST was in the spirit of God before all time, and was in heaven, just as he also remains with us, even unto the end of the world.[7] And for this reason alone, that his words were heavenly, you ought to have admitted that he himself was from heaven; for the baptism of John was from heaven, and *the second man is of heaven, heavenly.*[8] With regard to what you say, that he was sent by the Father, there seems to be no great difficulty. For John also is said to have been sent from God: *There was a man sent from God, whose name was John.*[9] Likewise Moses and the Prophets are said to have been sent by God.[10] And CHRIST, speaking to the Father about the Apostles, says, *As thou didst send me into the world, so send I them into the world.*[11] And, *As the Father hath sent me, even so send I you.*[12]

23. I am forced to light upon these illustrations, not because they furnish a complete analogy, but in order to persuade you that a man was sent; which you, led astray by your philosophy, undertake to deny. For it is a great mistake to say that the second being is said to be passively sent, when it is the very Na-

---

[1] Wisdom xviii, 15.
[2] John vi, 33.
[3] Deut. viii, 3; Matt. iv, 4.
[4] John vi, 53–56.
[5] Books II and III.
[6] John viii, 23.
[7] Matt. xxviii, 20.
[8] I. Cor. xv, 47.
[9] John i, 6.
[10] Matt. xxiii, 34; Luke xi, 49.
[11] John xvii, 18.
[12] John xx, 21.

ture of God. It is true that this unique sending of CHRIST, and his coming forth from the Father, has its roots fixed in God, as we shall explain when the mystery of the Word is disclosed.¹ Likewise, as for your saying that CHRIST came into the world, what wonder is it, when this is also true of others: *Every man coming into this world.*² Again, of what king do you understand this passage: *Blessed is the King that cometh in the name of the Lord.*³ Again, observe that those that are led by the spirit of God are not of the world; ⁴ and they are said to come into the world even as into the houses of publicans. And they are said to come into this earthly tabernacle of our body, and are said to put on flesh, even as when one puts on a garment. And he that speaks by the spirit observes that he is above the world. And Peter said that he was bound in this tabernacle as in something put upon him, speaking, that is, after the inward man.⁵

The third argument of the Pharisees.

24. Moreover, you can prove in what way CHRIST *thought it not robbery to be equal with God.*⁶ These words of Paul are so obscurely and variously interpreted by them that they can clearly convince no one by the words themselves; and that the more, since it is perfectly plain that Paul is simply speaking of CHRIST JESUS. In the first place, some interpret it as meaning that the second Person, apart from robbery, thought itself to be equal with the first. And again, they warp this ignorant explanation and make it refer to philosophical Natures, saying that he did not think that to be a matter of robbery which belonged to his Nature. Others say, He did not think it robbery that he should be equal with God; that is, he did not think it a robbery of the equality with God, did not care to seize for himself equality with God. This meaning is more plausible than the first, because Paul never thought of the Natures, and it is counter to Paul's purpose, who is treating of nothing but CHRIST'S modesty and humility. Also the force of the word, *but*,⁷ is clearly opposed to them, which, as the Lawyers say, is taken adversatively; and of necessity the meaning is bound to be this: He did not exalt him-

---

¹ Book III.
² John i, 9 (Vulg.).
³ Luke xix, 38.
⁴ John xvii, 14; I. John ii, 16.
⁵ II. Pet. i, 13, 14.
⁶ Phil. ii, 6 (Vulg.).
⁷ Phil. ii, 7.

self, *but* he humbled himself; he did not think it [robbery], *but* abased, emptied, submitted himself. But in vain do I waste my labor on these things (which are all false), when the true solution lies in the words of the Master. For the objection of the Pharisees, who assailed CHRIST, is that he made himself equal with God; and CHRIST, in reply, did not deny this equality, but said, *What things soever the Father did, these the Son also will do in like manner*; and, *As the Father raiseth the dead, giveth them life*, cleanseth lepers, giveth sight to the blind, healeth the deaf, the paralytics, the demoniacs, and others, *even so doth the Son;* and finally, *The Father hath given all judgment*, all power, *unto the Son, that all may honor the Son, even as they honor the Father.*[1] Behold how CHRIST was made equal with God, because all things whatsoever the Father hath are his.[2] Behold how the μορφή,[3] that is, the appearance of Deity, shone forth in him when he wrought such great miracles; and this is what Paul says, that he existed in the *form* and appearance of God.[4] From this let us observe the humility of CHRIST, which Paul cites to us as a model of all humility; for the greater the power he is endowed with, the greater is his humility, the more he submits and abases himself. For there are many good men who, if they are made magistrates, or have reached a higher estate, prove tyrants. But not so with CHRIST; for CHRIST did not think that this great equality which he had with God constituted robbery, and would not use it in the way of robbery. Firstly, because he did not accept the robbery when he perceived that they were about to take him by force, to make him king;[5] but he bore himself in humble fashion, and would that his kingdom should not be of this world.[6] And it is this discourse[7] that Paul has in mind. Secondly, he thought it not robbery to seize for himself twelve legions of angels[8] and defend himself by force against the Jews, but chose humbly to suffer.

25. This, then, is the equality which he had while existing in

---

[1] John v, 19, 21–23, loosely conflated with Matt. xi, 5.
[2] Matt. xi, 27; John iii, 35; xiii, 3.
[3] *Morphe*, form.
[4] Phil. ii, 6.
[5] John vi, 15.
[6] John xviii, 36.
[7] i. e., in John v, vi.
[8] Matt. xxvi, 53.

the form of God: he had in himself an equal power with God by reason of the authority that was given him in equal measure with God.[1] Because he was found to be God by his power, just as he was man by his flesh. And all things that the Father hath are his;[2] and through him all things are done that are performed by the Word of God, since he himself is the Word of God.[3] And he spoke thus of an equality of power because, *The Son of man shall be seated at the right hand of the power of God.*[4] And Stephen saw him at the right hand of the power of God.[5] And this equality and exaltation at the right hand of God Paul proclaims saying, not of the *being*, but of CHRIST, that he was placed *above all rule, authority, power, and dominion, and every name that is named, not only in this world, but also in that which is to come*;[6] finally, that all things were put in subjection under his feet, and that he was given to be head over all things to the Church itself, who filleth all in all.[7] Likewise equality in him with the power of God is noted in Daniel: *Behold, there came . . . a son of man, and he came even to the ancient of days*, and there was given him all kingly power.[8] And wonder at him is expressed in Jeremiah: Who is he that thus approacheth and hath been caused to draw near to God?[9] so that he even comes near being equal to [God] himself. And this is the mere truth, so that Joseph was made equal to Pharaoh, although strictly speaking he says, Pharaoh is greater than I.

19a

Their argument is turned the other way in many ways.

26. Again, Paul did not say that there are two beings and one Nature, or that the second Person is of equal Essence with the first. For had Paul understood that the second Person thought it not robbery to be of equal Nature with the first, wherefore did he not say that it was equal with the first Person, and not, with God? for the word of God is living,[10] and there denotes something distinct from God. Why should he also have dragged in the saying about robbery? What suspicion of robbery could there be in one who is the same being, the same Nature: for Paul would

---

[1] John v, 27.
[2] John iii, 35; xiii, 3.
[3] John i, 1, 3.
[4] Luke xxii, 69.
[5] Acts vii, 55, 56.
[6] Eph. i, 21.
[7] Eph. i, 22, 23.
[8] Dan. vii, 13, 14.
[9] Jer. xxx, 21.
[10] Heb. iv, 12.

have been speaking foolishly. Again, who does not see that the word, *thought*,[1] is altogether human? Who does not see that it is blasphemy for the sentence of robbery to be passed on the *beings*? Again, hear how he says, existing *in the form of God*.[2] How could he have said that the second Person had the appearance of Deity if it is itself a deity, and that by Nature, if it is God quite as properly, and as much by Nature, as the first Person? Paul spoke absurdly. He who said that the Father was greater than himself spoke falsely; for, to speak without caviling, the *being greater* is there spoken of with regard to the Son, as is evident from the word, *Father*, and from the related word, *I*. You ought also, if there is a Metaphysical equality, as readily and as properly to admit that the first Person is the Father of God, and is equal to the Son, as you would the reverse, which, however, the Scripture shrinks from saying. Again, consider the words of Paul which follow: *Wherefore God highly exalted him*;[3] for the reference is to the one who "thought." Was the second Person, then, so greatly exalted because it humbled itself? For I deem it ridiculous to say that the Nature of God humbles itself. Again, as I have said, taking into account Paul's aim, the blindness of Theophylact [4] is mitigated; for Paul is here treating not of CHRIST's Nature, but of his appearance. How, then, can the equality of his Nature be inferred from this passage? Again, take here the word ἴσα,[5] used in the Greek in place of the adverb, *equally*; for the expression, *equally*, denotes not his nature but his station; and he could pronounce himself on an equality with God in power, who promises that he can do all things soever that the Father does.[6]

27. The unmistakable explanation of the truth is this: that though existing in the likeness of God, having the power of God, he did not deem it robbery to be on an equality with God, did not think that he should use this power of God by way of robbery. For it really would have been robbery, had he violently

---

[1] Phil. ii, 6, "thought it not robbery."
[2] Phil. ii, 6.   [3] Phil. ii, 9.
[4] Comment. in Ep. ad Phil. ii, 9 (MPG. cxxiv, 1166).
[5] *Isa.*, equal.
[6] Matt. xi, 27; John iii, 35; v, 19; xiii, 3.

withdrawn from the work to which the Father had appointed him, or had he seized for himself a kingly tyranny over this world. And this is the proper meaning of the word ἁρπαγμός.¹ For CHRIST never cared to plunder, never violently robbed any one of anything. This idea is made clear by the Greek article, τό,² as if to say, the very fact that he was on an equality with God. As to this equality with God in him, he did not think that it constituted robbery. Nor does Paul, as some most groundlessly suppose, treat the word, *on an equality*, as of capital importance. But he brings this in by way of a consequence from his likeness to deity, for he says that he existed in the likeness of God. He did not think that τὸ εἶναι ἶσα θεῷ ³ — did not think that that was a question of equality, did not think that the equality (which, that is to say, he had when existing in the form of God) constituted robbery. And this meaning is clear from the passage above quoted,⁴ nor can any other equality be treated of here than is treated of there. For when his equality with God was being treated of there, CHRIST did not deny it. Indeed, he showed that it was actually in him, although he did not use it, as a tyrant or a giant, by way of robbery, but bore himself humbly, in the servile fashion of man, becoming obedient even unto death.⁵ When it is said that he took the form or appearance of a servant, he says this in order to mark a distinction from the form of God of which he had been speaking; for the word μορφή ⁶ is used in both clauses, and he spoke on purpose to express greater humility. For though he possessed both appearances, he used the humbler; not the appearance and might of God, but as one among men. And he is said to have been *found in fashion as a man*; ⁷ even as the Psalmist says, Ye shall die as men, though ye be gods.⁸ And Sampson, because he was very strong, as though he were not a man, but more than a man, said, I shall then be weak, as men are.⁹ These are all the passages of

20a

20b

---

¹ *Harpagmos*, robbery.
² In the Greek quoted just below.
³ *To einai isa theo*, the being on an equality with God.
⁴ John v, 19–23, in paragraph 23.
⁵ Phil. ii, 7, 8.   ⁶ *Morphe*, form.
⁷ Phil. ii, 8.   ⁸ Ps. lxxxii, 6, 7.
⁹ Judges xvi, 7.

Scripture that speak of equality, far removed from the disputes of our age; and the question as to equality or inequality of Nature was unknown to the Apostles.

28. Yet some reason out an equality of Nature, because it says, using the same word, *The Lord said unto my Lord.*[1] But they should be pardoned, for not knowing the original language of Holy Scripture they know not their own selves. Yet you, if you know Hebrew, will find the prophet saying, נאם יהוה לאדני.[2] It obviously also says of CHRIST *Adon*.[3] And this prophecy about sitting on the right hand is fulfilled in CHRIST, as is shown in the tenth of Hebrews.[4] Nevertheless the philosophers invent other sittings in the eternities of the ages. Again, this is known of itself from the words of CHRIST, nor does he make a point of applying the name יהוה [5] to himself; for in that case it would have been easy for the Jews to reply to him.

Ignorance of the divine names deceives the philosophers.

29. To sum up, that you may know the trend of my thought: I say that with the single exception of the passage in John,[6] all the Scriptures from first to last speak of the man CHRIST himself; and the passage in John speaks not of what is but of what was; and the mistake lies in not understanding *what* that was, and how it became flesh. And let not your fancies lead you astray, but lay this up in your inmost hearts: that in all the Scriptures the man CHRIST himself is speaking, and let your thoughts be ever directed to him. Pray God to grant you a cheerful mind to hear, and I will (without any pettifogging, hair-splitting, or equivocation) render the Scriptures as plain to you as day, and will place God himself before your eyes, provided that you always look upon the face of CHRIST.

There is in the Gospel not one letter which speaks of the Mathematical Son.

OF THE HOLY SPIRIT

30. The philosophers have invented besides a third separate being, truly and really distinct from the other two, which they call the third Person, or the Holy Spirit; and thus they have contrived an imaginary Trinity, three beings in one Nature. But in

---

[1] Ps. cx, 1.
[2] ibid., *Naam Jehovah leadonai*, Jehovah said unto my Lord.
[3] Heb., Lord; Mal. iii, 1.   [4] Heb. x, 12; cf. Mark xvi, 19.
[5] Jehovah.   [6] John i, 1.

reality three beings, three Gods, or one threefold God, are foisted upon us under the pretense and with the names of a unity. On this matter hear the view of recent writers which John Major states in his *Sentences*.[1] For with them it is very easy, taking the words in their strict sense, for three beings to exist which they say are strictly, simply, truly and really so different or distinct that one is born of another, and one is breathed out by the others, and all these three are shut up in one jar. I, however, since I am unwilling to misuse the word Persons, shall call them the first *being*, the second being, the third being;[2] for in the Scriptures I find no other name for them, and what is properly to be thought of the Persons I shall say later on.[3] Admitting, therefore, these three, which after their own fashion they call Persons, by reasoning from the lower to the higher they freely admit a plurality of beings, a plurality of entities, a plurality of Essences, a plurality of *Ousias*,[4] and in consequence, taking the word, *God*, strictly, they will have a plurality of Gods.

31. If this is so, why are the Tritoites[5] blamed, who say that there are three Gods? For they also contrive three Gods, or one threefold one. These three Gods of theirs form one composite *Ousia*; and although some will not use a word implying that the three have been put together,[6] yet they do use a word implying that they are constituted together,[6] and that God is constituted out of the three beings. It is clear, therefore, that we are Tritoites, and we have a threefold God: we have become Atheists, that is, men without any God. For as soon as we try to think

---

[1] Book I, dist. v, solution of the 6th argument. [2] See note 12, par. 3.
[3] Paragraph 51. [4] Greek for Latin *essentia*.

[5] The word *Tritoitae* has been the occasion of much discussion. The counterfeit reprint of this work uniformly replaces it by *Tritheitae*, as though a misprint; but that Servetus used the term deliberately is shown by the fact that it repeatedly occurs, both in this work (above, and in paragraphs 50, 55) and in his *Christianismi Restitutio* (pp. 30, 108, 394, 406). It has generally been inferred from the context that it means tritheists; and a precisely contemporary work, Sebastian Franck's Chronica, Argentorati, 1531, p. cccxxxviib, defines it thus: Tritoite oder Tricolite, die gleich wie sy drey person in der Trifeltigkeyt zulassen, also auch drey götter. But if etymology has any bearing (Greek *tritos*, third), it should mean worshipers of the third Person. The term with this meaning would involve tritheism, though not expressly charging it. Servetus seriously objected to the worship of the Holy Spirit, as this part of his work shows.

[6] *Compositionis verbo . . . constitutionis verbo.* cf. paragraph 57.

about God, we are turned aside to three phantoms, so that no kind of unity remains in our conception. But what else is being without God but being unable to think about God, when there is always presented to our understanding a haunting kind of confusion of three beings, by which we are forever deluded into supposing that we are thinking about God. And see how manfully they defend the one God. For even if they admitted a downright and absolute plurality of Beings and Entities, and consequently a plurality of absolute Gods, yet they have one connotative God. For they say (to refer to the passage cited above)[1] that these words, as they use, or rather misuse, them, are not taken in the strict sense, but in a sort of artificial, sophistical, and connotative way. They seem to be living in another world while they dream of such things; for the kingdom of heaven knows none of this nonsense, and it is in another way, unknown to them, that Scripture speaks of the Holy Spirit.

32. But since this matter requires more thorough investigation, let it be reserved for the following books.[2] For indeed Scripture treats strangely and almost incomprehensibly of this matter, especially for those who are not acquainted with its peculiar habit of speaking. For by Holy Spirit it means now God himself, now an angel, now the spirit of a man, a sort of instinct or divine inspiration of the mind, a mental impulse, or a breath; although sometimes a difference is marked between breath and Spirit. And some would have the Holy Spirit mean nothing other than the right understanding and reason of man. And with the Hebrews רוח[3] means nothing other than breath, or breathing, which is expressed indifferently as wind and spirit; and with the Greeks πνεῦμα[4] is taken for any spirit or mental impulse whatsoever. Nor is it any objection that a spirit is called holy; for all these operations of the mind, when they concern the religion of CHRIST, are called holy, and sacred to God, since *no man can say,* JESUS *is Lord, but in the Holy Spirit.*[5]

33. It remains to reply to certain passages of Scripture from which the Moderns suppose that the three beings can be de-

---

[1] i. e., from John Major, in paragraph 29.
[2] Books IV and VII.
[3] *Ruach,* spirit.
[4] *Pneuma,* spirit.
[5] I. Cor. xii, 3.

duced: as, *There are three that bear record in heaven, the Father, the Word, and the Holy Spirit, and these three are one.*¹ But in order to give this a more satisfactory answer, I shall reply first to two other passages of Scripture, which they also bring forward to prove this matter: *I and the Father are one*, and, *The Father is in me, and I in the Father.*² The first passage Augustine brings forward against Arius, because he said, *one*; and against Sabellius, because he said, *are*.³ And from this he argues the two beings as against Sabellius, and one Nature as against Arius. Yet I think that the words make simpler sense, for CHRIST is speaking, and he said, *are*; because, being God and man, he said, *one* in the neuter, as Tertullian says,⁴ and he did not say, *one* in the masculine. For the meaning of *one* in the masculine singular seems to be as if it denoted the singleness of one and the same being. But *one* in the neuter has reference not to singleness, but to oneness of mind, and harmony, so that the two might be credited with one power. And this is what the earlier writers rightly called one *ousia*, because there is one authority given by the Father to the Son. But later writers made a most wicked jest of the word *homousion*,⁵ as well as of *hypostasis*,⁶ and Persons, making Nature out of *ousia*, not only contrary to the proper meaning of the word, but contrary to all passages of Scripture in which that word is found. For in John and Matthew,⁷ and wherever Christ speaks of the authority given him of the Father, the expression *ousia* is used, which to the Greeks signifies not Nature, but wealth, treasures, possessions, riches, and power, which are all in CHRIST in rich measure; and he has one authority, one sympathy and will, with the Father. And both *unum* ⁸ for the Latins and ἕν ⁹ for the Greeks include those that are of one mind, are alike, and all mind the same

23a

---

¹ I. John v, 7 (Vulg.).   ² John x, 30; xiv, 10, 11.
³ In Joannis Evang., Tract. lxxi (MPL. xxxv, 182; NPNF. ser. i, vii, 328; Dods, xi, 261).
⁴ Adv. Praxean xxv (MPL. ii, 188; ANF. iii, 621; ANCL. xv, 391).
⁵ Of the same substance.
⁶ Substance, also Person.
⁷ John xvii, 2; Matt. xxviii, 18 (the word actually used in these passages is not οὐσία, but ἐξουσία).
⁸ One (n.).   ⁹ One (n.).

thing; and to take *unum* in the Scriptures for one Nature is more Metaphysical than Christian; nay, it is foreign to the Scriptures. Greece never knew of ἕν being taken for one Nature. Should you say, Why, then, do the Greek doctors take is so? let Basil the Great reply to this, where he says [1] that this is not in accordance with the proper meaning of the word, but is philo-
23b sophical reasoning. We ought therefore to get at the interpretation of the word either from its proper meaning, or from other passages of Scripture. But you will nowhere find that *unum* in the Scriptures means the Metaphysical unity of nature; indeed, quite the contrary, as appears from the words of CHRIST his own self, who like a faithful teacher explains himself where he prays the Father for the Apostles, *that they may all be one; even as thou, Father, art in me, and I in thee, that they also may be one in us . . . and that they may be one, even as we also are one.*[2] Repeating the word again and again, he prays that they may be one (*unum*). Does it then follow that we, who are one in the same way as they, constitute one Nature? Of course we are one, since we are of one mind, *keeping the unity of the Spirit in the bond of peace.*[3] Again, *I will give them one heart and one way;*[4] and, *The multitude of them that believed had one heart and one soul.*[5] And along with understanding this saying, Origen would have another saying expressly understood: The Father and the Son, he says, are one, for it is evident that they are two beings in Substance, but one in sympathy and harmony, and in identity of will.[6]

34. There seems to be a similar thought in Cyprian;[8] and Paul concludes from our unity of faith that we are one;[9] and,
24a *He that is joined unto the Lord is one spirit* with him.[10] Yet he never thought of one Nature. Nay, even had he said, I and the Father are not two, but one, you would draw no conclusion from it; for Man and Woman are *not two, but one flesh;*[11] yet one does

Erasmus also explains it thus in his Notes.[7]

---

[1] Adv. Eunomium, IV (MPG. xxix, 679).
[2] John xvii, 21, 22.   [3] Eph. iv, 3.
[4] Jer. xxxii, 39.   [5] Acts iv, 32.
[6] Contra Celsum, VIII. xii (MPG. xi, 1534; ANF. iv, 643 f.; ANCL. xxiii, 500), where he explains John x, 30 in the light of these texts.
[7] Paraphrases in N. T., ad loc.
[8] Ep. ad Magnum, v (MPL. iii, 1141; ANF. v, 398; ANCL. viii, 306).
[9] Gal. iii, 26, 28.   [10] I. Cor. vi, 17.   [11] Matt. xix, 6.

not reason from this that they have one Nature. If you say it is not necessary that in that passage [1] there be all manner of likeness, because the Apostles are as properly said to be one as the Son and the Father are one; in this you say well that there is not *all manner*, but you assume that there is *none*, whereas there is *some*. And that there is not all manner of likeness is undoubted, for he alone is in the bosom of the Father, he has one power together with the Father, has the same deity and authority. Hence he is said to be one with the Father in a far higher way, especially in those writers who understand the mystery of the Word; yet it does not therefore follow that you may argue from this the mathematical unity of nature, for that is a philosophical fancy, standing much by itself, and it is not set forth in the sacred records. Moreover, in that case, CHRIST's comparison would be inappropriate and irrelevant [if he meant] that we may be one Nature, and that we may be harmonious, when he says, *May be One, even as we are one*. Again, you will grasp CHRIST's meaning from another angle, if you do not take the words raw and undigested, but note the order and cause of what he says; for CHRIST added that he was one with the Father for the purpose of proving that no one can snatch his sheep out of his hand, because the Father hath given them to him.[2] And if no one can snatch them out of the hand of the Father, it follows that no one will be able to snatch them out of his own hand; since he and the Father are one power, and he holds them by the Father's consent.

35. As a result of this, another passage is explained: The Father is in me, and I in the Father,[3] and yet they are deluded about this. For Hilary says [4] that the nature of the human intelligence does not grasp the reason of this saying, and he concludes proportionably that some beings exist in other beings, that single beings exist in single beings, the first in the third, and the third in the second, and conversely. But one must wonder why he permits himself to be set at odds with his own good sense, and

---

[1] John xvii, 21.   [2] John x, 28, 29.
[3] John xiv, 11.
[4] Hilary of Poitiers, De Trinitate, III (Servetus says IV), 1 (MPL. x, 76; NPNF., Ser. ii, ix, 62).

pays no regard to the Master's explanation. It is a sheer waste of breath to call CHRIST master, if we pay no attention to his explanations. For in the same chapter CHRIST says to the Apostles, *I am in my Father, ye in me, and I in you*.[1] Yet the Apostles are not with CHRIST in the sense of being crowded into one Nature. Again, what is more, in that and the following chapter CHRIST explains himself by saying that he is in us when we keep his words;[2] and he is in the Father because he keeps his commands and loves him.[3] Again, what is yet more, in this chapter and the tenth he infers from the fact that he does the works of the Father that he is in the Father, saying, *Believe me*
25a *for the very works' sake . . . that ye may know and believe that the Father is in me, and I in the Father*.[4] Let Hilary consider what the Master's way of reasoning was, how from his works CHRIST infers the Metaphysics of the Natures, or the inherent existence of the beings in one Nature. Also in the chapter cited above CHRIST explains himself; and he is said to be in the Father in almost the same way in which he had said that he was one with the Father; for he says, *Even as thou, Father, art in me, and I in thee, that they may be one in us*, and, *That the love wherewith thou lovedst me may be in them, and I in them*.[5] And, CHRIST abideth in us, and we in him.[6] And from faith and love the conclusion is that CHRIST is in us.[7] And from love the inference is that we are in him;[8] and, *He that keepeth his commandments abideth in him, and he in him*.[9]

36. From this point on the main question is easily settled. In the first place, the Father testifies: *The Father that hath sent me, he beareth witness of me*;[10] for he testifies, saying, *This is my beloved Son*.[11] In the second place, the Word testifies; for the very language of CHRIST makes it plain enough that he is from God, as he witnesses concerning himself. From his words it is seen above all how great he is, although the world to-day makes

---

[1] John xiv, 20.
[2] John xiv, 23; xv, 7.
[3] John xv, 10.
[4] John xiv, 11; x, 38.
[5] John xvii, 21, 26.
[6] John vi, 56.
[7] Eph. iii, 17.
[8] I. John ii, 24.
[9] I. John iii, 24.
[10] John v, 37.
[11] Matt. iii, 17.

CHRIST'S words trifling and ineffectual. But when the spirit is given they will be found to be full of life. In the third place, the Holy Spirit testifies; but as to what this is, I say nothing here, meaning to set it forth in the following Book.[1] You shall also see what else can be understood by the Paraclete. For the present I say as CHRIST explains: For while I am present, the language that you have heard, or the words that I speak, bear testimony;[2] afterwards, when ye are clothed with power from on high, as Luke says,[3] ye shall bear witness; and when this power had been received through the Spirit coming upon them, he commanded them to bear witness.[4] And this is the witness of the Holy Spirit, even as Paul calls the witness of his conscience the witness of the Holy Spirit.[5] And these three are one, as has been explained above.[6] And the *Glossa Ordinaria* itself explains: *Are one*; that is, bearing witness of the same thing.[7] For John's intention is to show the force of the truth from the agreement of the witnesses; because their testimonies do not waver or vary so that they can be objected to by some exception taken, as often happens in the case of different witnesses in law. Besides, a note on Matthew xvii, 3 says, You may see Moses and Elijah talking with JESUS; for the Law and the Prophets and JESUS say one thing and agree together.[8] Thus three testify there to the Word itself: CHRIST himself, and Moses, that is, the Law given by the Father, and Elijah, that is, the spirit of the Prophets; because *the testimony of* JESUS *is the spirit of prophecy*.[9] And these three are one, and between them there is the most complete harmony of thought. Again, an explanation is found in the words of the Master, who cites three witnesses:[10] firstly, the witness of the Spirit, for John bore witness when the Spirit descended; secondly, his own witness, for the works that he does bear wit-

---

[1] Book II, paragraph 21 ff.
[2] John xiv, 25, 26; xv, 26.
[3] Luke xxiv, 49.   [4] Acts i, 8.
[5] Rom. ix, 1.   [6] Paragraphs 33–35.
[7] The *Glossa Ordinaria* of Walafrid Strabo served the West for five centuries as the chief source of biblical learning. (MPL. cxiv, 702 f.)
[8] Strabo, op. cit. (MPL. cxiv, 144).
[9] Rev. xix, 10.
[10] John v, 33, 36, 37.

ness; thirdly, he adduces the witness of the Father who bears witness; and these three agree.

37. We can now turn their argument the other way, showing that the saying in John can not be taken in their sense, since it is counter to his whole design and intention; for it is evident that it is there a question not of the nature of the three beings, but of the credibility and agreement of the testimony. Again, see for what purpose he introduces these testimonies; observe in what direction John's proof tends. For he is not aiming to derive one Idea from another, or to prove that the second being is the offspring of the first. But he is proving that the JESUS of Nazareth whom his eyes have seen, and his hands have touched, is the Son of God, and not the son of Joseph. And he exhorts us to believe this, as we strictly hold it. And he that does not so believe is no Christian; he that does not so believe is not founded upon the rock: *Thou art the* CHRIST, *the Son of the living God.*[1] For this is the rock (*petra*) from which he was named Peter (*Petrus*), the rock on which Peter was the first to be founded. To believe that JESUS CHRIST is the Son of God is the foundation of the Church. *Peter was the first stone, because he more firmly and earlier than the others believed that Jesus was the Son of God.*

26b This is the corner-stone upon which the whole building groweth unto the building up of the body of CHRIST, which is the Church.[2] You will say, CHRIST himself is the corner-stone; but what, pray, is CHRIST in us, but to believe that he is the Son of God? For CHRIST dwells in our hearts through faith.[3] It is an idle thing to say that CHRIST is of himself the rock, if you destroy that which builds us upon the rock.

38. A second authority which, according to Peter Lombard,[4] very evidently supports the Trinity is, *Of him, through him, and in him are all things.*[5] For Augustine[6] explains this as referring to the three beings: *of him*, referring to the first; *through him*, to the second; *in him*, to the third. But I do not believe that Paul, had he been questioned about this, would philosophize thus; for this would be contrary to his wont; and it would be irrelevant for him to treat of these things in that connection. For he is

---

[1] Matt. xvi, 16.   [2] Eph. ii, 20, 21; iv, 12; Col. i, 24.
[3] Eph. iii, 17.   [4] Sent. I, dist. ii, cap. v.   [5] Rom. xi, 36.
[6] De Trinitate I (Servetus wrongly cites II), vi, 12 (MPL. xlii, 827; NPNF. ser. i. iii, 22; Dods, vii, 12).

merely exclaiming at the depth [of the riches] of God the Father; and all the philosophy that can there be inferred is in the phrase, *through him.* For when in another place he says, *through the Word*,[1] and here, *through him,* it implied that all things that God made through the Word he made through him; and of this Irenaeus also bears witness.[2] The following Book,[3] therefore, will show that, according to him, this passage makes against them. And Paul here means nothing else than to commend the manifold *dispositions*[4] of God, and the greatness of his power, as when he says he is over all, through all, and in all.[5] And that the more because the Apostle is also, in this triple phrase, not including the third Person. *There is,* he says, *one God the Father, of whom are all things, and we in him; and one Lord* JESUS CHRIST, *through whom are all things, and we through him.*[6] Here are the three phrases: *of him, through him,* and *in him,* whereas he makes no mention of a third Person. And again the Apostle says of the Son alone, *All things have been created through him, and in him.*[7]

27a

39. Moreover, Jerome reasons to the three beings from the three measures of meal.[8] But it is exceedingly silly, and savors somewhat of Plato, to reason to numbers in beings from parables and numbers of words. If such reasoning is allowed us, why are Marcus Calarbasus[9] and his like blamed, who from parables, from the letters and numbers of the words of Holy Writ, reason to ternions, quaternions, and octonarions, and in like manner reason out a Demiurge, a Bythos, a Pleroma, and in fine the various Aeons? Only in name do the latter seem to differ from the former; and even as they declare that some beings arise from others as a result of the laughter and the tears of the

---

[1] Rom. x, 17.
[2] Adv. Haereses, IV. xx, 4 (MPG. vii, 1034; ANF. i, 488; ANCL. v, 441).
[3] Book II, paragraphs 5 and 7.
[4] See note 2, paragraph 41.   [5] Eph. iv, 6.
[6] I. Cor. viii, 6.   [7] Col. i, 16 (Vulg.).
[8] Comment. in Matt. xiii, 33. (MPL. xxvi, 91.)
[9] Colarbasus, or Colorbasus (Servetus spells, Calarbasus), is a supposed Valentinian Gnostic of the second century, referred to by Irenaeus, Contra Haer. I. xii. Marcus was his follower (ib. xiii–xvi). Unless a comma has dropped out from between the names, Servetus fuses the two, mistaking them for a single individual.

Aeons, so we say that the first being produces the second by being aware of itself, and that these two by loving each other breathe forth the third. Pray, where in the Scriptures did you read of these marvelous things? And beyond these, we add this the most dreadful thing of all: that these three beings, that so differ one from another, are yet one and the same being.

40. Furthermore, Lombard says [1] that almost every separate syllable of the New Testament agrees in suggesting this Trinity. But to me not merely the syllables, but all the letters, and the mouths of babes and sucklings, nay the very stones, cry out, One God the Father, and his CHRIST the Lord JESUS; *for there is one God, and one mediator between God and men, the man* CHRIST JESUS; [2] and, *To us there is one God, who is the Father, . . . and one Lord,* JESUS CHRIST.[3] John also, to whom the heavens were opened in the Apocalypse, saw only God the Father, and his CHRIST, and only God and the Lamb are there praised.[4] Again, Stephen, when the heavens were opened, *saw the glory of God, and* JESUS *standing on his right hand,*[5] yet he saw no third Person. And, *One is your Father,* and, *One is your Master, even the* CHRIST; [6] and, *I am not alone, but I and the Father.*[7] These words of CHRIST, uttered with such emphasis, often pierce to my very vitals. *I am not alone,* he says, *because the Father is with me;* [8] and, *They have not known the Father, nor me;* [9] and *That they should know thee the only true God, and him whom thou didst send, even* JESUS CHRIST.[10] He did not also command us to worship a third being, but the Father and himself, and the Father in his name.[11] Likewise, when he said, *No one knoweth the Father, save the Son; nor the Son, save the Father,*[12] was the third being asleep, or had it no knowledge of these? And John desires us to have fellowship with the Father, and with his Son, JESUS CHRIST; [13] yet of fellowship with the third being he does not speak. And Paul says, *I charge thee in the sight of God, and the Lord* JESUS

---

[1] Sent. I, dist. ii, cap. v.
[2] I. Tim. ii, 5.
[3] I. Cor. viii, 6.
[4] Rev. xxi, 22; v, 12, 13; vii, 10.
[5] Acts. vii, 55, 56.
[6] Matt. xxiii, 9, 10.
[7] John viii, 16.
[8] John xvi, 32.
[9] John xvi, 3.
[10] John xvii, 3.
[11] John xvi, 23.
[12] Matt. xi, 27.
[13] I. John i, 3.

CHRIST, *and the elect angels, that thou observe these things without prejudice.*[1] Mark that Paul's solemn protestation is made before God, CHRIST, and the angels, and not before the third being. Likewise, *I will confess his name,* says CHRIST, *before my Father, and before angels.*[2] Mark the grave affront to the third being, in that CHRIST says, *before angels,* and not, *before it.* Likewise he makes mention of himself alone, and the Father, and the angels;[3] and John desires for us grace and peace from Almighty God, *and from the seven Spirits that are before his throne, and from* JESUS CHRIST, *who is the faithful witness;*[4] yet from the third being he desires nothing for us. And Paul in all his epistles says, *God the Father, and the Lord* JESUS CHRIST; *from God the Father, and the Lord* JESUS CHRIST.[5] And in the Scriptures there is frequent mention of the existence of God the Father, and of the Son, and of seeing and praying to them; but of the Holy Spirit no mention is made, except where it speaks about doing something, as by a sort of casual statement; which is noteworthy, as though the Holy Spirit denoted not a separate being, but an activity of God, a kind of in-working or in-breathing of the power of God.

41. Lombard, following others, establishes his triad of beings by the passage: *The God of Abraham, the God of Isaac, the God of Jacob.*[6] If they were speaking of the Trinity in the proper sense, it might be let pass, even if this passage does not prove it. But it is proved by the passage, Baptize *in the name of the Father, and of the Son, and of the Holy Spirit.*[7] In the name of the Father, because he is the prime, true, and original source of every gift.[8] In the name of JESUS CHRIST, because through him we have the reconciliation of this gift, *neither is there any other name under heaven wherein we must be saved.*[9] And in the name of the Holy

---

[1] I. Tim. (Servetus says I. John) v, 21.
[2] Rev. iii, 5.
[3] Mark viii, 38; Luke ix, 26; xii, 8, 9.
[4] Rev. i, 4, 5.
[5] So in the greeting prefixed to each epistle, from Romans to Philemon.
[6] Ex. iii, 6. cf. Lombard, Sent. I, dist. xxxiv, cap. ii.
[7] Matt. xxviii, 19.
[8] James i, 17.
[9] Acts iv, 12.

Spirit, because all that are baptized in that name receive the gift of the Holy Spirit. Just as we say, in the name of his Imperial Majesty, in the name of the glory of God. And Peter, in the Clementine Recognitions,[1] speaks not of three equal beings, but of a threefold invocation of the divine name. Because there are three wonderful *dispositions* [2] of God, in each of which his divinity shines forth; and from this you might very well understand a Trinity. For the Father is the whole substance and the one God from whom these degrees and personations proceed. And they are three, not by virtue of some distinction of beings in God, but through an οἰκονομία [3] of God in various forms of Deity; for the same divinity which is in the Father is communicated to the Son, JESUS CHRIST, and to our spirits, which are the temples of the living God; for the Son and our sanctified spirits are sharers with us in the Substance of the Father, are its members, pledges, and instruments; although the kind of deity in them is varying, and this is why they are called distinct Persons, that is, manifold aspects, diverse forms and kinds, of deity. Nor are the older traditions of the Apostles at variance with his view; on the contrary, they agree with it. Now as for the reason: that the three beings are not denoted in it is proved by the fact that when God spoke to Jacob he said, *I am the God of thy father Abraham and Isaac.*[4] Yet you can not from this infer two phil-

29a

They say that to-day the Essence is communicable to the three beings.

---

[1] II. xlii (MPG. i, 1268 f.; ANF. viii, 108 f.; ANCL. iii, 220).

[2] *Dispositiones*. This term gives the key to Servetus's explanation of the Trinity. It is taken as the equivalent of the Greek οἰκονομία (*oikonomia*), and may be variously translated economy, management, disposition, dispensation, distribution, division, arrangement, modification; though perhaps aspects suggests the author's thought as well as anything. The idea is that God disposes or manages himself in three different ways for three different forms of his activity. Servetus has evidently taken his view from Tertullian, Adv. Praxean, ii, iii (MPL. ii, 156–159; ANF. iii, 598 f.; ANCL. xv, 335–339). The annotator of the Latin version of Irenaeus, Adv. Haer., I. vi (MPG. vii, 503) remarks: "*A dispositione*. So the translator is wont to render the Greek word οἰκονομία, . . . but I could wish that he had agreed with the other Latin writers in translating it *dispensatio*; for this word denotes what the Savior did upon earth to procure the salvation of the human race, of which the incarnation is the source and beginning, which the Greeks express by the one word οἰκονομία, and the Latins by *dispensatio*." Cf. Book II, paragraph 5.

[3] *Oikonomia*, disposition, or dispensation.

[4] Gen. xxviii, 13; cf. xxxii, 9.

osophical terms. And when he spoke to Isaac, he said, *I am the God of thy father Abraham.*[1] Again, if the three beings are understood there, how will the God of Abraham, the God of Isaac, the God of Jacob be called the Father of JESUS CHRIST?[2] Is the imaginary Trinity called the Father of JESUS CHRIST? For as the first Person begot this man, so also did the second; and thus we shall be admitting that the Son of God is the Father of JESUS CHRIST!   29b

42. Rejecting these things, then, let us understand that God is here seeking to keep the Jews from believing in more than one God, for to this belief they were prone (even as we ourselves also to-day); and the Jews were wont to multiply their gods in proportion to the number of their cities: *According to the number of thy cities were thy gods, O Judah.*[3] And God, taking care lest they multiply their gods in proportion to the number of the ages or generations of men, in the belief that there had been one God of Abraham, another God of Isaac, another God of Jacob, declared that he was the same God of them all, as he shows by the words which he spoke before, saying, I am the God of thy fathers.[4] And so he is wont to say, I am the God that brought thee out of the land of Egypt, and out of Ur of the Chaldees.[5] And he says that it is he that appeared to the others: I am God, he says, who *appeared unto Abraham himself, unto Isaac, and unto Jacob*.[6] And, *I am he, I am the first, I am the last*.[7]

43. The second explanation, which is gathered from the words of the Master,[8] is also agreeable to the first; because he said that he is the God of Abraham, Isaac, and Jacob in this respect: that he shows himself the God not only of present men, but also of those that have passed away. For from this saying CHRIST proves the resurrection; for if he is the God of those that have passed away, it follows that they are all living.[9] And in view of this, consider what deep meaning lies hid in the words of   30a

---

[1] Gen. xxvi, 24.
[2] Acts iii, 13.
[3] Jer. ii, 28; xi, 13.
[4] Acts vii, 32.
[5] Gen. xv, 7; Lev. xix, 36, etc.
[6] Ex. vi, 3.
[7] Isa. xlviii, 12.
[8] i. e., Peter Lombard. cf. paragraph 41.
[9] Luke xx, 37, 38.

the law, even though the literal sense seem to be plain. Here the Master gives us a wonderful doctrine, to which if you give heed, I will below clearly prove CHRIST to you from the law. Besides, the argument, according to their interpretations, can, if you weigh it quite correctly, be turned the other way; nor does the nature of the Holy Spirit denote a third being, for there it is an appearance of fire, which they say belongs to the nature of the Holy Spirit, as does also the appearance of a dove.[1] Yet hear the voice: *Thou art my beloved Son;* [2] *I am the God of thy fathers.*[3] These words are not suited to a third distinct being. Likewise, just as it is written, *The Holy Spirit spoke,*[4] so also, God spake by the mouth of his saints and prophets.[5] Not, therefore, to a distinct being, but to God himself, can those things which belong to the nature of the Holy Spirit be ascribed as accidents;[6] for God is a spirit,[7] and, *I, who sanctify you, am holy.*[8] Nor is the term *paraclete* a special name of the third being, for Christ himself is called a paraclete.[9] And when it speaks of another paraclete[10] than CHRIST, CHRIST himself is also indicated there as a paraclete; and he said, *another*, for the reason that then, while hearing him daily, they were being comforted by the Word itself, by CHRIST himself, and he himself was protecting them. But afterwards they will have protection not from the very presence of the Word, but of the Spirit; and they will be comforted by the Spirit through the truth revealed to them. Besides, it is not the third being, but God, that anointed us.[11] And that the Spirit of God abides in you [12] means nothing else than that the anointing which you received from him abides in you, and is that which teaches you concerning all things.[13] And to receive the Holy Spirit means nothing else than that when the heavenly messenger comes upon you, you shall receive power from on high.[14] And that this power is not a separate being is proved by

---

[1] Matt. iii, 16; Luke iii, 22.
[2] Mark i, 11.
[3] Acts vii, 32.
[4] Acts xxviii, 25.
[5] Acts iii, 21; cf. Heb. i, 1.
[6] i. e., in the logical sense of the term.
[7] John iv, 24.
[8] Lev. xxi, 8.
[9] Advocate. I. John ii, 1.
[10] John xiv, 16.
[11] II. Cor. i, 21.
[12] Rom. viii, 9; I. Cor. iii, 16.
[13] I. Cor. ii, 10, 13; John xiv, 26.
[14] Luke xxiv, 49; Acts i, 8.

the texts in which JESUS perceived in himself that power had gone out of him.¹ Say, if you can, what is the entity, or being, which is said to have gone forth from him; for in like manner I shall speak of another heavenly power. Again, that the Holy Spirit can not absolutely denote a third being, but that it is spoken of by way of an accident,² is proved by the fact that the Holy Spirit is said to be increased or diminished: *The Lord said unto Moses, I will take away from thy spirit*; and again, *Taking away from the spirit that was upon Moses, and putting it upon the seventy men.*³ And, *Let a double portion of thy spirit be upon me.*⁴ Again, because *God giveth not the Spirit by measure*;⁵ and, *The spirit of God was in Daniel in fuller measure* than in the others.⁶ Again, what does it mean that the Apostles were so often filled with the Holy Spirit?⁷ Did the third being come to them many times, uniting itself to them in the flesh? Verily, it means nothing else than that the Apostles, as they listened, grew fervent, and reasoned with and exhorted the Pharisees with the utmost warmth of faith and love. And that John was filled with the Holy Spirit, even from the womb,⁸ means nothing else than that the babe leaped in the mother's womb ⁹ by divine power. Nor can you infer that the third being was in that way united with him; for this is worse than carnal and profane; and by parity of reasoning you would conclude that the spirit of Elijah was united with him, because it says that he came with the spirit and power of Elijah.¹⁰ Again, what does it mean, pray tell, to grieve the Holy Spirit;¹¹ and, *The spirits of the prophets are subject to the prophets?*¹² Does the third being suffer grief? Again, to give the Spirit shows that this means just what it says: I will give them a new heart and a new spirit,¹³ and he giveth us understanding.¹⁴ And, as John says, *He hath given us a mind, that we may know him*;¹⁵ even as also to Solomon there was given a wise

31a

---

¹ Mark v, 30; Luke viii, 46.
² In the logical sense of the term.
³ Num. xi, 16, 17, 25 (Vulg.).
⁴ II. Kings ii, 9.
⁵ John iii, 34.
⁶ Dan. vi, 3 (Vulg.).
⁷ Acts ii, 4; iv, 8.
⁸ Luke i, 15.
⁹ Luke i, 41.
¹⁰ Luke i, 17.
¹¹ Eph. iv, 30.
¹² I. Cor. xiv, 32.
¹³ Ezek. xviii, 31; xxxvi, 26.
¹⁴ Ps. xxxii, 8 (Vulg.).
¹⁵ I. John v, 20.

heart,¹ and there is given *the spirit of wisdom, the spirit of counsel, the spirit of knowledge, and of piety.*² But why, as a result of this, the holy Spirit of God is said to be in us, I shall say in what follows. For the present, observe that it belongs to God, and by antonomasia ³ it becomes him to be wise, just as it does to be powerful, just, and merciful. Hence God, by sharing those gifts with us, is said to give us his Spirit; for those virtues are often

31b called copies, because just as their ἰδέα ⁴ shines forth in God, so when they shine forth in us, a copy of God, or his Holy Spirit, is said to be in us. And not only when such gifts are given, but for the mere reason that he gives the breath of life, he is said to give us his Spirit.⁵ Again, that the Holy Spirit is not a distinct being is proved by the fact that it is called the Spirit of CHRIST,⁶ and the Spirit of the Son.⁷ Likewise, *The Spirit of God dwelleth in you. But if any man hath not the Spirit of* CHRIST, *he is none of his.* . . . *But if the Spirit of him* (that is, of the Father) *that raised up* JESUS,⁸ etc. And because of these words Hilary says that by the Holy Spirit is meant now the Father, now the Son, now a third being,⁹ and consequently these names of three beings are confused among them.

44. There are other grounds on which many say that the Trinity is also established by logical proof, or by demonstration. Thus from the very nature of love Richard by an evident demonstration draws the conclusion that there can not but be a plurality in God.¹⁰ For if there is affection, it is directed toward another, that is, toward the Son. And if there is affection, then the affection itself is something, hence there is a third Person. Like-

32a wise Henry of Ghent, reasoning by analogy,¹¹ draws the conclusion from any begetting whatever here below that there must needs be begettings among divine beings; because in the Father

---

¹ I. Kings iii, 12.   ² Isa. xi, 2.
³ In Rhetoric, the substitution of an epithet for a name.
⁴ *Idea*, archetype, pattern.   ⁵ Ezek. xxxvii, 14.
⁶ I. Pet. i, 11.   ⁷ Gal. iv, 6.
⁸ Rom. viii, 9, 11.
⁹ Hilary of Poitiers, De Trinitate, viii, 25 (Servetus says vii, 3). (MPL. x, 254; NPNF. ser. ii, ix, 144.)
¹⁰ Richard of St. Victor, De Trinitate, III, ii (MPL. cxcvi, 916).
¹¹ *Per medium intrinsecum.*

there is only speculative knowledge, and in the Son practical knowledge, and in them there is no impulsive love as there is in the third Person, and consequently one can do nothing without the other unless they copulate together and beget.[1] Countless other arguments of this sort I deliberately pass by; and instead of solving all the things that might be brought up by philosophers at this point, you may observe this rule, which is that of the lawyer; namely, that those things which deserve special mention are, unless they are specially mentioned, understood to be disregarded.[2] But whether this article does deserve special mention, when it is the prime foundation of all faith, on which depends knowledge of both God and Christ, you must judge for yourself; and whether it is expressly mentioned, is learned from the reading of the Scriptures, although not one word is found in the whole Bible about the Trinity, nor about its Persons, nor about an Essence, nor about a unity of the Substance, nor about one Nature of the several beings, nor about their other babblings and disputes of words, which Paul says belong to the knowledge which is falsely so called.[3]

45. It remains for us to show by some reasons and authorities that these three beings can not exist in one God. In the first place I might attack this imaginary triad with the sixteen reasons which Robert Holkot states,[4] to none of which he makes a good reply, nor can he reply save by sophistry. On the contrary, he admits that this article is opposed to all natural reason. See also the *Preludes* of Pierre d'Ailly;[5] but for the present I set forth my theme in another way, and prove not only that the three beings can not exist in one God, but that they can not even be imagined, and that it is wholly impossbile to have any notion of them. For one having a notion of the Trinity would have distinct notions of the three beings; and this would amount to having a notion of one by not having a notion of another, which all deny. You will say that one has a notion of the Trinity because

---

[1] Quodlibet vi, q. 2.
[2] Corpus Juris Civilis, Digest xlvii, De Injuriis, x, 15, 26, § *Hoc edictum* (Servetus wrongly cites, § *Ait Praetor*).   [3] I. Tim. vi, 4, 20.
[4] Super quatuor libros Sententiarum, I. quaest. 5.
[5] Lib. I, quaest. 5.

he has a notion of God by conceiving that he is the three beings. O firm pillar of the Sophists! Why, pray, would you have us bound by faith to that of which your own Aristotle was never sure? Is it right that we should have so certain a faith depending upon such uncertain conceptions? How do you know? Who has revealed these conceptions to you? Indeed, as I shall show very clearly elsewhere,[1] there is no such difference in meaning, although those Nicanders [2] are found in words. Or, at least, since this is not altogether certain, no faith can be founded on these. Again, according to your philosophy, how can something be connoted by the term, *white*, without its being able to be absolutely imported by another abstract term, *whiteness*? And so of other concrete terms connoting a certain being; or will you say that here only a *disposition* [3] is connoted? There is also the rule of Porphyry, that from any essential term agreed upon, a concept may be derived having an absolute and simple meaning.[4] Again, according to their rules, I should ask whether the Trinity is unknown to CHRIST and the angels; whether they assume three notions of three beings in the soul of CHRIST and in the angels, and thus distinctly recognize three Gods. For CHRIST says that the angels behold the face of his Father,[5] but other forms they see none. Likewise CHRIST saw in himself nothing other than the Father, nor does he to-day see anything else in heaven. Dream as much as ever you will, fix your eyes on the mental images,[6] and you will find that the Trinity is not to be understood without three such images; because it is necessary for one who thinks to observe these images.[7] Indeed, you cherish a Quaternity in your mind, though you deny it in words. For you have four ideas,[8] and the fourth is a mental image with re-

---

[1] Book IV, par. 1.
[2] Nicander, a Greek poet and grammarian of the second century, B. C., who was given to hair-splitting and sophistical distinctions, for which his name therefore became a synonym.
[3] *Dispositio*, see note 2, paragraph 41.
[4] *A quacunque convenientia essentiali abstrahibilis est conceptus absolute et incomplexe singificans.* Porphyry, a third-century commentator on the Logic of Aristotle.   [5] Matt. xviii, 10.   [6] *Phantasmata.*
[7] See Aristotle, De Anima, III. vii, viii.
[8] *Simulachra.*

spect to an Essence, because it is necessary in understanding the Essence to observe the mental images; and when you have seen these, you will comprehend clearly what I shall say elsewhere [1] as to the formation of the notion. And even now, if you give heed, you can realize that your Trinity is nothing else than a kind of moving of forms in your imagination, which holds you deluded.

46. If you say, All cry with one voice that it is enough to believe, though the matter be beyond one's understanding, you expose your foolishness even in the fact that you accept a matter beyond your understanding, without sufficient warrant of Scripture; as it says, *Though they understand neither what they say, nor whereof they affirm,*[2] and *rail in those matters whereof they are ignorant.*[3] And that the more, because you yourself confess that the knowing is itself an object of faith; only, if you have faith, tell me what is the understanding of your own capacity? What is it that you believe in as known by yourself? Are you perhaps reflecting upon a mere disorder of your brain as a sufficient object of faith? Again, there can be nothing in the mind that was not first in the senses, either in itself or in something similar or corresponding.[4] But of three beings constituting one Nature, you have never had any sensation, either from near or from far; nor can you compare some degrees to others, since neither two beings, nor three, nor more, are found meeting together in one Nature. And consequently there is discovered no foundation perceived by the senses, from which the mind derives such a conception by logical reasoning. On the contrary, it is wearied and confused by the very fact that it tries to speculate about this, as though building upon the wind without foundation in the senses. Again, let us imagine the only Person to be that of the Father, as our opponents readily admit when they formally distinguish Persons from Essence: then the question arises, Since it is proper for any being to have an Essence of its own, and a Nature of its own, how shall I be able to imagine a multiplication of beings without a multiplication of Essence,

---

[1] Book V, par. 9. [2] I. Tim. i, 7.
[3] II. Pet. ii, 12.
[4] Aristotle, De Anima, III. viii; Anal. Poster., I. xviii.

and that a new being is added, but no new Essence? Did you ever perceive these or like things by the senses? Certainly not; then do not expect to perceive such things by the mind.

47. We are taught, not only by reasons but by numberless authorities, to avoid this plurality; and unless indeed I seemed out of my mind, I should bring into the discussion all the testimonies of the Gentiles, philosophers, poets, and Sybils cited by Firmianus Lactantius,[1] that from them you might realize what a laughing-stock you would be if you tried to sell them your three beings in place of one God. But let us prove the matter from Holy Writ, from the Old Testament as well as the New. *One is good, even God.*[2] *None is good save one, even God.*[3] Are those not content, then, with the mere name of unity, who do not acknowledge the One in very deed, and turn aside from their artificial, verbal Essence to a plurality of beings? And lest you permit any one here to misrepresent the matter, note that it is the Son that is speaking; from which it is evident that every sort of unity of God abides in the Father alone. And there is a weighty text to the effect that there is only God the Father and the Son,

34b JESUS CHRIST: *There is one God*, it says, *who is the Father*, . . . *and one Lord*, JESUS CHRIST;[4] and, *There is one God and Father.*[5] I know not what madness it is in men that does not see that in the Scriptures every sort of unity of God is always referred to the Father. And, *For there is one God, one mediator also between God and men, the man*, CHRIST JESUS.[6] Again, when the Apostle speaks so many times of one God and his CHRIST, and says that this God is the Father of JESUS CHRIST,[7] and that CHRIST JESUS is mediator,[8] and that through him we have access to God,[9] do you suppose it is to be understood that the first being is Father of the second, and that through the second being we have access to the first?

48. Again, when Ignatius, Irenaeus, and other early writers

---

[1] Divin. Instit. I. iv–vii (MPL. vi, 127–153; ANF. vii, 13–17; ANCL. xxi, 10–20).
[2] Matt. xix, 17 (Vulg.).
[3] Mark x, 18.
[4] I. Cor. viii, 6.
[5] Eph. iv, 6.
[6] I. Tim. ii, 5.
[7] Rom. xv, 6; II. Cor. i, 3; xi, 31; Eph. i, 3; Col. i, 3; I. Pet. i, 3.
[8] I. Tim. ii, 5.
[9] Eph. ii, 18.

dispute against heretics, saying that the Almighty God, who was the God of the Old Testament, the God of the Law and the Prophets, is also the God of the New Testament, and that the same one is the Father of JESUS CHRIST,[1] do you suppose it is to be understood that they were proclaiming the three separate beings? Likewise Tertullian, though he seems not to be self-consistent, nevertheless proclaims many of the plainest truths in accordance with the Apostolic tradition. Again, while it is an apocryphal book, still it is an ancient one, namely the Clementine Recognitions, in which CHRIST is very clearly proclaimed even to the ignorant; and in it you will find the odor of the ancient simplicity widely diffused. But, not to build on uncertain foundations, I pass that by, but will refer to the words of Ignatius to the Philippians.[2] If one, he says, has proclaimed the God of the Law and the Prophets as one, but has denied that CHRIST is his Son, he is a liar. Also if one confesses CHRIST JESUS, yet denies that the God of the Law and the Prophets is the Father of CHRIST, he does not stand fast in the truth.[3] And in the Epistle to the Tarsians, he says plainly of CHRIST that he is not the one who is God over all, but he is his Son.[4] Indeed, as Justin, the disciple of the Apostles, says, no faith would have been had in CHRIST himself had he said that another being than the Maker, Creator, and Father of all was God.[5] You have it also in Irenaeus that it was the heresy of Cerdo[6] that the יהוה[7] who was proclaimed in the Law and the Prophets to be God is not the Father of JESUS CHRIST.[8] Look in that and the following chapter and find out what is the reason why those ways of speaking are not found among our Trinitarians.[9] This reason alone is

35a

---

[1] Ignatius, Epist. ad Magn., viii; Irenaeus, Adv. Haeres., IV. ii, v. (MPG. v, 670; vii, 976–986; ANF. i, 62, 463–467; ANCL. i, 180; v, 378–388).

[2] A wrong citation. It should read, Philadelphians.

[3] Ep. ad Philad., vi (MPG. v, 702; ANF. i, 82; ANCL. i, 230–232).

[4] Ep. ad Tarsenses, v (MPG. v, 891; ANF. i, 108; ANCL. i, 457).

[5] Quoted by Irenaeus, Adv. Haeres., IV. vi, 2 (MPG. vii, 987; ANF. i, 468; ANCL. v, 390).

[6] A Syrian Gnostic of the second century, teacher of Marcion.

[7] *Jehovah.*

[8] Adv. Haeres., I. xxvii, 1 (MPG. vii, 687–689; ANF. i, 352; ANCL. v, 98).

[9] So far as has yet been discovered, this is the first use of the word *trinitarius* as a term of theology, although it had been used since the twelfth century for the

very strong, if you consider well that there is a whole book of Irenaeus on this subject, and yet he never mentions their nonsense.

49. Again, in the Old Testament we are commanded, and that more than once, not to acknowledge many gods, but only one.[1] *I am thy God*, and, *Thou shalt have no other gods besides me.*[2] And, *Hear, O Israel, that Jehovah is our God, and Jehovah is one.*[3] This he [I?] wished to translate thus, because those that know not the proper meaning of the word are here most horribly deceived. And, *Know therefore this day, and ponder it in thy heart, that God is God in heaven above and upon the earth beneath, and there is none else* besides him.[4] And in countless other passages he is said to be the God of Israel, the only God, even he alone.

50. To these things they think that they can easily reply; but they make a show of words, and do not get the sense when they say that several beings are one Essence, as if each being did not have its own existence. Indeed, as I shall show below,[5] it is more fit that one being have several Essences than that several beings have one Essence. Although I have often enough sought to learn from them the difference between the beings and the Natures, I have never been able to find out any other reason than

Yet they are unwilling that he be called the only one, but instead they wish him to have three associates.

---

title of a monastic order. It was one of the items in Calvin's indictment of Servetus that the latter had applied this term to orthodox believers in the Trinity. It was thus resented, and had doubtless been intended, as a term of reproach. Servetus seems to have used it to suggest that orthodox believers had substituted belief in a Trio for belief in the one and only true God. In the second half of the sixteenth century Catholic writers adopted the term, singularly enough, to designate deniers of the orthodox doctrine of the Trinity in Poland and Transylvania, and to denote what they regarded as practically a form of tritheism; since the Unitarians of that period, while more or less admitting a divinity of Father, Son, and Holy Spirit, considered separately, did not properly admit the unity of the three in one Substance. *Trinitarii* are thus among the heretics named in the bull of excommunication (*In coena Domini*) published annually from Gregory XIII. in 1583 to Clement XIV. in 1770. Those so called never admitted this designation, but came toward the end of the century to call themselves by the opposed term, *Unitarii*, apparently coined at this time in contradistinction to the objectionable term, *Trinitarii*. The Catholic connotation of *Trinitarii* at length became obsolete, and the term became the accepted designation of those holding the orthodox doctrine of God. cf. Book VII, paragraph 3.

[1] *Pluralitatem . . . unitatem.*
[2] Ex. xx, 2, 3.
[3] Deut. vi, 4.
[4] Deut. iv, 39.
[5] Book V, paragraph 9.

that רז״ל[1] had this usage. Again, their defense may seem artificial, without the witness of the Scriptures; for of the one God there is no question, but of the three beings which they call Persons I find no mention, nor does Scripture speak of an Essence, nor of all their other doctrines, disputes of words, and profane babblings. *O Timothy, turn away from novelties of words, which some professing have erred concerning the faith.*[2] And elsewhere, *Be not carried away by diverse and strange questions.*[3] Again, Paul forbids us to be led astray by disputes about words.[4] But that their defense is merely verbal is now plain from what has been said; for admitting that there are three beings, which they call Persons, by reasoning from a substitution of terms,[5] they admit three entities, and consequently three Substances. If *God*, therefore, has an absolute meaning, it plainly follows that they are real Tritoites,[6] and in consequence are really opposed to the Scriptures and to the unity of God, and that they are sophistically defending one connotative God, wherefore they are hateful to God.[7] Pray look at another foundation: for while admitting that there are three beings, they deny that there are three entities and three Substances, for the reason that these nouns end in *-tia*,[8] hence relate to an Essence.[9] O monsters of the world, that God should be a jest to us because the ending of words requires it; and that we should confess a plurality in God because one word requires it, and not because another does; as though Hebrews, Greeks, and Barbarians ought to have nouns ending in *-tia*, so that all languages may have a fixed rule for making sport of God. Are these the verbal disputations which Paul abhors? And if you ask them why they utter those utterly meaningless

---

[1] In both the original and the counterfeit reprint, the second of these three Hebrew characters is not the ז here printed, although that this was in the printer's font is shown from its use elsewhere in the text; nor is it clear what the character is. But if it be taken as a misprint for a ז, the enigmatical word in the text is (so Buxtorf, De Abbreviaturis Hebraicis, s. v.) an abbreviation for a phrase common in rabbinical Hebrew, רבותינו זכרונם לברכה, meaning, Our Masters, of blessed memory; which fits perfectly with the context at the end of this paragraph.

[2] I. Tim. vi, 4, 20 (Vulg.).
[3] Heb. xiii, 9.   [4] II. Tim. ii, 14.
[5] *A convertibilibus arguendo.*   [6] cf. note 5, paragraph 31.
[7] Ecclus. xxxvii, 23 (Vulg.). *Qui sophistice loquitur, odibilis est.*
[8] *Entia, substantia.*   [9] *Sunt essentialia.*

ON THE ERRORS OF THE TRINITY 57

things as fundamental truths, they will reply that they learned so by the usage of their masters. It is no concern of theirs if they make void the word of God, provided they preserve the leaven of their tradition.[1]

51. Again, hear what view Scripture holds about Persons, that you may understand that their usage is mightily like that of Scripture! For in Scripture the outward form and appearance of a man is called his *person*, as when we say, He has a beautiful person; and it is so taken when it is said that God is no respecter of persons,[2] because he has no respect to those outward differences, as to whether one is male or female, bond or free, Jew or Greek.[3] And it is so taken when it says that we are not to respect the person of the poor, or the countenance of the mighty.[4] And so the Greek word πρόσωπον[5] is used, which in Latin is rendered *vultus, persona, aspectus*, and *facies*.[6] But, apart from the Scriptures, the meaning of the word *persona* is in itself so well known to the Latins that some devil must have suggested to them to invent mathematical Persons, and to thrust their imaginary and metaphysical beings upon us as Persons. For in CHRIST shone forth one Person of the Deity; and in the appearances or utterances of God the Father, another; and in the sending of the Spirit, another; and thus in the Gospel we know three Persons, that is to say, by a divine manifestation. And it says, another Comforter[7] according to Tertullian,[8] not as representing the Substance, but the Person; because there was another aspect, and another form and *disposition* of Deity. For Scripture considers the manners of the appearances, and not the metaphysical Natures of the beings. Here investigate the causes from the beginning, what view tradition formerly held of Persons, and how all things have been corrupted by the damage of

---

[1] Mark vii, 13; Matt. xvi, 6, 12.
[2] Rom. ii, 11; Eph. vi, 9; Col. iii, 25; Acts x, 34; I. Pet. i, 17.
[3] Gal. iii, 28.
[4] Lev. xix, 15. cf. I. Sam. xvi, 7; Jas. ii, 9; Deut. i, 17.
[5] *Prosopon.*
[6] Countenance, person, looks, face. II. Cor. i, 11; ii, 10; iii, 7, 13, 18; iv, 6; viii, 24; x, 1, 7; xi, 20.
[7] John xiv, 16.
[8] Adv. Praxean, ix (MPL. ii, 164; ANF. iii, 604; ANCL. xv, 350).

the times. What a monster they have also made of the *hyposta-sis* I shall say later on, when we speak of the Word.¹

52. Again, referring to what is proclaimed in Mark; *Hear, O Israel, thy God is one . . . and there is none other but him*;² and the second commandment is about one's neighbor, on which two commandments it says that the whole law hangeth, and the prophets.³ Thus among all the commandments of the Law there is no command to believe in an imaginary Trinity. But there is one alone who said, *I am, I am, and besides me there is no saviour*;⁴ and, *I am the Lord, and there is none else besides me, there is no God apart from me, there is no Lord: I am the Lord, and there is none else.*⁵

53. The Hebrews are supported by so many authorities that they naturally wonder at the great division of Gods introduced by the New Testament, and they deem our Testament schismatical when they see us hold their God in such abhorrence. But if we have to dispute against them, we ought to follow the example of the Apostles, namely, say to them plainly that this Jesus is the Christ,⁶ and the Son of God: which the Master also teaches us, who in this way sought to persuade the Jews, saying, The יהוה ⁷ of whom ye say that he is your God, he is my Father.⁸ 37b See how plainly and intelligibly he addressed their minds concerning his God; *and for this cause they sought to kill him, because he had said that God was his own Father*.⁹ And, *He is worthy of death, because he made himself the Son of God*.¹⁰ Why not consider in what sense they said these things? Nor does Christ deny this sense; on the contrary, he confirms it, replying, *Ye say that I am the Son of God*.¹¹ Again, if Paul were in Damascus to-day, trying to persuade the Jews that *this* is the Son of God,¹² what do you think he would be referring to by the pronoun? What sort of reasoning should you rely upon in order that such Jews might be persuaded as you see expecting the Messiah to-day, even as

---

¹ Book III.
² Mark xii, 29, 32 (Vulg.).
³ Matt. xxii, 40.
⁴ Isa. xliii, 11 (Vulg.).
⁵ Isa. xlv, 5, 6 (Vulg.).
⁶ Acts xvii, 3.
⁷ Jehovah.
⁸ John viii, 54.
⁹ John v, 18.
¹⁰ Matt. xxvi, 66; John xix, 7.
¹¹ Luke xxii, 70.
¹² Acts ix, 20.

the woman who expected the Messiah was persuaded by the word of CHRIST?[1] Nevertheless, some seem to themselves so grand that they do not deign to turn their eyes to look at the man, and deem it something improper and absurd for a man to be called the Son of God. But it is something else, more exalted, that they make the Son of God; and as for the Son, they say that it is necessary that he be of the same Nature, or, as they say, of precisely the same kind [2] with the Father; and so from the very start they reject this sonship of the man as blasphemy. But let the Master himself answer for me, who shows himself the Son of God by comparison with other men: For if he called other men gods, say ye that I blaspheme because I said, I am the Son of God, when the Father has sanctified me beyond all my fellows?[3] See plainly that he who was sanctified is called the Son of God; this is he that *shall be called holy, the Son of God*;[4] this is he of whom the Apostles say, *Thy holy child* JESUS.[5] That precisely his kind is unknown also in dumb beasts is evident; and they supply that lack by inventing something out of their own heads. I would that they might get a little nearer to God, for they judge of him too much from afar.

54. Again, let them bring the Old Testament into harmony with the New. Why is it that with the Hebrews it is so often said of the Messiah-king, He glorified, adorned, crowned him; glorious, comely, renowned, noble; glory, praise, comeliness, beauty, majesty, honor — which things in the New Testament also are very often attributed to JESUS CHRIST, the Son of God? But they attribute none of these things to the man, nor do they care about the Old Testament Messiah. They ascribe everything to the second being by the *communicatio idiomatum*; for they say there are not two kings, nor two glorified ones.

55. Let us now hear the monstrosities which this Trinity controversy has brought forth, for it will be a sufficient confutation of all the philosophers to drag them out into the light. The Tritoites, since this philosophy about three beings entered into the world, have said that there are three Gods; because, although

---

[1] John iv, 25, 29.
[2] *Eiusdem speciei specialissimae.*
[3] John x, 35, 36; Heb. i, 9.
[4] Luke i, 35, margin.
[5] Acts iv, 27, 30 (Vulg.).

they deny it with the mouth, our brethren confess it in fact. The Arians divide the second being from the Substance of the first, as being less than it. Macedonius [1] denies that the third being is God, but says that it is subject to the Father and the Son. Behold how, when a wrong foundation is once laid, men are driven out to sea utterly lost, adding a greater matter to a less; and any one who pleases thinks up a new God and forever joins blasphemies to it. Moreover, the Aetians and the Eunomians [2] say that these beings are unlike. The followers of Origen rave that the Son can not see the Father, nor the Holy Spirit the Son. Maximinus [3] said that the Father is a part of God, and that whichever Person you please is a third part of the Trinity. The Metangismonites [4] said that the second being is in the first, just as a smaller vessel is contained in a larger one. The Nestorians say that Jesus is one Son of God, and another son of man; and this in fact our brethren confess. For, as appears in the disputations of Maxentius [5] of Constantinople, Nestorius never admitted that there were two Sons, but defended himself by certain sophistical tricks, quite in the manner of men to-day. Read what is said there, and you shall clearly see that these are Nestorians. The Eutychians asserted that the only nature in CHRIST is a divine one, as though it were a phantom fallen from heaven, as the Marcionites said. The Monarchians, such as Praxeas and Victorinus,[6] said that JESUS CHRIST was God the Father almighty, and that he sat at his own right hand. And after them the Sabellians confuse the person and the names of

---

[1] A heresiarch Bishop of Constantinople about the middle of the fourth century; cf. Sozomen, Eccl. Hist. IV, xxvii (MPG. lxvii, 1199; NPNF. ser. ii, ii, 322).

[2] Aetius, a deacon of Antioch, reviving Arianism a generation after the Council of Nicaea, and his pupil Eunomius, Bishop of Cyzicus in Mysia, taught that the Son was of different Substance from the Father; cf. Epiphanius, Adv. Haeres., lib. iii, tom. i, haeres. lxxvi (MPG. xlii, 515–550); Basil. Magn., Liber Eunomii Apolog. (MPG. xxx, 835–868).

[3] Arian Bishop of Hippo, contemporary of St. Augustine; cf. Augustine, Coll. cum Maximino (MPL. xlii, 709 ff.).

[4] cf. Augustine, De Haeres., lviii (MPL. xlii, 41).

[5] Dialogi contra Nestorianos (MPG. lxxvxi, 124 f.).

[6] Praxeas, a heretic at Carthage and Rome late in the second century, against whom Tertullian wrote his Adv. Praxean (MPL. ii, 153 ff.; ANF. iii, 597 ff.; ANCL. xv, 333 ff.). Victorinus Afer, a Roman rhetorician and theologian of the fourth century; cf. MPL. viii, 993 ff.

CHRIST and the Father, and are also called Patripassians, since they believe that the Father suffered. The Alogi, not understanding the mystery of the Word, say that John lied when he said that the Word was God. Very recently, as the Decretal relates,[1] Joachim was arguing against the Master [2] that there is a Quaternity in the divine beings, for the reason that the Essence, according to Master Lombard, is a kind of Nature, not begetting like the Father, nor begotten like the Son, nor proceeding like the Holy Spirit; but it is a kind of supreme being, and according to this it seems to be a kind of fourth appearance.[3] Hence Joachim admitted that the three beings are not a Substance, nor an Essence, nor a Nature; but they are said to be one in a collective sense, just as many men are one people. He was certainly right in arguing for a fourth appearance, though he drew his conclusion stupidly. A good many others spew out errors in other ways, because, according to them, when one inconsistency occurs more follow, and the last error is worse than the first.

The Essence is a fourth appearance.

56. Not only among heretics, but in our own Church, countless monstrosities have arisen, countless questions have arisen, not only doubtful, insoluble, and knotty, but also most absurd, confirming what the Master says, *He that walketh in darkness knoweth not whither he goeth.*[4] The first of these questions to arise is, What is the difference between *proceeding* and *being begotten*, and why is the third being not called Son, and not said to be begotten like the second? Of this [Peter Lombard speaks in the passage [5]] where Gregory [6] says that it is not possible for him to know, although he confesses that he believes; but God knows what sort of faith he had, when placed in such a difficult situa-

39b

---

[1] Joachim of Flora (c. 1132–1202), a Calabrian monk, held heretical views on the Trinity, and also attacked Peter Lombard, for which he was condemned by Innocent III; cf. Innocent's Decretal in Corpus Juris Canonici, Lib. I, tit. i, De summa Trinitate, cap. ii, Damnamus.

[2] i. e., Peter Lombard, called "Master of Sentences."

[3] *Simulachrum.*

[4] John xii, 35.

[5] Sent. I, dist. xiii, cap. iii.

[6] A mistake in citation for Augustine, Contra Maximinum, II. xiv, 1 (MPL. xlii, 770).

tion. Likewise Augustine,[1] John of Damascus,[2] and all the rest have a great horror of this question. But I dispatch the matter in a very few words, and say that the flesh is begotten in the natural way, but the Spirit is not begotten at all; for to say that the Word is begotten is a mere dream, and a great misuse of words. This will come out very clearly when I have said how the Holy Spirit is said to proceed.[3] Moreover, they say that one Essence is derived from another; yet the Essence does not beget, while the Demiurge does beget. They ought therefore to have said that he had a kind of spiritual wife, or that he alone was masculo-feminine or hermaphrodite, was at once father and mother; for the meaning of the word does not allow that one be called a father apart from a mother. And so they surpass Ptolemy,[4] the Valentinian, in this, that they tacitly contemn their own dreams, which are included in their very notion of God, as he explicitly and separately states. They also say that the first being is continually begetting, not from another, nor from nothing, but from itself, one who is identical with itself. Not that it begot but once, as Valentinus [5] said, but by abusing its spiritual wife is forever breathing forth, is forever in travail; nor can he cease from this intercourse, for he is continually bound to it, and the spiritual Bythos is said to be brought forth daily, though it is the same in nature with the eternal Demiurge (I use Valentinus's own words), because between these and those there is only a verbal distinction. Besides, they say that by these two Aeons a third Pleroma is naturally brought forth; and this third one in *proceeding*, like the second one in *being born*, receives the fact that it is an Essence. And you must forever insist upon the conclusion that these three spirits, or these three beings, with origins so different and unlike one another,

40a

---

[1] De Trinitate, XV. xxv, 45 (MPL. xlii, 1092; NPNF. ser. i. iii, 223; Dods, vii, 430).

[2] De fide orthodoxa, I. viii (MPG. xciv, 819, 823; NPNF. ser. ii. ix, 8, 9).

[3] Book II, paragraph 27.

[4] A second-century Gnostic; cf. Irenaeus, Adv. Haeres., I. xii (MPG. vii, 569 ff.; ANF. i, 333 f.; ANCL. v, 49–51).

[5] A second-century Gnostic; cf. Tertullian, Adv. Valent.; Irenaeus, Adv. Haeres. (MPG. vii, 433 ff.; MPL. ii, 525 ff.; ANF. iii, 503 ff.; i, 315 ff.; ANCL. xv, 119 ff., v, 1 ff.).

are one and the same being; and this one is not that one, and that one is not the other one, and all are one — which is something so monstrous that I had rather, like Valentinus, break in pieces a hundred octonarions of demons than thus to despise and break up the nature of the supremely Good and Great God, and to cut it up in various ways into three unlike beings. Try as they may to cloak this division under various kinds of names, yet unless you were used to speaking of these beings with great reverence, you will easily decide, if you open your eyes, that to make God out so unlike is of all blasphemies the greatest. Moreover,
40b notwithstanding these derivations, they say, in opposition to Donatus, that the three beings are equal and of the same power; so that, according to Augustine,[1] the Son is able to utter a son for himself, and a grandson for the Father; and consequently the third Spirit is able to impregnate a Chimaera, and to breathe forth offspring; yet he says that the Son did not beget because it was not necessary. Moreover, they say that the third being is ours, but the second is not ours but the Father's; and they say that the second being is united with the human nature hypostatically, that is, asswise,[2] and that the other two are not in Christ. But I should like to know why when the Master himself spoke he did not say, The Son, or the second Person, that abideth in me, instead of, The Father that abideth in me, The Father is in me.[3] Likewise, when it says that the Spirit of God is in him, why did it not say that he had not the third, but the second, being included within himself? Nor can I see whence come so many profane babblings,[4] to the effect that only the second Person sustains, cries out, takes up into the unity of the Substance,[5] limits its dependence; especially since they so glue the Persons together that they act without division. For they say that the works of the Trinity are outwardly undivided, and they themselves can neither say nor understand how the human nature depends upon the second being alone, and not substantially [6] upon the others; and that only the second being is there united

---

[1] De Trinitate, XV. xiv (NPL. xlii, 1076; NPNF. ser. i. iii, 213; Dods, vii, 407).
[2] *Asinaliter*; cf. paragraph 16, note 5.
[3] John xiv, 10.
[4] I. Tim. vi, 20; II. Tim. ii, 16.
[5] *Suppositum*.
[6] *Suppositaliter*.

with the flesh, for here God is manifestly divided. Or it is necessary to reason like Scotus; and the Realists say that Occam,[1] when he was devising relations on this subject, was forced to confess the truth. But God is truth, and they are both liars: he that speaketh from himself, says CHRIST, is a liar.[2]

<small>All things that pertain to God, if they are not proved by the Scriptures, are lies, because every man is a liar.</small>

57. Moreover, if the second Person assumes Mary as it assumed CHRIST, then the Sophists admit that Mary is CHRIST, CHRIST bore the Son of God, CHRIST is his own mother, CHRIST is man and woman (pray restrain your laughter, if you can); and with all this they keep a brazen front so that they know not how to blush. Moreover, they say there is a great difference between constitution and composition;[3] for they assume a constitution in divine beings, because the Son is constituted of an Essence, but is not composed. Moreover, just as they assume two births of the two beings in CHRIST, and different ones, so also they assume two inbreathings in the third being. In the first place, it flows from within the first two by a kind of chimerical[4] and monstrous branching off. In the second place, they say that by another mutation it is breathed in from without, and in time, by the other two. Furthermore, they say that this and the second being are being daily made or produced. These are clearly the artificial emissions of aeons which are being daily produced, begotten, born, and made; and at this point, strangely enough, they would have the fourth appearance a very simple one, so that notwithstanding these deformities in its womb, the two beings when brought forth, together with the other being begetting but not begotten, constitute one inactive Nature, not begotten nor begetting, nor breathed upon nor breathing. Moreover, there is great controversy as to what names belong to the human nature and what to the second being; for at first they apply the title of Son not to the man but to the second being. And in consequence of this, when JESUS CHRIST is called the Son of God, the words JESUS and CHRIST both flocked together to

---

[1] Johannes Duns Scotus, c. 1265–1308; William of Occam, c. 1280–1349, distinguished scholastic theologians.

[2] John v, 31; viii, 44.

[3] cf. paragraph 31.

[4] The Chimaera of classical mythology was part lion, part goat, and part dragon.

that. Finally, they maintain that he is called Son of man not from a man but from this being. Nay more, they deny that the man himself is a man, and so his human nature has remained nameless. Moreover, Basil the Great [1] maintains with singular mistakenness that he is called *begotten*, and not a *created being*; a *Son*, and not *born*. And the great theologian Nazianzen, in his Theology [2] holds that the third Spirit was neither begotten nor unbegotten, a view which Augustine [3] and others follow. And whether the third Person proceeds from the Father and the Son, or from the Father only, as the Greeks say, is a very bitterly debated, vain, and ancient problem, which I shall later [4] solve with ease. In fact, I wonder why they do not also debate whether the second proceeds from the third, just as the third does from the second, so that each in turn may be the cause of the other. For it is written, *And now the Lord hath sent me, and his Spirit.*[5]
42a Hence the Son is sent by the Spirit, and is said to have been conceived of the Holy Spirit,[6] and the Spirit of the Lord is said to be upon him.[7]

58. Again, whether the Father and the Son are called one breather collectively, or are called one beginning because they are one Essence; and thus, whether the Essence is the beginning of the inbreathing, is an intelligible question. For they would have the fourth appearance, which they call Essence, be inactive in all respects — at least the Moderns would. Furthermore, it is of great importance whether the notions are the common ones, or are those of Persons by [technical] definition. Likewise, it makes a great difference whether a thing is said to be a Substance [8] or not; it even makes so great a difference that the whole kingdom of heaven depends on it. For they deny that the man JESUS CHRIST is a Substance. And there is a long discus-

---

[1] Adv. Eunomium, ii (MPG. xxix, 615–618).

[2] Gregory Nazianzen, Fifth Theological Oration, de Spiritu Sancto, viii (MPG. xxxvi, 142; NPNF. ser. ii. vii, 320).

[3] De Trinitate, V. vi, vii (MPL. xlii, 914–916; NPNF. ser. i. iii, 89–91; Dods, vii, 150–154).

[4] See Book II, par. 27.

[5] Isa. xlviii, 16. [6] Matt. i, 20.

[7] Matt. iii, 16; Mark i, 10; John i, 32.

[8] *Suppositum*.

The Sophists, rejecting Christ, chose this master for themselves.

sion, from the 25th to the 35th distinction, in which Occam¹ strongly insists, while they lay the foundations of our faith upon certain notions, relations, formalities, quiddities, and filiations of which Paul never thought. They are founded upon the sand, and not upon the solid rock; and regarding the majesty of the faith as not firm, they seem to make game of it. Pray hear the sound reasoning of the Lombard Rabbi² in his *Sentences*,³ where he treats of the very subtle question, as to what befits the truest majesty of God; that is, what is the reason of the difference, that the Father is said to love with the love which proceeds from him, and is not called wise with the wisdom which proceeds from him; and being wholly and thoroughly terrified by the difficulty, he wavers, and knows not whither he goes. Likewise in another chapter⁴ is a question which, though difficult, is yet ridiculous: namely, What is the reason of the difference, that properties can not be in the Persons without limiting them, and yet they are in the Essence without limiting it? Pray what Turk, Scythian, Barbarian could bear these disputes of words, as Paul calls them,⁵ without laughter? But it would be superfluous here to follow them through one by one, although there are among them many other horrible inventions on the subject of the incarnation, both far removed from the terms of the law, and foreign to them. Reflect only upon this: whether these questions savor at all of the Apostolic mind. See whether this is the teaching of our Master, CHRIST. At present we have grown accustomed to them, but future generations will judge these things amazing. Verily they are amazing, more so than the things that Irenaeus relates of Valentinus;⁶ nor is there in the whole Bible one letter which leads to these fancies.

59. Furthermore, and worse than all this, how much this tradition of the Trinity has, alas! been a laughing-stock to the

---

¹ Quaestiones et Decisiones, dist. 26.

² *Longobardus Rabinus.* Servetus here employs the Hebrew title as an equivalent for the title *Magister* commonly applied to Peter Lombard as the "Master of Sentences."

³ Lib. I, dist. xxxii, cap. vi.

⁴ Lib. I, dist. xxxiii, cap. ii.

⁵ I. Tim. vi, 4.

⁶ Adv. Haeres. I. i (MPG. vii, 445–452; ANF. i, 316 f.; ANCL. v, 4–6).

ON THE ERRORS OF THE TRINITY

Mohammedans, only God knows. The Jews also shrink from giving adherence to this fancy of ours, and laugh at our foolishness about the Trinity; and on account of its blasphemies they do not believe that this is the Messiah who was promised in their law. And not only Mohammedans and Hebrews, but the very beasts of the field, would make fun of us did they grasp our fantastical notion, for all the works of the Lord bless the one God.[1] Hear also what Mohammed says; for more reliance is to be given to one truth which an enemy confesses than to a hundred lies on our side. For he says in his Alcoran [2] that CHRIST was the greatest of the prophets, the spirit of God, the power of God, the breath of God, the very soul of God, the Word born of a perpetual virgin by God's breathing upon her; and that it is because of the wickedness of the Jews toward him that they are in their present wretchedness and misfortune. He says, moreover, that the Apostles and Evangelists and the first Christians were the best of men, and wrote what is true, and did not hold the Trinity, or three Persons in the Divine Being, but men in later times added this.

60. This most burning plague, therefore, was added and superimposed, as were the new gods which have recently come, which our fathers did not worship. And this plague of philosophy was brought upon us by the Greeks, for they above all other men are most given to philosophy; and we, hanging upon their lips, have also become philosophers. Perhaps some will deem it a slight fault if I admit that they may have erred. But I prove this in no other way than by showing that they never understood the passages of the Scriptures which they adduce with regard to this matter. If they distinguished the brightness that then was from their own darkness so utterly confused, they might realize that Paul well said that the Church of God is the ground and pillar of the truth;[3] which is no more than to say that the word of the Gospel is true; and the word of the Gospel is this, namely, that JESUS CHRIST is the Son of God. For, as I

---

[1] Dan. iii, 57 (Vulg.).

[2] The statements following are apparently not quoted, but only loosely based on Surahs iii, iv, v, and xix *passim*.

[3] I. Tim. iii, 15.

have said, and shall say more at large below,¹ the most solid support and foundation of the truth on which the Church is founded is to believe that JESUS CHRIST is the Son of God; and it was on account of this foundation that Paul said, *pillar of the truth*. Therefore our Church is not said to be founded without a foundation, for its observation of this firm truth gives it the name of rock, pillar, and Church of God. For a church can remain without remaining the Church of God; Peter ² can remain in it, though no rock ² remains. These are matters too small to deserve mention, were there not some who have teeth of iron, so that if they bite hold of but a single passage of Scripture, they are content. But I would that they might as diligently observe other passages of Scripture.

61. Again, what good, pray, does it do them, that CHRIST said to the Apostles, *I am with you always, even unto the end of the world*?³ For CHRIST remained with the Apostles, and with all who were of their number, and is to remain, unto the end of the world. But we are not of their number; for had we been of their number, we should have abode in their teaching.⁴ Again, mark what follows and you shall understand the condition. *Preach the Gospel*, he says, *teach them to observe all things which I commanded you; and lo, I am with you*.⁵ Where, pray, are those who are preaching Christ; where are those who are keeping his commandment, namely, about believing that he is the Son of God, that Christ may be with them? I will show you at the end of Book III,⁶ something that you do not know: what this Gospel is that is committed to them to be preached. Nay more, I will prove to you that you are no Christian. They believe that a congregation is a kind of mathematical body, holding the Spirit of God bound by the hair, even though none of them knows Christ nor his spirit. *As often*, he says, *as you are gathered together in my name*.⁷ But how are those gathered together in the name of

All the promises of the Law are made on this condition. The same is clear from Matt. x and xv and Psalm lxxxix.

44a

---

¹ Paragraph 37; also Book III, paragraphs 20–22.
² *Petrus . . . petra.*
³ Matt. xxviii, 20.
⁴ I. John ii, 19.
⁵ Mark xvi, 15; Matt. xxviii, 19, 20.
⁶ Book III, par. 21.
⁷ *Congregati.* Matt. xviii, 20.

Christ who know not who the Christ is? Besides, how will the Holy Spirit be in the congregation, if in individuals of it there be a spirit full of fornication and robbery? Beware, then, lest by mere persistence in saying, The Church can not err, you oppose knowledge of Christ, and defend the error of ignorance of him. May the Lord grant you understanding, that you may conform to the simplicity of the Scriptures. If you have sought after CHRIST with your whole heart, he will without fail be gracious to you.

BOOK II

Argument

CHRIST, the Son of man, who descended from heaven, was the Word by uttering which God created the world. He became flesh as God's firstborn, and was the Son of God. He was both human and divine. God's Spirit, moving all things, operates within us as the Holy Spirit, which is a person of the Godhead. It proceeds from the Son, not as a separate being but as a ministering spirit. It is holy, one of three persons in the Godhead, and sanctifies us by dwelling within us.

Synopsis

1. Christ, the Son of man, ascended into heaven; and we are in heaven when we believe that he is the Son of God. 2. Christ, the Son of man, came down from heaven. 3. One who sees Christ sees the Father through him. 4. The Word which was in the beginning was simply the utterance which God gave when first creating the world. 5. Christ was thus the voice of God become flesh, and intrusted with the function of speaking for God. 6. It was the Word originally with God, not a second being, that became flesh. 7. All things were made through the Word, not through a being. 8. It is Christ, not a being, that was firstborn, 9. and born of the flesh, as Christ and the ante-Nicene writers taught. 10. The expression, firstborn, has no reference to time, since to God all time is one, 11. who uttered his begetting Word at the beginning of the world, thus making him firstborn. 12. Jesus is proved to be the Son of God by his resurrection, 13. through which he was born again, as we shall be. 14. Being begotten also expresses escape from perils. 15. The passage must be taken in both its literal and its spiritual meaning. 16. Christ was a prophet, though the whole of God was in him. 17. Christ is not merely human, but the Word of God, both human and divine; 18. both man and God; though a man, yet inseparable from God. 19. God's Spirit animates all men and things, 20. moves all things, and fills the earth. 21. When acting within us it is known as the Holy Spirit. 22. It is sometimes represented as an angel, 23. but not when the angel acts from without. 24. Holy Spirit denotes a closer

personal relation than Spirit of God. 25. It is a Person of the Godhead. 26. Spirit originally means a breathing, but here has a restricted meaning. 27. The Holy Spirit proceeds from the Son, being sent by Christ. 28. It is not a separate metaphysical being, but a ministering spirit. 29. It is properly called holy, 30. and is distinct from Christ. 31. There is one Godhead in the three Persons, but not in three beings. 32. The Holy Spirit is not spoken of in the Old Testament, which is concerned with outward sanctifications, whereas in the New Testament it relates to inward sanctification. The difference between the two is complete. 33. The Comforter was the Spirit sent for a special purpose. 34. The Spirit is given by God, filling all things with divine power, and dwelling in us.

BOOK THE SECOND

1. *No one hath ascended into heaven, but him that descended out of heaven, even the Son of man, who is in heaven.*[1] Some wonder as to this: Who is this Son of man who was then in heaven? and they do not observe that heaven is wherever CHRIST is. In other circumstances they would also wonder, if CHRIST said to them, *The kingdom of heaven is within you.*[2] Nor would they believe Paul when he says, *Our citizenship is in heaven;*[3] and, *God raised us up with* CHRIST, *and made us to sit with him in the heavenly places.*[4] We are in heaven when we lay up treasures in heaven.[5] Likewise, when it says, *He that is but little in the kingdom of heaven, is greater than John the Baptist,*[6] it means nothing else than that any one of those that are under the Gospel is greater than one that was wholly under the Law. Therefore we too are least in the kingdom of heaven. Moreover, CHRIST said that he that was not far from knowledge of the Gospel was not far from the kingdom of heaven.[7] And the Apostle said, *Say not in thy heart, who shall ascend into heaven?* for this is the same as if thou didst ask, Who shall bring CHRIST down from heaven?[8] as though he said, In vain dost thou excuse thyself from the diffi-

---

[1] John iii, 13.
[2] Luke xvii, 21.
[3] Phil. iii, 20.
[4] Eph. ii, 6.
[5] Matt. vi, 20.
[6] Matt. xi, 11.
[7] Mark xii, 34.
[8] Rom. x, 6.

culty of the thing, in vain dost thou ask for what thou hast within, for all this difficulty has been overcome through CHRIST; he has been brought down from above, and brought back from the dead, so that heaven is now within us. Lo, heaven is here. *The word is nigh thee, in thy mouth.*[1] But if thou believest that CHRIST is the Son of God, thou hast ascended into heaven. The spiritual sense, therefore, in John iii. is gathered from the literal order; and as CHRIST there bears witness, those words are not earthly, but heavenly. Hence we ought not to understand them, like Nicodemus, in a carnal sense. And the sense is, Unless one has been born from above, he can not see the kingdom of God; that is, come to knowledge of the Gospel, through which we are made heavenly, having cast off the shadow of the law of those that are earthly. And most of all is he wholly in heaven who brings heaven with himself. And the kingdom of heaven is at hand when CHRIST is at hand; and no one had ascended thither as yet but the Son of man himself, who is in heaven; because *he that cometh from above is above all.*[2] CHRIST means to say that the kingdom of the Gospel, which is heavenly, was as yet known to none but himself alone; nor can it be made known save to those that believe that he is the Son of God. And note that he says that he has already ascended into heaven; for $\dot{\alpha}\nu\alpha\beta\acute{\epsilon}\beta\eta\kappa\epsilon\nu$ [3] here is in a past tense, and this can not be understood of another heaven. Nor could the second being then be understood to have ascended. But it was right for him then to say of himself that he had already ascended into heaven, which ascent of the Son of man you will understand in Book IV.[4] For the present, you may say that he had already ascended to the bosom of the Father; heaven was to him the light unapproachable in which the Father dwells,[5] and that he ascended into heaven, and is in heaven, means nothing else there than that he is treating of spiritual things in the fulness of the Spirit, and thus was in heaven while he was speaking of heavenly things. And unless you understand it in this way, you will not understand why Paul said, *even to the third heaven.*[6] And with regard to this you ought to know that

---

[1] Rom. x, 8.
[2] John iii, 13, 31.
[3] *Anabebeken*, hath ascended.
[4] Book IV, paragraph 8.
[5] I. Tim. vi, 16.
[6] II. Cor. xii, 2.

for the Hebrews nouns in the dual number have a dual meaning. Hence to them שמים¹ means the two heavens beyond which they do not ascend, because they are flesh. One heaven is that of the air; as, the birds of the heaven, the clouds of heaven, the waters of heaven. The second is that of the ether, the region of the stars. But the spirit, not content with these, ascends further, though I do not mean in a local sense. And thus the spirit of Paul penetrated the third heaven, and this very one is within us. If these heavens are open to any one, as to John and Stephen, he will see CHRIST where he is, will see what it means to say, God created *hashamayim*,² that is, the spiritual dwelling-places of God; and, the light unapproachable³ with which God covers himself as with a garment;⁴ and just what this is, I shall say below.⁵

2. If you do not receive this heavenly teaching of the Master, tell me, why did CHRIST say that he was the Son of man, who had ascended into heaven?⁶ What do you understand by Son of man? For it is a great misuse of language to say that Son of man is the name of a *hypostasis*; and that the more, because this could not be proved of the *hypostasis*. Hence, speaking against you, he said in plain terms, *the Son of man*; nor could he have spoken more clearly unless perchance you would have had him say, after your own fashion, this human nature, this body, this flesh is in a definite place above the expanse there on high. Again, CHRIST also asks you one thing: *The baptism of John, was it from heaven or from men?*⁷ And you must reason, along with the Pharisees, whether you admit that it was from heaven. They thought better of heaven than you, since they dared not deny that the baptism of John was from heaven, while you deny that the Son of man, or what you call his human nature, is from heaven. Note also CHRIST's argument from a sufficient enumeration of parts, *from heaven or from men*, as much as to say, that which is not according to man is from heaven. Hence CHRIST is from heaven, because *the second man is from heaven, heavenly*;⁸

46a

---

¹ *Shamayim*, heavens.   ² Heb., the heavens.
³ I. Tim. vi, 16.   ⁴ Ps. civ, 2.
⁵ In paragraph 2.   ⁶ John iii, 13.
⁷ Matt. xxi, 25.   ⁸ I. Cor. xv, 47 (Vulg.).

whatever is above flesh and blood is both from heaven and in heaven.

3. The second question is as to the meaning of the words, *He that seeth me seeth the Father*.[1] If you understand how the Father was in him, and how he was in the Father to such an extent that he did nothing but those things that are the Father's, you will easily understand that in seeing the Father's glory one sees the Father, even as one sees the sun through its radiance. For after he said, *He that seeth me seeth the Father*, he at once added, *Believest thou not that the Father is in me, and I in the Father?*[2] And consequently he that considers the unsearchable riches of CHRIST,[3] and his divinity, will easily arrive at knowledge of the Father; for his very Son, JESUS CHRIST, is called the Word of the Father, because he declares the Father's mind, and gives knowledge of it. This interpretation is confirmed by the text, *No man hath seen God at any time; the only begotten Son, who is in the bosom of the Father, he hath declared him*.[4] And, *Ye have neither heard his voice, nor seen his form . . . for whom he sent, him ye believe not*.[5] And, *If ye had known me, ye would have known my Father also*.[6] He that has known the power of Holofernes[7] easily knows how great Nebuchadnezzar was who sent him; for he that sees one sent by another, and receives him, sees also him that sent him.[8] When the Son is glorified, God is glorified in him.[9] But neither the Apostles, nor the angels of heaven, have seen any other glorification than the glorification of the Son of man. In fine, to see CHRIST is to know that he is the Word of the Father, and to know what power is in him, and to know whence he came forth, even as he himself said, *Ye both know me, and know whence I am*.[10] Only it is not possible to know these things without knowing the Father. Again, the argument is controverted, for it is impossible that the saying should be understood as referring to the metaphysical being, and to seeing it. For CHRIST says that we are led to knowledge of the Father through him; but how is

---

[1] John xiv, 9 (Vulg.).
[2] John xiv, 10.
[3] Eph. iii, 8.
[4] John i, 18.
[5] John v, 37, 38.
[6] John viii, 19 (Pagn.); cf. xiv, 17.
[7] Judith ii, 4.
[8] John xii, 45; xiii, 20.
[9] John xiii, 31.
[10] John vii, 28.

that being which is more unknown than the Father himself to lead us to knowledge of the Father?

4. *In the beginning was the Word*;[1] that is, the utterance or voice of God; because *In the beginning God said, Let there be light: and there was light*;[2] and this Word became the true light, when he said, Let there be light. And this same Word, this same light, is the man CHRIST, who is the light of the world,[3] *the true light, which lighteth every man, coming into this world.*[4] See how the words correspond to one another. Paul makes this very thing clear by the word εἰπών,[5] that is, *said*.[6] Likewise also Irenaeus;[7] for who will bear to wrest Scripture to another sense than that which the proper meaning of the word bears? For λόγος[8] means not a philosophical being, but an oracle, a saying, a speech, a discourse, a declaration of God; for it is derived from the verb λέγω,[9] which means *say*; and that the more because the very Genesis of the world indicates the meaning, since God even from the beginning was speaking of CHRIST, and was acting by speaking this Word, so that thus all things are said to exist through CHRIST himself. Origen also says,[10] What is the word of the Lord which came to Jeremiah or to Isaiah or to any prophet you please? I know, he says, of no other word than that of which John said, *In the beginning was the Word*.[11] For in order to seek the meaning of a word, the passages must be sought in which the Holy Spirit has employed that word; and there is not in the whole Bible a single letter which supports their imaginary meaning of the word. Hence they are rash, and it is far more rash to make out of a word a Son. How, pray, does their doctrine differ from the fictions of the Gentiles, who have the tradition that Mercury means the word through which instruction is conveyed to the understanding, that Paris means feeling, and Minerva bravery? For in like manner they say that the third being means love, and the second knowledge. They take great

---

[1] John i, 1. [2] Gen. i, 1, 3. [3] John ix, 5.
[4] John i, 9 (Vulg.). [5] *Eipon*, said.
[6] II. Cor. iv, 6, Seeing it is God that *said*, Light shall shine out of darkness, etc.
[7] Adv. Haeres., III. xi, 8 (MPG. vii, 887; ANF. i, 428; ANCL. v, 293).
[8] *Logos*, word. [9] *Lego*.
[10] Homilia ix (Servetus says vi) super Jeremiam (MPG. xiii, 347).
[11] John i, 1.

pride in Platonizing, by multiplying separate beings. To sow disagreements and inconsistencies in the Scriptures is their delight. They explain, *In the beginning* [1] as meaning, in the Father; and, *In the beginning* [2] as meaning, in the Son. What am I to understand? Do you suppose that the son of Zebedee [3] would have been acquainted with such subtle philosophy? I would rather be ignorant of this inharmonious harmony of the Scriptures than know it. But assuming with Tertullian [4] that each word had its proper meaning, I say that *principium* means beginning, and was thus an appropriate word to be used for things commencing to be made; for nothing that has to be made is without a beginning. And thus the Word is the commencement or beginning of an undertaking, and not the name of any Substance; as though we said, In the end God will do this or that. And when we mean the order of a work, we say, In the beginning a potter made a basin or an urn. Without controversy, then, explain *in the beginning* as meaning, before all things; and wisdom is said to have been made before all things; [5] because before a man speaks, a meditation of the mind is first required; and because the speech of God is itself wisdom, for God can not speak foolishly. And so Ecclesiasticus explains himself; for after he said, *Wisdom hath been created before all things*,[6] he at once added, *The word of God is the source of wisdom*; [7] and, *I came forth from the mouth of the Most High, firstborn before every creature*.[8] But, that which comes forth from the mouth is speech.

5. Before I proceed further, in order fully to get at John's aim we must know that the older tradition of the Apostles understands by the mystery of the Word a kind of *disposition* [9] or dispensation in God, by which it pleased him to reveal to us the secret of his will. And this Tertullian very often calls οἰκο-

---

[1] John i, 1. [2] Gen. i, 1.
[3] John, as author of the Fourth Gospel.
[4] Adv. Hermogenem, xx (MPL. ii, 215; ANF. iii, 488; ANCL. xv, 83).
[5] Prov. viii, 23–31.
[6] Ecclus. i, 4.
[7] Ecclus. i, 5 (Vulg.).
[8] Ecclus. xxiv, 5 (Vulg.).
[9] cf. the note on these words, Book I, paragraph 41.

νομία,¹ and Irenaeus calls it *dispositio*.² And just as the speech³ was God, so also according to Irenaeus⁴ the Father himself when he speaks is said to be a *logos*;⁵ that they may be distinguished from each other just as a being and the *disposition* of the being; as though the being itself were unseen, but were made evident through the sound of words.⁶ For we shall prove below that here is an explanation of this saying.⁷ Hence the Word, in God when he utters it, is God himself speaking. After the utterance is the flesh itself, or the Word of God. Before the speech became flesh the very oracle of God was understood to be within the darkness of the clouds, not being yet manifested; for the speech was God. And after the Word became man, we understand by the Word, CHRIST himself, who is the Word of God, and the voice of God; for, like a voice, it is uttered from the mouth of God. And there is a clear text to prove that he is now the Word of God, for it is he that John saw sitting upon a white horse, whose name is the Word of God.⁸ When, therefore, the change has been made from Word to flesh, the Word is called flesh. For of what use would it be to us that the Word became flesh, if the Word is not now called flesh? For John saw the Word of life, and handled it with his hands.⁹ And Irenaeus especially derides all those that say that the Word of God is a kind of philosophical being; but he declares that JESUS of Nazareth, the very one who was born of Mary, was the Word of God after the Word became flesh. And he says that those who do not acknowledge that this JESUS is the Word of God have no sense.¹⁰ Moreover, who is the bread, what is the flesh from heaven?¹¹ Surely it is the Word of God, which is the very body of Christ,

48b (margin)

Those that admit that the Word of God is a man because the Word became man, must needs admit that the Word of God is flesh, because the Word became flesh; or else flesh will be the name of a *hypostasis*.

---

¹ *Oikonomia*. Adv. Praxean, ii, iii (MPL. ii, 156–159; ANF. iii, 598 f.; ANCL. xv, 335–339).

² Adv. Haeres., I. vi (MPG. vii, 503; ANF. i, 324; ANCL. v, 25).

³ *Sermo*.

⁴ Adv. Haer., IV. v, xx (MPG. vii, 983 f., 1031 ff.; ANF. i, 467, 487 ff.; ANCL. v, 387, 439 ff.).

⁵ Word.

⁶ Deut. iv, 12; Ex. xx, 18. ⁷ See paragraph 6.

⁸ Rev. xix, 11, 13. ⁹ I. John i, 1.

¹⁰ Adv. Haeres., I. i, 3; III. xxi, 10; xvi, 6; (MPG. vii, 450, 955, 926; ANF. i, 317, 454, 442; ANCL. v, 6, 358 f., 329).

¹¹ John vi, 50, 51.

the very flesh of CHRIST. For whatever is in him has been uttered from the mouth of God, is the Word of God. And the eating of which it there speaks[1] is the food and drink of the Word. And this is just the word of the Gospel, namely, that JESUS CHRIST is the Son of God, without which there is no eating of his body, as the Master there clearly explains himself. Come, he says, and believe in me, and ye shall never hunger nor thirst.[2] I always speak of the flesh, after the manner of John, instead of the man CHRIST himself; and John used this word on purpose to express the man CHRIST more and more, lest perchance one say that CHRIST is a phantom. Into the error which he had once condemned we have slipped in the same way; for it makes no difference whether one says that what appeared to be flesh is a phantom fallen from heaven, or whether we say that a like phantom fallen from heaven is in the flesh, and is united to the flesh in the common and carnal way; since John does not say that the Word was united with, but became, flesh. For quite in the same way Valentinus said that the Savior put on an animal body.[3] Let us therefore understand the meaning of John as to how the Word of God became flesh; because God determined his own *dispositions* to be manifested in the flesh, and all those things which God hitherto wrought by his Word, or by his own voice, are now wrought by the flesh, CHRIST, to whom has been committed the rule and all power, who reconciles, renews, sums up all things in himself. It is also understood in very truth that the Word which was in the beginning became flesh, because this flesh was begotten by a voice uttered from the beginning, not otherwise than as if I, uttering a word from my mouth, produced gold or pearls; for then it might be said, properly speaking, that my voice became gold. For the almighty Word of God was able, without the bond of material things,[4] to change into fleshly substance; and therefore CHRIST himself is now called, the Word become man, the Word become flesh. The Word may also be understood to have become flesh in fulfilment of what is said of CHRIST, *I will put my words in his mouth, and . . . he shall speak*

---

[1] John vi, 50–58. [2] John vi, 35.
[3] Adv. Valent., xvi–xviii (MPL. ii, 569–573; ANF. iii, 512 f.; ANCL. xv, 142–145). [4] *Rerum coagulum.*

*in my name.*¹ And CHRIST himself says, *I speak not of myself, but as the Father has taught me, so I speak.*² He is said to be the speech of the Father for the reason that he declares the Father's will, and gives knowledge of him. In the fourth place, the oracle from the darkness of the cloud became flesh, and the answers from God which Moses then received we now receive from the mouth of CHRIST; indeed, the former was a shadow of the latter, and herein is concealed the true meaning which the ancients favor, the deeper mysteries which lie here concealed, of which below.

6. John, therefore, contrary to the Ebionites who denied that Christ was divinely begotten, when about to make known his ineffable birth, shows how he was first of all made CHRIST by the Word of God, saying that he who is now flesh was formerly the *logos*;³ and that the *logos* was even from the beginning; *and the Word was with God,*⁴ that is, the second being was with the first. What flavor, pray, have these most insipid words: the second being was with the first? For the sound teaching of Christ takes it in another sense, that the Word was with God, since this was a mystery hidden from the beginning in the mind of God, until the fulness of time came, and it was then manifested when the Word became flesh. And so the same John says in his Epistle that the Word of life, which was from the beginning with the Father, was afterwards manifested.⁵ And so Tertullian says, He held discourse with, and in, the very reason within himself, secretly meditating and determining with himself what he was presently to express in speech.⁶ And that speech was God. John foresaw the philosophers who reason thus: *The Word was with God,* hence it was a kind of distinct being; and to make null their misrepresentation he at once added, *And the Word was God;*⁷ that is, as Irenaeus says, the Father himself, when speaking, is said to be the *logos.*⁸ Again, the philosophers ought to have rea-

---
¹ Deut. xviii, 18, 19.
² John viii, 28.   ³ Word.
⁴ John i, 1.   ⁵ I. John i, 1, 2.
⁶ Adv. Praxean, v (MPL. ii, 160; ANF. iii, 600; ANCL. xv, 342).
⁷ John i, 1.
⁸ Adv. Haeres., V. xviii, 2 (MPG. vii, 1173–1174; ANF. i, 546; ANCL. ix, 104–105).

soned thus: The Word was with God, therefore it was a kind of being distinct from God; and in that way they might fairly have deduced a plurality of Gods. They will not have it that the Word was with the third being, nor even with the divine Essence, but only with the Father; and thus the divine Essence is something else than God, or else John did not do well to say that the Word was with God.

7. *All things were made through him.*[1] God made all things by his Word: that is, the first being through the second. The first being wrought through the second, took it in his hand as a beast, or as an axe, and therewith cleft and brought wood. Pray search the Scriptures, bring them into harmony, and see whether it could have been more clearly said that all things were made by the Word of God, unless in accordance with what Genesis declares, that God said, let it be made, and it was made.[2] And the Psalmist says, *By the Word of the Lord were the heavens made, . . . for he spake and they were made.*[3] And thus Irenaeus distinctly explains.[4] And in this sense Hebrews xi, 3 and Wisdom ix, 1 are taken.[5] Nor would John ever have imagined that we should make an utterance of God the proper name of some particular being, especially since he himself refers to that speech which God spoke in the beginning, when he made the world. Also from other passages of Scripture let it be evident that this speaking or utterance of the Word is a naming of CHRIST, by which in Isaiah CHRIST is named under the figure of Abraham; for it says, *Calling a bird from the east, the man of my counsel from a far country; I have spoken, I will also bring it to pass.*[6] And, *From the rising of the sun he called upon my name.*[7] And because of this naming or calling it says, *Before the sun*

---

[1] John i, 3. [2] Gen. i, 3.
[3] Ps. xxxiii, 6, 9 (Vulg.).
[4] Adv. Haeres., II. ii, 5; I. xxii, 1; IV. xxxii, 1 (Servetus wrongly cites the last two as I. xix and IV. lii) (MPG. vii, 715, 669, 1071; ANF. i, 362, 347, 506; ANCL. v, 123, 85; ix, 5).
[5] *The worlds have been framed by the Word of God. Who madest all things by thy Word.*
[6] Isa. xlvi, 11.
[7] Isa. xli, 25. Servetus has *vocavit* in place of the Vulgate's *vocabit*, perhaps through a Spaniard's natural confusion of *v* with *b*.

ינין שמו,¹ that is, Before the sun will his name be brought forth; for, looking into the future, he said, *He shall be as a son*;² yet the plan of this sonship is *before the sun*, and this is called, *the dew of his birth: From the womb, from the morning, thou hast the dew of thy birth.*³ Likewise in Isaiah, *The Lord hath called me from the womb*; and, *He hath caused my name to be remembered.*⁴ Read there from chapter xl. to the end, and you shall discover this naming, and how the mouth of the Lord hath spoken.

8. It remains to ask with regard to his generation in what way he is said to be, as the Apostle says, *the firstborn of creatures.*⁵ This primogeniture the Philosophers attribute to the second being, saying, *Who shall declare his generation?*⁶ But the words of Isaiah are forcibly and perversely wrested with respect to his generation; for he says, *He was rejected among men, a man of sorrows . . . he will be led as a lamb to the slaughter, as a sheep before its shearer will he be dumb . . . who hath declared his generation? For he was cut off from the land of the living, for the transgression of my people was the stroke given him.*⁷ And so Philip explains to the Eunuch that the man CHRIST is referred to.⁸ For it is he that is the Melchizedek of unknown race, as to whom no one knew whence he was.⁹ For indeed the mere thought is absurd to utter, that one angel is the son of another, is born of another, or is begotten by another, or that another being is said to be begotten without a body; for that is an affair of the flesh. Nor does one ever read in the Scripture of a begetting of the Word, or of a begetting of the second being, which by a misuse of language they call the *logos*. But properly speaking it is called an utterance of the Word, upon which the begetting of the flesh follows.

9. Again, note this: that when CHRIST is called the firstborn among creatures, he is also noted as being himself the creature

---

¹ *Yinnin shemo*, his name shall be continued. Ps. lxxii, 17 (Vulg.).

² *Filiabitur*. Ps. lxxii, 17. Servetus here follows a Hebrew text represented in the marginal reading of the English R.V.

³ Ps. cx, 3.   ⁴ Isa. xlix, 1 (Pagn.).

⁵ Col. i, 15.   ⁶ Isa. liii, 8 (Vulg.).

⁷ Servetus's quotation here (of Isa. liii, 7, 8) conflates Vulg. with Pagn., and by another confusion of *v* with *b* (as above) he makes *enarrabit* read *enarravit*.

⁸ Acts viii, 35.   ⁹ Heb. vii, 1-3; cf. John vii, 27.

of God, as well as the firstborn from the dead;[1] because he also was dead. Again, Wisdom says that she was created, and, *He that created me*, and, *I the Lord have created him*.[2] Paul also, and John, say that he *was made*, nay, was *made out of a woman*.[3] Also it is said that he *was made of the seed of David*, and it adds, *according to the flesh*,[4] in order to distinguish the begetting of the flesh, which is from his mother, from the begetting by his father, which through the Spirit and power of God is from everlasting. And this is the meaning of the very saying of Paul, *according to the flesh*, as appears from Ephesians vi, 5 and Colossians iii, 22, where those having servants are called *masters according to the flesh*; for the reason that through the Spirit of God in CHRIST JESUS there is neither bond nor free, but we are all one.[5] Likewise they are called *kinsmen according to the flesh*,[6] because, through the spirit of CHRIST, those that do the will of his Father are his brother and sister.[7] And all these things are explained according to the thought of John, whose aim was to confound Ebion and Cerinthus,[8] who asserted that in CHRIST there was only a begetting of the flesh, since from his mother he is born physically, but from his Father he is born from everlasting. Nor is there more than one son born and begotten. Nor could the Philosophers, even had they expressly meant to jest, have spoken more absurdly than by saying that one of the two was begotten and born of a father without a mother, but the other of a mother without a father, all of which they make up out of their own heads. Who ever heard of a begetting without a father, and of being born without a mother? They are so fascinated by their own Ideas that they wonder that I say that flesh is born. But what, pray, can be born but flesh? Nevertheless it is not born from the father; for it is one thing for flesh to be born, another to be physically born. Again, if the Son was the *logos*, born of his

52a

---

[1] Col. i, 15, 18.
[2] Ecclus. i, 4; xxiv, 8; Isa. xlv, 8 (Vulg.).
[3] John i, 14; Gal. iv, 4 (Vulg.).
[4] Rom. i, 3 (Vulg.).   [5] Gal. iii, 28.
[6] Rom. ix, 3.   [7] Matt. xii, 50.
[8] Ebion, supposed founder of the Jewish Christian sect of Ebionites; Cerinthus, Gnostic of Asia Minor; both of whom about the end of the first century denied the virgin birth, and taught that Jesus was mere man.

Father without a mother, tell me, how did he bear him; through a womb, or through his side? Nor will I permit you here to make up various reasons to suit yourself. For you have learned such errors not from the Scriptures but from the Philosophers. For the begetting of the Son of God was made like the begetting of ourselves. Nor does the Scripture attribute to God either speech, or sonship, or other accidents, save in so far as they are adapted to the usage of men. Whence, then, is this great foolishness that we thus abuse God to suit ourselves? I would rather speak after the manner of common men and not go beyond Scripture, than philosophize foolishly. This manner of speaking the Master taught me; and not only he but all the Scriptures exhibit this manner of speaking. For the words of CHRIST are so familiar that it is utter madness to outrage them by such monstrosities. Again, with regard to what has been said above, the earlier writers admit that the Son is God's creature, and hence created. Thus they do not speak of the metaphysical Nature; and as touching this, I remember having read a quotation of the testimony of Clement,[1] the disciple of Peter whom Paul mentions. Likewise the testimony of the other Clement, of Alexandria,[2] and of Dionysius, Bishop of Alexandria,[3] whose writings, as well as those of all the others that wrote before the Arian schism, I would that I had seen.

10. Now as to the question why he is called firstborn, Irenaeus says[4] that neither the Prophets nor the angels in heaven know, nor do I know, how to explain this kind of begetting; yet I will try to argue for it a little. And you should know first that our chief cause of error is that we judge after the flesh about a before or an after in time, regarding actions of God which are not subject to time. With him we do not find *was*, but always find *is*, even as he said, *He that is hath sent me to you;* . . . *I am that I am*:[5] Nothing is past to him, all things are present to

---

[1] The allusion is perhaps to Clementine Homily, XVI. xv (MPG. ii, 378; ANF. viii, 316; ANCL. xvii, 252).

[2] Perhaps referring to Paedagog., I. ii, viii, or Strom., VII. ii (MPG. viii, 251 ff., 326 ff.; ix, 407 ff.; ANF. ii, 209, 227 f., 524; ANCL. iv, 115 ff., 155 ff.; xii, 409).

[3] Ep. ad Dionysium (MPL. v, 125; ANF. vi, 92 ff.; ANCL. xx, 189 ff.). Dionysius in fact here denies this inference from what he had said.

[4] Passage not identified.   [5] Ex. iii, 14 (Vulg.).

him, all live unto God;[1] all things are naked and plain in his eyes;[2] *he calleth the things that are not as those that are;*[3] with him a thousand years are as one day, and one day as a thousand years;[4] and it was said, *This day have I begotten thee,*[5] for the reason that from the beginning of the world even to CHRIST is one day in which the begetting of CHRIST is accomplished. Besides, that there is no difference of times in God is argued by the proper meaning or the usage of the utterances of the Prophets; for they relate future things as past, and then again contrariwise.[6] And one tense is often used for another, signifying not only the constancy of the matter, but also that in God there are not the three distinctions of time, namely present, past, and future; for the things that are seen are already constant, and are perpetual, to him who sees them. Again, consider how it was before the creation of the world; for the order of the seasons arose as necessary not to God but to man; and to mark these, the lights in the heavens were set in their places. *They shall be,* he says, *for seasons and for days and years.*[7] Thus neither did he who made time have any time before time began, nor did he who fixed the beginning have any beginning before there was a beginning. And this is in the sight of God a strong reason; nor did God submit himself to time by creating the world.

11. If you now, having drawn back the veil of the intervening time, observe that the hour of the nativity or begetting of Christ is, or was, present to God at the very beginning of the world, you will readily admit that God then uttered his word, spoke, and in uttering begot the Son, namely, him who was manifested in the latter days. But that middle wall of partition[8] hinders sensual flesh from this sort of knowledge. This is what Isaiah says in great astonishment, *Before she travailed, she brought forth, before the time for her delivery came, she was de-*

---

[1] Luke xx, 38.   [2] Heb. iv, 13.
[3] Rom. iv, 17 (Vulg.).   [4] II. Pet. iii, 8.
[5] Heb. i, 5; v, 5.

[6] The reference is to the peculiarity of the Hebrew verb, which has only two tenses, representing actions as either finished or unfinished; hence the latter may refer to either future or past time.

[7] Gen. i, 14.

[8] Eph. ii, 14.

livered of a man child; ¹ for the time of travailing is the very hour of delivery and of birth, only before these things took place, even from the beginning, he called, conceived, and brought him forth before the dawn.² Behold, how gloriously God brought forth the Son whom he decided to beget as his only begotten. It was meet that he be so gloriously begotten, who had been ordained to be the judge of the living and the dead.³ At the very lifting of my eyes to see him at the right hand of the Father in heaven, I tremble when I hear him called *the human nature* by you. Do you not see that it is he that governs all things? This alone, if you look on high, is sufficient reason for his being called not only Son of God, but God and Lord of the world. Hence by reason of the utterance made at the beginning, he himself is said to be the beginning, and for the same reason must be said to be the firstborn, for he must be said to have been born in the beginning; for the utterance made in the beginning is its very self the begetting of the flesh, as the wisdom which is the mystery of Christ makes clear to us; for it calls itself the firstborn among creatures ⁴ for the reason that from the beginning, as I have said, it was made together with speech. And Paul, noting this mystery, calls CHRIST the firstborn, who he says is the wisdom of God.⁵ Moreover, Paul also confirms this view, for he says that God foreordained the elect, whom he also called *to become conformed to the image of his Son, that he himself may be the firstborn among many brethren.*⁶ For the elect are said to be called after his likeness, and to follow the image of his begetting; because he himself was elect first, and was called and brought forth first of all as a pattern of every calling, and thus is called the firstborn among the elect in a more exceptional way than among other creatures.

54a

12. I had said in the discussion why it was said, *This day have I begotten thee,* in order not only to overthrow the proof which they draw from this, but also to show that their philosophy is vain who from this saying conclude that the second being is begotten, is produced, and emanates from the first daily and by

---

¹ Isa. lxvi, 7.
² Ps. cix, 3 (Vulg.).
³ Acts x, 42.
⁴ Col. i, 15.
⁵ I. Cor. i, 24.
⁶ Rom. viii, 29 (Vulg.).

continuous succession. Nor do they blush to fasten upon God a transient action so imperfect and changeable, as though the Son were a kind of something left over, brought forth in the same way in which they dream of time and motion; and what is more, I have explained from Scriptures not understood by them, therefore in view of their comparative foolishness, on what day of the world it could have been said, *This day have I begotten thee.* But now let us look further into the meaning of this saying, so that they may realize that they can not go astray, as to why Paul said Jesus was raised, *as it is written in the Psalm, Thou art my Son, this day have I begotten thee.*[1] For although Paul seem to have spoken foolishness, yet is his wisdom profound. And the meaning of this matter is found where Paul also says that JESUS CHRIST *was through the spirit* ἁγιοσύνης [2] (which was in David himself) *determined to be the Son of God with power, by the resurrection from the dead.*[3] And this determination or declaration of David is found in Psalm ii, 7, and in II. Samuel xxii, 51; xxiii, 1. And this determination from the fact that he rose again is made for the reason that by his resurrection CHRIST is glorified. All authority, inheritance, and rule were then given to him, even as he himself testifies, *All authority hath been given unto me in heaven and on earth.*[4] Paul therefore said, *in power*; and those that rise in his likeness will rise in power,[5] as CHRIST declares against the Sadducees.[6] For it is sown in weakness, and it will rise in power.[5] And with respect to this power of the resurrection of CHRIST, David said, in the Psalm cited above, *Ask of me, I will give thee the nations for thine inheritance, and the uttermost parts of the earth for thy possession, and thou shalt rule them with a rod of iron.*[7] And what is there spoken of as *a potter's vessel*, it elsewhere calls *the mire of the streets.*[8] This I say that you may not despise history. Of the same *rod of iron* and fulness of power which CHRIST received through his resurrection, John makes mention.[9] Referring to this day, CHRIST said, Hence-

The passage in Rom. i. was never understood.

This declaration of sonship furnishes the strongest proof that the Son is not the being, but a man.

---

[1] Acts xiii, 33.
[2] *Hagiosunes*, of holiness.
[3] Rom. i, 4.
[4] Matt. xxviii, 18.
[5] I. Cor. xv, 43.
[6] Matt. xxii, 29.
[7] Ps. ii, 8, 9.
[8] II. Sam. xxii, 43.
[9] Rev. ii, 27; xix, 15.

forth the Son of man will be sitting at the right hand of the power of God.¹ Then also, The kingdom of God cometh with power,² even as the Son of God also comes with power.³ For here, as also in Romans i, 4, it says ἐν δυνάμει,⁴ that is, with power, or in strength. And it not only says, with power, and because of the special power of CHRIST himself and his kingdom, but also because *with great power gave the Apostles their witness of the resurrection of* CHRIST;⁵ and because God employed his great power, strength, force, and might in CHRIST when he raised him from the dead.⁶ And so Paul is wont to employ the saying of the Psalmist for no other purpose than that in a new way he may show CHRIST's glorious power after his resurrection; how seated above angels at the right hand of the Father he abides there a priest forever.⁷

55b   13. David, therefore, considering that he was then to be born again, and that salvation was then being procured for us, proclaims that he, as it were a new-born man, was made the mighty Son, for on that day will be manifested the great power with which *I have begotten thee*; on that day it will be manifested that *thou art my Son*,⁸ as if I had then begotten thee. And so the Chaldaean paraphrast⁹ reads, *as if I had created thee on that day*; for unless he had risen from the dead it would not have been meet that he be believed to be the Son of God, nor would the Apostles have believed it, for they had all lost hope. So in every way, with respect to both himself and us, he is called to-day the Son of God, he is born to-day who now is, and before was not; he has passed over to-day from the birth of a mortal body to an incorruptible birth. Hence he is understood to have been then born, because he was born again, and born as it were with full authority, a new man newly created king; and so CHRIST said, new in his Father's kingdom.¹⁰ Others explain it as meaning, This day have I begotten thee as king. Paul begets new men;¹¹

---

¹ Matt. xxvi, 64.
² Mark ix, 1.
³ Matt. xxiv, 30; Mark xiii, 26; Luke xxi, 27.
⁴ *En dunamei.*
⁵ Acts. iv, 33.
⁶ Eph. i, 19, 20; Phil. iii, 21.
⁷ Heb. i, 3, 4; v, 6.
⁸ Ps. ii, 7; Heb. i, 5.
⁹ i. e., the Targums.
¹⁰ Matt. xxvi, 29.
¹¹ I. Cor. iv, 15.

for all these things relating to his image apply to us, that we may become conformed to the image of the Son of God.¹ And after the likeness of him that was born again, we say that we are born again, since, when the flesh has been buried through baptism, we rise again through the power of the Spirit and are born again; and he that is born again is said to be born. And we are all said to be born and begotten in Zion, and Zion is called our mother,² and he is said then to be born in a new way, because in a new way he is the firstborn from the dead.³

14. Again, this meaning is rendered indubitable from history, for that Psalm as well as the following one was written when the princes of the Jews had conspired with Absalom against David, as was also done against CHRIST.⁴ For they raged, and with Ahithophel they imagined vain things against David his CHRIST;⁵ and there, as also in the Psalm following, mention is made of his resurrection, namely, that he was rescued from perils; and then he says, To-day have I been begotten. And this we, too, when we escape from great peril, are wont to say: To-day I have been born. And the most correct explanation is this: This day have I begotten thee as king, as clearly appears where David says of the same day, *I know that I have this day been made king over Israel*;⁶ and to this meaning he adds his escape from the hand of Saul;⁷ which things all speak of the resurrection of CHRIST. And in II. Samuel xxiii, as well as in Psalm ii, according to Paul,⁸ he proclaims CHRIST as the Son of God through the Holy Spirit, applying to him from this day all the explanations concerning the resurrection. This, saith he, has been ordained concerning me, so that this day I have been born to God as Son and king; Son, I say, exalted and with power, even as he said, I will give thee an inheritance, and a rod of iron.⁹ Marvelous Paul, and marvelous explanation! for in the words, *This day have I begotten thee*, lies the explanation of his sonship; and the prophet at a single stroke includes the two things as following from the resurrection.

¹ Rom. viii, 29.   ² Gal. iv, 26.   ³ Col. i, 18.
⁴ Acts iv, 26.   ⁵ i. e., anointed.
⁶ II. Sam. xix, 22 (Vulg.).   ⁷ II. Sam. xxii, 1, 49; Ps. xviii, 50.
⁸ I. Cor. xii, 3.   ⁹ Ps. ii, 8, 9.

15. I can not here refrain from sighing, when I see the replies that Rabbi Kimchi made against the Christians on this point.[1] I find the reasons with which they sought to convince him so obscure that I can not but weep. They said it was understood as speaking of the mathematical Son: *this day*, that is, before all worlds, *have I begotten thee*. They most foolishly make an aeon out of *this day*, although in the Hebrew the demonstrative pronoun is used, indicating *this* day. While leaving the literal meaning, neither he nor they knew to what the spiritual meaning refers. They argued against him that the literal meaning did not refer to David; he argued against them that the spiritual meaning of the prophet did not refer to CHRIST. Yet since the one reasoning can not stand without the other, it would else be idle to say that David is a type of CHRIST. Moreover, what blinder thing can be said than to deny that it was said of Solomon, *I will be to him a Father, and he shall be to me a Son?*[2] There is a clear text referring to him in I. Chronicles.[3] It speaks of them, but in a higher sense than can be appropriate to them, so that from this it easily appears that the spirit refers to something else, especially since there are words intermingled which can by no means be appropriate to them, as of the eternity of his throne and kingdom. For this is said to Solomon himself; but it is not said of him on his own account, but only in so far as he is a representative of CHRIST. Here you clearly see that it is under the type of a man that the man is called Son. This reason is very strong, if you have an understanding of history; or else you will say, with the Jews, that here is only sonship in a parabolic sense; for the true sonship, which is in JESUS CHRIST, was under a shadow in Solomon and David. These words are not parabolic, but they have very great force; yet to infer the sonship of the second being from the type of a man is a blind fancy; neither a kind of type nor any form of representation can be applied here.

[1] cf. The Longer Commentary of R. David Kimḥi on the First Book of Psalms, tr. R. G. Finch, London, 1919, p. 15, com. on Ps. ii, 7: "Every one who is obedient to the voice of God he calls his son." So Deut. xiv, 1; II. Sam. vii, 14; Hos. ii, 1 . . . "On this day there was born in him the spirit of God." So I. Sam. xvi, 13.
[2] II. Sam. vii, 14; Heb. i, 5.
[3] I. Chron. xxii, 11; xxviii, 6.

16. Some are scandalized that I call CHRIST a prophet, for inasmuch as they have not this custom themselves, it seems to them to be Judaism or Mohammedanism if CHRIST is called a prophet. Nor do they care whether Scripture and the earlier writers call him a prophet. They ask me whether I assume two Natures as hypostatically united in CHRIST. But how far they are off the track in this matter by taking the name of the Word as meaning a Nature, and how great is their profane abuse of this hypostatic union, will appear below.[1] For the present, I say, to satisfy the purpose of their question, that the whole Nature and Essence of God is in CHRIST, though they would have one part in him represent the Nature of God. Just as the Ebionites 57b make JESUS a mere man of the seed of David, not the same as the Son of God, so it seems to them that we call CHRIST simply a kind of prophet, or purely a man, even as any of us; nor can they otherwise see any difference except they bring in a kind of incarnate being, which they declare is by a carnal and more than profane union joined to his whole human nature, both flesh and bones and sinews, so that from this there arise as many and as foolish questions as possible. And the words which CHRIST spoke they do not understand as referring to him that spoke them, but all the glory is referred to the being, as Valentinus ascribed it to his aeons; as though CHRIST lied, or spoke of the separate being under a sort of deceitful disguise. And do not speak to me of one Substance, or one Person, after you clearly see that these inventions are not derived from the Scriptures; and in what follows you will realize that you have been deceived by these misuses of terms. Can there be a greater insult than for you, while I am speaking, to deny that I exist, or to deny that what I ascribe to myself belongs to me? CHRIST was not speaking to philosophers, who were already learned with regard to the *hypostasis*, but to the common people, to children and women.

17. That you may therefore have knowledge of the true CHRIST apart from the imaginations of the philosophers, give heed how these more than Ebionites despoil the true Christ of 58a all but his bare human nature, nor raise their eyes to regard his

---

[1] Book IV, paragraph 12.

ineffable generation which took place from the beginning from the Substance of God; nor regard him, all full of the divinity of the Father, all radiant with divine light. Oh, that you had beheld his glory on the mount, when his raiment was white as the light, and his face shone as the sun,[1] and you would say with John, *We beheld his glory.*[2] But if no one knoweth who the Son is, save the Father,[3] why am I here tormented? Knowledge of him is wisdom hidden in a mystery, which had they known they would by no means have crucified the Lord of glory.[4] And if you would understand the mystery, he is himself the ineffable voice of God which spoke to Abraham, Moses, and the rest; he himself is the Word which gave commandments to Adam himself, and that same Word against which Adam sinned gives remission, after sins, to them that believe. Nor shall you marvel that he is the Son of man. *Greater works than these will God show him, that ye may marvel.*[5] For *who is this*, think you, *that the wind and the sea obey him*,[6] to whom *all authority hath been given in heaven and on earth*,[7] and *all things whatsoever the Father hath are his*,[8] and whom the Father *made to sit at his right hand*[9] on an equality with himself? And the Son himself, and the *hypostasis* of the Creator, since he is God in spirit, is able to lay down his life, and to take it again,[10] because the Word of God does not die. For since God *giveth not the Spirit by measure*,[11] so great is the power of his spirit that all things that are said of him are more than human; and although they say that this being died and suffered even as a man, and that thus two died and were crucified, yet I maintain with the earlier writers that he was God and man — in one respect born, in another not born; in one respect flesh, in another spirit; in one respect weak, in another very strong; in one respect dying, in another living — and in fact the earlier writers admit that man was mingled with God, since God was born as a man, Emanuel. Yet it is not God that dies, but man; it is not the soul that dies, but the flesh. Who can but

These words are warped and twisted by them to bear another meaning, and yet they evidently prove our case.

---

[1] Luke ix, 29. [2] John i, 14. [3] Matt. xi, 27.
[4] I. Cor. ii, 7, 8. [5] John v, 20.
[6] Mark iv, 41. [7] Matt. xxviii, 18.
[8] John xvi, 15. [9] Eph. i, 20.
[10] John x, 18. [11] John iii, 34.

laugh at the *communicatio idiomatum,* which bids me believe that angels of God can die?

<small>This they admit: that if angels put on an ass's body, then angels too will be asses.</small>

18. And note this one teaching of the Master: that all words soever that are from CHRIST are spirit and life. Hence it is spiritually to be understood that CHRIST is God; for as he is not called man without having flesh, so he is not called God without having the Spirit of God. And thus if you regard the spirit you should no more deny that one who shares both Substances is God than you deny that he is man; because *that which is born of the Spirit is spirit,*[1] and *God is a spirit*;[2] and since his spirit was wholly God, he himself is called God, even as from his flesh he is called man. And do not marvel that I adore as God him whom you call the human nature; for you are wont to treat the human nature as though it had no part in the Spirit; you regard the flesh, and judging after the flesh you can not comprehend what the spirit of CHRIST is like, which gives the matter its being, and is that which giveth life, when the flesh profiteth nothing.[3] All this is, as it were, only a prelude to arriving at the ineffable divinity of CHRIST (of which we shall speak below).[4] Let this suffice for the present, that you may know those to be the true Ebionites who make him out a man, or a mere human nature, and take from him all that should be ascribed to the true CHRIST, that they may philosophize at their own pleasure. Their magisterial metaphysics knows only this: that CHRIST, or the Son, must not be separated from the Nature of God. To which, though it be their invention, I shall reply, and in replying I ask of what CHRIST or Son they are speaking; for the one whom they portray, whether as the Son or as CHRIST, I do not so separate, because he is nothing. For the Word of John once existed, but now there is no such Word, as I shall show below;[5] and this John clearly indicates, always saying of this being, *was,* though it never says, *is.* To declare that, therefore, to be null which is nothing is no blasphemy in them, yet it is a great and evident blasphemy; for that he whom I call CHRIST is really something, they can not deny; yet once fallen to disputing about

<small>They speak of man as if of pure flesh.</small>

---

[1] John iii, 6.
[2] John iv, 24.
[3] John vi, 63.
[4] Book VII, paragraph 4, 5.
[5] Book IV, paragraph 8.

ON THE ERRORS OF THE TRINITY 93

Christ, they deny that he is the CHRIST, and they reject a mere man as being far removed from the Father. Hence I do not separate him from God any more than a voice from him that utters it, or a ray from the sun; for CHRIST is in the Father as the voice is in him that utters it, and he and the Father are one, as the ray and the sun are one light. For it is a wonderful mystery that thus joins God to man and man to God, and wonderfully has God made the body of CHRIST his own, that it might be his own tabernacle for him to dwell in.

19. Of the Holy Spirit I have already said that God gives us his Spirit only in this way, that he gives us the breath of life.[1] For life is not derived from us, nor from our nature, but is given according to the grace of God; and by the breath of God upon a mass of clay man is made a living soul.[2] Yet the philosophers believe thus: that God bestowed his power upon elements and stars, as though he despoiled himself of it; they believe that we are kept in being by breathing the very air, as though by a property of nature, no account being taken of the grace of God; which is a most ungrateful falsehood. Nay, it must be said that the energy and life-giving spirit of the Godhead are in that substance which is breathed in and out; for he by his spirit keeps the breath of life in us, giving breath unto the people that are upon earth, and spirit to them that walk therein;[3] he alone shaketh the heavens,[4] bringeth forth the winds out of his treasuries,[5] bindeth up the water in the clouds of heaven,[6] giveth rain in its season;[7] he alone doing all these things, always doing marvelous things alone.

20. To come bluntly to the Holy Spirit, we begin with the Spirit of God; for the philosophers, not knowing this energy of the Deity, have been unable to understand why the blowing of the wind could be called the Spirit of God.[8] Nor do they care whether God sends it to us out of his treasuries and flows into us through it. Therefore let them know henceforth that God his

---

[1] cf. Book I, paragraph 43.   Ezek. xxxvii, 5, 6, 14.
[2] Gen. ii, 7.   [3] Isa. xlii, 5.
[4] Hag. ii, 21.   [5] Jer. x, 13.
[6] Job xxvi, 8.   [7] Jer. v, 24.
[8] Gen. i, 2.

very self is acting in the wind's very substance. Lo, God himself is as present in thy mouth, in thy breath, within and without thee, as though thou shouldst touch him with thy hand.[1] By the moving of his Spirit are the powers of the heavens moved.[2] The matter of which the world is made is a lifeless thing unless it were kept in motion by the Spirit of God. All this the philosophers admit, yet forthwith, because they are speaking of the Spirit of God, they forget what I by myself have well enough learned from their teachings, speaking of meeting God as though his dwelling-place were above and not near at hand. In speaking of the Spirit of God it was enough for me if I understood that the third being was in a sort of corner. But now I know, what he himself said: *I am a God at hand, and not a God afar off*;[3] now I know that God's universal Spirit fills the earth, encompasses all things, and produces the power in every man. With the prophet I would cry out, *O Lord, whither shall I go from thy spirit?*[4] since neither above nor below is there any place without the Spirit of God.

The difference between the Holy Spirit and the Spirit of God.

21. This about the Spirit of God is a prelude to [what I have to say of] the Holy Spirit; for the kind of holiness which is joined to the action of the Spirit of God means nothing philosophical; for the Spirit of God acts within and without, but it is what is within that is sanctified. Hence let us note the difference between breath and spirit, for it is called breath when it comes from without; but when acting within it illuminates and sanctifies the spirit of man. The Spirit is called Holy; for we are not said to receive a breath; but when the breath comes, we receive the Spirit, so that when he has breathed on them with his mouth, CHRIST says, *Receive ye the Holy Spirit.*[5] Wind also differs from spirit, because properly speaking a spirit is said to be in the wind as in a substance, in so far as it is a life-giving power; and wind is taken as an evil, as when it is called a pestilent and consuming wind. But when he sends his Spirit, he acts kindly. Spirit is also a more general term than wind. From this, the subject of the Spirit, so far as concerns the Old Testament,

---

[1] Acts xvii, 28.
[2] Matt. xxiv, 29; Luke xxi, 26.
[3] Jer. xxiii, 23.
[4] Ps. cxxxix, 7.
[5] John xx, 22.

is much cleared up; for the Spirit of the power of God can not be understood without the instruments with which its action is bound up.

22. I have said above¹ what else can be understood by the paraclete, and this is also drawn from their words; for they say that appearances of fire are something proper to the Holy Spirit, though these occur by means of angels, as when the Lord appeared to Moses in the bush;² and through an angel the voice of the Lord there came to Moses.³ Hence, according to this, the voice of God uttered through the mouth of the angel is called the voice of the Holy Spirit. And after the Holy Spirit descended upon JESUS, he said, *Verily I say unto you, ye shall see the angels of God ascending and descending upon the Son of man.*⁴ And Isidore, from the fact that it says, *He shall declare unto you the things that are to come,*⁵ infers that it was an angel, because angel bears the meaning of messenger.⁶ Add to this the fact that all angels are called *ministering spirits, sent forth to do service,*⁷ and, *He maketh his angels spirits, and his ministers a flame of fire.*⁸ And this is the flame of fire which appeared in Acts ii, 3. Again, just as an angel is called a lying spirit,⁹ so in a contrary passage an angel is to be called the spirit of truth and the Holy Spirit, even as it also says, Spirits of God.¹⁰

23. It is true that in the Scriptures separate mention is made of angel and spirit, for what is done by outward understanding, speech, or revelation is said to be done by an angel, as though it were done by some man; but what is done inwardly, or so to speak by way of a breath, or of a dove, as it were a winged breath, is said to be from the Spirit. In consequence of this, note that neither the appearance of fire in the bush, nor the appearance of a cloud, is ever called the Holy Spirit, although the service of the angel was there quite as well. The reason of the dif-

_{Scripture observes the manners of the appearances.}

---

¹ Book I, paragraph 43.   ² Ex. iii, 2.
³ Acts vii, 30.   ⁴ John i, 51.
⁵ John xvi, 13.
⁶ Isidore of Seville, Etymologiae, VII. iii, 3 (MPL. lxxxii, 268).
⁷ Heb. i, 14.
⁸ Heb. i, 7.
⁹ I. Kings xxii, 22, 23; II. Chron. xviii, 21, 22.
¹⁰ Rev. iv, 5; v, 6.

ference is that there he did not appear by way of a breath; only that which is not spirit can not be called the Holy Spirit.

24. Likewise there is a distinction between the Holy Spirit and the Spirit of God, because it is called Holy when it is sent to make our spirits holy, as I shall say below;[1] but it is called the Spirit of God when it is sent into all the earth.[2]

25. Again, note that it is a Person of the Godhead; that when the angel speaks he says, *I am the God of thy fathers*;[3] as also the angel said to Jacob, *I am the God of Beth-el*;[4] for the name of God is said to be in him;[5] and, *In hearing his voice*, it says, *thou shalt hear the things that I speak*.[6] Wherefore Origen says, I think that just as the Lord was found among us men in form as a man, so among angels he was found in form as an angel;[7] and although this saying be false in its intention, yet how far it has regard for the truth I shall say below.[8]

26. These things contribute to our purpose in this respect, that we understand that the *dispositions* of God which are performed by angels are marvelous; nor let any one's feelings be provoked if I call the Holy Spirit an angel, as well as an outward breath; since he calls himself God. Nor is Holy Spirit the natural name for him any more than for a breath of air. Besides, an angel is nothing else than a breath of God.[9] And this very thing is by the Hebrews called a blowing and a breathing. In its original sense, therefore, it is appropriate to God alone, as an affair of one who breathes, and of holiness. But in an instrumental sense it is applied to a breath which he uses as his messenger; and however many discussions about the Holy Spirit there are in the Scriptures, they would all be easy if we understood how those spirits are in God, and what name and power of God is in them, of which below.

They all speak sophistically of this procession.

27. That we may define the Holy Spirit more clearly, let us see how the Spirit also *proceeds* from the Son; for he gives us the Spirit, saying, *The words which thou gavest me, I have given unto*

---

[1] In paragraph 29.
[2] Rev. iv, 5; v, 6.
[3] Ex. iii, 6; Acts vii, 32.
[4] Gen. xxxi, 13.
[5] Ex. xxiii, 21.
[6] Ex. xxiii, 22.
[7] In Genesim, Hom. viii, ad Gen. xxii, 10 ff. (MPG. xii, 208).
[8] In Book IV, paragraph 6.
[9] Ps. civ, 4.

them.¹ For the Spirit is derived from the Word, and if his words abide in us, the Spirit flows from us as rivers of living water.² See also the reasoning of the Master: *He shall take of mine*, saith he, *and shall declare it unto you. All things whatsoever the Father hath are mine: therefore said I, that he shall take of mine.*³ And when it says, *proceeds*, the Greek is ἐκπορεύεται, which some would have mean, *sets out*, rather than *proceeds*; likewise it also means to *go out*;⁴ and as many as are sent by God, as messengers, are all said to go out from his face, and also to proceed and to set out, as I could prove from many other passages of Scripture where the same Greek word is used. Indeed, when a man sets out anywhere, it is expressed by this word. But investigate for yourself, for Scripture interprets itself clearly if you rightly compare passage with passage.

As for the interpretation, they seek it not from other passages of Scripture, but by metaphysics.

28. Nor will other passages of Scripture suggest to you those metaphysical and inner emissions of beings; but setting out in visible character from the Father, sent by CHRIST, it came to the Apostles. And CHRIST sent it, just as if I, drawing something forth from the bowels of my father, imparted it to my brethren. And this is what CHRIST says: Whom I will send unto you from the Father;⁵ and it is sent by God through JESUS CHRIST.⁶ For all things are given us by the Father, yet through JESUS CHRIST. And Peter, proclaiming this very thing, says, *Having received of the Father the promise of the Holy Spirit, he hath poured forth this gift, which ye see.*⁷ And in this the Psalmist agrees with Paul: *When he ascended on high, he* received and *gave gifts* — received them from the Father, and gave them *unto men.*⁸ For in the saying of Peter there is a clear agreement, and CHRIST said that he was from the Father, as much as to intimate that the Spirit would not be a deceiver, but would be from God; as John says, *Prove the spirits, whether they are of God.*⁹ For the words of the Master present a teaching rather than philosophical disputes. CHRIST suggests here nothing metaphysical except what is often

---

¹ John xvii, 8.
² John xv, 7; vii, 38.
³ John xvi, 14, 15.
⁴ *Proficiscitur . . . procedit . . . egredi.*
⁵ John xv, 26.
⁶ Tit. iii, 6.
⁷ Acts ii, 33.
⁸ Eph. iv, 8; Ps. lxviii, 18.
⁹ I. John iv, 1.

said in the Hebrew: I will put my Spirit within you, He sent his Spirit, A Spirit went forth from God.[1] Yet nothing else had gone forth but some outward breath. Of these Hebrew expressions, which led them astray as to the Word, I shall speak in Book VII.[2] For as the Word sets out from God, when he speaks, in order that a thing may be done anywhere, so his Spirit sets out from him anywhither when he intends some result anywhere. In fine, expound it thus: He who sets out from the Father, that is, whom the Father gives. The Master there teaches us to ask the Father for the Spirit, since he is himself the Father of spirits; and unless he himself has given us the Spirit, there is no light at all in us. And CHRIST teaches that the Spirit is from the Father, saying that he gives the good Spirit to them that ask him;[3] for he pours it out plentifully and liberally.[4] Again, if you read with clear sight, all the words of Christ are concerning the Spirit which he was going to send upon the Apostles.[5] It is something altogether silly to infer from these words eternal processions of aeons, and to be mad with this Cabalistic[6] metaphysics. But this matter is settled on other grounds. First, that the *disposition*[7] is a power and gift from God. Second, that the being that comes is itself a messenger, or a ministering spirit sent by CHRIST. Third, that in this messenger is the *hypostasis* itself, or the very image of the Godhead, as I shall show below.[8] Fourth, that all these things aim at the sanctification of our spirits. Yet the one who thus visibly sets out, who shall not speak from himself,[9] who shall take of Christ,[10] is truly a ministering spirit, or else there is no ministering spirit in heaven.

29. And he is also called the Spirit of truth, and the Holy Spirit; and consequently, as we have spoken of an external breath, much more may we speak of a ministering Spirit. It is not to be wondered at if, being separated by God for a certain

---

[1] Ezek. xxxvi, 27; Judith xvi, 14; Ps. civ, 30; Wisdom ix, 17.
[2] Paragraph 12. [3] Luke xi, 13 (Vulg.).
[4] Joel ii, 28; Tit. iii, 6. [5] Acts ii, 1–4.
[6] The Cabala was a mystical system of interpretation of the Scriptures, current in the Middle Ages among both Jews and Christians, and assigning an occult meaning to the letters and numbers of Scripture.
[7] cf. note to paragraph 41, Book I. [8] Book VI, paragraph 4.
[9] John xvi, 13. [10] John xvi, 14.

work, he is called Holy Spirit, or Spirit of God; for they set out from the profounder treasures of God, and in a far more remarkable way God makes them his own by his own acts. CHRIST also often calls the holy ones angels.[1] If, then, what God employs is a spirit, and a sort of holiness is appropriate to it, why shall it not be called the Holy Spirit? And, to make few words of it, every breath, every breathing and impulse of the mind through which God breathes, is called holy, and accordingly the Holy Spirit, or a holy spirit, or the Spirit of God. Nor is there any other briefer explanation of this word; and it is not a single expression, but two: holy, and spirit. And in Greek it is written now the Holy Spirit, now a holy spirit;[2] indeed, in Hebrew it is expressed, Spirit of holiness. This at least is a good point against those who hold to their usage so strictly that they are scandalized if one little word be changed. And I would that they might give up their metaphysical habit of speaking, because they would then consider the heavenly spirits not in accordance with the Nature of a being (for of this Scripture never makes mention), but as to how far the very image of the Godhead shines forth in them, that all things may at length tend to the glory of God. For for this reason they are called the souls of God, and the spirits of God; and the very names of the angels indicate this, since nothing else about them is perceived by us save the power of God, the healing of God, which are God, as it were, and manifest nothing else than the brightness of the *hypostasis* of God, although they are appointed for our service.

[64a]

[Sidenote: Scripture never takes Natures into account.]

30. After this, it is for me very easy to say, another Comforter; and I speak truly of an otherness of the being, for he said of a distinct being without qualification, *He shall take of mine.*[3] And he is said by CHRIST to be another, and something other, unless perchance you take *other* as marking a lack of harmony; for in that case I shall not admit that the comforting Spirit is something other than CHRIST. On the contrary, they are one.

31. In this sense the Holy Spirit testifies as to what I refrained from mentioning above: that when the Spirit descended

---

[1] Matt. xiii, 39, 41, 49; xxvi, 53; Mark xiii, 27; Luke xvi, 22.
[2] *Sanctus spiritus . . . spiritus sanctus.*
[3] John xvi, 14.

upon CHRIST in the Jordan, he bore distinct witness to John, distinctly witnessed that this JESUS is the Son of God,[1] whom you deny to be the Son of God. And to prove this, John appealed to his witness; and these three are one because they agree, and they are one because they are distinguished by marks of one and the same divinity. Behold the singular, *one*, which you were seeking; and in a most singular way are they said to be one, because in the three there is one and the same Godhead. And so I admit one Person of the Father, another Person of the Son, another Person of the Holy Spirit; and I admit Father, Son, and Holy Spirit, three Persons in one Godhead; and this is the true Trinity. But I should prefer not to use a word foreign to the Scriptures, lest perchance in future the philosophers have occasion to go astray. And I have no controversy with the earlier writers, because they employed this word sensibly. But may this blasphemous and philosophical distinction of three *beings* in one God be rooted out from the minds of men.

32. By this means another account is settled, of which many stand in dread, namely, why the term Holy Spirit is more frequently employed in the New Testament than in the Old. For from this it seems to them that the new being is revealed anew, just because, by the addition of a single note, CHRIST said, *the Comforter, even the Spirit*.[2] To the first it is replied that this is not for the reason that in the New Testament God has just arrived; for there is no other God than the God of our fathers, יהוה,[3] and he is the Father of JESUS CHRIST. And the reason of the difference, which you are seeking, is this: that the Jews were not concerned, as we are, with making the Spirit holy. Therefore they neither knew the Holy Spirit, nor had they heard whether there is a Holy Spirit.[4] For with them the question was only about a certain material sanctification, which is effected by outward anointings and touchings, so that a thing that one has touched is called sanctified.[5] But now our ointments and spiritual sacrifices have a greater odor of sweetness than their fatted sacrifices or the whole burnt offerings which God then smelt.

---

[1] Matt. iii, 17.
[2] John xiv, 16, 17, 26; xv, 26.
[3] Jehovah.
[4] Acts xix, 2 (Vulg.).
[5] Ex. xxix, 37; Lev. vi, 18, 27.

ON THE ERRORS OF THE TRINITY

And the latter differ from the former as the spirit from the letter, the truth from the shadow. For we have to do with an inward anointing and sanctification, which is effected in the spirit and by the Spirit; therefore we call the Spirit holy, and we are all holy. And we are baptized in the name of the Holy Spirit for the reason that, being dead to the law [1] and buried in the flesh, we may always be mindful only of the sanctification of the spirit. And although they, when the question is about the Spirit, are content with the outward breathing, yet in the New Testament the consideration about the Holy Spirit is different; because since we are always dealing with an inward sanctification, we consider the Holy Spirit as it is in us, and not as it comes from without. But in the Old Testament the breathing coming from without is called a holy Spirit, or the Spirit of God.[2] And 65b when the spirit is prayed for, they could understand it as an outward spirit. But we, when we pray for that, understand an enlightening of the mind. Hence in these matters the usage and intention of Scripture is to be heeded. And mark these differences; for they always treated of things in an outward fashion. They called upon the Spirit of God, whereas we always call upon the Holy Spirit for the different reason which I have mentioned, that a kind of sanctity was not yet ascribed to the Spirit. Neither the word spirit, nor the word holy, is new. But formerly spirit was regarded otherwise, and there was another kind of holiness, than now. Then the flesh was made holy; but now the spirit is holy. And this is indicated when the words are joined together, and a kind of holiness is ascribed to the Spirit. From this it is evident that it is not a separate being; but every holiness of spirit is referred to man; and, excepting the messenger who when he descends is called the Holy Spirit, I say that nothing else outside of man is called the Holy Spirit. And John well said, *The Spirit was not yet*,[3] though they are unwilling to have the words stand as God uttered them, as though God were in need of their lying. For in the very act of giving it says, Holy Spirit; nor is it said to be before it is given. And now I say that

---

[1] Rom. vii, 4.
[2] Ps. li, 12; Wisdom ix, 17; Gen. i, 2; Ex. xxxi, 3; Num. xxiv, 2; II. Chron. xxiv, 20.   [3] John vii, 39.

there is no longer a Holy Spirit, it is nowhere, because no one believes that JESUS CHRIST is the Son of God; for in the same passage this proof is conclusive.

33. Nor let it vex you that CHRIST, adding the article, said *the* Comforter; for, if I have decided to send one of my messengers to you at a certain time, I shall say to you, The messenger whom I send from my father's house will be a truthful man, or he will do thus and so. Again, if you refer to what was said above, the sense of the words of CHRIST is very clear. For he says, The messenger (he, that is, who I said is to be sent to you), *he shall teach you*.[1] And this sense is so appropriate that it can be understood by a mere grammarian. For after CHRIST had said that they should have another true Comforter in place of him, he added to it, *The Comforter*, that is, the one of whom I spoke, is not any man, but is *the Spirit*, separated by the Father, to be sent to *teach you all things*. Add to this that the Greek article has not so much force as a relative pronoun, so that you may suppose that a being is there indicated. Again, the office of the messenger was there a single one, and the appearance, or person, of the divinity was single. Thus it could be represented by the singular article, and by a special mark, because the like was never seen either in the Prophets or in other men.

34. Finally, if we wish to compare the Spirit with the Word, let us say that as the Word is said to come forth from the womb and the heart, so our spirit should be said to have been given us by God from the inner chambers of his heart. And God is said to give us his Spirit, as if I said, I give you my bowels, which expresses the highest degree of his love toward us.[2] Moreover, as the whole Word is God, so is the whole Spirit; and as he speaks by thinking, so he breathes by speaking, and commands by the authority of his power. And therefore it is said that all things were made by his Word[3] and his Spirit, because he spoke, and ordered them to be made by the power of his Spirit. As he created them by his Word, so he adorned and strengthened them by his Spirit; and just as no plurality of beings is proved by bringing forth things by his Word, but he speaks and they

---

[1] John xiv, 26; xvi, 13 (Vulg.). [2] Rom. v, 5; I. John iii, 1.
[3] John i, 3.

are made; so it is not to be proved by adorning, fortifying, and quickening things by his Spirit. For those things which he speaks by a word he commands by the power of his Spirit; and as by the very fact that he spoke, a thing is at hand, so by the very fact that he commanded by the power of his Spirit, the thing stands completed. For it is the property of the Spirit of God to quicken and strengthen; and as no thing is made without his Word, so there is no thing, nor stone, nor plant, which has any power without the Spirit of God. Again, all that is made by the power of God is said to be made by his breath [1] and inspiration; for there can be no uttering of a word without a breathing of the spirit, just as we can not utter speech without exhaling; and therefore it says, *the breath of his mouth,*[1] and, *the breath of his lips.*[2] From this it is sufficiently shown that the Spirit of God in us is not the created being, as Eunomius held,[3] nor is it the metaphysically distinct being which we imagine. And that you may understand this more in detail, note that although in the time of the Law an angel was said to go in and go out of a man, and to be in the Prophets,[4] yet God himself dwells in us through Emanuel, as it is written: *I will dwell in them.*[5] Through CHRIST we have become heaven. Again, to the Jews angels were in the place of God, so that according to the letter of the law God speaks indifferently of himself and of angels: *Behold, Adam is become as one of us; Let us make;* and, *Our.*[6] Moreover the angel, speaking to them, said, *I am God,*[7] because the invisible God, who is manifested to us through Christ, was manifested to them through angels; or rather, was concealed, was covered by an angel's skin, as by a curtain; and there is now no angel who says to us, I am God. Indeed, all are ministers of CHRIST; nay, under the type of Christ, as I shall prove below,[8] they were called gods. For CHRIST is very God, of whose Godhead the shadow, and not the truth, was in the angels. I say, therefore, that our spirit

This prophecy indicates a new dwelling of God in us.

---

[1] Ps. xxxiii, 6.   [2] Isa. xi, 4.

[3] v. Eunomius, Liber apologeticus; and Basilius Magnus, Adv. Eunomium, III, in Thilo, Bibliotheca Patrorum Graecorum, ii, 78, 124, 596, 598, etc.; cf. MPG. xxix, 654 ff.

[4] Ezek. ii, 2; iii, 24; Zech. i, 9, 13, 14, 19 (Vulg.).

[5] II. Cor. vi, 16.   [6] Gen. iii, 22; i, 26.

[7] Gen. xxxi, 13.   [8] Book IV, paragraph 6.

dwelling in us is God his very self; and that this is the Holy Spirit in us, according to the saying of the prophet, is shown by the Apostle, saying, *The Spirit of God in us*,[1] because God said, *I will dwell in them*.[2] And he who contemns us contemns God, because he put his Spirit in us; and he who lies to the Holy Spirit lies not to men but to God.[3] And herein we bear witness that there is in our spirit a certain powerful and hidden energy, a certain heavenly feeling, and a hidden divine something, for when it bloweth where it will, I hear the voice thereof, but know not whence it cometh, or whither it goeth; and so is every one that is born of the Spirit.[4]

<small>Scripture takes the Holy Spirit as it is perceived, and not metaphysically.</small>

[1] Rom. viii, 9; I. Cor. iii, 16.
[2] II. Cor. vi, 16.
[3] Acts v, 3, 4.
[4] John iii, 8.

BOOK III

Argument

THE pre-existent Word, first uttered by God in creation, was afterwards incarnate in Jesus as the Son of God. Christ's spirit manifested the power of God's Word in creation and in the world, and he deserves our holy service; yet the Father did not suffer in Christ's body. High praise is ascribed to Christ as the wisdom of God. The Word was not the Son, but a disposition of God, who is above all distinctions of time. Belief that Jesus is the Christ, the Son of God, is the essence of Christian faith, and the foundation of the Church.

Synopsis

1. The Word, existing before creation, was begotten when first uttered by God, and was afterwards incarnate in the flesh of Christ. 2. The witness of John the Baptist shows the pre-existence of Christ, begotten as Jesus, the divine Son of God. 3. Jesus' statement that he is from the beginning also shows his pre-existence. 4. Christ's spirit was the eternal power of the Word of God. 5. The various actions of God in the world are the actions of Christ in God. 6. "Spirits in prison" means the minds of men imprisoned in darkness. 7. God works in the spirits of those asleep, as men are now; but not forever. 8. The creative power of the Word of God dwelt in Christ, 9. through whom, as the Word, all things were made. 10. He had the power to rise from the dead, though the Father raised him. 11. Free-will offerings are to be made to Christ as sovereign, even of ourselves in holiness. 12. The teaching that the Father is in the Son does not justify the inference that the Father suffered, or that he became flesh. 13. The titles applied to Christ do not mean that he was an abstract being, but are used to ascribe high praise to him. 14. He is the wisdom of God, 15. and came forth from God. 16. The Word was never the Son, 17. but was a disposition of God at the beginning of the world. 18. Past, present, and future are indifferent to God, who is above distinctions of time. 19. God and the Word existed before the world not by temporal sequence, but only causally. 20. Belief that Jesus is the Christ, the

Son of God, ensures our salvation, and makes us sons of God. 21. *Gospels and Epistles teach that this belief is the test of one's being a Christian.* 22. *Some hold only a blind, or a nominal, or a partial belief; but the complete belief is the foundation of the Church.*

BOOK THE THIRD

1. *The Word became flesh* [1] is John's clear proclamation which must always be premised when we investigate the mysteries of CHRIST; and from this we easily understand the saying, *Before Abraham was born, I am.*[2] For I am the oracle of God which was uttered and manifested before Abraham, was heard and seen by Abraham himself, uttered with a voice visible indeed before Abraham, nay, before Adam. Even from the beginning CHRIST goes forth from the mouth of God, of which going forth from everlasting Micah speaks: *Out of thee shall a leader come forth unto me; his goings forth are from of old, from everlasting.*[3] He that was born in the beginning can be said to have been born before Araham, indeed must be said to have been born before the dawn.[4] And note always the commanding words of the Master, note the actually present way of his being, be not deceived by distinct differences of times in God; for he did not say, Before Abraham was born, I was, or I had been, flesh, as it were; but, I *am.* It is as if he said, My existence began to be before Abraham; because his existence depends essentially upon his Father's utterance, which took place in the beginning. And so John says that he is from the beginning;[5] and he is before all men,[6] because his existence is from the beginning. And in that way he says that he came out from the Father, and was come into the world;[7] because his existence and his going forth from the bosom of the Father has an eternal beginning. Just as in writers on Law one is said to be dead from the day of the infliction of the wound that caused his death, so JESUS the Son of God is said to have been born and begotten from the day of the

---

[1] John i, 14.
[2] John viii, 58 (Pagn.).
[3] Micah v, 2.
[4] Ps. cx, 3 (Vulg.).
[5] I. John ii, 14.
[6] Col. i, 17 (Vulg.).
[7] John xvi, 28.

uttering of the word from which he essentially has every kind of existence; and the son of God became the son of man because, though eternally born of God, he is afterwards born of man in time, although he is only one being. Moreover, what if I admit that the Son of God put on the flesh, or, if you please, was incarnate; for Paul also, speaking of his earthly tabernacle, says that he is unclothed, and clothed upon,[1] because Paul speaks in the power of the Spirit, hence according to the inward man, as if it were some other being that puts the flesh on and off like a garment. Likewise Job says, *Thou hast clothed me with skin and flesh.*[2] Therefore far more clearly, and incomparably more easily, is this proved clear about CHRIST; for it is the Spirit that speaks, who is in CHRIST without measure. Take this as an illustration: if power were given me to beget a son in a woman by the breath of my mouth instead of by the seed of a man, then if I withdrew after the breath was emitted I could say to the woman, I have begotten a son, I leave a son in you who, when the fulness of time comes and he has become a man, will be born

68b of you. And although that is absurd to say, my breath is a son, nay, my word will be a son to me; yet we say that a son was then begotten by reason of the power of seed, not because there was a real begetting of the breath or of the word uttered by God, but the begetting of the flesh took place in the outward uttering of the word. These illustrations will perhaps seem to you crude; but be not amazed. Those that are not very strong must drink milk; moreover, in what follows you shall have solid food.

2. From this is understood what his forerunner the Baptist said: *This is he of whom I said, He who followed with me is become before me; for he was before me; and of his fulness we all received.*[3] And so ὅτι [4] is used to begin the following clause; and the sense can not be, He is become before me *because* he was previous to me; but the sense is, This is he of whom I said, He that cometh after me was already made long before me. And again, as if recapitulating [5] and explaining this, he adds, *For he was before me,*

---

[1] II. Cor. v, 4. [2] Job x, 11. [3] John i, 15, 16.
[4] *Hoti*, that; used in introducing quotations; also, since, because.
[5] *Repilogans*, a baffling word, which has escaped the dictionaries. *Repilogare* = re + *epilogare* (Gr. ἐπίλογος); to recapitulate, summarize, epitomize, repeat.

and, *Of his grace we all received.*¹ Nor does the word ὅτι in John make so crude a conjunction, and his whole gospel is full of this usage; and he does not usually take it in another sense. On the contrary, in the same chapter he several times repeats it, saying *Hoti* he was before me, *Hoti* the law was given through Moses, *Hoti* I am not he, *Hoti* he was before me, *Hoti* I have beheld the Spirit, *Hoti* this is the Son of God.² And John's meaning would be sufficiently explained by saying, Surely he was before me, since indeed, if indeed, he was before me, and I knew him not; although the best reading is also by the expression, *since*. Again, the conjunction does not express the cause of the statement, as he shows below, repeating the statement without the conjunction; and he repeats this again farther down, saying, I bore witness that after me will come a man who was already made long before me; and giving reason for this afterwards he adds, for he was before me, and was not known; and therefore the Spirit bore witness to me that he should be made manifest to Israel.³ In consequence of this witness of John, plain as it is, I have often exhorted you not to deny that JESUS CHRIST is the Son of God. Weigh also this strong evidence, that they may tell you who he is that was already made long ago; for the controversy of the Arians and others about this statement is altogether groundless, and the rest, who speculate about other beings, confound their very selves. I should have liked to ask them all this one thing: whether this begetting of CHRIST which I have mentioned as taking place from the beginning seems to them to be divine, or rather human. If, then, it is truly divine, for what are those seeking who speculate about other begettings among the gods? If JESUS the Nazarene, whom Scripture foretells, was so admirably born through this begetting, he who was born will be called a son. Hence there is no use in speculating about another son. For here you see clearly that this is that Melchizedek whose origin was unknown to men.⁴ And from the manner of his begetting it is known who the Son is. See what the language of Matthew leads to: *Now the birth of CHRIST was on this wise.*⁵

Note these two words, made, and long ago.

¹ John i, 15, 16.   ² John i, 15, 17, 20, 30, 32, 34.
³ John i, 30, 31.   ⁴ Heb. vii, 3.
⁵ Matt. i, 18.

Is he speaking of the birth of a second being, or is he rather disclosing to us the birth of a man, which had been kept secret? Therefore he who was born will be called a son; nor will you read in Scripture of the birth of another being. You see clearly that he was born, and from God alone; and you deny that he is the Son of God.

They have this distinction in readiness, but they do not prove the other part of the birth.

3. Hereby is rendered more clear the difficult passage in which the Master had said that he was, and, *Except ye have believed that I am he, ye shall die*;[1] and the Jews, wishing to understand this being of his, ask, *Who art thou . . . whom makest thou thyself*,[2] who sayest that thou art he? JESUS answered, Τὴν ἀρχήν, that is, I am from the beginning, ὅτι καὶ λαλῶ ὑμῖν;[3] as if he said, I am from the beginning, however I also speak unto you; and the word ὅτι is sometimes employed pleonastically: I am from the beginning, and I speak unto you; or, he there shows an occasion of wondering, as if he said, How can this be; for however I speak unto you, yet I am from the beginning; and this is his way of speaking in order that we may observe more carefully how this is. And so CHRIST speaks to them commandingly, that he might arouse their dull minds. Be astonished, therefore, and wonder, that he who speaks is from the beginning. And this is the most reasonable way of understanding the words of CHRIST, who speaks consistently, always declaring that he is, is before all, is from above, is sent from the Father; and in addition to this, he repeats below, *Before Abraham was born, I am.*[4] And although there is in Latin no word which fully brings out what is meant by the expression ὅτι, yet the sense is, I am surely from the beginning, and I speak unto you; I am from the beginning, however I also speak unto you. And so he himself was wont to say, *I that speak unto thee am he.*[5] So clearly and intelligibly does he bear witness of himself that one is more than blind who does not see; and this is marvelous in our eyes, so that being blinded along with the Pharisees we do not understand him who says that he is that Melchizedek who hath *neither beginning of*

---

[1] John viii, 24. [2] John viii, 25, 53.
[3] *Ten archen hoti kai lalo humin*, from the beginning what I also say to you.
[4] John viii, 58 (Pagn.).
[5] John iv, 26.

days nor end of life;[1] for CHRIST there clearly intimates that he has no beginning of days, nay, that he is from the beginning before all days. If, with the Pharisees, you object to this: *Thou art not yet fifty years old, and hast thou seen Abraham?* [2] you make him a liar; for see who it is that was speaking. It is clear that he was speaking of himself, and not of the second being. See how you admit that Abraham saw the days of CHRIST, apart from the fact that you assume some being hypostatically united in Abraham himself. For if you say that he saw in spirit, you could have said correspondingly that CHRIST was in the Spirit of God earlier than Abraham; for having also a pure spirit he could have said, Before Abraham was born, I am, as though not a man but the spirit itself spoke. Hence much more strongly could this hold true of CHRIST, for CHRIST in the Spirit of God came before all time.

4. This spirit of CHRIST is the eternal power of the Word of God, as it says, *Who through the eternal Spirit offered himself.*[3] In the same manner Peter speaks of the eternal spirit of Christ when he says, *Being made alive in the spirit; in which also he went and preached unto the spirits that were in prison.*[4] Which passage I shall here explain, because it contributes much to the knowledge of CHRIST. Some understand it in one way, others in another; but I should never venture to declare what is in my own opinion the proper meaning, save after comparing other Scriptures, especially since Peter is here obviously referring to something said in Genesis.[5] And Rabbi Moses, the Egyptian,[6] in his *Liber Perplexorum*, agrees with Peter, relating how the generation rebelled in the time of the flood. And in Wisdom it says, *When the nations had exalted themselves.*[7] It is just these that Peter calls disobedient and rebellious; and Peter here shows CHRIST'S spirit as an eternal power, and that CHRIST was formerly a Saviour through water, as he now is through baptism.[8]

---

[1] Heb. vii, 3. [2] John viii, 57.
[3] Heb. ix, 14. [4] I. Pet. iii, 18, 19.
[5] Gen. vii, viii.
[6] Moses Maimonides, in his *Moreh Nebukhim*, or Guide for the Perplexed, a religio-philosophical work published 1190. English translation by M. Friedländer, 1885. The reference here is to I. 29 (Servetus wrongly says 28).
[7] Wisdom x, 5 (Pagn.). [8] I. Pet. iii, 20, 21.

71a For the Master also, from whom Peter received this, in the Gospel compares the days of Noah to himself;[1] and the preaching of the Apostles does not go beyond the limits of the Master's words, for so they are truly called disciples. Yet we shamelessly go beyond both at our own pleasure, nor have we anything that savors of the disciples of CHRIST.

5. Therefore, just as God went out into Egypt, went and passed through the midst of Egypt, slaying the firstborn; so in the time of Noah he passed through the midst of the world, and having thus set out he made his will known to them. Passed through, I say, by his declaration, by doing to them the evils which he had said. What our translator renders, *preached*, is in Greek ἐκήρυξεν,[2] which means, to herald abroad; that is, he published the decree, he made his power known to them as well as to Pharaoh. It tells in favor of this, that in the following epistle of the same Peter, speaking of the same matter, a word of the same meaning is repeated, saying, *Noah a herald of righteousness*;[3] for κήρυκα,[4] which our translator has rendered *herald*, properly means an officer with a flag of truce in time of war. And thus CHRIST declared war upon them. Note also the word *righteousness*, for there was a judgment [5] there. Πορευθείς,[6] that is, having set out when he had come, when he had ordered them to be punished, as he himself is wont to say: I will come, I will pass through, I will descend, I will speak about them, I will do 71b as I said. The sense therefore is that having set out he proclaimed, or pronounced, judgment upon them. And this is what *He condemned the world*[7] means. Likewise, Against the Egyptians, the nation to which they have been in bondage, will I pass judgment, saith the Lord.[8] And in this sense the expression, *to give judgment* [9] is taken. You will note the wonderful interpretation of the spirit of Peter; for all the movements of יהוה,[10] all

---

[1] Matt. xxiv, 37; Luke xvii, 26.   [2] *Ekeruxen*, proclaimed.
[3] II. Pet. ii, 5 (Vulg.).   [4] *Keruka*, herald.
[5] The original reads *indicium*, a palpable misprint for *judicium*, as corrected in the counterfeit reprint.
[6] *Poreutheis*, having set out.
[7] Heb. xi, 7.   [8] Acts vii, 7.
[9] Jer. i, 16; xxxix, 5; II. Kings xxv, 6.
[10] Jehovah.

his actions that you will ever find in the law, as when he says spoke, went, came, passed through, came down, and wrought, were movements of Elohim, were the personal actions of CHRIST in God, because CHRIST was then with God. This will serve for what needs to be said, and below you shall understand all these things more clearly. Already from of old Habakkuk ascribes them to CHRIST, saying, *God will come from the South, . . . he hath given the earth to other nations, he hath ground the eternal mountains in pieces, he hath made the everlasting hills to bow, his ways are everlasting ways*,[1] I say, because already from everlasting he makes his way, comes, and passes through all things; and to the word הליכות[2] well corresponds what Peter says, πορευθείς;[3] for הלכ[4] and πορεύομαι[5] mean the same thing.

6. When Peter said, *to the spirits*, he indicates their thoughts, oppressed by evil spirits. God saw that every thought of his heart was intent upon evil;[6] even as Paul, when the subject was about bringing the thoughts of men into captivity to the obedience of CHRIST,[7] says that the warfare is against evil spirits, who hold captive the minds of the reprobate. And the sense is, To those spirits in prison, that is, who were held in a spiritual prison, or in whose spirits they were in prison; for he spoke in a figure, though not without great emphasis. And when he calls them spirits he is alluding to that which the angels were called. But there was a spiritual prison, and they were made disobedient by wicked spirits; for a wicked spirit, according to Paul, is *the spirit that worketh in the sons of disobedience*.[8] For that is why they are said to have been rebellious and disobedient. Note also that the meaning of the word φυλακή[9] is taken from the words of the Master, and we must always recur to what was said by him, for it is used in Matthew.[10] It is the same word, and the same subject, of which mention is made here and there; and

---

[1] Apparently Servetus's independent translation or paraphrase of Hab. iii, 3, 6.
[2] *Halikoth*, ways.
[3] *Poreutheis*, went; I. Pet. iii, 19.
[4] *Halak*, to go.
[5] *Poreuomai*, to go. [6] Gen. vi, 5 (Vulg.).
[7] II. Cor. x, 5. [8] Eph. ii, 2.
[9] *Phulake*, prison, also watch.
[10] Matt. xxv (Servetus says xxiv), 36, 39, 43, 44.

as Valla¹ here observes, φυλακή ² is the night-watch, when thieves come and men are asleep, and then the unclean spirits hold sway. And so mention is made both of spirits and of prison.³ Those wretched angels, therefore, were asleep in the dark night, and the day seized them suddenly, as a thief. CHRIST, and also Peter, suggests that a flood overwhelms them by night; for this very thing is the prison of our spirits, the hour and the power of darkness. Moreover, he slew the firstborn in Egypt in the silence of the night; and in the same passage φυλακή is taken for a watching in the night.⁴ Note how the discourse of CHRIST is interwoven with what he had said of Noah, and how the words of Peter answer to it.⁵ Hence he upbraids the spirits because they did not watch as CHRIST commanded; and when the spirits are asleep in the watches of the night, the sudden lightning, so to speak, gives them no time to awake. There are also other circumstances which were the cause of Peter's speaking of the spirits, namely, from Genesis' literal way of speaking, which Peter observes; for it says there, He smote every soul, he took away every spirit from their midst.⁶ Also God said in his heart, and being inwardly grieved at heart, seeing that their thoughts were intent upon evil,⁷ he expressed his purpose by his spirit, saying, I will take away their spirits. For strictly speaking, when a man is asleep his spirit is said to be taken away; and especially so when it happens by drowning, in which case the breath is cut off by the entrance of water. And so in the case of the spirits he put his purpose into execution. Just as also in the spirits there was a slumber of the night *phulax*; ⁸ and both of these things Peter finely expressed.

Would that we took as much pains to observe Scripture ways of speaking.

7. From this we may learn that the almighty Ruler of the spirits of all flesh is working in our spirits when we are not thinking, or are sleeping; which is highly suitable to our times, for all

---

¹ Laurentius Valla, Italian humanist and critic, 1405–1457, one of the precursors of modern New Testament exegesis. The reference is to his In Novum Testamentum Annotationes, ad loc.
² *Phulake*, prison, also watch.   ³ Rev. xviii, 2.
⁴ Ex. xii, 42 (cf. R.V. marg.).
⁵ Matt. xxiv, 37, 38; Luke xvii, 26, 27; I. Pet. iii, 20.
⁶ Apparent reference to Gen. vi, 7, 17; vii, 4, 21–23.
⁷ Gen. vi, 5.   ⁸ Watch.

are sleeping in the night watch. Nor do CHRIST and Peter refresh 73a
our memories of this without reason. For what do we see to-day
on the face of the earth but sons of Elohim,[1] sons of the great,
adulterous pastors of the Church, all led astray by idle thoughts;
who eat, and drink, and devote themselves to luxury even as
did they. There is none that seeks after CHRIST; and they say,
We can not err. There seems to be a contradiction in what has
been said. Why did God say, My Spirit in man,[2] if they were
led by evil spirits? To this it must be said that the spirit of man
always has either the Spirit of God or the spirit of a devil resident in it; and over this a life-and-death struggle takes place.
For even if we are driven by a wicked spirit, yet the Spirit of
God always warns us at some time; and when it sees us incorrigible it says, *My Spirit shall not strive in man, for that he is
flesh.*[3] And this reads here in the Hebrew, לא ידון,[4] that is, my
Spirit shall not judge, shall not dispute, in man, and forever.
But the sentence was then once for all, and final; and this is
what Peter's saying ἐκήρυξεν [5] meant, for if you compare all,
they agree admirably.

8. Paul says that God created all things through JESUS
CHRIST his Son;[6] and the meaning of this matter we ought to
look into, for the interpretation of those who would have it un- 73b
derstood that the worlds were made by the second being is altogether perverse, for the whole language of Paul speaks of the
man JESUS CHRIST. It is to be understood, therefore, that when
the Word was made flesh, so great a mystery lies hid in this
matter that the same power of the oracle of God by which the
worlds were made, the same and as great as it then was, is now
in CHRIST, made his very own, so that CHRIST says it is his own,
as when he says, *All things whatsoever the Father hath are mine;*[7]
and the power of the Word became the power of the flesh as
clearly as the Word became flesh. Thus CHRIST can say that
the worlds were made by his power. And it means the same,

---

[1] Gen. vi, 2.   [2] Gen. vi, 3.   [3] Gen. vi, 3.
[4] *Lo jadon*, shall not judge, or contend.
[5] *Ekeruxen*, preached, proclaimed.
[6] Eph. iii, 9; Col. i, 16; I. Cor. viii, 6; Heb. i, 2; ii, 10.
[7] John xvi, 15.

ON THE ERRORS OF THE TRINITY 115

whether I say, Was made through me, or, Was made by my power. And note the *by him*;[1] for it means one thing to say, CHRIST created, and another to say, Were created through CHRIST. And herein is the wisdom of Paul, for he alone mentions this matter. And it is not without significance that Paul so often repeats, *Through his Son, through* CHRIST, *through whom, through him*; that is, through the secret power of his word. For you can say that that was made through you which had once been made through your spirit, if the spirit had preceded the flesh. And observe that such a spirit as this is in you, and some such evil spirit was in Simon Magus,[2] when he said that the worlds had been made by his power; for he had adopted that way of speaking from the discussions of the Apostles, so that the Apostles were no more believed when they said that the worlds were made through CHRIST, than was he when he boasted such things of himself. If then, in imagination, the power of the Word, and the eternal Spirit, were in you as they were in CHRIST, then if you speak by the Spirit you can say that you were there, because the flesh is nothing, and you would remember all those things, and would be observing the creation of things face to face, present to you within yourself; and you would say that the worlds were made through you, that is, by the word of that power which is within you. And this is what the Apostle means in the chapter cited;[3] for just as he spoke of the creation, so he continues about the government and direction, so that those things are said to be made and governed through CHRIST which are made and governed by the word of his power;[4] for God girded him with power and might, even because the Word which was in the beginning was the very power of CHRIST. Thus it says, *With thee is the beginning, in the day of thy power*;[5] and it is not without significance that Paul, among other things, calls CHRIST the power of God.[6]

The cunning of a heretic teaches us.

9. In this same way the Apostle, in the chapter cited from Ephesians, declares that all things were made through CHRIST, exclaiming throughout the whole epistle at the exceeding great-

[1] John i, 3.
[2] Acts viii, 9 ff.
[3] Heb. i.
[4] Heb. i, 3.
[5] Ps. cix, 3 (Vulg.).
[6] I. Cor. i, 24.

ness of the power of God in Christ, and the working of the strength of his might, the surpassing wealth of his grace, the unsearchable riches, the breadth, length and height;[1] and so he indicates that in a mysterious way the worlds were made through CHRIST. The same thought is indicated in the chapter cited from Colossians: so that through CHRIST, that is, through all the fulness that is in him, working unto a mystery, God is said to have created and reconciled all things.[2] That this is the thought, John also indicates to us, being led by the same spirit with Paul, and in agreement with him; for what Paul says was made through CHRIST, John says was made by the Word itself, as if the power which was once that of the Word were to-day CHRIST'S. Just as CHRIST, therefore, felt within himself the majesty of the Father abiding in him (as when he said, *No one knoweth the Father, save the Son*[3]), and just as he perceived in his spirit the reasonings of the Pharisees,[4] so also when he was in the Spirit of God before all times, he uttered his words in the way in which he considered in his spirit that they had from eternity been with his Father; and he perceived that all things created by God were made by the power which is in himself. And so one who observes his spiritual power will admit that all things were created through CHRIST, and through his power. Through CHRIST, therefore, the worlds were made, because I say that all things which my hand has made have been made through me; and the power of the Word uttered from the beginning is that of CHRIST himself, and is his own, and is as appropriate to CHRIST as hand to body. And the demons cast out by the finger of God were said to be cast out by CHRIST; and this is itself the Word of God, and the Spirit of the power of God.[5] Therefore the worlds were made through CHRIST, because they were made by his finger.

10. Now that we realize the power of God in CHRIST, by which we say that the worlds were made through him, we shall verify what he said: that he has power to lay down his life, and to take it again;[6] for since divinity is joined with man, all the

---

[1] Eph. i, 19; iii, 8, 18.   [2] Col. i, 16, 20.
[3] Matt. xi, 27; Luke x, 22.   [4] Mark ii, 8.
[5] Matt. viii, 28 ff.; xii, 22 ff.; Luke xi, 20.   [6] John v, 26.

Father's authority is in me and is mine. Thus I have authority to do all things, and the power of divinity which will arouse me from the tomb is my own; thus I have power and authority to lay down my life and to take it again. *The Father gave to the Son to have life in himself*,[1] he has authority over life and death. But after I have died I do not raise myself up, but the Father raiseth me up. For you ought to notice that in Scripture it reads, not once or twice, but often and yet more often, that the Father raised him up.[2] Hence the statement, He raised himself up, is sophistical, and foreign to the Holy Scriptures. I keep within the limits of Scripture, and say that he had the power; but nevertheless after he died the Father raised him up.

11. Following the Vulgate translation from the Greek I said, *With thee is the beginning*,[3] lest any one say that I misrepresent, if I do not satisfy him to the very letter. But I suppose they derive *principium*[4] from his *principatus*[4] over the people; for ἀρχή[5] is here taken for rule over the people, as we may show from the etymology of the Hebrew. In Exodus it is written that the rulers and the people offered gifts for building and adorning the sanctuary.[6] It says the like in the passage under discussion; and as a matter of history David there speaks of a free-will offering of the people made in the time of Solomon to adorn the holy edifice.[7] And under this figure of history David foretells a free-will offering to be made to CHRIST, and with a greater glory of holiness. In the Hebrew it runs thus: עמך נדבת ביום חילך;[8] that is, Thy people are making free-will offerings in the day of thy warfare. He said *free-will* to distinguish it from נדר.[9] Of this free-will offering it speaks with the same word נדבה.[10] Nor

(margin: A misprint can not be interpreted save by conjecture.)

---

[1] John v, 26.
[2] Acts ii, 24, 32; I. Cor. xv, 15; II. Cor. iv, 14, etc.
[3] Ps. cix, 3 (Vulg.); cf. end of paragraph 8.
[4] Beginning (also precedence) . . . sovereignty.
[5] *Arche*, dominion.
[6] Ex. xxv, 1–9; xxxv, 20–29; xxxvi, 3–7.
[7] I. Chron. xxix, 6–9.
[8] '*Ammeka nedaboth beyom cheleka*, Ps. cx, 3.
[9] *Neder*, a vow; Lev. xxii, 18, 21, 23; Deut. xii, 6.
[10] *Nedabah*, a free-will offering; Ps. liv, 6; Ez. i, 4. Similarly Ezek. xliv, 30; xlv, 1, etc.; xlviii, 8, etc.; and this is also spoken of in Isa. lxvi (Servetus says lxiv), 20; Ps. lxxii, 10.

is it any objection that we do not see gold from Arabia given to CHRIST; for the Prophets are wont to prophesy in terms of law or of history. Literal truth belongs to history; the Spirit, the offering, and spiritual sacrifices look toward CHRIST. It is enough that Solomon was given tribute and was offered of the gold of Arabia and Tarshish.¹ Again, that the prophet is speaking of this offering is proved by what he said, *in the splendors of holiness*;² which saying is explained in another place,³ where the discussion is also about this offering and this splendor, or the glory of holiness; for the holy place, beautiful and glorious, they call the *beauty of holiness*. *Bow down to the Lord in the glory of holiness*, that is, in the holy temple.⁴ And this is expressed in the plural, *beauties*, to intensify the meaning, because the splendor of the glory is manifold. Hence the very same thing is said here as in Psalm lxviii.: *In thy temple at Jerusalem kings shall bring presents unto thee.*⁵ And just as we care not for the earthly Jerusalem, so we inquire to no purpose about the gold of Arabia; for CHRIST requires greater things, since in this discussion he is teaching us about the temple of his body; and speaking in this case of the Queen of Sheba he said, *Behold a greater than Solomon.*⁶ Here CHRIST is not seeking what things are ours, but us ourselves.

12. That the Father is in the man (as I positively maintain, being instructed from the words of the Master) some deny, as though this appeared to be patripassian.⁷ But I know not from what this most idle fancy follows. If the sophistical *communicatio idiomatum* were effaced from the minds of men, this difficulty would easily vanish; for when I say Son, I refer to the flesh, and I do not say that he who was in the Son suffered, but that the Son suffered. Just as it is an affair of the flesh to be born, so it is an affair of the flesh to suffer, to be scourged, to be crucified, to die, and to rise again; nor do these things in any wise

---

[1] I. Kings iv, 21; x, 11, 22; II. Chron. ix, 10, 21.
[2] Ps. cx, 3 (Vulg.).
[3] Ps. xcvi, 9 (Pagn.), cf. R.V., marg.; I. Chron. xvi, 29.
[4] Ps. xxix, 2 (Pagn.).   [5] Ps. lxviii, 29 (Pagn.).
[6] Matt. xii, 42; Luke xi, 31.
[7] A sect of heretics in the early Church who held that the Father suffered, as well as the Son.

pertain to the spirit. Moreover, it is not the soul that dies, but the flesh. Who would be so wicked as to admit that the angel existing in me is dead when I die; and who, unless bewitched, dare say that the second Nature of God is dead? How ridiculous the death of one who feels the torments of death no more than that stone! I call them Deipassians, because they admit that the Nature of God is dead, or that the being which they say is the Nature of God is dead. But I shall never admit that anything dies which does not suffer the pains of death. And the Sabellians were called Patripassians because, not understanding the dispensation [1] of the Word, they admitted that another Son, who they said was also the Father, was crucified, dead, and buried, saying that the Father became flesh. But they were wretchedly mistaken, because they were speaking of the Word in a metaphysical way, inquiring as to its Nature, which is a misuse, as I shall show in the following book.[2] And the cause of all their error was that they were philosophers, and made one other a Son, besides CHRIST; and identifying him in all respects with the Father they fell into this confusion. And, as Athanasius relates, they attributed to this imaginary Son every property and name of the Father. Thus they argued: The Word became flesh, and the Father is the Word, therefore the Father became flesh. But this paralogism [3] is plainly sophistical, and a fallacy of the accident, since for the Word to become flesh means nothing else than an act of the divine *disposition*. Nor can anything be inferred from this any more than it can be inferred from some change of accidents that you prove to be a stone. Nay, that the Father became flesh is far more absurd. And when you have seen the following Books, you will judge that these things are not worthy of mention. Again, to argue, The Word is the Father, is as absurd as to say, Flowing is drinking. Again, you may infer, The Word became flesh, and the Essence, the supreme being, is the Word; hence the Essence became flesh; and thus you will be an Essentiaepassian. Yet what I have said, that the Father is in CHRIST, the Master himself

---

[1] *Oeconomia.*
[2] v. Book IV, paragraph 12.
[3] In Logic, an unconscious fallacy.

teaches me, saying once and again, *The Father is in me, . . . the Father abiding in me.*[1] And, *God was in* CHRIST *reconciling the world.*[2] And, *He that created me rested in my tabernacle.*[3] Now what but the flesh itself is the tabernacle which was created?

13. It may be asked, Why is CHRIST called the wisdom of God, the power of God, and the effulgence of his glory?[4] This question about abstract nouns will perhaps cause difficulty to Scotists,[5] but it is none to Hebrews. With them there are numberless nouns ending in *-el*,[6] and *-iah*,[7] which have this meaning, although we translate them by abstract nouns. It is also a Hebraism that whenever any exceptional quality or *disposition* of God is appropriate to anything, it is itself called by the name of that *disposition*: for instance, a strong thing, the strength of God; a wise thing, the wisdom of God; the healing of God, the health of God; so also, a great mountain, the mount of God; and lofty cedars, cedars of God; a beautiful and holy thing, as I have said, is called the beauty of holiness, and the splendor of holiness, and the glory of holiness. We often call some other man the distinguished ornament and honor of his country; indeed, these things are appropriate to CHRIST *par excellence*. Is not the one whom he called *the effulgence of his glory* the same as he whom God appointed heir?[8] Who can endure equivocation in so plain a matter? I ought therefore rather to introduce these passages against you, to prove that these are the accidents[9] of a man; for it is absurd to exalt the nature of God by these titles. Moreover, what if I say that CHRIST is the justice of God? Shall you be able to make any speculation out of this? See how they said of Simon Magus, *This man is the power of God which is called great*:[10] from which words we learn the usage of the language, so that we are not confused by this plain way of speaking, by saying that CHRIST is the power of God, he is our peace, our justice, and our sanctification. Now here are abstract

---

[1] John xiv, 10, 11. [2] II. Cor. v, 19.
[3] Ecclus. xxiv, 8 (Vulg., 12).
[4] Eph. iii, 10; I. Cor. i, 24; Heb. i, 3.
[5] Scholastic philosophers, followers of Duns Scotus.
[6] God.   [7] Lord.   [8] Heb. i, 2, 3.
[9] In the logical sense of the term.
[10] Acts viii, 10.

nouns. He is the soul of the world; nay, more than the soul, for through him we live not only a temporal life, but an eternal one. He has given us a temporal life in the Word, and has won an eternal one in the flesh. I would say more than, *the effulgence of his glory*; for Paul said that the Lord of glory was crucified.[1] He is the bright and morning star;[2] but they have conceived so great an error concerning the human nature that they can not think rightly of CHRIST. They are ashamed to call him, *the effulgence of his glory*, though he himself said, *I am the light of the world*.[3] From what is to be said, you will see that far greater things are appropriate to him; for he is the light of God, the light of the Gentiles;[4] the brightness of his countenance gives light to all the heaven, and will give light in the world to come.[5] That he is the power of God, by which all things were created,[6] has been sufficiently said above. Nevertheless, in the thought of the Apostle, this saying tends to this: that the preaching of CHRIST crucified, although to some it is foolishness, is yet to others the power of God;[7] for by his marvelous power he subjected the world to his dominion, and will subject it, and without clash of arms he leads the minds of men captive.

14. Concerning the wisdom of God, in which are hidden all
78b the treasures of wisdom and knowledge,[8] you shall in what follows come to know the wisdom which passeth knowledge, hidden in a mystery, and manifested by the manifested Word. In this place alone learn wisdom, although with you its words be of little weight. In CHRIST is all the wisdom of the Father; in his mouth, the new law and the interpretation of the old law, the Word of God, which gives knowledge of the Father. Do you deem it absurd when the Master says that he repeats to us the words which he had heard from the Father? In the chapter just cited, therefore, the thought of Paul tends to this: he says of CHRIST, Who was made unto us wisdom from God, and righteousness and sanctification;[9] was made wisdom from God, while

---

[1] I. Cor. ii, 8.
[2] Rev. xxii, 16.
[3] John viii, 12; ix, 5; xii, 46.
[4] Isa. xlii, 6.
[5] Rev. xxii, 5.
[6] Col. i, 16.
[7] I. Cor. i, 23, 24.
[8] Col. ii, 3.
[9] cf. I. Cor. i, 18–25.

he manifests to us the wisdom of God, for the word of the cross is the wisdom and power of God, all of which Paul introduces in opposition to the wisdom of this world, which is foolishness in the sight of God. And he speaks expressly against Aristotle concerning the wisdom of the Greeks; and the wonder is that we seek wisdom from Aristotle rather than from God, and pay the more diligent attention that we may excuse his words. If he was in darkness, how can he give us light? Our Master gives a teaching which can not escape notice: namely, that the blind can not lead the blind.[1] If the book came down from heaven, think you that anything superfluous or not pertaining to learning can be contained in it? In the Bible I find all philosophy and wisdom. Do you not clearly see how Paul here says that the wisdom of the Greeks is false and worldly? Let it not mislead you that the sons of this world are wiser than the sons of the light.[2] Pray read the Bible a thousand times, for if you have no relish in reading it, it is for the reason that you have lost CHRIST, the key of knowledge, which you shall easily get again if you knock without ceasing.

15. Furthermore, it is asked how CHRIST is said to have come forth from the Father. As to this, see how Isaac came forth from the bowels of Abraham;[3] how the law, which is the shadow of the body of CHRIST[4] came forth from God speaking from heaven; how the Gospel springs out of the spirits of the law, how the spark of fire comes forth from the stone, how the manna was given from heaven, how Moses made water come out of the rock, for that is properly the coming forth of JESUS CHRIST,[5] who is the stone which came forth from the mountain, cut out without hands.[6] Again, from the fact that, *Thou knowest all things, . . . we believe that thou camest forth from the Father;*[7] and from the miracles which he did, he infers, *They knew of a truth that I came forth from thee.*[8] But how was the metaphysical coming forth known from his miracles, when it can not even be properly called a coming forth? Again, he himself declares that

---

[1] Matt. xv, 14; Luke vi, 39.
[2] Luke xvi, 8.
[3] Gen. xv, 4.
[4] Heb. x, 1.
[5] I. Cor. x, 4.
[6] Dan. ii, 45.
[7] John xvi, 30.
[8] John xvii, 8.

THE ERRORS OF THE TRINITY

he came forth, because the Father sent him,[1] and this he declares again, saying, For *I am not come of myself, but he sent me.*[2] It also says, *There came forth a decree from Caesar Augustus*;[3] and, *There came forth a wind from the Lord*,[4] and messengers come forth from him.[5] And if you desire to be more intimately acquainted with this coming forth, it will appear in what follows, if you observe that from the beginning CHRIST was personally in God, but now is really among men; and that is preeminently his coming forth from God.

16. Another question: whether we admit that the Word was ever the Son.[6] This question will be fully cleared up in the last Book; but for now I say this, that in the Prophets the Son of God was always proclaimed as one that was to come; and if you wish here to represent something according to your own view, first hear the Prophets. *Unto you . . . shall the sun of righteousness arise.*[7] And, *The earth shall open, and bring forth a Savior.*[8] And, *There shall come forth a man out of the stock of Jesse.*[9] And, *Its leader shall arise from it, and a Prince shall proceed from the midst of it.*[10] And, *there shall arise a star out of Jacob.*[11] Split hairs as you please, for that which *shall arise* will be a son. And, *Behold, a virgin shall conceive, and bear a son.*[12] And, *I will be to him a father, and he shall be to me a son.*[13] And the angel says, *He shall be called the Son of the Most High.*[14] Again, do you think that John, speaking in a human sense, said Word rather than Son? And you can not produce one iota in which Scripture called this Word the Son. Again, John says of this Word, both in his Gospel and in his Epistle, that it was in the past; but it never says of it, *It is*, which difference and way of speaking you do not notice. But later on I shall make this beyond doubt to you if you attentively note the scripture ways of speaking; but

---

[1] John vi, 39, 49, 57; vii, 16, 33, etc.
[2] John vii, 28.
[3] Luke ii, 1.
[4] Num. xi, 31.
[5] Ezek. xxx, 9.
[6] Book VII, paragraph 1.
[7] Mal. iv, 2.
[8] Isa. xlv, 8 (Vulg.)
[9] Isa. xi, 1. Servetus here reads *vir*, man, instead of the correct *virga*, shoot.
[10] Jer. xxx, 21 (Vulg.).
[11] Num. xxiv, 17.
[12] Isa. vii, 14.
[13] I. Chron. xvii, 13; II. Sam. vii, 14.
[14] Luke i, 32.

meanwhile I shall here inquire into the eternity and beginning of the Word.

17. From what has been said above in the second Book, it is well enough known that the going-forth of the Word is from the beginning of the world; for before that (if one may say, before that), one could not speak of a *logos*, which is a kind of speaking; and it is against the nature of the term to say that it meant an inner knowledge as to what is within the mind; for that this is a mistaken invention, I shall show below. And had there been another world, perhaps there had been no mention of either speech or spirit; but God might have employed new arguments,[1] for this *disposition* of the Word is a dispensation [2] of the world, and is like a mustard seed in proportion to the mouth of an elephant. You ought to bring the world back to its proper meaning as an utterance of the mouth of God. They themselves say that the three beings ought to have remained even in spite of God; for they say that this is by the requirement of their nature. But Tertullian [3] expressly contradicts them, saying that God, of his mere good pleasure, employed as many *dispositions* as he wished — that is, for the government of the world. And this the founding of CHRIST's kingdom anticipates, as I shall presently say. And had God created other worlds, he might, in place of our speech, spirit, and reason, have made new creations, with other powers, quite different from ours, and have employed *dispositions* according to what they required for themselves; and then the philosophers of that world would have said that those *dispositions* were distinct beings. And so any world would worship new beings as God in its new Trinity; and some would have a Trinity, others a Quaternity, if God ever employed four *dispositions*; and in that way, according to the number of thy worlds would thy Gods be multiplied, O Judah.[4]

18. Some here invent imaginary questions about the eternity of the aeons, and do not pay attention to the sense in which

80!

---

[1] *Disputationibus;* but this would seem to be a slip for *dispensationibus*, as in the next clause. The thought would then run: The *disposition* of the Word is intended for this world; but for other worlds God might have made some other *dispositions*.   [2] *Oeconomia*.

[3] Adv. Praxean, iv, (MPL. ii, 159; ANF. iii, 599 f.; ANCL. xv, 339 ff.).

[4] cf. Jer. ii, 28.

Scripture speaks of eternity; which comes of their ignorance of the Hebrew tongue. They ask whether God was alone and idle before he created the world; and they say, No; but he was walking about with the three beings. Thus they speak of *before* as though in God there were found a before and an after. Moreover, they argue that there was in God a change, according to the time; because before this being was, he wished it as future, and afterwards he did not wish it as future; and the object in this proposition being thus fixed, as they say, this being is future, they admit positively that God first had to wish with regard to that being, and afterwards had to be unwilling with regard to the same being in the same sense. But to all this I reply

81a that in God predestination is not distinguished from that which is; nor are wished, wishes, future, past, found in God; but he wishes this being to be made thus and so, and such to be its limit. Nor do I therefore say that there is no foreknowledge in God; for Scripture speaks to men, and to us who are subject to time it really means something, nor is it possible for the depth of the wisdom of God to be made clear to us otherwise; lest perchance one think God ignorant of future events, since after all nothing is future to him. I do not on that account detract anything from God, for that which I say with regard to God is more than foreknowledge, nay, is the supreme presence [1] of all things. And note this, for some, judging of this foreknowledge of God in terms of time,[2] make God bound by necessity with regard to all things in future; for they say that all things come to pass of necessity (are necessary even in the sight of God), so that after all the will of God concerning future events is not free,[3] and since all things that will be are indicated, God can neither prevent nor change any of them, which is a most horrible thing to say; and they are built on a false foundation. Their roots being set, that is, in the past knowledge of God (though nevertheless nothing is past to him, his knowledge has neither time nor num-

Of the will of God as free and not free, according to the Lutherans.

---

[1] The text actually reads *praesentia*; but this may perhaps be a misprint for *praescientia* (foreknowledge), which occurs just before and just after; although in the counterfeit reprint the latter occurrence also reads *praesentia*.

[2] *Temporaliter.*

[3] *Servum arbitrium.*

ber), they say that they consider that thing follows thing even to God, and they do not consider that God is above time, and that the *dispositions* of God are above their consideration.

19. I say therefore that neither God nor his Word existed before the world by any interval of time, nor does Scripture speak of an eternity of the Word in the way that you imagine; for all eternity is, in Hebrew, עולם,[1] which means nothing else than world, and the days of the age; and, from the beginning, from everlasting, from the days of old, from everlasting days, are expressions taken in Scripture for the same thing, as is also shown by the adding of the word *days*, for that is eternal which is not limited to a certain number of days; nor can it be understood how with its eternities of aeons a being is said to have begun to be, and how the Son is said to be begotten and brought forth from everlasting; for these are figments of the imagination, which go beyond the limits of Scripture. For when John said, *He was made before me*,[2] he is referring to the beginning of the world, just as when he said, *In the beginning was the Word.*[3] Again, CHRIST's kingdom is called eternal a thousand times, yet at the end he will deliver it up to God the Father;[4] not that anything will be detracted from CHRIST's glory, indeed it will be his supreme glory to have ruled all things well even to the end, and to have made them subject to the Father as he intended. And this will be to deliver up the kingdom to God the Father, just as the general of the whole army offers the Emperor the palm of victory. Again, inasmuch as then all manner of ruling will cease, all authority and power will be abolished, all ministry of the Holy Spirit will cease, we shall need no advocate nor reconciler, but God will be all in all. And thus the dispensation[5] of the Trinity will then cease. Tertullian also says[6] that the Trinity will cease, which note, just as even now the Trinity is otherwise than it once was, as I shall show in what follows. God and his Word therefore were before the world in another sense than by priority in time, namely, just as cause is

---

[1] *'Olam*, age, world.
[2] John i, 15 (Vulg.).
[3] John i, 1.
[4] I. Cor. xv, 24; Acts iii, 21.
[5] *Oeconomia.*
[6] Adv. Praxean, iv. (MPL. ii, 159; ANF. iii, 600; ANCL. xv, 341 ff.).

before effect, and this is a natural, true priority, and one more appropriate to God than priority in time, since with him there is no time. Again, as Tertullian says,[1] the manifestation of speech, which led to the begetting of the Son, was from the beginning made before the beginning; and in the very beginning, because the first beginning was the utterance of the Word, *God said, Let there be*;[2] and upon this follows the creation of the world, and it was done; nor could speech be expressed before, because speech is not expressed save when it is manifested by utterance.

20. Finally, I would exhort you here to tremble when you deny JESUS CHRIST; and consider with what power, what emphasis of words, John said, *Whosoever shall confess that Jesus is the Son of God, abideth in him, and he in him*;[3] and, *Whosoever shall believe that JESUS is the CHRIST is begotten of God*.[4] And, *Who is he that overcometh the world, but he that believeth that JESUS is the Son of God?*[5] And, believing that JESUS CHRIST is the Son of God, ye shall have eternal life in his name.[6] What shall I say more? All the words of CHRIST tend to this end: that they might all believe that he is the Son of God, might trust in his salvation. And this is to me the chief foundation, for CHRIST is to me the sole Master, CHRIST first preached the Gospel, and in his words I see the whole teaching of the Apostles shining forth. All the preaching of the Apostles in the Acts aims at this very point: that they might persuade men that this JESUS visibly shown to them is the CHRIST, the Son of God, the Saviour. For us that believe this, CHRIST prays the Father. *For them*, he says, *that are to believe in me through the word* of the Apostles.[7] All Paul's teachings about justification[8] have regard to this faith in CHRIST. The Lutherans, departing from this foundation of faith, have never been able to understand what justification is. Paul says that his Apostleship was appointed *unto this obedience of faith* in CHRIST.[9] For verily it is obedience, and in the highest

To this end was the Holy Spirit given, that he might teach them the meaning of the words of Christ. John xiv, 26.

---

[1] Adv. Praxean, v. (MPL. ii, 160; ANF. iii, 600; ANCL. xv, 339 ff.).
[2] Gen. i, 3. [3] I. John iv, 15.
[4] I. John v, 1. [5] I. John v, 5.
[6] John xx, 31. [7] John xvii, 20.
[8] *Omnes Pauli justificationes.* [9] Rom. i, 5; xvi, 26.

degree acceptable to God, when we thus bring our thoughts into captivity to the obedience of CHRIST; [1] that so we may persuade ourselves, may believe, and trust. Indeed, God so loved his own Son that this sole command concerning faith in Christ was substituted in place of the whole law; and there is far greater profit in the keeping of it. Again, from the fact that we believe that he is the Son of God, we too are made sons of God.[2] Again, from this faith in CHRIST comes the giving of the Holy Spirit: He that hath believed in me, out of his belly shall flow living waters; for this, John explains, he spake of the Holy Spirit, which they that believed on him were to receive.[3] The same thing is shown in Ephesians i, 5; Galatians iii, 26; Acts xi, 17; xix, 6, which passages see, and say what it means where it says, *after we believed,* and, *after you believed.* Believe therefore that JESUS CHRIST is the Son of God, and immediately you shall feel the Holy Spirit given to you, which will make you understand all things.[4]

21. I would now know whether you are a Christian. Tell me, What is the law of Christians? What do you understand by *a new testament,* or covenant?[5] What is the *covenant of peace?*[6] What do you understand by the Gospel of CHRIST? What does it mean where CHRIST said, *Believe in the Gospel?*[7] What is the Gospel committed to the Apostles,[8] that they might preach it? Nor do you satisfy me when you show that this book was composed by four Evangelists; for this is nothing else than the relation of a story, aiming at this end alone, that we may believe that CHRIST is the Son of God. And for this there is a clear text: *These are written that ye may believe that JESUS is the CHRIST, the Son of God.*[9] The Epistles of Paul likewise are nothing but documents for building upon this foundation of CHRIST; for he had already preached face to face to those to whom he was writing, that JESUS is the CHRIST, and the Son of God. Again, before the Apostles wrote, the Gospel had already been preached by

---

[1] II. Cor. x, 5.
[2] John i, 12; Gal. iii, 26.
[3] John vii, 38, 39.
[4] John xvi, 13.
[5] Jer. xxxi, 31.
[6] Ezek. xxxvii, 26.
[7] Mark i, 15.
[8] Gal. ii, 7; I. Thes. ii, 4; Tit. i, 3.
[9] John xx, 31.

CHRIST, when he proclaimed the good tidings, and the kingdom of God, to those that believed that he was the Son of God. The Church was already founded on this point. He died on this point, because he said that he was the Son of God. On this point a voice from heaven once and again bears witness. The law of faith was already given by him, and the covenant confirmed by his blood, as once before.[1] Compare the one covenant with the other, and you shall find yourself without a covenant. For if you know not that the religion of Christians is to believe that this JESUS is the CHRIST and the Son of God, the Saviour, I say to you that you are no Christian, you have no covenant with CHRIST, and no peace. This is the covenant of our salvation, and the Spirit is given for a sign, and as a pledge of this covenant. Of this it was said, *He that disbelieveth shall be condemned.*[2] This is *the Word of the Gospel, . . . cleansing their hearts.*[3] This is what was committed to the Apostles to preach. *He charged us*, says Peter, *to preach, and to testify that this is he.*[4] And to those that believe these things good tidings are proclaimed, and this is the Gospel of the kingdom. From that time the kingdom of God alone is preached to us; and he that does not believe that he is the Son of God, knows not what the Gospel is, nor does he understand what the kingdom of God is like, which we that believe have already obtained, because it is within us,[5] although the world knows not the fruit of this kingdom.

22. Note also the order of the Apostolic preaching in their Acts; for first they visibly show JESUS the man from Nazareth; and our faith does not rest upon him. But afterwards they urge us to believe that this JESUS is the CHRIST, and is the Son of God. Yet we turn the whole order around; we are content if we say that we believe on JESUS CHRIST, not who he is. Nor do we take the trouble to inquire, with the blind man who had received his sight,[6] who the Son of God is; yet we believe on the Son of God. Nor is it any wonder if it was unto Gentile philosophers foolishness[7] to preach that JESUS is the Son of God,

---

[1] Ex. xxiv, 8.
[2] Mark xvi, 16.
[3] Acts xv, 7, 9.
[4] Acts x, 42.
[5] Luke xvii, 21.
[6] John ix, 36.
[7] I. Cor. i, 23.

since even to-day they think this to be most foolish; indeed, they will neither hear nor acknowledge that he is the Son of God, and they cry out with Caiaphas, *He hath spoken blasphemy*, because he said, I am the Son of God.[1] For very evidently, if no consideration is herein paid to the Word, he proclaimed full circle that he was the Son of God; as you will most clearly discern from the very first preaching of Paul.[2] Some only admit in words that he is called the Son of God, since they add that he is called Son in a dependent sense, and conjointly with another invisible Son; and all this is one aggregate, and one Son. Others confess that JESUS CHRIST is the name of his human nature, yet they refuse the man the relation of a son. But what else is this than to deny that CHRIST is the Son of God; for they say that there is one Nature of the Son, there is another Nature of JESUS CHRIST, and the Son of God united himself with CHRIST, as Valentinus[3] said. I therefore simply and candidly admit and believe that this JESUS is the CHRIST, and is the Son of God; and he that does not thus believe hath been judged already.[4] Against this rock, said CHRIST most truly, the gates of hell shall not prevail;[5] nevertheless, we are in marvelous ways finding out that they have prevailed over us, and we heed not that the rock is gone. From this *rock* [6] he is called *Peter*,[6] because he was ahead of the rest in his firm faith in CHRIST. On account of this faith CHRIST made supplication for Peter, that his faith might not fail,[7] by which, that is to say, he had confessed that he was the Son of God. Ponder the four Gospels, because you will not find one letter which does not speak of this faith.

84b

---

[1] Matt. xxvi, 63–65.   [2] Acts ix, 20.
[3] A Gnostic of the second century. cf. Tertullian, Adv. Valentin. xxvii (MPL ii, 581 f.; ANF iii, 516; ANCL xv, 152).
[4] John iii, 18.   [5] Matt. xvi, 18.
[6] *Petra, Petrus*.   [7] Luke xxii, 32.

BOOK IV

Argument

GOD *has manifested himself in three different* dispositions. *Of these, the Holy Spirit is his activity in the spirit of man, and is the minister of the Word. God is seen in the Person of Christ, represented in Scripture under the imagery of angels; but the real image of God is Christ. The term Nature is appropriate only to God; the Word no longer exists; Person means a representation of another being; Christ, incarnated, is the image of the Substance, but not of the Nature, of God.*

Synopsis

1. God has manifested himself in three different Persons, or dispositions. 2. The Holy Spirit is God's activity in the spirit of man, acting upon his heart and mind. 3. The Holy Spirit is to be distinguished from the Word, as its minister. 4. The invisible God is seen through the person of Christ, as is shown in many passages of Scripture which speak of God's face, etc. 5. Christ is repeatedly represented in scripture imagery by angels and cherubim, who herald his glory. In his face God's glory is seen, and in him God fully dwells. 6. The real image of God is Christ, who was one in Person with the Father, but was represented in angels. 7. The term Nature should be applied only to God. 8. The Word ceased to exist when it became flesh in Christ. 9. Person means not an aggregate of two beings, but a representative of another being. 10. Christ, who had pre-existed in God, came down to earth and took flesh. 11. He is the very image of the Substance, or Essence, of God, 12. which has no reference to the divine Nature.

BOOK THE FOURTH

85a 1. God, in assuming a person in time past,[1] showed us that the Trinity was to be manifold. The Scripture describes his acts now under the appearance of a breath, now under the Person of the Word. The Persons of the Deity also appeared after-

---

[1] *Seipsum olim personando.*

wards in various ways, as under the form of a man, and under the form of a spirit. And God, when he began to employ in himself those *dispositions* which he was afterwards to manifest to us in various ways, *by his Word created the heavens, and all the powers of them by the breath of his mouth*.[1] Yet they all then existed only by a *disposition*, but now in very fact; and the appearance of the Persons which then in some secret way were *dispositions* with God, has now really taken place in diverse beings, and thus a real distinction of Persons has been made; one Person, that is, with the aspect of Deity, appearing in the Son, another in the Holy Spirit. And the absolute and distinct beings in which the Persons have appeared are, God the Father, a man the Son, and an angel the Holy Spirit. And just as the JESUS of Nazareth who preached in Judaea is the CHRIST, the Son of God, so the flame of fire which appeared [2] was an angel and a sanctifying Spirit. And just as when I speak of the man CHRIST JESUS, I do not separate from him the divinity of the Father; so when I speak of a messenger or a ministering spirit, I do not separate 85b from it the character of divinity, that there may be in the Persons one divinity of the Father. For the difference between the Persons is to be judged in their ways of appearing, not just in a metaphysical plurality of beings of one Nature; in which matter all the philosophers have gone astray; for Scripture never pays attention to Natures, but to appearances and *dispositions*.

2. With regard to the Holy Spirit, I speak of an appearance in bodily form, in consequence of the Spirit's descending; but I speak of a *disposition* in us, and the former is limited to the latter. Hence I always say that the Holy Spirit is the activity of God in the spirit of man; and that outside of man it is not properly called the Holy Spirit. Here it should be noted that when it says, *The Lord is spirit*,[3] many suppose that it means nothing else than to say that the nature of God is incorporeal. But Scripture cares for nothing less than for these philosophies. For according to this, when it says, God is a fire,[4] you would infer, following the view of the Chaldaeans, that the nature of

<small>Outside of man the Holy Spirit is nothing.</small>

---

[1] Ps. xxxiii, 6 (Vulg.).   [2] Acts ii, 3.
[3] II. Cor. iii, 17.
[4] Heb. xii, 29.

God is fiery. When therefore it says, *God is a Spirit*,[1] a spiritual *disposition* of God is denoted; for from the fact that God is a Spirit it is inferred that he is to be worshiped in spirit. And from the fact that the Lord is a spirit, Paul infers that *where the Spirit of the Lord is, there is liberty*.[2] Similar is the conclusion of John: *He that loveth not is without God; for God is love*.[3] With equal reason it may be inferred that the spiritual movement of God in the heart of man is his Spirit in us, because God is a Spirit; and this is more proper than to call God a Spirit because he is incorporeal. Indeed, no being is called a spirit from its own nature, but in so far as its action is spiritual; and it means another thing to say, God is in him or with him, than to say, The Spirit of God is in him, or upon him; for the latter signifies a spiritual illumination of the mind, but the former both protection of the body and direction of every act.

3. Moreover, it should be known that the eternal *disposition* of the Spirit of God is said to have been distinguished from the Word in this way: that God both began to act and determined that he would act by his own Spirit, by an action distinct from the Word. Nor do I ever call an angel of God by itself the Holy Spirit; but it is so called on account of a *disposition* of the Spirit of God inseparable from the ministry of angels. Nor does Scripture call any more spirits holy, although more are ministers; for all sanctification is wrought by one, there is one Spirit of God who works these things in us. Nor does any Macedonian [5] subjection of the third being prevent me from calling angels ministers. Nor can any subjection be argued from the fact that God particularly wishes to employ one *disposition* of himself for the administration of those things that he accomplishes through another one. Or, if he distinctly separates the Person of his Spirit for the sole administration of the Word (since for this purpose angels were made spirits for him, who are ministers, fulfilling his word, in order that obedience might be given to the

It said, The Spirit of God, but not the Holy Spirit.[4]

---

[1] John iv, 24. [2] II. Cor. iii, 17.
[3] I. John iv, 8. [4] Gen. i, 2.

[5] The Macedonians, a heretical sect of the fourth century, followers of Macedonius, Bishop of Constantinople, held that the Holy Spirit is a mere creature or divine energy.

voice of his word [1]), even the Spirit is, with regard to the Word, as are the angels with regard to Christ; hence I call the Holy Spirit, as Ignatius does,[2] a minister of the Word, just as angels are ministers of Christ, so that the sacred terms agree very well with the facts. And to inquire here concerning an equality or inequality of Nature is to feed upon wind; since there is only one being, and neither Scripture nor the ancient writers ever mentioned equality or inequality in this being, nor indeed thought of it. But Eunomius first devised this theory with regard to the Spirit, just as Aetius did with regard to the Word.[3]

4. In connection with the Person of the Word, the Person of Christ must be investigated. But before this, I say (and to this the preaching of John leads) that the Word was from the beginning already uttered, prepared, and appointed to the end that it might become flesh; and it was already in him, with God, as the representation and likeness of the man that was to be. And τὸ πρόσωπον,[4] this mask, this countenance, this face, this representation of man in God, is mysteriously hidden in all the passages of Scripture which speak of image, face, person, and countenance. In the first place, Wisdom [5] shows the likeness of a man, and represents the Person of Christ, when it says that it was born and created. Again, the Prophets, when they saw, saw Christ, for no other reason than that they saw a representation of the man that was to be. Of this likeness, figure, and image in God Moses speaks: [6] for the people saw voices,[7] but in confusion, because they did not see the true image of Christ.[8] And in that passage תמונה [9] denotes the form, figure, likeness, and image of Jesus Christ, as appears in the sixteenth Psalm, which the Hebrews call the seventeenth.[10] Balaam also sees this

87a

---

[1] Ps. ciii, 20, 21.

[2] Ep. ad Philad. ix (MPG. v, 703–706; ANF. i, 84; ANCL. i, 235).

[3] Eunomius and Aetius, heretics of the fourth century, taught that the Son was of a different substance from the Father, and unlike him.

[4] *To prosopon*, the face or mask, hence person; equivalent of the Latin *persona*, in both senses.

[5] The Wisdom of Jesus the son of Sirach, i. e., Ecclus. i, 4, 9; xxiv, 8, 9.

[6] Deut. iv, 12. [7] Ex. xx, 18.

[8] Deut. iv, 15. [9] *Temunah*.

[10] Ps. xvi in the Vulgate, but xvii in the Hebrew and the English version. See Ps. xvii, 15. This and many other instances show Servetus's independent use of the Hebrew in preference to the current Latin version.

image from afar: *I shall see him*, he says, *and not now: I shall behold him, and not nigh.*[1] Habakkuk saw the same thing.[2] Again, observe in how many passages David desires to see this glorious face: *Shine, O Elohim, show thy face, and we shall be saved.*[3] It says the same thing of his countenance in the fourth and the forty-fourth Psalms;[4] likewise in the above-quoted sixteenth Psalm: *When justice reigns, I shall behold thy face; and I shall be satisfied when thy image is spread abroad.*[5] In the same way in the eighty-eighth Psalm[6] he watches for the face and countenance of CHRIST in God. Again, see how clearly Isaiah saw this countenance sitting high upon a throne, yet his face was covered with wings of fire.[7] The same thing is evident from Ezekiel.[8] And this very thing John saw, though without a covering.[9] This image of the son of man Daniel saw, though beneath a covering and a cloud.[10] This is just what Zechariah saw in the darkness of the night.[11] This presence, this face, as CHRIST says, many desired to see.[12] And this desire appears in the twenty-fourth, twenty-seventh, sixty-seventh, and eightieth Psalms, and in II. Chronicles.[13] Indeed, it was commanded in the law that when they wished to bless one they should say, *The Lord show thee his face.*[14] This face Isaiah and Habakkuk looked for.[15] Seeing this countenance of the divine face, they cried out, *Oh, that thou wouldest rend the heavens, and come down.*[16] To the same purport Isaiah speaks again.[17] These and other things, as John witnesses,[18] Isaiah said when he saw the glory of Christ; for of such glory and brightness Isaiah is there speaking, and he proves CHRIST himself to be the brightness of glory.[19] *And his brightness will be as the light.*[20] The glittering brightness of the

It was always seen dimly before, but now clearly.

---

[1] Num. xxiv, 17 (Pagn.).
[2] Hab. ii, 1.
[3] Ps. lxxx, 3, 7, 19.
[4] Ps. iv, 6; xliv, 3.
[5] Ps. xvii, 15; Servetus's own rendering of the Hebrew.
[6] Ps. lxxxviii, 14.
[7] Isa. vi, 1, 2.
[8] Ezek. i, 1. 26–28; x, 4.
[9] Rev. iv, 2, 3.
[10] Dan. vii, 13.
[11] Zech. i, 8.
[12] Matt. xiii, 17; Luke x, 24.
[13] Ps. xxiv, 6; xxvii, 8, 9; lxvii, 1; lxxx, 3, 7, 19; II. Chron. ix, 23.
[14] Num. vi, 25.
[15] Isa. viii, 17; Hab. ii, 1; iii, 3, 4.
[16] Isa. lxiv, 1.
[17] Isa. lx, 2; lxii, 2.
[18] John xii, 41.
[19] Isa. lx, 3; lxii, 2.
[20] Hab. iii, 4.

face of Christ appeared to Paul above the brightness of the sun.[1] Again, when it is said that they saw the Lord face to face,[2] we have it made clear in the Gospel that it was the countenance of Christ, for introducing this as something understood of Christ, they say that God neither had been nor could have been seen.[3] As though, it says, he had seen him who was invisible.[4] And Jacob says that he has seen Elohim face to face.[5] But that Elohim was Christ will be shown by what follows. Even Jacob himself clearly declares that this was the face of a man, by the comparison which he makes in the following chapter, when he says to his brother, *I have seen thy face as if I saw the countenance of Elohim.*[6] Christ also confirms this by a verb in the past tense, saying, *He that hath seen me hath seen the Father.*[7] John also says of Christ, *He hath declared him,*[8] as if he said, Knowledge of God was had through Christ not only by us but also by them of old. Again, what does it mean to say that the grace which has now been made open to all was *given to us through* Jesus Christ *before times eternal?* [9] Verily, it was given by God through the Jesus Christ that then was, when he established a pattern of Jesus Christ in his Word; and this was before times eternal. This is just what Peter said, He called us unto his eternal glory through Jesus Christ.[10] Some say that this likeness of the Word is denoted by the word πρὸs,[11] *the Word was with God,* πρὸs τὸν θεόν,[12] as if it said, in the sight, in the face, of God; and the meaning here is that the Word was the εἰκών [13] of the Father, because it was nothing else than the likeness of a man. Again, let us understand the veil on the face of Moses,[14] and we shall understand the glory of the Lord of which Paul speaks;[15] and there he is watching for this glorious face and image of Christ, which from everlasting shone out in God.

---

[1] Acts xxvi, 13.
[2] Gen. xxxii, 30.
[3] John i, 18; Heb. xi, 27; I. John iv, 12; I. Tim. vi, 16.
[4] Heb. xi, 27.
[5] Gen. xxxii, 30.
[6] Gen. xxxiii, 10 (Vulg.).
[7] John xiv, 9.
[8] John i, 18.
[9] II. Tim. i, 9.
[10] I. Pet. v, 10. (Servetus says iii.)
[11] *Pros*, with.
[12] *Pros ton theon*, with God, John i, 1.
[13] *Eikon*, image.
[14] Ex. xxxiv, 33; II. Cor. iii, 13.
[15] II. Cor. iii, 18; viii, 19.

And upon this depends what he says, that CHRIST *is the εἰκών of the invisible God*.¹ And he states the substance of the matter when he says that the glory of God is seen in the face of JESUS CHRIST.² Nor can this be proved true in any other sense than that the glorious face of CHRIST already shone out in God from the beginning. O wondrous glory! This, he says, is *the glory which I had with thee before the world was made*.³ And παρὰ σοί ⁴ here denotes a person. Moses therefore desired to see his face; he saw some things and rejoiced, he saw his back, but he saw not his face.⁵ For they feared when they turned their eyes upon this face, and they feared lest they die.⁶ And the veil signifies that the glory of God was not yet revealed to them.⁷ Nevertheless we, now that the veil of the temple has been rent in twain, are permitted to look into the Holy of holies, that is, into the face of CHRIST, which was veiled from them. To us there is no other veil, except the flesh of CHRIST itself, with which the divinity of the Father is covered.⁸ Moses therefore saw the countenance of his face, but not his face; he saw the representation, but not the thing itself. *They desired*, says CHRIST, *to see the things which ye see, and saw them not*.⁹ Hence John points out that, because that glorious face was concealed from them, they were all in darkness, when he says, *And the darkness apprehended it not*.¹⁰ And, *To shine upon them that are in darkness*.¹¹ What Habakkuk says leads to the same thing: *There was the hiding of his power*.¹² With which agrees Deuteronomy;¹³ for on Mount Sinai, at the time when the law was given, although his power was great and terrible, yet הביון,¹⁴ there was a hiding, when the countenance of him who spoke was not seen, who nevertheless is distinctly manifested to us; hence he that is but little in the kingdom of heaven is greater than they all.

---

¹ Col. i, 15. ² II. Cor. iv, 6.
³ John xvii, 5. ⁴ *Para soi*, with thee.
⁵ Ex. xxxiii, 23.
⁶ Ex. iii, 6; xx, 18, 19; Judges xiii, 22.
⁷ Heb. ix, 3. ⁸ Heb. x, 20.
⁹ Matt. xiii, 17. ¹⁰ John i, 5.
¹¹ Luke i, 79. ¹² Hab. iii, 4.
¹³ Deut. xxxii, 20. (Servetus says xxxiii.)
¹⁴ *Hebyon*, a hiding.

5. Again, if you wish to understand the glory of CHRIST, mount up to the cherubin, consider the wheels and animals of Ezekiel; for in them all the image of the man Jesus Christ is represented in the glory of God. And above the wheels and animals Ezekiel saw CHRIST, and this he calls *the appearance of the likeness of the glory of the Lord*.[1] And this itself is the CHRIST whom John saw.[2] And *the voice of many waters* there is the same that Ezekiel heard.[3] Again, *cherub*, according to the Hebrews, is interpreted as painted, or fashioned, or a picture, or a figure; and the angels with the image of a man represent CHRIST; and both cherubim and seraphim are angels, heralds of the glory of CHRIST.[4] And he described all these things as an image and pattern of CHRIST, which Moses had seen in God.[5] For the pattern of which Exodus speaks [6] is that of which mention is made in the preceding chapter; that is, Elohim, the CHRIST, whom he had there seen.[7] And David saw this image of CHRIST above the cherubim,[8] and he gave the pattern and likeness of it to Solomon his son;[9] the *pattern*, I say, and likeness of all that he had seen by the spirit; and he says, He made me understand all the works of the pattern; moreover, all things, he says, were written by the hand of the Lord.[10] But what can be said to have been written by the hand of the Lord more properly than that very thing which had been expressly portrayed and fashioned in him, and had been fashioned for them, yet under a veil, with which the cherubim covered and overshadowed the oracle of God with their wings?[11] In fine, all things that are in the law are a shadow of the body of CHRIST, and this is represented to them through the angels, since to them Gods are often literally called angels; though after all, properly speaking, what are called Gods are God the Father and the Lord JESUS CHRIST. And for the glory of God to be seated above the cherubim means for JESUS CHRIST to be superior to the angels; because he him-

---

[1] Ezek. i, 28.
[2] Rev. iv, 2, 3.
[3] Rev. i, 15; Ezek. i, 24; xliii, 2.
[4] Isa. vi, 2; Luke ii, 9–14; Rev. iv, 6–9.
[5] Acts vii, 44; Heb. viii, 5.
[6] Ex. xxv, 40.
[7] Ex. xxiv, 10.
[8] II. Sam. xxii, 11.
[9] I. Chron. xxviii, 11.
[10] I. Chron. xxviii, 12, 19.
[11] Ex. xxv, 20; Heb. ix, 5.

self is the Lord of glory, and sits upon the throne of his glory.[1] And he is to come with this brightness of his Father's glory.[2] And the glory of the Lord which so often appeared in the cloud above the cherubim has now been revealed;[3] and, now that CHRIST is known, we all with unveiled face (by the very fact that we turn our eyes upon him) see and know the glory of the Lord;[4] for that, according to Paul, is seen in the face of JESUS CHRIST.[5] You will say that it profits little to see the outward face; but I say that it profits much if you see by believing. But you look upon his face unworthily; yet after you have believed may you never turn your eyes away from it, and you will realize that it is useful; for the eyes of the flesh draw with them the eyes of the mind. Again, all the angels that once appeared to them were nothing else than the likeness of CHRIST represented by angels; and they said that in seeing this they had seen God, just as under this figure an angel also is said to be God to them. And the saying of Origen, which I have mentioned above,[6] aims at this; for the name of God then dwelt among the angels, and his dwelling among the cherubim[7] denotes this very thing. For the dwelling of God is in heaven, that he may nowhere dwell more truly than among spirits; for thus the spirits are open wide to God, just as tents are to us. And, as I declared above, this is the light unapproachable,[8] this is heaven, and the dwelling-place of God. *He stretcheth out the heavens like a skin,*[9] and *spreadeth them out as a curtain, and as a tent to dwell in.*[10] He covereth himself with this light as with a garment.[11] These are the curtains of his tabernacle.[12] This light of God means his Essence, and the heavenly creatures, as I shall say below. For all these were angels, foreshadowing CHRIST as the dwelling-place of God. For the name of God, which according to the letter of the law dwelt in the midst of the angels, now dwells in CHRIST; and angels manifested the light when God said, *Let*

---

[1] Matt. xxv, 31.
[2] Mark viii, 38; Matt. xvi, 27.
[3] Isa. xl, 5; xlvi, 13.
[4] Isa. lxvi, 18; Hab. ii, 14.
[5] II. Cor. iv, 6.
[6] Book II, paragraph 25.
[7] II. Sam. vi, 2.
[8] I. Tim. vi, 16.
[9] Ps. civ, 2 (Vulg.).
[10] Isa. xl, 22.
[11] Ps. civ, 2.
[12] Ex. xxvi, 1 ff.

there be light,[1] and yet this light is really JESUS CHRIST. I call all the heavenly creatures spirits and angels, although angels and spirits are spoken of only when they are sent; and we call them so in general because we do not perceive them in any other way. Yet neither angel nor spirit is the name of a Nature. Again, just as the angels, in hearing a voice, heard the voice of God, quite so is it with regard to CHRIST. Indeed, that was a shadow of this truth; and in hearing the voice of CHRIST, Paul heard the voice of God, as Ananias witnesses;[2] for in CHRIST alone does the name of God now wholly dwell. And even as in seeing him, just so in hearing him is the Father heard; and on account of his blood it is said that we are redeemed by the blood of God.[3] God is in him entirely, and to such a degree that all things that are in him are God's; and the things that are done through CHRIST are not man's works but God's. *All things, he says, that are mine are thine*;[4] and, *The Father abiding in me, he doeth the works*;[5] and, We are justified through CHRIST;[6] we have become the righteousness of God,[7] and have become the body and members of CHRIST.[8] We are the congregation of God.

6. Again, you will not find that man is directly called the image of the invisible God יהוה;[9] but it says, Let us make man in our image and likeness;[10] and, He was made in the image and after the likeness of Elohim.[11] Or it says, Made in the image of the likeness of God,[12] because the real and chief likeness is the representation of man in God, which is CHRIST JESUS himself, in whose image we are made, being conformed, as Paul says, to the image of the Son of God.[13] And although when it says, Let *us* make ... after *our*, it is literally understood of angels, just as when it said, *Adam* ... as one of *us*;[14] yet the real spirit of it refers to CHRIST. Just as wisdom also was not said to be created,

---

[1] Gen. i, 3.
[2] Acts. xxii, 14.
[3] Acts xx, 28.
[4] John xvii, 10.
[5] John xiv, 10.
[6] Rom. iii, 24; v, 9; I. Cor. vi, 11; Gal. ii, 17.
[7] II. Cor. v, 21.
[8] I. Cor. xii, 27.
[9] Jehovah.
[10] Gen. i, 26.
[11] Ecclus. xvii, 3.
[12] Wisdom ii, 23 (Vulg.).
[13] Rom. viii, 29.
[14] Gen. iii, 22.

except from the person of CHRIST; even as also of Solomon and David more things are said, and more excellently, than can be appropriate to them. They are said of them, but not on account of them. Moreover, of an angel it is literally said, *My face shall go before thee*,[1] although nevertheless the true face is CHRIST. It is he that attended the children of Israel on their journey.[2] Nor does God number the angels with himself so that he says, as though they were one of *us, our*, and let *us* make. But because the person of the Son is foreshadowed in them, this is indeed correctly understood of the Son, who is one with the Father; for hitherto the Son was one with him, in one Nature, that is, personally; but now he is one with him in power and authority. And he said, *our*, for the reason that the same likeness of CHRIST belonged to each. Hence many of the Jews, as though dreaming of CHRIST, imagined that there are bodily forms in God, because צלם [3] and דמות [4] are attributed to him in Scripture; and Rabbi Moses undertakes to oppose this view in his *Director Neutrorum*, Book I, chapter i;[5] saying that it is a metaphorical use of Scripture. But I deem that in such figures of speech mysteries lie hidden, and that nothing was said by the divine oracles without a meaning. And this whole difficulty is easily solved by CHRIST, for it must be borne in mind that the Scriptures employ various ways of speaking. It is not without mystery that Scripture attributes such things to God in the Old Testament rather than in the New; it is not without significance that in the Old Testament you so often read of his hands, fingers, eyes, face, and feet, and that none of these is found in the New Testament, but quite the contrary: *God is a Spirit*.[7] For the reason is clear; because CHRIST was then with God. And that same pattern after which man was made is the דמות [8] which Ezekiel saw,[9] that is, CHRIST, whose face did shine as the fire.[10] Through an angel, therefore, the countenance of CHRIST was

I will open my mouth in parables, I will utter things hidden, etc.[6]

---

[1] Ex. xxxiii, 14 (Vulg.). [2] I. Cor. x, 4.
[3] *Tselem*, image. [4] *Demuth*, likeness.
[5] The same work cited in Book III, paragraph 4, as *Liber Perplexorum*.
[6] Matt. xiii, 35; Ps. lxxviii, 2. [7] John iv, 24.
[8] *Demuth*, likeness. [9] Ezek. viii, 2.
[10] Matt. xvii, 2.

represented as shining forth in God;[1] for, as Cyprian says,[2] he is at once angel, and God, and CHRIST; he is here covered by a wonderful tabernacle.[3] The same thing is proved in Exodus.[4] Paul notes the same thing in Galatians: The law, he says, *was ordained through angels by the hand of a mediator.*[5] For there already existed a mediator in God; and notwithstanding this, God was one, although (in view of the fact that no sort of mediator can here be asserted of one only) Paul here acutely assumes, indeed, an inconsistency, so that by resolving it you conclude that CHRIST was with God. For so great is the glory of CHRIST that the person of CHRIST was figured in God, in angels, in men, in rocks and other things. These things are the ineffable mysteries of CHRIST which, had they been understood by the ancient heretics, they would never have said that angels created the world, and were the gods of the Old Testament. From the same ignorance of CHRIST it resulted that others conceived that above the angels there were yet more Gods as creators of the world, because in Genesis *Elohim* is used in the plural; which nevertheless clearly proves our case, as what follows will indicate. And explain *Elohim*, that is, God and his Word, God and CHRIST, and God through CHRIST. Nor does it say that *they* created, but *he* created, because God created by the Word; yet it was the Person of Christ that was creating.

<small>This was formerly the view of certain Hebrews, against whom Paul of Burgos wrote in his *Scrutinium*.[6]</small>

7. From this is discovered the truth of the common opinion by which they say that two Natures united in CHRIST make one Person, and one Son, because there is one Nature of the Word, another Nature of the flesh; and these two are one Person, because the Word became flesh. In which opinion there are as many errors as there are words; and they do not understand what *Person* means; and they misuse the term when in this metaphysical fashion they speak of the Nature of the Word. But properly speaking one says, the Nature of God, and not, the Nature of the Word; because the being of the Word is a

<small>92b</small>

---

[1] Gen. xxii, 11, 15; Jud. vi, 22.
[2] Testim. adv. Judaeos, ii, 5 (MPL. iv, 728; ANF. v, 517; ANCL. xiii, 102 f.).
[3] *Caelatura.*   [4] Ex. iii, 2–6.
[5] Gal. iii, 19.
[6] Paulus Burgensis, or de Sancta Maria, formerly R. Salomon Levita; Dialogus qui vocatur Scrutinium, 1434.

Person assumed in the Nature of God. Indeed, hitherto it ill suggests the Nature of God, which we know not how to call into court; and we transgress the limits of Scripture. And I shall never take the Nature except for the being itself, which is God.

8. Moreover, John did not say, the Word was united to the flesh, but, *The Word became flesh*,[1] because a change was made from the Word into flesh; a change was made from a Person into a being,[2] as if the Person of the Word, when it became flesh, withdrew from God and came to man. Yet it did not really withdraw from God, but CHRIST ascended to God, and CHRIST is now just as really in God as the Word was with God before.[3] And this is the Son of man who had already ascended into heaven, and was in heaven,[4] as I said in Book II.[5] That which before was the Person of the Son, now that the Word has become flesh is JESUS CHRIST himself, who is the true, real and natural Son of God. Nor is there now in God any other *hypostasis* or form but the man Christ himself, for when the being itself comes, its personal representation ceases. Reflect upon this continually; for I say that the Word was in the law as a prefiguring of CHRIST; the Word was the shadow, and CHRIST is the truth. John, both in his Gospel and in his Epistle, says of the Word, *was*;[6] but now, after its being manifested, there is no such Word, but the very being itself of which the Word was a type. For we never read of the Word, *is*, but, *was*. But now there is the Son, JESUS CHRIST, because what was in the Word exists as flesh, and the Word became flesh; that is, the Person became a being, the shadow became light, as Paul says, *Our glorying became truth*;[7] that is, just as we gloried in the Word, so it was in fact. The Word, which was in the law as a shadow, became the truth. Even as he adds, *The law*, that is the shadow, *was given through Moses; truth came through Christ.*[8] There was

[1] John i, 14.
[2] *De persona ad rem*; from the mask of a being into the being itself.
[3] John i, 1.
[4] John iii, 13.
[5] Book II, paragraph 1.
[6] John i, 1; I. John i, 1.
[7] II. Cor. vii, 14 (Vulg.).
[8] John i, 17.

The separate words of John have reference to the face of Christ.

then a Word concerning the being which now is; that is, the being itself did not exist, but there was a Word concerning it, like a conversation about an absent being, which was then being represented by the Word. The very thing which was the πρόσωπον[1] of the Word, and the light shining in darkness,[2] is now in heaven, the face of Jesus Christ which on the mount did shine as the sun.[3] For the Person of the Word was prepared to this end, that the glory of Christ might be manifested, which was also done, *and we beheld his glory*;[4] and at this the preaching of John very clearly aims. We ought now, therefore, with clear and simple contemplation, to attend solely to Jesus Christ and God the Father. Nor does any other Word now remain, nor has one ever been heard, either in Paul's mouth or in his preaching, except God the Father and his Son Jesus Christ; which differences and modes of speaking I would have you note, how, that is, it means one thing to say the Word, means another to say the Son; means one thing to say, was once, means another to say, is now. Reflect on this, for you have fallen short in the chief foundation. If you show me one iota by which the Word is called the Son, or mention is made of the begetting of the Word, I will confess myself as one beaten, though he has kept my language to the very letter, as Christ says; who when Scripture says the Word will himself also say the Word; when it says the Son, will say the Son; that is, once the Word, but now the Son.

9. As for what they say of *Person*, it is a gross misuse of the term to say that one Person is an aggregate of two beings, or of two Natures united into one mass. But properly speaking, one being is called the person of another, as Job's friends, assuming the person of God, wished to speak and to judge as though they were themselves Gods;[5] and the false apostles speak in the person of the apostles, and Satan speaks in the person of a good angel, when he fashioneth himself into an angel of light.[6] And wisdom speaks in the person of Christ, David and the Prophets often speak in the person of Christ, and Christ in the person of the Church; which things were all hidden types or signs of the

---

[1] *Prosopon*, face.
[2] John i, 5.
[3] Matt. xvii, 2.
[4] John i, 14.
[5] Job xiii, 7, 8.
[6] II. Cor. xi, 14.

Word. For in a way altogether similar we say that the Word in the Person of CHRIST was once the Son, and that CHRIST was with the Father from the beginning in the Person of the Word; and CHRIST is the Person of the Word, and the Word is the Person of CHRIST, and there is but one Person and one aspect, because the very thing that shone forth in the Word is CHRIST himself; so that if I have a mirror, although you see me face to face, and also in the mirror, yet you see but one person. And thus it amounts to the same thing when, having mentioned Christ, or having mentioned the eternal Word, you say this: He was the Son from the beginning; because, whatever you may mention, he was from the beginning the Son in Person, not in reality. Indeed, Persons are spoken of because of the absence of beings, and Persons are incompatible with beings. Therefore it is not argued from this that there was any real begetting up there among the Gods, for this speculation is very beastly and harmful, and deserves such great derision that it needs no recommendation.

All things that are in the law are signs of the hidden Word.

94b   10. From this, if you understand what has been said, you will have an answer to all the arguments in the world. Indeed, there will be no argument against you, but you will very plainly admit that the Son of God was with the Father from everlasting, came forth from the Father, came down from the highest heaven, came into the world, entered the world, and put on flesh. Let those now keep silence who say that the Son was sent by the Father in no other way than one of the Prophets; for one was sent and manifested who aforetime was the hidden God of Israel, while his countenance lay concealed within the shadow of the Father;[1] for he dwelt in the secret place of the Most High, and in the shadow of the Almighty.[2] There was his power placed and hidden.[3] And John says that not the Son alone, as they say, but JESUS CHRIST himself came in the flesh.[4] And this is itself the appearing of our Savior CHRIST; though to what purpose is his appearing, unless that he too formerly was hidden in secret? To such a degree did the Prophets see CHRIST in God, that he says that in the beginning he laid the foundation of the earth.[5]

---

[1] Isa. xlv, 15.   [2] Ps. xci, 1.   [3] Hab. iii, 4.
[4] I. John iv, 2; II. John 7.   [5] Ps. cii, 25.

And although many think that these words are forcibly made to apply to Christ, yet that is their proper sense, as the Apostle teaches.¹ For after the Prophet spoke of God as יהוה,² and said, His name is to be declared in Zion, that all may be obedient to him through Christ,³ he afterwards speaks of the affliction of Zion, that is, of the people of Christ. And in addition to this he calls upon אל ⁴ Christ, and adds a consolation, proclaiming the power and eternity of Christ. He it is of whom the whole sixty-eighth Psalm speaks, whom he desires to arise. He is El; the heavens declare his glory; that is, the spiritual creatures, and also literally the superior powers and the worlds which he created.⁵ But more about this in what follows,⁶ for there is also a similar opinion about other Psalms, although they explain them otherwise if they have no knowledge of Christ. It is he that formerly was hidden in wisdom, and afterwards *did appear upon earth, and was conversant with men.*⁷ From this is solved the question as to how he took the seed of Abraham, to which a reply has already been given.⁸ For he, coming from heaven, enters the world, takes ⁹ and puts on flesh. But this meaning, although it be true in itself, yet seems to me in this passage to bear some other meaning along with this. Nor does the Apostle compare the seed of Abraham to a single angel whom he had been on the point of taking as a human nature, but to the whole company of angels; as though he were saying, he came to set free not angels but men. He is said therefore to take the seed of Abraham, which we are, thus: *Moreover, I will take thee;* ¹⁰ and, *He took me, and drew me out of many waters.*¹¹ Quite so our merciful and faithful High Priest, when he set us free from bondage to the Devil, drew and took us from death to life, from the power of Satan to his own bosom. *I will take you,* he says;¹² and, *Take ye one another, even as Christ took us to the*

95a

95b

---

¹ Heb. i, 10.   ² Jehovah.
³ Ps. cii, 21, 22.   ⁴ *El*, God.
⁵ Ps. xix, 4.   ⁶ In Book VII, paragraphs 4, 5.
⁷ Bar. iii, 37.   ⁸ Book III, paragraphs 1 ff.
⁹ *Assumit*, and so in the following quotations, following Pagnini's rendering, except the last, which follows the Vulgate.
¹⁰ I. Kings xi, 37.   ¹¹ II. Sam, xxii, 17.
¹² John xiv, 3.

*glory of God.*¹ And, *He will take thee, will gather thee, and will bring thee* ² into his rest, that is, *into the land* of Canaan, into which rest we have already been brought, although just what this is the world knows not; but it will know when it is known that Jesus Christ is the Son of God.

11. There remains to be explained the passage in Hebrews,³ how the Son is called the very image of the Substance, or *hypostasis*, of God. In order to get at the meaning of this, let us see what the Apostle means by Substance. In the first place, the *substance* of a lawsuit is spoken of, its theme, its marrow, or that in which the knot of the question chiefly consists. And in this way the same Apostle takes it in the same epistle; for he wishes us particularly to consider the beginning of the *substance* of Christ unto the end; ⁴ that is, that with a living spirit we consider the marrow of the matter, whose *hypostasis* is to bring the whole order of the law back to Christ, as to its very goal. And we thus bring straight to Christ that part which speaks of rest, knowing that now at the end of the ages is the seventh day on which God rested from the works of the law. And into that rest into which they did not enter because of unbelief, we that believe in Christ enter to-day; and we observe a perpetual, true, and spiritual keeping of the sabbath, even sabbath after sabbath, now that our eternal high priest is forever within the tabernacle.⁵ Moreover, he says that faith is the *substance* of those things which are hoped for; ⁶ for that which is hoped for is eternal salvation, and the chief root, marrow, and infallible way of attaining to this salvation consists in faith. Hence faith is said to be the *substance* of this matter, just as we say that the wealth on which human progress is founded is our *substance*. I am always speaking not of the Lutheran faith, but of the faith of CHRIST, which alone justifies. That is the door entering through which we are purified; and being thus cleansed, laboring worthily in the Lord's field, we earn our talent. The whole faith of the Gospel has regard to the Person of Christ; that is, that we believe him; and in him is all our trust. For he himself al-

---

[1] Rom. xv 7.
[2] Deut. xxx, 4, 5.
[3] Heb. i, 3.
[4] Heb. iii, 14 (Vulg.).
[5] Heb. iii, 19–iv, 4.
[6] Heb. xi, 1.

ways cries, Be of good cheer, and, Believe in me; and as a result of this preaching of Christ the Gospel of the kingdom of God is alone proclaimed to us; and the *hypostasis* of eternal salvation is to believe that JESUS Christ is the Son of God. Therefore *hypostasis* is properly subsistence: that which chiefly subsists in anything is its essence and *hypostasis*.

12. From this it is plain what the Apostle means by *hypostasis* in the chapter quoted from.[1] And they are deceived who explain it as meaning the Nature of the Father; for Scripture has nothing to do with Natures, nor does the proper meaning of the term allow that sense. And the *substance* of things to be hoped for is not the thing itself that is to be hoped for, or the *nature* of things to be hoped for; but by *substance* of the Father the Apostle means his way of subsisting, and the *being* of the Father. And this is what the expression $\upsilon\pi\acute{o}\sigma\tau\alpha\sigma\iota\varsigma$ [2] means; for the *hypostasis* of the Father shines forth in the Word, and the likeness of the Word is the man CHRIST JESUS himself, who is the very image of this being, of which very image I shall speak more at large below.[3]

---

[1] Heb. i, 3, where the Greek *hypostasis* is translated substance, its etymological equivalent.

[2] *Hypostasis*.   [3] In Book VI, paragraph 4.

BOOK V

Argument

EXAMINATION *of the Old Testament usage of the words for God — Elohim and Jehovah— shows that both refer to Christ, as centre of all, and essence of all things.*

Synopsis

1. Elohim, plural in form, means God and his Word; 2. but is singular in construction because the Word was God; and Christ is indifferently called Elohim or Jehovah, Jehovah in the Law, and Elohim in the Prophets. 3. The word for salvation, or Christ, is used not with Jehovah but with Elohim. 4. Usage of Scripture shows that Christ is Elohim. 5. Our justification through Christ is for those that believe that he is the Son of God. 6. The meaning of the name Jehovah also points to Christ. 7. He is the creator of all things, 8. as John also shows. 9. God is the source of light, and the Essence of all things.

BOOK THE FIFTH

1. The more notable names of Divinity are *Elohim*, and *Jehovah*; the one the name of Christ, the other that of the Father, and of these we have now to speak with a view to a fuller knowledge of Christ. I have interpreted Elohim as meaning God and his Word; and I say more plainly that Elohim was in Person man, and in Nature God. And by this analogy they call great men and distinguished persons *elohim*, be they of men or of angels. Moreover, the Hebrews attribute this plural number to the usage of their language, but as usual they quench the Spirit. Yet of us greater things must be required, since we know that *the testimony of* JESUS CHRIST *is the spirit of prophecy*.[1] For this usage was established before there was any other usage; and that it was thus established in this sacred language by God is not without mystery. I say the same of *Adonai*, or *Adonim*;[2]

---

[1] Rev. xix, 10.   [2] Heb., Lord, Lords.

For there are many Elohim or Adonim, whether in heaven or on earth. I. Cor. viii, 5.

for it might reasonably have been established for this being, and it can also be employed for other lords, just as *elohim* is also employed. Again, that a plural is indicated in *elohim* is proved in Joshua, where it not only says *elohim* of God, but אלהים קדשים,[1] as though it said, holy Gods. It therefore can not be denied that some plural is here indicated. Likewise in Jeremiah, אלהים חיים,[2] that is, live Gods, living Gods; and in the Psalms, אלהים שפטים,[3] that is, Gods that judge. This plural, as I have said, was indicated by Paul in Galatians, saying, *Now a mediator is not of one*.[4] And there is this plural because Elohim was then in Person man, and in Nature God; so now Elohim is Christ, man according to the flesh, God in spirit and in power.

2. It is in the highest degree appropriate to this matter that, although *elohim* is interpreted in the plural, that is, God and his Word, yet it is placed in the singular construction, because the Word was God. In the same way Christ, as he was with God, is, upon consideration, indifferently called Jehovah or Elohim; for in the Law the name Jehovah is not separated from Elohim. Therefore he who was then Elohim was Jehovah, because the Word was God; and, as it frequently reads, no one was Elohim except Jehovah, and Christ himself was Elohim, the source of being, from whom emanated all things in the world. But when a prophecy is directed to the Christ that is to come, the name Jehovah is never applied to him. Evidence in support of this matter is in the fact that though the same words are repeated in the Law and the Prophets, in the Law *Jehovah* is used, and in the prophecy which refers to Christ *Elohim* is used.[5] Likewise, Jehovah is thy Maker, and thy Redeemer shall be called the Elohim of the whole earth.[6] And in many other passages this usage is found: And Jehovah said, I will be *Elohim* to you.[7] For the sovereign rule[8] of Jehovah comes to us through the dispensation[9] of Elohim, just as God reigns through Christ,

---

[1] *Elohim kedoshim*, Josh. xxiv, 19.
[2] *Elohim chayyim*, Jer. x, 10; xxiii, 36.
[3] *Elohim shophetim*, Ps. lviii, 11.
[4] Gal. iii, 20. cf. Book IV, paragraph 6.
[5] Deut. xxxiii, 2; Hab. iii, 18.   [6] Isa. liv, 5.
[7] Lev. xxvi, 12; II. Cor. vi, 16; Heb. viii, 10.
[8] *Monarchia*.   [9] *Oeconomia*.

for otherwise Jehovah is a separate name by itself. Again, the reason that chiefly moves me is that the word Elohim has reference to Christ; for all the Psalms which the Holy Spirit has in the gospel records interpreted as relating to Christ, and any other passages of Scripture that attribute to Christ a divine name, employ the word *EL, Elohim*, or *Adonai*, especially *Elohim*. And this Christ himself clearly shows: *Be still*, he says, *and see that I am Elohim*.[1] And the Apostle explained that in the preceding Psalm Christ is said to be *Elohim*.[2] And in the one before that he is said to be *Elohim* and *Adonai*.[3] Likewise other Psalms before and after all declare that he is *Elohim*, thus:

98a *Elohim* is greatly exalted;[4] This is *Elohim*, he will rule us forever;[5] Out of Zion will *Elohim* come with glorious beauty.[6] For that this *Elohim* here is Christ, who rejects the ceremonies of the law, is plain from the argument of Paul in I. Corinthians x, and Hebrews x. Again, who that has even a moderate knowledge of Hebrew or Chaldee will fail to know that Thomas did not call on Jehovah when he said, My Lord, my God.[7] Did you ever see this affix, *my*, added to the name Jehovah? Search, then, and let him be ignorant who will.

3. Again in another way, and it is a mystery worth noting; for ישע [8] (which means saved, and salvation, Christ) is never joined to the name Jehovah, but to the name *Elohim*,[9] as in very many passages where, besides the name Jehovah, something about אלהי ישעי [10] is usually added, which means judge, prince, our Savior, saved and salvation, Christ; and the Gospel interprets this salvation as meaning Christ.[11] In the same way the angel interpreted the name Jesus as meaning Savior.[12] To the same purport spoke Mary, following a saying of Habakkuk, *My spirit will rejoice in God my salvation*;[13] for Habakkuk had said, *In Elohim is my salvation*.[14] And although Jehovah is said

---

[1] Ps. xlvi, 10 (Vulg.). [2] Ps. xlv, 6; cf. Heb. i, 8.
[3] Ps. xliv, 21, 23. [4] Ps. xlvii, 9.
[5] Ps. xlviii, 14 (Vulg.). [6] Ps. l, 2.
[7] John xx, 28. [8] *Jesha'*.
[9] Hab. iii, 18; Ps. xviii, 46; xxiv, 5; Isa. xii, 2; Micah vii, 7.
[10] *Elohei jesha'y*. [11] Luke ii, 30; iii, 6; Acts xxviii, 28.
[12] Luke ii, 11. [13] Luke i, 47.
[14] Hab. iii, 18.

to save because he saves through Christ, yet they are never joined together, it never reads יהוה ישע.[1] But, what is also worth noting, there is generally an addition about ישועתו,[2] that is, about his salvation, Christ.[3] And so Simeon said, *Mine eyes have seen thy salvation.*[4] Isaiah shows me this difference plainly. For in composing the history the spirit often suddenly intermingles sublimer things; in composing the history the Prophet is all at once caught up into heaven to gaze upon the glory of the world to come, where they shall see Christ and the Father eye to eye, and shall say, This is Elohim, Christ the Savior. Likewise, when the Father is pointed out, This is Jehovah, and we will rejoice in *Jesuato*, that is, in his Jesus, in his salvation, Christ.[5] For his name is ישועה, Jeshuah, which is also used in the Psalms.[6]

4. Again, the name Elohim is never put before the name Jehovah, but on the contrary it always says, Jehovah Elohim; so that it not only is noted there that the Word was God, but it can also be explained in accordance with what is to be said, that is, one who forms the Essence, or will give the Essence to Elohim Christ himself. Again, Christ is clearly proved in another way to be Elohim; for, since Christ is the Word, no mention is ever made of the Word of Elohim, nor does Elohim send or set in motion his Word, because he does not set in motion nor send himself. But, since the Father is Jehovah, he is rightly called the Word of Jehovah himself, and mention is always made of his own Word, and of his Word. And although mention is never made of the Word of Elohim, yet mention is properly made of the spirit of Elohim, for this very thing was the breath of Christ,[7] just as also to-day Christ sends the Spirit from the Father. Again, the fact that Elohim is Christ confirms what I said above,[8] that man was not made in the image of Jehovah, but in the image of Elohim.

Note the mystery: that it says, the spirit of Elohim, and not, the Word of Elohim.

---

[1] *Jehovah jesha'*.
[2] *Jeshu'atho*.
[3] Ps. xcvi, 2; xcviii, 2.
[4] Luke ii, 30.
[5] Isa. xxv, 9.
[6] Ps. ix, 14; xiii, 5; xx, 5; xxi, 1, 5; cvi, 4, and in a great many other passages.
[7] Gen. i, 2.
[8] In Book I, paragraph 20.

5. To some what is said of the name Jehovah in Jeremiah [1] will cause difficulty. But even if Jerusalem is there called, Our righteous Jehovah, they could infer little from it. For names are often given to things with these additions. Yet I suppose that there is here another sense; for in the one passage the relative masculine is used, which refers to the tribe of Judah; in the other passage the feminine, which refers to Jerusalem; for in both passages it had made mention of them just before. And afterwards it adds וזה שמו אשר יקראו יהוה צדקנו,[2] that is, And this name of him who called him, namely Judah, is, Our righteous Jehovah. And in the other passage it says likewise, He who will call her, namely Jerusalem, is our righteous Jehovah; just as if you said, The God of peace called us, that is, he called us in peace. It means to say that they will be called under the name of righteousness, he will be our righteousness, we shall all be righteous, after he has freely justified us. I have pointed out above [3] that this righteousness is not according to the Lutheran faith, but is for those that believe that Jesus Christ is the Son of God. For we were acknowledged by God, and justified from our sins, when we believed in Christ.[4] For though we were dead through sins, he made us alive and made us heavenly.[5] It is not needful that we seek righteousness and the friendship of God through works of the law; indeed, this would be to distrust Christ, as though he had not sufficiently and freely justified us once and for all. They sought this in the law, although they were unable to obtain it; but we have been justified, purified, and sanctified by Christ.[6] The enmity between God and the world which could not be removed through the law has been removed through Christ. God has become to us a merciful Father, and we his sons. And not only this, but he has given us the pledge of the Spirit, that we may be already partakers of the glory to come.[7] O wonderful χάρις [8] of God, that we most wicked men should have been made righteous in the sight of

Made righteous by this alone, that we have believed in Christ.

---

[1] Jer. xxiii, 6; xxxiii, 16 (Vulg.).
[2] *Wezeh shemo asher yikreu Jehovah tsidkenu,* Jer. xxiii, 6.
[3] Book III, paragraph 20. [4] Acts xiii, 38, 39; Rom. iii, 21–28.
[5] Eph. ii, 1, 5, 6. [6] Heb. viii, 10; x, 10, 14.
[7] Eph. i, 13, 14. [8] *Charis,* grace.

God! We are reconciled to God through Christ, by his not imputing our sins to us; and thus without works we have been made the righteousness of God, and friends of God,[1] in which grace already gained we now firmly stand, as follows in the same passage.[2] But what now remains to be done, now that we have believed in Christ and have been justified? Let the Lutherans inquire. If they do not find out, let them sleep with their faith. It was not enough for them to be without faith in Christ, unless they also robbed the people of the reward of love, and of every act of virtue. They keep men suspended in the mere wind of faith, and make an exhibition of themselves. They say they have faith; but I have never been able to understand what it is that they have, which they call faith. I would that they might take the Scriptures more freely, and without doing them violence, also casting off their most unfortunate prejudice. For Christ did not speak falsely when he said that by love, fasting, and prayers we lay up treasure in the kingdom of heaven, and prepare for ourselves an abundant reward in the world to come. Indeed, without this, justification is in vain, and we have received the grace of God in vain. Yet they think to bring the people forcibly to do these things. Have love, they say, but it will profit you nothing. Thus their imagining makes men slothful, so that they neglect everything, they pay no heed to prayer; to give alms is useless; if you speak of continence, mortification of the flesh, or fasting, they will laugh with a great guffaw. I will speak of this more at large elsewhere;[3] for it was necessary for the present to touch upon these things, in order thereby to show my purpose, namely, what that Evangelical faith is which they are seeking. For this foolishness is our faith and salvation, namely, that Jesus Christ is the Son of God, the Saviour, because he died for us, and rose again. By this foolishness of preaching it is God's good pleasure that they that believe should be saved; foolishness, I say with Paul,[4] in the judgment of the philosophers, which is nevertheless the wisdom of God.

Justified like Abraham, who by the fact that he believed one Word was made the friend of God.

100a

6. The other name, most holy of all, יהוה,[5] some say means

---

[1] II. Cor. v, 21; Rom. iv, 13.   [2] Rom. v, 2; II. Cor. vi, 1.
[3] This promise was fulfilled in the *Dialogues*.
[4] I. Cor. i, 21–25.   [5] Jehovah.

100b Essence; others, begetting. Yet it includes both, and can be interpreted thus: יהוה, that is, source of being, parent of beings, one who causes to be, gives being, cause of being. I leave to the Cabalists [1] their own secrets; and I simply say that (as the *Jod* with the *Sheva* [2] shows us) it is the future *Piel*,[3] which has an active meaning, formed from the root הוה,[4] or rather היה,[5] by changing the *Jod* to a *Vav*, and small words to great, as frequently happens; and it is interpreted יהוה,[6] that is, he will give being, or will cause to be; which applies rather well to Christ, as much as to say, He will cause Christ to be. Note the greatness of the mysteries, that even in the very name of God, there was a sign, an indication, or a prophecy of the Christ to come. Christ is he whom Jehovah caused to be from the beginning; and not only caused him to be, but all things to be through him. The change of points [7] was made for the sake of likeness to those of the word אדני,[8] even as it also sometimes has the points of the word Elohim, as though it also included in itself the meaning of those words.[9]

7. We can settle this meaning of the word by a passage where he was about to do great deeds and lay Egypt waste; hence he says that his name Jehovah, which is the name of the one that does these great deeds, was not known to the patriarchs.[10] For God appeared to the patriarchs, and was known under the name EL Shaddai;[11] and from the meaning of these names in this passage it is ascertained that far more is conveyed through the name Jehovah; for שדי[12] comes from שד,[13] which means deso-

---

[1] The Cabalists devoted themselves to the esoteric doctrines of Judaism, and gave Scripture mystical interpretations.

[2] *Jod* is the Hebrew J; the *Sheva* is a half-vowel, equivalent to an unaccented *e*. The reference is to the *Je* in Jehovah.

[3] The *Piel* is a form of the Hebrew verb denoting intensity or repetition.

[4] *Havah*.   [5] *Hajah*.   [6] *Jihveh*.

[7] The Hebrew vowel signs, written under the consonants.

[8] *Adonaj*.

[9] The true vowels were never written with the sacred name whose consonants were *Jhvh*, lest it be profanely pronounced; and those of *Adonaj* (Lord) were substituted, thus giving the artificial name, Jehovah.

[10] Ex. vi, 2, 3.

[11] God Almighty; Gen. xvii, 1; xxviii, 3; xxxv, 11.

[12] *Shaddai*.   [13] *Shod*.

lation, as though he were a desolator, or one able to lay all waste. And so it is explained in Joel,[1] and in Isaiah;[2] כשד משדי,[3] that is, like desolation from a desolator. Likewise אל[4] means strong, and powerful; whence EL Shaddai, as though he were a mighty desolator; and under this name he was first manifested to Abraham;[5] and that for this reason, that Abraham might be mightier in not fearing others, then also that he might walk more perfectly before him in the fear of the Lord, as it says, *I am a jealous God,*[6] *a consuming* and terrible *fire.*[7] Therefore, although I have appeared to them with this name, although they have realized that I laid waste Sodom and Gomorrah, yet they have not fully known hitherto that I am omnificent, have not known me under the name of Jehovah, which is a more complete name of one that causes to be, that does so great and so many things, as you shall see in the things that I am now about to do against Pharaoh. And this preface concerning the things that he was about to do God premised before he went on to the explanation of his name. So also he afterwards said, The Egyptians shall know that I am Jehovah[8] that cause all things to be. The conclusion is valid, that we are to know by such great plagues and desolations of Christendom that he is EL Shaddai and Jehovah. But we have no eyes; the heart of Pharaoh is hardened. The Prophets, when they prophesy some great thing to come, are wont to make the same inference.[9] For us to know that he is Jehovah who does such great things against us, it is not enough for you to say, Now we know that it is the finger of God, for Pharaoh's magicians also said this;[10] but they did not inquire what he demanded who wrought such great evils. Nor are we willing to take warning from it. The priests of the Philistines gave more earnest heed to this.[11] And shall we not blush for shame that the Gentiles surpass us in regard for the Scriptures? Moreover, this name of one who creates, or causes

---

[1] Joel i, 15.
[2] Isa. xiii, 6.
[3] *Keshod mishshaddi,* Joel i, 15.
[4] *El.*
[5] Gen. xvii, 1. Modern scholarship does not support these etymologies.
[6] Ex. xx, 5.
[7] Heb. xii, 29.
[8] Ex. vii, 5; xiv, 4, 18.
[9] Ezek. xxv, 7, 11, 17; xxix, 6, 9, 16, 21; xxx, 8, 19, 25, 26; I. Kings xx, 13, 28.
[10] Ex. viii, 19.
[11] I. Sam. vi, 1–9.

to be, is made plain from the creation of the world, and from the first passage in which the voice began to be uttered by the Holy Spirit; for during the six days God was never called by that name, because the creation was not yet completed. But on the seventh day, when the creation was completed, he first began to be called by this name, the names of the generation and creation being repeated. *These, it says, are the generations of the heaven and of the earth when they were created, in the day on which Jehovah made them.*[1] Hence he is there called the creator of things and of beings; he himself is the father of the rain, because he hath begotten the drops of dew from the womb, whose outgoing is the frost, and he hath begotten the hoar-frost of heaven.[2]

8. Again, according to the Gospel of John, this name of God is explained by the mere fact that he said, *was*;[3] for this *was* is the *hypostasis* of the Word, as I shall say in Book VII.[4] Again, by way of the Word John explains that Jehovah himself is the one who gives being and causes to be, saying, *All things were made through him, and without him was nothing.*[5] Moreover, he is explained to be one who begets through the Word or Christ, because he was begetting the Son from everlasting and always by a word; and through Christ that name best fitted him, because he first of all gave the Son being by the uttering of a word, through which he also caused other things to be. For, as I said, Christ is before all. And he himself, by saying, I am, I am from the beginning,[6] shows the name of the Father, because the Son has eternal being from the Father.

9. Just as God is called the source of being, so is he also called the source of light, the Father of Spirits,[7] the Father of lights;[8] nor do I understand light as meaning here the assertion of a quality. But inasmuch as the rays of being, and shining angels, flow from God, the breath of being comes out of his storehouse, from the Father's breast, as sons from a father's bosom; manifold rays of divinity proceed, which are all Essences of God,

---

[1] Gen. ii, 4.
[2] Job xxxviii, 28, 29.
[3] John i, 1: In the beginning *was* the Word.
[4] Book VII, paragraph 8.
[5] John i, 3.
[6] John viii, 58.
[7] Heb. xii, 9.
[8] James i, 17.

and he is in them. Nor is there anything in the world that can more truly be called Essence than that which God disposes to exist in his own character. For his Accidents are more essential than our Quiddities; and no celestial messenger is ever sent to us in whom his Essence is not. He sends his light to us, and this itself is God his very self. He sends his Spirit to us, and this itself is God his very self. For the express image of the *hypostasis* of God is always there; and for this reason Jehovah is called Sabaoth, that is, of hosts; because his Essence fights in the number of the multitude. He arms all the hosts and armies of heaven with the splendor of his Essence. And Jehovah of Sabaoth, as I have said, can be called Jehovah Elohim, as much as to say, he that gives being to the hosts. And hence it comes to pass that the name of divinity is mingled with the names of angels, because his Essence is mingled with them. You see here that God has several Essences; for there can not be said to be several beings in one Essence, but quite the contrary. Indeed, I say that God himself is the Essences of all things, and all things are in him.

102b

BOOK VI

Argument

THE *incomprehensible God is known through Christ, by faith, rather than by philosophical speculations. He manifests God to us, being the expression of his very being; and through him alone God can be known. The Scriptures reveal him to those who have faith; and thus we come to know the Holy Spirit as the divine impulse working in us.*

Synopsis

1. God, incomprehensible in himself, is known through Christ, who was an aspect of him; while abstract philosophical conceptions of him are meaningless, and such are the phantasms of the philosophers. God is manifested through his Word in the face of Christ. 2. The vision of God is given to those who see Christ, for God is in him. 3. The Word, or oracle, originally with God, through which he spoke in the Old Testament, is now seen in Christ. 4. Christ is not the mere image of God, but the character, or expression, of his very being. 5. The philosophers do not understand what the character of God's hypostasis *can mean. 6. Christ is so called because in him alone God exists or can be known; the disposition of God which wrought everything in the world. 7. The Scriptures give us a revelation of the invisible God, if we have faith in Christ. 8. My conception of God comes by faith in Christ, through whom we approach him; but abstract philosophical conceptions are a delusion. 9. Knowledge of Christ leads to knowledge of the Holy Spirit, which is also invisible, and known by inner experience, 10. and illuminates us, as the divine impulse within us.*

BOOK THE SIXTH

102b 1. You will (if you have examined your capacity with the sober judgment of reason) easily recognize the knowledge of God which we obtain through CHRIST. For in himself God is incomprehensible; he can be neither imagined, nor understood, nor discovered by thinking, unless you contemplate some aspect[1] in him. And the likeness of Christ and the Person of the Word are just this. For the impersonated oracle of God, the Person of Christ, as I have said above,[2] which was with God, was God himself; nor was there in him any other aspect than that. And the face of Jesus Christ is just this. And the other conceptions which the Sophists boast of having concerning indivisible beings mean nothing. It is foolishness in the sight of God; they are bewitched by their own phantasms and phantoms, as I shall, please God, show elsewhere.[3] For this is the most certain truth, and evident to any man of sense, that we can have no conception of anything in the world, unless we observe some aspect or appearance in it. And if you force me to come down to fine points, a conception is not said to alter a thing by representing it in living form, except in so far as the image of that thing is presented to the mind by the phantasm itself. Again, every one knows that it is necessary for a thinking man to examine his phantasms. Let them tell me, then, what sort of figure it is, or what resemblance that phantasm has, which they examine when they have a conception of God. For it is quite certain that the phantasm, whatever it is, manifests a visible likeness, because there is no phantasm in the world which is not limited to a visible thing, just as they are also produced in us by visible things. Nor do they grasp how, by means of these visible things, things invisible are said to be understood in a mirror, darkly. As by means of a visible likeness of the Word we understand God, so from effects we argue that there is one first cause, from movements we reason that there is a prime mover, although of this Aristotle never had any real conception. These, says Paul, are things that can be known about God,[4] yet not that God himself is therefore known. Indeed, the whole discussion is nothing else than a shifting about of visible phantasms. But, waiving these matters, this becomes quite clear to us from the Scriptures alone; that God is manifested to us through his Word. And you ought to acknowledge this face in God, that you may know the glory of God in the face of Jesus Christ,[5] and may now know

---

[1] *Vultus.*   [2] Book IV, paragraph 6.   [3] Paragraph 8.
[4] I. Cor. ii, 11, 12.   [5] II. Cor. iv, 6.

God, whom you never knew before, nor ever saw his form. And εἶδος [1] here means the outward appearance and form and face of God, so that Christ here says that God can not be known save in his face. But in the face of Jesus Christ he is known, as though God manifested himself to me without a veil, with that visible countenance with which he appeared to Moses face to face. And if he plainly manifested to me that face which Moses did not see, I should see nothing else than the face of Jesus Christ. And this itself was the likeness of the Word, and in this way the invisible God manifests himself to us through the visible Word. And for this reason Christ is called the face of God, for that is called the face of anything through which that thing is seen and known. And, consideration of the Word apart, God is entirely invisible and unimaginable; nor would all the philosophers in the world be enough to form any conception of him; and all that they say about these things are blasphemies against Christ. For it ought to be found simply and frankly true, that God is seen through his Word, and, *He that seeth me seeth the Father*; and, no man hath seen him but through the Son.[2]

104a 2. But just as the accursed philosophers would have *God is a Spirit*[3] understood in a metaphysical sense, so they suppose that when it says, *No man hath seen God at any time*,[4] it is understood only of the vision of God with the bodily eye. Nor can they grasp the fact that the meaning of the Gospel aims at anything else when mention is so often made of the vision of God, who is seen through JESUS CHRIST, and who was never before either seen or heard. Do not wrest the meaning of the words in the raw way of the sophists, but always keep the order of the process. Bear in mind that the Apostles were as yet untaught men; and Christ says that they had already seen the Father. It says the same in I. John,[5] yet he had seen nothing else than the face of CHRIST. Notice in what sense they were asking these things, and the reply of Christ to the question they had put. And when it says, He that seeth me seeth the Father, note the expression, *seeth the Father*, and call this mental vision a con-

---

[1] *Eidos*, form.
[2] John i, 18; v, 37; vi, 46; viii, 19; xii, 45; xiv, 9.
[3] John iv, 24.   [4] John i, 18.   [5] I. John i, 1–3.

ception, a knowledge, or an understanding, or whatever you will; and in a corresponding sense admit to me that God was never seen before. Otherwise CHRIST would have brought us nothing new, would claim in vain that the Father was seen through him. If, then, God is seen in a new way through CHRIST (indeed, a complete vision of God was never had before through God himself), what can this vision be but the person of Elohim, which now shines forth in the face of JESUS CHRIST? And he expressly said he was *seen*, in order to disapprove the imaginary conceptions of the philosophers. Would that God might give them a mind that they might know him, and might say with John, We have seen his glory whom no man hath seen at any time.[1] Nor did John ever see anything else than this Person that was with God, and was himself God. And through the contrivance of God this reasoning is sound; by visibly looking into his face, God was seen, because God was just this, and the face of CHRIST is now just this; therefore God is seen in the face of CHRIST; and so, strictly speaking, JESUS CHRIST is now in God, just as that Word which was God himself was with God. And for this reason CHRIST proves that the Father is seen through him, because the Father is in him, and he is in the Father.[2] For you ought always to reflect upon what the looking at the oracle of God once was, and you should compare it with the face of CHRIST. And now say that God is seen more clearly, never forget, hear him still crying from heaven to-day, In seeing me you see God, in seeing me you see the Father.

3. From this it appears that the Word impersonated in such a countenance was not an articulate voice, and that it has no actual existence.[3] For John would not have said of it in itself, *The Word was*; but he said, *Was*, for the reason that it appeared to be self-existent.[4] Indeed, nothing else than the oracle seemed to exist, as though the invisible God lay concealed in it. And agreeably to the thought of John I would rather say *oracle* than *word* or *speech*;[5] and the thought of John is this: In the beginning there was a certain oracle with God, and this itself was the

[1] John i, 14, 18. [2] John xiv, 11.
[3] *Subsistentia.* [4] *Per se subsistens.*
[5] *Oraculum, verbum, sermo.*

light that could not be comprehended by those that were in darkness. But we saw him after he became flesh, because this itself is to-day the shining countenance of CHRIST. Moreover, the word oracle is appropriate to this subject, for this itself was the oracle which was covered and overshadowed by angels' wings,[1] the oracle through which God made answer to Moses;[2] and so this oracle was in the secret place of the house, just as CHRIST was hidden in the shadow of the Almighty. Again, the Hebrew word confirms this interpretation of the mystery; for from דבר,[3] which means *logos*, comes דביר,[4] which means the oracle of the temple.[5] For Christ is the true oracle, through which we receive God's answers, even as he is also called the propitiatory, that is, the propitiation for our sins;[6] a covering, on whose account blessed are they whose sins are covered.[7] And just as CHRIST is now the oracle, so once not only in the temple, but before that in the tabernacle, and even before the construction of the tabernacle, his person was the oracle whence Moses within the cloud received answers. There, moreover, was the light which according to John shone within the darkness of the cloud,[8] which ought to elicit all things from the law, though we care little for it.

105b

4. In consequence of this, notice that CHRIST is improperly called the image of God. Indeed, he is more than an image; for an image is when two things are formed in a similar way, and either one is called the image of the other. But in the case of CHRIST and God it is not just as if the angel Gabriel came to me in the form of a flying eagle. Should I say, This is the image of Gabriel? Even if it be truly called an image, it is more than an image, that is, a likeness or character representing, nay containing, his *hypostasis*. And the oracle could not properly be called the image of the Father, but more than an image; for it was its very self the face of God, and God himself was the likeness or a

---

[1] Ex. xxv, 20; xxxvii, 6–9 (Vulg.).
[2] Num. vii, 89 (Vulg.).   [3] *Dabar*, word.
[4] *Debir*, sanctuary (Vulg., *oraculum*).
[5] Ps. xxviii, 2; II. Chron. v, 7, 9; I. Kings vi, 5, 19–22.
[6] I. John ii, 2; iv, 10.
[7] Ps. xxxii, 1 (Vulg.); Rom. iv, 7.
[8] John i, 5.

kind of form containing the very being of God. Likewise CHRIST is more than an image, though words fail me in which I can explain this with my slow tongue. Nor can I say more clearly than Paul did, the *character* [1] of the *hypostasis* of God; that is, the carving in which the very being itself shines forth as if with its own face. David and Moses call it תמונה.[2] And mark well in what sense it is there called an image, when it says, *Ye saw no image*;[3] for if you take image here in that sense, you will judge rightly. For the image was there the very form of the face, with no regard to its resemblance to another imagined thing. And in this sense CHRIST will be called the εἰκών,[4] that is, the image of God, because he is the likeness, is a kind of representation of his *hypostasis*, or the very exhibition of a being by its outward appearance.[5] CHRIST is therefore properly called the εἰκών, that is the likeness, or a kind of carving-in, exhibiting the very being of God.[6] In like manner he is called the χαρακτήρ,[7] that is, the especial mark, of the *hypostasis*, that is, of the existence, of God, by seeing which I am said to see God, just as in seeing the Eagle I should be said to see Gabriel. Otherwise God would not be able to reveal himself to us in visible form. For if this could have been done, it has been done through a veiled view of the oracle, and at length through the unveiled face of JESUS CHRIST. For the very vision of his face is a vision of God, just as to Tobias himself the vision of the youth was the vision of an angel;[8] and when the dove was seen John said, *I have seen the Spirit of God descending.*[9]

5. From this it is plain that the philosophers are far astray in their investigation about this *character*. This argument, which they supposed was an Achillean[10] one against me, hasbecome a sword of Goliath[11] for them; nor were they ever able to prove why the Son is called the *character* of the *hypostasis* of God. They are strangely deceived when they speak of the

---

[1] Heb. i, 3, in the Greek.
[2] *Temunah*, image, form; Ps. xvii, 15; Deut. iv, 12, 15.
[3] Deut. iv, 12.   [4] *Eikon*, image.
[5] John v, 37.   [6] II. Cor. iv, 4; Col. i, 15.
[7] *Charakter*, an engraved or stamped figure; Heb. i, 3.
[8] Tobit v, 4.   [9] John i, 32.
[10] i. e., unanswerable.   [11] I. Sam. xvii, 51.

106b *hypostasis* of the Father, and not of the *hypostasis* of God; as if they were speaking of a metaphysical likeness of another being, and not of an image of God, although this is nevertheless the Gospel way of speaking, and even that of the Old Testament. Yet they avoid scripture ways of speaking by deriding everything. Nor is an image of the Father spoken of in their sense of the word, but a likeness of God, a *character* of God; indeed, Paul adds significantly, *the likeness of the invisible God*,[1] as though he said that in a visible man there was an εἰκών of the invisible God. And all this tends to explain the words of the Master, *He that hath seen me hath seen the Father*;[2] and, *If ye had known me, ye would have known my Father also*.[3] And to these sayings the Old Testament also gives the fullest testimony in the passages quoted above, in which mention is made of this image. And God calls this image *ours*,[4] because the one and the same face of CHRIST is that of both, and the very person of the oracle was the face and countenance of God.

<small>We ought to imagine some face in him who is called the image.</small>

6. CHRIST, therefore, is called an aspect, a face, a likeness, a sign, a character, a seal, a distinguishing mark, a kind of engraving, of the *hypostasis*, that is, of the being, of God; because in him alone God exists, nor can God be known through any one else. And just as the face of the sun appears in the midst of immensity and of light unapproachable, so in the midst of the heights and depths of God has appeared his oracle, the Person 107a of JESUS CHRIST. This itself was God, this itself is now the vision of God, this has been appointed to us for a sign, and in none other is there salvation,[5] nor is there any other vision of God, nor did John see anything else when he said, ἦν πρὸς τὸν θεόν.[6] This is the height and depth of the knowledge of CHRIST. This is the power, *disposition*, and *economy*, of God which wrought everything in the world, even as John also said, *All things were made through him*.[7] And to this end CHRIST ascended, was made the power and might of God, as the Master himself well taught us, saying, *Without me ye can do nothing*;[8] even as

---

[1] Col. i, 15. [2] John xiv, 9.
[3] John xiv, 7. [4] Gen. i, 26. [5] Acts iv, 12.
[6] *En pros ton theon*, was with God, John i, 1.
[7] John i, 3. [8] John xv, 5.

without God we can do nothing. For all the might of God is through him, all things were made through CHRIST in power, all things were made through CHRIST in the Word, all things were made through CHRIST in Person — not only made, that is, created from the beginning, but the whole process and order of the world was carried on through his *economy*. His own glorious face, which was once covered by a cloud in the midst of light unapproachable, to-day shines forth revealed. And with equal propriety [it may be said that] CHRIST is now in God, even in reality, just as he was formerly with him in Person. And the energy flowing from that oracle, as it were the breath of his mouth, was called the Spirit of God; for it was the breath of Elohim CHRIST,[1] since to-day it is holy to us, flowing from the mouth of CHRIST.[2] And in the same book[3] he gave a natural spirit of life, even as also to-day by his own inspiration he has given us a supernatural one. And more mysteries yet lie concealed here; for after the likeness of this oracle, the Holy Spirit proceeds in us from the oracles of Scripture, as rivers of living water. For it is the same spirit of his mouth, from the eternal oracle, and from the mouth of CHRIST, and from the oracles of Scripture; and this very energy and power of the oracle is the eternal spirit of CHRIST, of which I have spoken above.[4]

He hath made the darkness his hiding-place.

7. If you ask why we speak of God, and say so much about him, if we do not know him, nor have any conception of him, Paul replies to this that *the Spirit searcheth all things, yea, the deep things of God*;[5] and those things which are invisible God reveals unto us through his Spirit,[6] which is hidden in the sacred Scriptures. For I endeavor to learn those things which are contained in the Bible concerning God. But the things that I have acquired through philosophical conceptions are of no value for instructing us. A book has been given us from heaven, so that in it we may search after God, faith assisting us to this end, which is not the superficial assent of the sophists, but an emotion of the heart; as the Scripture says, *With the heart man believeth*,[7] and, *If thou believest with all thy heart*.[8] And for the

---

[1] Gen. i, 2. [2] John xx, 22. [3] Gen. ii, 7.
[4] Paragraph 3. [5] I. Cor. ii, 10. [6] I. Cor. ii, 7–10.
[7] Rom. x, 10. [8] Acts viii, 37 (Vulg.; cf. R. V. marg.).

object of this faith any outward manifestation of God suffices, without the philosophical conception of God. This consideration alone destroys the philosophical conception, because any man has his own imagination of God, and one different from any other man. Again, faith in CHRIST helps wonderfully toward this end, because through it we receive the Spirit; and unless you have first believed that JESUS CHRIST is the Son of God, you will never understand yourself. This is the foolishness, or rather, the heavenly philosophy, which is derived not from Aristotle, but most fully and clearly from divine sources, if we follow the scripture manner of speaking. For in the words themselves lie hidden the Spirit and wisdom, as well as the style of wisdom; for every word, every Scripture inspired of God, is profitable for teaching, correction, and instruction.[1]

Nor are we capable of understanding a single letter, except he reveal it by his Spirit.

8. And I reply to the question,[2] that I have a conception of God, and this conception is the vision of his oracle; and it is the vision itself by which, when I see it, the Father is seen in a mirror, darkly. And here is learned the Christians' true faith in CHRIST, which is therefore called an indication of things not seen.[3] Yet the Philosophers, who know everything, who have conceptions of everything, have no need of faith. Indeed, CHRIST has really become superfluous for them, because they do not know God now otherwise than before. But we know that a visible manifestation of the mystery has been made; we know that God is seen through CHRIST. God determined thus, and wished to regard himself in that mirror, as he had before done through the sight of the oracle. And for Christians this vision of God suffices to the fullest degree, so that through it we enjoy the invisible Spirit of God. For CHRIST is the way, and we ought to approach God in the spirit through him, and not through these conceptions; which is quite the opposite of what they have done. They have seemed to themselves to touch the three mathematical beings with their own senses, although there is nothing of which they had less knowledge than of these. They say that a conception is a sort of quality abstracted from phantasms, and

---

[1] II. Tim. iii, 16.
[2] i. e., raised in the previous paragraph.
[3] Heb. xi, 1.

also located in their heels. But God will sometime put an end to this nonsense. It distresses me that it is not only a mathematical delusion of the imagination, but also a horrible slander against the teaching of Christ. Let it suffice for them to pretend to have imaginations in their heads, without seeking for conceptions in their heels. Other than those through CHRIST, let them not trifle with visions about God. For even if they saw all the angels in heaven with open eye, yet God is still more deeply hidden, clad in angelic raiment, like a skin spread out. Nor let the philosophers here assail me regarding the nature of the angels, as to which I have no knowledge; for I do not say *spread out* in a local sense, for the skill of God is superior to place. Most foolish of men, they reduce to a kind of point all that is outside their bodies. They have reached such folly as to say that God himself is, as it were, a point many times repeated in the same plane. Is this the conception of God of which they boast? I pray God that his Spirit may touch them when they read these things, lest perchance they be to them a savor of death unto death.[1]

All the heresies in the world have arisen from ignorance of Christ.

9. If they admit this very plain way of seeing God, they will better understand what the Spirit of God, and the Holy Spirit, is; for it all depends upon knowledge of CHRIST, and if we are ignorant of this, we are ignorant of everything. And it should be known that although three *hypostases* are commonly admitted, yet more properly speaking I say that in God there were two *dispositions*, namely, an oracle and a Spirit; and the visible *hypostasis* was in the oracle alone. For no kind of seeing is properly attributed to that which is in its nature a spirit, nor is there in it the face of a permanent being as there is in an oracle;

There was but one hypostasis, namely, the Person of the Word.

nor is the Spirit said to have been made any such thing as the oracle was made flesh. But we know it not by the sole fact that we see a breath, but because we perceive it within;[2] and, as it were, by hearing, as CHRIST says.[3] And so there appeared, as it were, tongues of fire, and a mighty sound was heard;[4] and it pleased God that the Spirit be poured upon them in a visible Person that we might have the greater certainty concerning

---

[1] II. Cor. ii, 16. [2] John xiv, 17.
[3] John iii, 8. [4] Acts ii, 2, 3.

this divine *disposition*. And though that vision does not remain for us, yet we know by experience that it is in us.¹ Hereby we know, as John says, that we abide in him, because we perceive the working of the Spirit in us.² Give heed, I beseech you, to 109b CHRIST, and you shall know his Spirit; for the glorious advent of JESUS CHRIST has wrought such great things that all things have been changed, a new heaven, a new earth.³ He has made us to ascend into heaven, heaven has been opened, and his oracle having been made visible, God has disclosed himself to us. We have entered the gates of God, seeing the things that lay hidden in him, and touching his Word with our hands, and perceiving his Spirit within ourselves. I have already at the beginning ⁴ said of the oracle that there is no other Person of the oracle in God except Christ JESUS himself, as though the oracle had withdrawn from God when it became flesh; yet it did not really withdraw, but CHRIST ascended to God, and thence he brought heaven with himself to us. *We perceive all these things by faith in Christ, for want of which the Lutherans know not what the kingdom of Christ is, nor his Gospel.*

10. Correspondingly I say of the Spirit, that the Spirit of God, as it were, withdrew from God when it was sent to the Apostles.⁵ Yet it did not really withdraw, but we ascended to God, and he has made us to sit with CHRIST in the heavenly places. Nor is the Holy Spirit to us a being placed on high. But by the wonderful contrivance of God a dark being is made bright because of his presence, just as the face of JESUS CHRIST became bright on the mount, apart from union with any being coming upon him; and this comparison you will find in Scripture.⁶ Say, then, that the Holy Spirit is a divine impulse in the spirit of man. Thus what God illuminates by impelling, he also 110a sanctifies by illuminating. Nor is any quidditative ⁷ definition required here; for the word *spirit* is used of a kind of movement, like the motion of an impulse and of a breath; and because God, by thus moving them, sanctifies those that believe in CHRIST, therefore the Spirit in man is called Holy, and that because of faith in CHRIST. *Explanation about the Holy Spirit.*

¹ John xiv, 17; II. Cor. xiii, 3, 5.   ² I. John iv, 13.
³ Rev. xxi, 1, 5.   ⁴ Paragraph 1.
⁵ Acts ii, 3, 4.   ⁶ Matt. xvii, 2; II. Cor. iii, 18.
⁷ Constituting the essence of the thing.

BOOK VII

Argument

THE eternally begotten Son was a spoken word by which God made himself known. The Hebrew shows that the whole nature of God abode in Christ as Elohim, man being blended with God. The Word was a disposition of God, who begot the Son, a visible being. The Holy Spirit also is a real being, as Christ was. The Word was an actual being, creating all things, manifesting God in bodily form.

Synopsis

1. The Word was the Son, eternally begotten, not by way of emanation, but as a spoken word. 2. God used the Word to make himself known, though unseen, and this we know as the Son. 3. The Monarchian heresies as to the deity of Christ came of ignorance of the Hebrew. 4. Christ was Elohim, really the Father. 5. The Father abides in him, the whole Nature and glory of God are in him. In Christ man was blended, rather than united, with God. 6. The Word is a disposition of God, and shares all his qualities, as a statue shares those of the stone from which it was carved. 7. God especially begot the Son, and thus gave us life through him. 8. The hypostasis was a visible being, hence called a Person. 9. The Holy Spirit also is audible to the senses, hence is a real being and not a mere philosophical abstraction. 10. David speaks of Christ by the name, Jah, thus indicating an actual being, which Simon Magus tried to counterfeit. 11. The Logos, then, had actual existence in the body of Christ, as Irenaeus and Ignatius clearly show. 12. This is confirmed by the Hebrew use of the term, word, as applied to any objective existence or act. 13. Every event is thus a word of God. 14. All things came into being through Christ, the creative Word. 15. The transcendent God has been manifested to us in the law, in the Prophets, and in Christ. 16. John teaches that God had no bodily form, but that he became flesh in Christ.

BOOK THE SEVENTH

110a 1. With regard to filiation among divine beings, and the divinity of CHRIST, and the *hypostasis* of the Word, questions are usually asked which I shall clear up with a few words. I say that from the beginning there was among the divine beings a filiation, not real but personal. The Son was the Word; the Son was not real but personal, in so far as it was the Person of CHRIST. Nor is he in Scripture ever called Son, but an eternal kind of generation is attributed to CHRIST, and the things that were in the law were a shadow of the body of Christ. Yet some dream here of an emanation of a conception, or of a Word, from the divine mind, by means of an emanating filiation. But their dreams carry little conviction unless they prove by Scripture that the Word was a real Son; and these emanations are remains left over from the emissions of the Valentinians;[1] these emissions or emanations from within are mathematical, and un-
110b known to the Scriptures. Even the word emanation smacks somewhat of the philosophical, which can not be included in the Nature of God. For that which has emanated from God is CHRIST himself, who came forth from the Father. But in God, within, there are no goings forth, nor emanations; but CHRIST was formed beforehand in the divine mind. There was a certain way of keeping himself which God arranged in himself in order that he might manifest himself to us; namely, by representing in himself the likeness of JESUS CHRIST, for all this was foreordained for exhibiting the glory of CHRIST. And John did not say that the Word emanated from God, but it was in God, and, *the Word was God.*[2] And *logos* does not signify reason, that is an inner and philosophical conception of the understanding, or a mental concept, as some fancifully say; but the *logos* is called a sort of speaking, it means a vocal reason, as it were, an oral reasoning, corresponding to the nature of the word λέγω.[3] Nor

The logos, a way of speaking.

---

[1] A sect of second-century Gnostics. cf. Tertullian, adv. Valentin. (MPL. ii, 525 ff.; ANF. iii, 503 ff.; ANCL. xv, 119 ff.), and Irenaeus, adv. Haer. (MPG. vii, 433 ff.; ANF. i, 315 ff.; ANCL. v).   [2] John i, 1.
[3] *Lego*, to speak, as etymologically related to *logos*.

is it otherwise ever found in place of reason among Greeks of approved speech; which you should note constantly. For the deception consists solely in the imaginary nature of the word *logos*. And consider well what the word λέγω properly signifies, and you shall see that it means oracle, of which I have made mention above.

The end of the disposition of the Word: that God may manifest himself.

2. Again, their false imagination is seen in consequence of the establishment of the divine *economy*; for God, of his mere good pleasure, employed this kind of word for the purpose of disclosing himself to us, just as he formerly disclosed himself (though dimly) through it. For the Word was visible; and to all this John has regard, adding at once, *No man hath seen God at any time.* [2] For he related the progress in the Old Testament, comparing Moses with CHRIST; and you, unless you have regard to the Old Testament, will never understand the New, because it is wholly derived from the Old. But why do I search for other proofs, when it has been shown in the preceding Book [3] that these conceptions of the philosophers are nothing but imaginatively mathematical delusions; and to any man of sense this will be the strongest of reasons; so that it is necessary here to look upon the face of Elohim. There was, then, an oracle, a *hypostasis* of God, a Person of CHRIST, the divinity which was Son to God himself alone. Yet to us CHRIST alone is called Son. The being was future to us; but to God nothing is future. There was in God the very image of a being that to us was future; as if I now saw in a mirror a being that is not, but will be tomorrow. For this is the height and depth of the divine *economy*; and the Word, which formerly was with God, has to us become the Son. And it makes no difference, even if you say that the Son was with God; indeed, I say that CHRIST was with God, who afterwards came and was incarnated.

111a

According to Irenaeus the Word is visible.[1]

As to the second question.

3. Paul is forever trying to explain to us the deity in CHRIST, even with greater fulness than can be thought out; but not through the union with a metaphysical Son. For why should the Apostle exclaim at the great fulness and breadth, the unsearchable brightness of the Godhead, the riches, glory, etc.,

111b

---

[1] Adv. Haer. IV, vi, 5 (MPG. vii, 989; ANF. i, 468; ANCL. v, 391).
[2] John i, 18.   [3] Book VI, paragraph 8.

that are in CHRIST? What need would there have been of so many words, except to say that the second being was carnally united with CHRIST, although this was never heard of in the Scriptures? If therefore you consider well, an investigation of Paul condemns their metaphysics. But that I may the better explain this matter, I shall relate the origin of these fancies about the Godhead. Paul of Samosata, previous to the Arian and trinitarian[1] philosophers, being entirely ignorant of the mysteries of CHRIST which are hidden in the Hebrew, by maintaining that CHRIST was a mere man, not God, and that he first existed then and not previously, scandalized the Greek philosophers, who were also ignorant of Hebrew, and infected by the contagion of Aristotle, and forced them to ascend to heaven without wings, where any one who would began to hunt for divinities in his own sense; and immediately there arose a countless swarm of heretics. And I suppose it was a sentence of divine punishment that the Pope was made King at the same time at which the Trinity arose; even as God also raised up many adversaries against Solomon at just the time of his sin.[2]

<small>Two very serious plagues, a leaven of Aristotle, and ignorance of the Hebrew language, deprived us of Christ. And then we lost Christ.</small>

112a 4. Let us then, that we may avoid such labyrinths of error, speak of his divinity more soberly; and we have above in many ways searched into these riches in CHRIST, although I seem to myself to have said nothing in comparison with his worth; nor could Paul set this forth otherwise than by exclaiming, Length, breadth, treasures, mysteries![3] Nevertheless I shall recall to mind certain things that proclaim his divinity, of which the root is that you keep in memory that he was Elohim. And from this you will consider the depth of the mystery, how he was in the oracle with the Father from the beginning, and in what way he is really the Father now, as he was personally in him before. We have mentioned above the brightness of his face, from which the whole world is to be lighted; although the philosophers consider that the face of his human nature, like that of another man, is now in heaven, and superfluous. But the divine transfiguration on the mount, and the vision of Paul, confounds

<small>Christ makes much of this light, for it was not the quality, but the natural splendor, of God.</small>

[1] See Book I, paragraph 48, note 2.
[2] I. Kings xi, 14, 23.
[3] Eph. iii, 18; Col. i, 27.

them. They close their eyes, lest they see him shouting from heaven and saying, He that seeth me seeth the Father.¹ This vision alone, if you often enjoy it, will transport you quite to heaven, and cleanse you from all error.

There is no other face, nor person, nor hypostasis of God, save Christ.

5. Another proclamation of his divinity, which surpasses all these, is the Father abiding in him, who is seen by him alone. He himself is the face of the Father, nor is there any other Person of God but CHRIST; there is no other *hypostasis* of God but him. Christ is honored by the presence of the Father more than he can be honored through their metaphysics. They say that one portion, I say that the whole Nature, of God is in him. In him is the whole Deity of the Father, in so much that even the angels marvel at this. And not only is God present in him, but the whole authority of God has been given him. Although they ascribe none of these things to the man, yet I say that he is God and the Lord of the world. The glory of the Father is in his spirit to a much more exceptional degree than the light can appear in his face. It would then dim this manifold fulness of Deity to be contented with a mere union with the second being; nor can this be done, unless you make the Son separate from the Father, or remove the Father from CHRIST; for there is in him nothing that can be called Son save the Father himself alone; therefore CHRIST is called the Son, and the Father is in the Son. If they speak to you of some ray ² in the man, you may quote against them the words of the Master, namely: *The Father is in me; the Father abiding in me.*³ And in heeding these words no one can ever be deceived; nor have they been able to find out like words against you. And their error as to the mathematical ray arises from the Word of John not being understood. They believe that the ray was united with CHRIST through the Word become flesh; though it is one thing to be united, another to become flesh. Again, John did not say, The Word *became* flesh,⁴ as they take it; but, The Word *was* flesh, the Word *existed* as flesh; and this is the most proper meaning of ὁ λόγος σὰρξ

Here are two Natures in Christ: the whole Nature and power of God are in the man.

---

¹ John xiv, 9.

² As the ray to the sun, was one of the illustrations by which was explained the relation of the Son to the Father.

³ John x, 38; xiv, 10, 11; xvii, 21.　　　　⁴ John i, 14.

ἐγένετο.¹ For that which was the Person of the Word is now Christ himself. Would that we had read, The Word *was* flesh; just as it says in the same place, There *was* a man sent from God;² for it is the same word in Greek.³ Likewise, all things *were* through him, and without him there *was* nothing;⁴ as also, He spake and they *were*;⁵ God said, Let there be light, and light *was*.⁶ For the Hebrew word here has this perfectly clear meaning; and John used the word which God used at the beginning of the world; and in place of היה⁷ he used ἐγένετο, as the Greek translation also clearly shows; even as he also used λόγος⁸ in place of דבר.⁹ The older writers say that man was blended, rather than united, with God. But even if you say that man was united with God, or God united with man, or that a kind of Deity was united with CHRIST, I shall not condemn you; this, however, is not by way of filiation, for this ἰδιότης¹⁰ or kind of filiation is in man alone, nor was this ἰδιότης naturally appropriate τῷ λόγῳ,¹¹ except in so far as it was a *figure*¹² of the man. And this is the view of Irenaeus,¹³ and also of Tertullian,¹⁴ who say that the change was made from the Word to flesh, and that along with this a kind of Deity was blended and united with the man, because God in CHRIST is just this.

6. For there are two things to be considered, the being and the Person. God is the being itself, and the Word is the *disposition*, and the Word was God; and every quality in the Nature of the Word has passed over to the man, who is now in God in the same way in which the Word was formerly with God. And with this the being itself is altogether united and blended;¹⁵

[Marginal note: Elohim, in Person man, and in Nature God; which you should keep perpetually in mind.]

---

¹ *Ho logos sarx egeneto*, the Word became flesh.
² John i, 6.
³ ἐγένετο, became, or was; also in the three references following.
⁴ John i, 3.   ⁵ Ps. xxxiii, 9.
⁶ Gen. i, 3.   ⁷ *Hahyah*, was.
⁸ *Logos*, word. ⁹ *Dabar*, word.
¹⁰ *Idiotes*, peculiar quality.
¹¹ *To logo*, to the Word.
¹² *Caelatura*, a figure carved in relief; and so where the word is used below.
¹³ Adv. haer. V, i, 3 (MPG. vii, 1122 f.; ANF. i, 527; ANCL. ix, 58).
¹⁴ Adv. Praxean xxvii (MPL. ii, 190 ff.; ANF. iii, 623; ANCL. xv, 396).
¹⁵ Assuming that *innixa* in the text is a misprint for *immixta*, as used in the preceding paragraph.

because *God was in* Christ, *reconciling the world*.[1] Again, consider what the expression, *figure* means, and you shall see that you have been deceived by your mathematical fancy, for the very thing that *was*, was a *figure* of Christ. A text is clear which to former ages was unintelligible: I will carve, he says, his *figure*.[2] In the Hebrew this is what it says: הנני מפתח פתחה,[3] that is, Behold I, carving, or laying bare, his figure or image, just as an artificer fashions a statue by carving a stone and laying it bare. For פתח [4] means, as it were, to carve a stone by laying bare, and with a graving-tool to uncover a hidden form; and in this way, when the divine stone was cut out of the mountain,[5] the form in it which formerly lay hidden in darkness was laid bare. With this the Chaldee interpreter [6] agrees, who renders it, Who turns his face to be revealed; for thus the Targum of Jonathan has it, הא אנא ללי הזייתהא [7] that is, Behold, I reveal, or open, his vision. And, to say it in a word, both the law and all the prophets very frequently mingle with their histories and prophecies of Christ the words *face, statue, hidden, concealed, habitation, shadow*, because the Spirit of the Lord has *carved* these words (which, as Christ says,[8] were all written of him in the law and all the Prophets), that under the silver figure may be hidden the golden word which by the secret purpose of God is concealed in historic types as if under a kind of covering even as Christ himself was covered under figures; and to wish, apart from this consideration, to apply the prophecies to Christ is to be wanting in sense, in which matter the Jews accuse us with good reason.

To the third question.

7. It is nothing to the prejudice of the *hypostasis* of the Word that I have said that it is the voice of God. For even Peter says that there was a foreknowledge of Christ, by which he was foreknown and foreordained before the foundation of the world, and was manifested afterwards.[9] And this is just

---

[1] II. Cor. v, 19. [2] Zech. iii, 9.
[3] *Hinneni mephatteach pittuchah*, Behold, I will engrave his engraving.
[4] *Pathach*, to open, hence to carve.
[5] Dan. ii, 45.
[6] i. e., the Targum, the Aramaic version of the Old Testament.
[7] Aram., *Ha ana laley hezyathaha* (the third word is a misprint for וגלי).
[8] Luke xxiv, 27; Matt. xi, 13. [9] I. Pet. i, 20.

what Jeremiah calls *the intents of his heart*.¹ Yet the Sophists here will hear of nothing else, generally speaking, than that CHRIST was predestined even as one of us. But far from me be such folly. They will not marvel at miracles of divine contrivance, so that they prefer to admit that God can not have especial regard to one particular being rather than another without any qualities. The Son was begotten of God by a distinct and special word, as truly begotten as the world was created. Indeed, by the same power of utterance by which he begot him, he created the world, made the light, and gave beings their life; and in no other way will he give us life than by the generation of the Son. Again, God made himself visible according to the likeness of CHRIST; and he governed the world by that oracle just as CHRIST now governs it. CHRIST was then with God in power, in the Word, and in Person. If all these things apply to them as well as to CHRIST let the Sophists say that they were predestined to be Christs.

[margin: 114b] [margin: Light and life are through him. John i, 4.]

8. This *hypostasis*, therefore, John commends to us by saying, *The Word was*,² and he shows that it was visible. For he declares to us a being that can be perceived, just as he, also, understood it by perception. Nor is it any objection if you say that he knew this by revelation of the Holy Spirit; for the revelation of the Holy Spirit is adapted to the capacity of man, otherwise it were delusion and not revelation. For John was a man, and had a common intelligence, even as we. Paul also appeals to visions and revelations;³ and so it always says, The vision of the Prophet, the vision of the Prophecy. Reflect and consider what it is that is representing itself to the mind of John when he begins to relate. For when we relate a deed we say that only that was which we perceive, and only the likeness of the oracle was in the mind of John; hence that was a divinity, he well said, which began to be called a Person by the older writers for the reason that a face was represented. And the Greek article helps somewhat here, as if pointing out visibly; and a like article is wont to be added in the Hebrew: in the beginning was *the* speech, *the* oracle. Lift up your eyes and see.

[margin: 115a] [margin: Consider here why it began to be called a Person.]

¹ Jer. xxiii, 20; xxx, 24.   ² John i, 1.
³ II. Cor. xii, 1.

9. Nor is the case different with the Holy Spirit; for he who feels that there is a spirit in himself speaks of it as distinctly as if he would point it out with his finger. But this being is unknown to the philosophers. Nevertheless, the power of the *dispositions* of God is in the highest degree admirable, so that they thus exhibit the *hypostasis* of a visible being. And Scripture speaks distinctly of those things that are distinctly perceived; attends rather to our capacity, or ways of perceiving, than to our philosophies. But we are mad, being unwilling to be instructed from that which adapts itself to us so closely, and bids us try and prove ourselves whether we perceive the Spirit in us, rather than inquire what being it is, or of what Nature. For I have often borne witness that in Scripture there is never any treatment of the Natures. Consider furthermore whether (if you were John the son of Zebedee, and not a philosopher), if you heard the voice of a being whom you do not see, having kept the thought of the voice, you would say, when about to tell of it afterwards, The voice was so and so, and it kept itself thus and so. Much more, then, could this be said of the Word that was visible and had existence. This is the *hypostasis* of the oracle which John and his elder disciples recommend by the word, *being*; for there was an existence there which could be perceived by itself, and a clear apprehension of the Person whose brightness, as John says, the darkness did not apprehend.[1] Indeed, nothing else than the oracle seemed to exist; hence it says of the Word alone, *It was*.

That very one whom you see before your eyes moves the spirit within.

It never says of the third being, It was.

10. This same *hypostasis* David recommends to us by the word, *Jah*. Speaking of Elohim CHRIST he bids us praise him by his name, which is יה,[2] that is, the existing Substance of a *hypostasis*. Exalt by his name Jah, he says, him that rideth through the deserts.[3] Likewise, speaking of CHRIST, he says that a people which shall be created shall praise Jah,[4] that is, him who exists, who is, CHRIST; just as he himself says, I am.[5] Moses also in his song calls him Jesua, Jah, EL, and Elohim.[6] And because he is called Jah, the Father is called Jehovah;

---

[1] John i, 5.
[2] Jah.
[3] Ps. lxviii, 4.
[4] Ps. cii, 18.
[5] Ex. iii, 14.
[6] Ex. xv, 2.

that is, he will give being to him that exists, or will make him to be CHRIST. Elohim CHRIST himself recommends the same *hypostasis* of himself, saying, *I shall be that I shall be.*[1] And after he became flesh, CHRIST himself said that he was, and was from the beginning,[2] because the Father caused him to be Jah, that is, a *hypostasis*, even from the beginning. And CHRIST is called ישב קדם,[3] that is, he that abideth of old, or remaineth from the beginning. Wonderfully well, then, did John, being instructed by the Master, say, *He was*; since Christ said before, *I shall be*; and David said, *being*. And once again the Master, I am from the beginning,[4] and in the Apocalypse, *Who was, who is, who is to come.*[5] And see the craftiness of the devilish spirit, by which the truth is nevertheless praised. Simon Magus, in order that he might throw the preaching of Christ into confusion, had himself called, *He that standeth*, and said that he was *He that standeth* from the beginning, so that those that did not believe him might not believe Christ either. Indeed, after the likeness of Christ he said that he was the one that had given the law to Moses on Mount Sinai; for all this is very truly said of Christ.[6]

11. Since, then, in consequence of this examination, things stand thus, reflect whether, if the Gospel by John had not yet been written, if no mention had ever in the world been made of the Trinity, but a question had arisen only about the Person of Christ, and Ebion and Cerinthus [7] were appearing again, you could explain the matter in more suitable words. Nor do I think that a mind capable of reasoning can penetrate the subject so that so great a matter can be better related in few words,

---

[1] Ex. iii, 14 (Pagn.).   [2] John viii, 58.
[3] *Josheb kedem*; Ps. lv, 19.   [4] John viii, 58.
[5] Rev. i, 4, 8; iv, 8.

[6] cf. Acts viii, 9–24; Clementine Recognitions, I, lxxii; II, vii, xi; Homilies, II, xxiv (MPG. i, 1246, 1251, 1254; ii, 91; ANF. viii, 96, 99, 100, 233; ANCL. iii, 189, 196, 199; xvii, 43).

[7] Ebion, erroneously supposed founder of the Ebionites, heretical Jewish Christians who denied the virgin birth of Christ. cf. Origen, contra Celsum, v, 61; Tertullian, adv. omnes haeres., iii (MPG. xi, 1278; ANF. iv, 570; iii, 651; ANCL. xxiii, 330 ff.; xviii, 265).

Cerinthus, a Gnostic teacher at the end of the first century, who taught that Jesus was the son of Joseph. cf. Irenaeus, adv. haeres. I, xxvi, 1, III, xi, 1 (MPG. vii, 686, 880; ANF. i, 351 f., 426; ANCL. v, 97, 287 f.).

and so agreeably to all other Scriptures of both the Old Testament and the New. For by just raising my eyes I see the oracle 116b coming from everlasting in the vision of John,[1] see JESUS CHRIST coming on the clouds of heaven with Daniel watching him,[2] riding in the chariot of Ezekiel,[3] and among the myrtle-trees of Zechariah,[4] and seated upon the throne of Isaiah.[5] And since this was a contrivance of the divine reason, I am bound to say that it was the Logos. Nor can I better explain this otherwise than by saying, It was; and for this reason Irenaeus,[6] while never abandoning the words of John, even though he does not actually distinguish the Logos from the Father, yet never fails to magnify this *hypostasis* of the Word, always employing this distinct way of speaking. And along with this, he always had his aim fixed upon Christ; and if you have yours fixed likewise, you will admit far more concerning the Word or oracle, provided that when there has been mention of the Son you do not turn away from Christ, for the Word came to be flesh.[7] *Behold, I myself that spoke am here;*[8] and, *They shall see eye to eye.*[9] What blind man even does not see this? I am he, the very one whom you perceive with your eyes and touch with your hands. The likeness of God is now a body. This was the same as God, and this is now the same as man, and remains God, and is in God as heretofore. It was hitherto a certain kind of divine reason, hence a *logos*; but it is now in form as a man, like unto us, the form of God shining forth in man; it has put on flesh, as it were, although this is the same as man mingled with divinity. Likewise, if you read Ignatius,[10] the disciple of John the Evan- 117a gelist, you will find the same expression as in Irenaeus; and I

Note that the said visions prove that it was the Logos.

---

[1] Rev. i, 7.   [2] Dan. vii, 13.
[3] Ezek. i.   [4] Zech. i, 8, 10, 11.
[5] Isa. vi, 1.
[6] Adv. haeres. II, ii, 4, 5; IV, vi, 1–6; xx, 1–4; V, xviii (MPG. vii, 714 f., 986–989, 1032–1034, 1172–1175; ANF. i, 361 f., 467–469, 487 f., 546 f.; ANCL. v, 122 f., 389–392, 439–441; ix, 103–106).
[7] John i, 14.   [8] Isa. lii, 6 (Vulg.).
[9] Isa. lii, 8.
[10] Ep. ad Ephes. vii, xviii, xx; ad Magnes. vi, viii, xi; ad Trall. x; ad Smyrn. i, ii; ad Polyc. iii (MPG. v, 650 f., 659, 662, 667, 670 f., 682, 707–710, 722; ANF. i, 52, 57, 61–63, 70, 86 f., 94; ANCL. i, 153 f., 165, 168, 177 f., 180, 184, 202, 240 f., 260).

beg you to observe this and not to depart from the ancient tradition in a single point, and then you will easily reject all the new inventions, blasphemies, and follies of our age.

12. The matter will turn out to be far more easy if we do not overlook the Hebraisms here, seeing that John was a Hebrew. For everything that exists, of whatever kind it is, and the doing of anything whatever, is called by the Hebrews a *word*; and in this sense the Word concerning the Christ to come was already from the beginning with God, since it was already being discussed in the secret counsels of God. And the Hebrews, when they have any business to do, say, I have a word for you; and, *He sent his word*,[1] when he spoke in order that anything might be done anywhere; and, *A word went forth from the face of the king*;[2] *I will bring my word*;[3] *Thy word shall come*;[4] *When that comes which thou hast said*.[4] And thus Manoah said to the angel, *When thy word comes*, and, *When thy word has come*,[5] namely, that which thou hast spoken concerning Samuel. And, *Until there come word from you and ye tell me*;[6] and, *When the word of the prophet shall come*.[7] And in this sense came the Word which was already with God from the beginning, until the matter went on so far that the mystery was revealed, and the Word came to be flesh. And thus these Hebraisms teach us not a little as to the *hypostasis* of the Word, as I said,[8] without being at all prejudicial. By a like Hebraism is verified what the shepherds said: *Let us see this word that is come to pass*.[9] And, *To you is the word of this salvation sent forth*;[10] and, *The word told to you through the Gospel*;[11] and, *He committed unto us the word of reconciliation*.[12] But, passing by these things which are rather remote from our design, let us take others which are more to the purpose; and there is an example which manifestly pertains to this figure of the Word of CHRIST, where it says, when the Israelites were pining away in the desert, *He sent his word and healed*

---

[1] Ps. cvii, 20; cxlvii, 18.
[2] Dan. ii, 15 (Vulg.).
[3] Jer. xxv, 13; xxxix, 16.
[4] Apparently two different renderings of Jud. xiii, 17.
[5] Jud. xiii, 12, 17 (Pagn.).
[6] II. Sam. xv, 28 (Pagn.).
[7] Jer. xxviii, 9 (Pagn.).
[8] See paragraph 7.
[9] Luke ii, 15.
[10] Acts xiii, 26 (Vulg.).
[11] I. Pet. i, 25.
[12] II. Cor. v, 19.

them.[1] And Joseph, being sent by God into Egypt, was kept in fetters *until his word came.*[2] And, *The Lord sent a word into Jacob,*[3] because he declared the overthrow of the ten tribes; and, *After seventy years are passed in Babel, I will arouse my word.*[4] And he afterwards aroused the same word concerning CHRIST.[5] Likewise it says, *Thine all-powerful word, leaping from heaven,*[6] because he said that at midnight the firstborn should be slain. For this going forth is the interpretation of what the Lord had said, *I will go out in the midst of Egypt.*[7] For Peter explained to us above that CHRIST was the author of all these things; for יהוה[8] went forth by his oracle; and thus the Chaldee version[9] very often interprets these things through the noun, *word.* You see, therefore, that the expression of the sacred language in which all these mysteries are laid down, constrains us to say that on account of the divine action and *disposition,* the Word went, came, and was sent; for CHRIST wrought all these things, and the oracle went to kill and to save them, just as afterwards it came to save us by the manifestation of itself.

118a

13. If we would here add anything else in our sense, we can not but go astray, and in the end there will be a war of words. For these two rules are infallible: first, that we can not divide the Nature of God; second, that which is an accident of the Nature is a *disposition.* From the fact that דבר[10] means *thing,*[11] some draw the conclusion that there are several beings. But this meaning of the word points in another direction; for when it says that God makes a good word, a bad word, it is a Hebraism, which is not free from mystery, but indicates a causal quality of the word. Just as *no word* means to them much the same as *nothing*; because in that case God did not speak. And the Prophets, when they prophesy some future thing, are wont to add that the Lord hath spoken it; for they intimate that the word of God belongs to everything, to every action. For he speaks, and they are done, and nothing is done unless he speaks;

Evils come to pass in Christendom because the Lord speaks.

---

[1] Ps. cvii, 20 (Vulg.).
[2] Ps. cv, 17–19 (Vulg.).
[3] Isa. ix, 8.
[4] Jer. xxix, 10 (Pagn.).
[5] Jer. xxxiii, 14.
[6] Wisdom xviii, 15.
[7] Ex. xi, 4.
[8] Jehovah.
[9] The Targums.
[10] *Dabar,* word, thing.
[11] *Res,* thing, being.

yet this is not to say that *dabar* is the absolute equivalent of *res*.

118b   14. In fine, you shall consider the divine purpose as though the world were to be created to-day, and in what way God determined to do it; and from this you will understand his *oeconomy*, both in the creation of the world and in the giving of the law, which things all lead to the glory of CHRIST. For all things take their rise from the personal existence of CHRIST in God. For CHRIST is Elohim our king, who even from the beginning is *working salvation in the midst of the earth*.[1] Even as according to the Apostle it also says of the same one, *Thou in the beginning didst lay the foundation of the earth*.[2] It is he whose voice shook the heaven and the earth.[3] And he whom we saw ascending into heaven is the same who had first descended.[4] The same one said in the Apocalypse and in Isaiah, *I am the first, I am the last*.[5] He is the visible God who created the world, and appeared to Abraham, Isaac, and Jacob. He is the God of the law and the Prophets. And with this we absolutely admit that the God of the law and the Prophets is the Father of JESUS CHRIST, which seems a contradiction. From this teaching of the Apostles, wrongly understood, some of the ancient Heretics said that above the God who created the world there was another invisible God. For they were dreaming about the mystery of CHRIST. They did not understand that it could take place without contradiction

119a   that this very oracle was with God, and was God himself; and that, although the oracle was God, yet it was the oracle, and not God himself, that came to be flesh. The spirit here settles wonderful oppositions. The very profound words of John not only explain the whole law concerning Jehovah and Elohim, but they also dispose of all the heresies. I am speaking of the ancient heresies, which were rather near the truth; for the absurdities of the Greeks arose afterwards. They do not approach the teaching of John, but are worthy of philosophers without sense.

[margin: Nature and Person; for it is the hypostasis itself, or the Person made flesh; but by no means the being itself, and this is the Patripassian fallacy.]

15. Finally, I describe to you visibly the practice and the

---
[1] Ps. lxxiv, 12.   [2] Heb. i, 10.
[3] Heb. xii, 26; Ps. lxxvi, 8.   [4] Eph. iv, 9.
[5] Rev. i, 17; xxii, 13; Isa. xliv, 6; xlviii, 12.

way of coming to Christ, that by seeing him you may see the Father. It is first to be premised that God is in all ways incomprehensible, unimaginable; nor can we form any conception of God himself unless he adapts himself to us under some form which we are capable of perceiving; and this the Master shows us in John v, 37. Secondly: he, out of the mere good pleasure of his will, determined to manifest himself to the world through his oracle, as if I were to make my voice heard among those who do not see me; and thus, at the time of the law, he was manifested to all the people.[1] Thirdly: he manifested himself to the Prophets by his oracle more clearly, yet obscurely under the form of a kind of pattern, in whose likeness Adam was formed; since in his oracle there shone forth the original image, or the first figure of the world, namely, CHRIST. Fourthly: from what has been said above, learn what has been clearly and distinctly manifested to us; for the oracle has come to be flesh, and we have seen him.

Questions had then arisen concerning the Person of Christ.

16. Out of this two questions seem to arise, namely: that God was a body, or that Christ may be a phantasm, each of which John disposes of. Yet note how clearly the fancies of the ancient heresies about this dilemma teach us the truth. The Trinity had not yet come within the memory of man. From the time of the Arian philosophers the way for investigating the truth has been closed. John, therefore, that no one might fancy that there are bodily forms in God, explained that this was the *logos*; that is, that in the very reason of God there existed a *disposition* of this mystery. For in whatever way God had assumed a personal form, he must needs have been the *logos*. Secondly: that he might dispose of the phantasm, he called it flesh, saying that the divine being came to be flesh, and we have seen him, and he has given us a mind to know him, and the Father through him, to whom be glory and dominion forever, Amen, Amen, ever world without end. Selah.

[1] Ex. xix, 16.

THE END

DIALOGUES ON THE TRINITY

TWO BOOKS

ON THE RIGHTEOUSNESS OF CHRIST'S KINGDOM

FOUR CHAPTERS

BY

MICHAEL SERVETO, *alias* REVES,
A SPANIARD OF ARAGON

MDXXXII

BOOK I

Synopsis

1. Christians lack true knowledge of Christ, thinking him altogether different from man. 2. The Word foreshadowed Christ. 3. The invisible God, by speaking the word of creation, assumed a new rôle as a visible Creator, the Logos, or Elohim, manifested in the Person of Christ, who has taken the place of the Word that once was. 4. In seeing him we see the light of God reflected. 5. In creation God also became a Spirit, again foreshadowing Christ, in whom alone we can worship him. 6. The manifestation of God through angels also foreshadowed Christ. 7. The fulness of God and of all his properties dwells in Christ, who is of the same Substance with the Father. 8. Christ alone is the one in whom the Word became flesh. 9. In Christ the Substance of God also shared the Substance of flesh in the incarnation, making one being; thus he really came down from heaven. 10. Salvation comes only by faith that Christ is the Son of God, as is taught by Paul, Peter, and Christ himself. 11. The schools teach two beings in place of the one man Christ, the Son of God. 12. As Christians we are made like Christ in regeneration, 13. just as in our old life we were like Adam.

TO THE READER, GREETING

A1b All that I have lately written, in seven Books, against the received view as to the Trinity, honest reader, I now retract; not because it is untrue, but because it is incomplete, and written as though by a child for children. Yet I pray you to keep such of it as might help you to an understanding of what is to be said here. Moreover, that such a barbarous, confused, and incorrect book appeared as my former one was, must be ascribed to my own lack of experience, and to the printer's carelessness. Nor would I have any Christian offended thereby, since God is wont sometimes to make his own wisdom known through the foolish instruments of the world.

I beg you, therefore, to pay attention to the matter itself; for if you give heed to this, my halting words will not stand in your way.
Fare you
well.

DIALOGUES ON THE TRINITY
BOOK THE FIRST

MICHAEL. PETRUCIUS

A2a 1. Necessarily, according to the Scriptures, these three ought to agree, the Logos, Elohim, and Christ; as is proved by a mere comparison of the beginning of Genesis with the beginning of the Gospel of John.

Petrucius. I hear the man speaking whom I was looking for. Ho there! What are you saying to yourself here alone?

Michael. I am greatly tormented in mind when I see that the minds of Christians are so estranged from any knowledge of the Son of God.

Pet. I too have seen some carried away with their minds perfectly enraged against you because you are bent upon taking away from them a large part of their Gods.

Mich. With what reasons, or by what Scriptures, do they censure me?

Pet. By none, so far as I have heard; but by shouting, and by appeals to the great Councils. I have even seen some who fear that this may perhaps be to us a tradition like the Talmud and Alcoran, because it does not savor of the spirit of the Lord, and the Scripture in many ways suffers violence.

Mich. There are some whose blindness is so dense that if Christ were again to preach that he was the Son of God, they would crucify him afresh. Just as they do not see that he is the A2b head, so they do not acknowledge that they are the members. I should not expect ever to become a son of God, unless I had a Nature in common with him who is the true Son, upon whose sonship our own sonship depends, as members depend upon the head. Yet they would have the Son be something altogether different, although they can never prove it, nor does it contribute to the purpose of our salvation.

2. *Pet.* You seem to assert some things that you can not prove.

Mich. What things?

Pet. That the Word has ceased to be, or that it has become a mere shadow.[1]

Mich. I have never admitted that the Word has ceased to be. On the contrary, I am ready to admit that the same Substance of the Word is in the flesh to-day. As for my saying that there is now no such Word as there once was, that will soon be explained. Moreover, I called it a shadow by force of necessity, being unable otherwise to explain this mystery. Nor am I willing to go so far as to say that the Word was a shadow which has passed away and does not abide. On the contrary, this body now has the same Substance that the Word once had. But Christ was there typified and prefigured; for in the law were anticipated the mysteries and types of things to come, which we can also call shadows. And in this very fact I disclose the glory of Christ, since God is light, who typified Christ in the very substance of light and of the Word. Nor does this fact detract from the Word of God more than from God himself; even as I also do not disparage the angels, even if I have said that a shadow of Christ pre-existed in them.[2] I wished with Paul to call whatever is seen in the law a shadow, in order that the body, that is, the truth itself, may be Christ's.[3] And you came up opportunely with questions of this sort, for I was meditating of this very thing when you saw me talking to myself.

A3a

Pet. What is it that you were saying to yourself?

Mich. In order to prove that the Word is Christ himself, I was saying that the Logos and Elohim were the same thing.

Pet. Our fathers do not make it clear enough how the words of John agree with the words of Moses,[4] even though they suppose that the one ought to be understood by means of the other. Express, then, what you think, and take your start from the words of Moses, *In the beginning Elohim created.*

3. *Mich.* The invisible God, as he was before the creation of the world, is altogether incomprehensible and unimaginable to us, and by the mere good-pleasure of his will he determined to

---

[1] De Trin., Book IV, paragraph 8.
[2] De Trin., Book IV, paragraph 6.
[3] Col. ii, 17.
[4] John i; Gen. i.

create the world, and to manifest himself to us. Else were the creation of things useless, if God remain unknown. Hence God then said, *Let there be.* Lo, he is already creating by the Word; lo here, the Logos, and Elohim, and Christ. Then is Christ's kingdom established, and then is grace conferred upon us before times eternal, according to the dispensation of the mystery of Christ until the fulness of the times hidden in God.¹ By the very fact that God speaks, he disposes himself in a certain way, and does something within himself by the very fact of making himself Creator; for he is otherwise than he was before. By the very fact that he is speaking, he is already manifesting himself, who hitherto in the silence was known to no one. By saying, Let there be light, he brings himself forth from the unknown darkness of the ages into light, and presents himself to view in some distinct character. This John calls the Logos, and Moses Elohim; and this itself was Christ with God, and the Word was God, and God himself was the very light itself. Which light, according to that dispensation, represented by the figures of angels, lay hidden until its appearance in the face of Christ. I was right, therefore, in saying ² that there is now no such Word, because there is now none according to the dispensation under which the oracle was in the darkness of the cloud, in the time of Moses. Again, if there is now such a Word as there once was, where is the oracle, where the tabernacle, where the cloud, where the darkness, where the Cherubim, where the glory of the Lord which appeared there? Is not the fulness of all these in Christ? You do not notice how much the coming of Jesus Christ accomplished, and what a manifestation of God took place, and why Paul exclaims, *Great is the mystery of godliness,* that *God was manifested in the flesh.*³ Of necessity therefore I always meet in the face of Christ what I see called Logos by John, and Elohim by Moses; especially since the whole law expresses this image to me, as I have said above in the fourth Book.⁴ To the philosophers all this will seem foolish, but they have not sufficiently

¹ Matt. xxv, 31; II. Tim. i, 9; Tit. i, 1; I. Pet. i, 20.
² De Trin., Book IV, paragraph 8.
³ I. Tim. iii, 16 (Pagn.).
⁴ De Trin., Book IV, paragraph 4,

weighed what great force there is in these words of Christ: *He that hath seen me hath seen the Father.*[1]

4. Again, if God was manifested in the flesh, it must be that in seeing this flesh you see God; and since the vision is the same, it must be that he was seen before in the same character. And since he was seen before through the Word, and that which was seen was Elohim, it must follow that the Logos and Elohim and Christ were one and the same. Again, what is said of light is confirmed by the same John in his Epistle; for that the Word was light does not presuppose that he was a ray really distinct from the Father, but because God is light, the Word was God himself, and the light was with God. Moreover, that this may be the more clearly understood, I say that before the creation of the world God was not light, because it can not be called light unless it shines. Again, according to Paul, God said that light should shine out of darkness,[2] hence there was darkness. But after the creation, the light shone in the darkness, shone in the gloom of the cloud, although men apprehended it not.[3] We were with eyes half-blind, so that we could not bear that brightness, nor dare to turn our eyes to that face. And it said expressly that this is the reason why the prophet Christ was raised up for us,[4] because the people were not able to bear the terrible sight of the fire and lightnings. But now without that terror, and with unveiled eyes, we behold the glory in the face of Jesus Christ; indeed, we always have it in our spirits as an illumined mirror, so that we too are transformed into the same image by the Spirit.[5] You now see that the light reflected in the face of Moses was the same light which formerly was the gleaming and shining face of Christ, and the face of Elohim. The light was therefore the Logos, and Elohim, and Christ, who is the light of the world, the true light, which lighteth every man coming into this world.[6] The words of Genesis confirm the same view, for by the very fact that God said, *Let there be light*, he created light in himself by a divine dispensation; and he made himself to be the

Marginal note: Before the creation of the world God was not light, nor Word, nor Spirit, but something else ineffable; and all these are words of dispensation.

---

[1] John xiv, 9.   [2] II. Cor. iv, 6.
[3] John i, 5.
[4] Deut. xviii, 15, 18. With this agree Heb. xii, 18–21; Ex. xx, 18, 19.
[5] II. Cor. iii, 18.   [6] John i, 9.

light; and also, as I have said, he formed the light itself, Christ, in the shape of angels, and also shined in our hearts, that we might be enlightened to know him, and the light in the face of Jesus Christ.[1] You see here the mysteries of the light, and its relation to the face of Christ, which Paul wonderfully teaches. I pray you then, by Jesus Christ, that in comparing the beginning of Genesis with the beginning of the Gospel of John you reflect awhile; for it is altogether needful that each of these beginnings be explained by means of the other, and that thus Christ be known.

5. From the same beginning, since Moses speaks of the Spirit of God as blowing upon the waters,[2] one may understand how God there became a Spirit; for before God breathed there was no Spirit, nor could there be a Spirit before God spoke, since God breathed in speaking.[3] Also in the same beginning it is indicated in a figure what the Holy Spirit is; and the truth of the Gospel answers to this. For as God founded the world, and determined to be manifested by the Word, he at the same time also communicated his Spirit to the world. And this order was also observed in Christ; and when Christ had been manifested, his Spirit was given, which was once the Spirit of Elohim. And this dispensation is here noted in an outward figure, just as through Christ his Spirit communicates itself to us inwardly. Here you see another reason why we can say that they had a shadow not only in the Word but also in the Holy Spirit; because they there had an outward and foreshadowing figure. And so God himself, and his Word, and his Spirit, and his angels, foreshadowed Christ. Again, in order the more strongly to confirm what I have said of the shadow, I say that the worship of God was a shadow, and God was never truly worshiped in the law; because even as God can not be seen, so also he can not be worshiped, apart from Christ. Christ himself confirms this, saying that now is the first time in which God is worshiped in truth.[4] Previously he was worshiped not in truth but in a shadow, in a temple of stone, and a tabernacle of wood, where

After the speaking of God, his Spirit blew upon the waters.

A5a

---

[1] II. Cor. iv, 6.   [2] Gen. i, 2.
[3] *Spiritus* means both spirit and breathing.
[4] John iv, 23.

the darkness of the glory of the Lord appeared. But now, since Christ himself is the temple of God, we ought to worship there, and with spiritual worship, even as Christ is also seen with the inward eye. Once more I tell you that apart from Christ you are no more worshiping God than some Turk would worship him. And all who, apart from Christ, seek for the vision or the worship of God, worship after the manner of Saracens, so that they make Christ superfluous to us. But I affirm that God is seen and worshiped in Christ alone; and in general I say that every way of coming to God is in Christ, even as he himself testified that he was the way, and, He that worships me worships the Father.[1] And, *The time now is*, that is, it is given to the world through me, *that the true worshipers may worship the Father* in me, *in spirit and truth*.[2] This I would have you consider, that Christ condemned in Thomas and Philip all anxiety to inquire into God by other ways, and visions, and notions; but he would have us wholly regard him, and presents himself to be worshiped openly. Those arguments about seeing in order to worship are sound; for worship presupposes seeing, and what is worshiped in spirit ought to be seen in spirit, and it must be seen where it is worshiped, and how it is worshiped. Otherwise Christ will justly say to us even now, *Ye worship ye know not what*.[3] It is always that the law sets God before us as one to be known, shows him to us in person, because there was nothing else than Christ. Likewise Christ taught that God was seen in his own person; yet the philosophers press other visions of God upon us, and they say not only that there is one God, but that they understand that there are three Chimaeras in him.

A5b

6. *Pet.* How was the light hidden, and manifested through angels?

Mich. It was manifested through angels in a figure, and it was the shadow of the true manifestation to come. For the light and the Word had a Substance of their own, never known to the world until Christ was revealed and his Substance was touched and felt with the hands. No human reason can attribute to God any name of Substance or Nature, for he exists

---

[1] John xiv, 6.   [2] John iv, 23.
[3] John iv, 22.

outside of all Substance and Nature; but, when about to create the world, he created in himself a Substance in the likeness of the things of this world, and this was the Word, and the light, and the cause of all nature. Indeed, some have called this Substance the body of the Word; and of this Substance of the Word without a body we shall speak below.[1] But now, since we are treating of shadows, let us just speak of the mystery foreshadowing Christ; saying that in the angels there was a mystery of the Christ to come, there was the name of God, which dwelt in the angel.[2] That is, it was God himself, who then manifested himself through angels under the person of Christ, and obscurely. If you wish to trace this ministry of the angels further, you should know that the angels were created for our sakes, and minister unto us, and good angels guard us, even as bad ones tempt us. And the ministry of angels began in man, as God was at that time to be manifested to man through them. And the angels were not the creators of the world, but their office then began when God said, *Let us make man.*[3] For before this God had not spoken to the angels, but had created alone. Moreover, he brought in angels for the creation of man, signifying that their ministry would be necessary for this creation. Hence it presently followed that God was manifested to Adam himself through an angel; bad angels presently began to beset man, and first the woman is led astray by the serpent, then again man is led astray by her, as by an instrument of the devil. Then again man is driven out of the garden of delights by angels. It is an angel that appeared to Abraham, Isaac, and Jacob. And all this was the oracle; for Abraham heard the Word, and walked with the Word, and it was an angel that talked with him. Again, the three men whom Abraham saw were two ministering angels together with Christ, and these two he expressly calls angels in the chapter following.[4] Likewise, Elohim appeared to Moses, and it was an angel and Christ. Adam also saw Christ, walking in the cool of the day.[5] By angels slaughter was inflicted upon the Egyptians; and this was the oracle by which the firstborn

[1] Paragraph 9.
[2] Ex. xxiii, 21.
[3] Gen. i, 26.
[4] Gen. xviii, 2; xix, 1.
[5] Gen. iii, 8.

were slain, for the oracle had already been made known to Moses, though not yet dwelling in the tabernacle. It was at one and the same time the Logos, Elohim, and Christ. All this is proved by a single example; for he that went before the children of Israel was God himself,[1] and was an angel,[2] and was Christ,[3] and all this is the face of God.[4] Therefore God, and the angel, and Christ, were the same thing. These are great and marvelous things of God, and great is the fulfillment of them all in Christ. All these things the Master teaches very boldly, saying that he has all glory, both the Father's and his own and that of the angels.[5]

7. *Pet.* I suppose that Paul also, in writing to the Colossians, referred to this fulness when he said that in Christ all fulness dwelt.[6] But why did he afterwards add something about the fulness of the Godhead?[7] Was it appropriate to a man to have the fulness of deity?

Mich. I should like to ask you this: If you believe that the Godhead has a habitation anywhere, do you suppose that it dwells elsewhere than in man? All this fulness is in fact in man, and is greater than the world ever understood. And before this it would first have to be said how all the fulness of the law is in Christ, for what has been said above of shadows points to this. I shall speak of this matter in a tract on circumcision,[8] and in a tract on the righteousness of Christ's kingdom,[9] where it will be shown how Christ is the fulness and the fulfillment of the law, which it is highly necessary for our age to know. For Paul impresses all this upon the Colossians in opposition to those who by argument from the law would have us bound by decrees and would deceive us by a verbal proof. Paul, therefore, touching upon this fulness, also treated of sublimer matters, namely, of the Godhead, which exists fully in Christ together with the fulness of the law, and bodily. Indeed, the body of Christ is itself

A7a

---

[1] Deut. i, 30.
[2] Ex. xxiii, 20, 21.
[3] I. Cor. x, 4.
[4] Ex. xxxiii, 20, 23.
[5] Luke ix, 26.
[6] Col. i, 19.
[7] Col. ii, 9.

[8] This tract was not published, but there is a chapter on this subject in the third part of *Christianismi Restitutio*, published twenty-two years later.

[9] This tract is found later on in the present work.

the veriest fulness, in which all things are fulfilled, meet together, are summed up, and are harmonized; namely, God and man, heaven and earth, circumcision and uncircumcision, etc. Indeed, the body of Christ is itself the body of the Godhead; so that deity is plainly said to be in him bodily. The body of Christ its very self is divine and of the Substance of deity. Besides, from the fact that Paul says, *dwelleth*, it is proved what the Godhead is. And the Rabbis call the Godhead שכינה from the word שכן,[1] which means, to dwell; hence the Godhead means the dwelling-place of God. From this also the tabernacle where the Godhead was, was called משכן.[2] And to such a view of the Godhead, along with his consideration of the law, Paul accommodates himself; for he wishes to show all that was in the law, likewise that the Godhead of both the tabernacle and the angels was a shadow, and that the truth is in Christ. Therefore he said, *Which are a shadow of the things to come; but the body is Christ's.*[3] That is, the truth itself is in him, represented by those shadows; even as he also distinguishes God's express image, or εἴκων,[4] which is in Christ, from the shadows of the law, in which there was no bodily reality. Note here in passing that this general statement about all the fulness of deity can not be verified in the humanity of Christ in accordance with the imagination of the philosophers, for the reason that the second being is united to it. But the whole fulness of God, the whole of God the Father together with all the fulness of his properties, whatever God has, this dwells fully in this man. Indeed, if you note more carefully how great a thing it is for Christ to be the bodily and express image of the Godhead, you will clearly see that there is substantial Godhead in the body of Christ, and that he is himself really of the same Essence, and consubstantial, with the Father. The bodily Godhead in the Substance of Christ is such that it was seen and touched by John with the bodily eye and the bodily hand, as John himself observed, not without pointed meaning, in his Epistle.[5] Yet that being of which the philosophers speak can not be seen nor touched, nor can a

A7b

---

[1] *Shekinah*, dwelling-place; *shakan*, dwell.
[2] *Mishkan*, dwelling.
[3] Col. ii, 17.
[4] *Eikon*, image. Heb. x, 1.
[5] I. John i, 1.

bodily Godhead exist through it. All these things will be clearer below,[1] when we speak of the Substance of the Godhead of Christ. This one thing we detest here and always: that the philosophers do not grant to us that the Word became flesh, but will have the Word united to the flesh, and would laugh everything to scorn with their *alloeosis*,[2] and metaphors, and *communicatio idiomatum*.

8. *Pet.* They themselves say that you do not sufficiently prove that this Christ alone was the Elohim and the Logos;[3] for we were all with God.

Mich. In consequence of what I am about to say, that Christ, both in flesh and in spirit, exists in that Nature or Substance in which Elohim once existed in the Word and the Spirit of God, the question will be settled very clearly; but at present we are treating only of the mystery of his manifestation. And that there was in God a unique regard for Christ can not be proved more clearly than by showing this regard in all the Scriptures, so that there is seen here a unique marvel of divine contrivance. It is proved, again, through that efficacy and power which shines forth complete in Christ alone, and through that fulness which is complete in him through whom all those things are fulfilled, and because all the mysteries of the law prefigured him. Again, what can be said more clearly than to say, That Word became this flesh? Again, if they admit that this Christ is God, let us ask of them whether God is a recent being; for if God is not recent, he must needs have been before all worlds. This argument proves that he was in God not only in a figure, but in his Substance; else he were really recent. Yet he is not recent, but, as Isaiah says, *It was I, and thou hast not known me*; and, *Behold, the former things are come to pass*; and, *I am he that did speak; behold, I am here.*[4] As for their saying that we were with God, it is true; but we were in the mystery of Christ.[5] Grace was then conferred upon us through Christ; and then we are all called Christians, elect in Christ, inasmuch as Christ's kingdom, which is in us, has been established. And just as Christ's kingdom, which is now within us, was established before the founda-

A8a

---

[1] Paragraph 9.   [2] Gr., change, alteration.   [3] cf. De Trin., Book V.
[4] Isa. xlv, 4; xlii, 9; lii, 6 (Vulg.).   [5] Eph. iii, 4; Col. iv, 3.

tions of the world were laid, so from that time this grace is spoken of as predestined, which was revealed at his coming.

9. *Pet.* I should like to understand better how all things were made through Christ, and about the incarnation and the coming down from heaven.

A8b

Mich. You will indeed understand if you acknowledge Christ as begotten of the Substance of God; nor indeed can you otherwise believe that he is the Son of God. All things depend upon this begetting; so that it is said that in his Substance he came from God into the world, and came down, by making his divine Substance partaker of the flesh; which is the true incarnation.[1] And he assumed flesh, who made the carnal Substance partaker of the divine Substance, so that the one man is partaker of both Substances. It is in this way that the ancient writers used the word incarnation, although they knew not that union. That this is the true incarnation, the words of John teach, which are clear: *The Word became flesh.*[2] The Law also teaches this very thing in that memorable figure when Aaron's rod, being thrown upon the earth, was incarnated.[3] Even his embryo is said to be incarnated and to take flesh, since there was milk and blood before he became flesh. In this sense Irenaeus takes the word incarnation, where he says that the incarnated rod is a type of Christ's incarnation: as the Word became flesh, so the rod became flesh.[4] There is also another figure pertinent to this matter, for even after the incarnation the rod remains; and the serpent itself when incarnated was called a rod, even as in the Apocalypse Jesus himself is called the Word of God.[5] It is not to be imagined that the Word of God is turned into flesh by a change of elements, but to the Substance of the Word there was added a partaking in the flesh, so as to make one *hypostasis*, although our moderns misuse the word *hypostasis* because they do not understand that the Substance of the Word and the Substance of the flesh are one Substance. The Word became flesh; that Word became this flesh. In consequence of this the

B1a

---

[1] Heb. ii, 14. [2] John i, 14. [3] Ex. iv, 3.
[4] Adv. Haer. III, xxi, 8 (MPG. vii, 953; ANF. i, 453; ANCL. v, 357); cf. Ex. iv, 3; vii, 10.
[5] Rev. xix, 13.

blasphemy of those is repelled who will not grant to us that this Christ came down from heaven, but say that there is another being from heaven, though by no means a human being. I, however, say that if you are a Christian you must needs grant that this flesh came down from heaven. For there are words of Christ which can by no means be misinterpreted, in which he declares that he and his flesh came down from heaven; for he says that the bread which came down from heaven is his own flesh.[1] Again, the type of the manna given from heaven clearly proves this very thing; for the falling of the manna is to be ascribed to the flesh of Christ, since it is the food represented by that food. Again, the second man, Christ, came from heaven as a heavenly being.[2] Again, there really descended from heaven one who was formerly in heaven as the Word, in a Substance of the same nature in which the flesh now exists, as the following Book will indicate.[3] In the same way we shall say that all things were made through him, because he was formerly in heaven as Creator in the same Substance in which he now exists both as flesh and as spirit. We ought therefore to close the mouths of our adversaries in this sole way, asking of them whether when they mention the man Christ they admit that he came down from heaven, and came forth and is come from God; whether they admit that this man is the firstborn man, is before all, and is from the beginning. And I do not believe there will be any Christians who will deny this. And if they grant us this, B1b we shall not trouble ourselves further to hunt for Chimaeras through this sort of sayings of the Apostles. Moreover, we shall expect them to bring forward other Scriptures, which prove another Son, and do not apply to our Christ. For we do not wish that one, but this one, to be the Son of God given us as a Saviour, and we pray that our faith regarding him may be firm.

Christ has eternal Substance both as flesh and as spirit.

10. *Pet.* Do you actually wish us to have faith in a man, and do you say that Paul always preached this faith, and always speaks of this faith when he treats of righteousness?[4]

Mich. You seem to call him a man by way of contempt; but I say that he is God and creator of all things, and I declare that

---

[1] John vi, 51. [2] I. Cor. xv, 47. [3] Book II, paragraph 1.
[4] cf. De Trin., Book III, paragraph 20.

you can not get saved by another faith, if you do not believe that he is the Son of God, who was given for your salvation, and suffered to expiate your sins. Although this matter has been settled in few words, yet it is a great thing if you truly believe. Nor can you believe in God otherwise than by believing this; for what else is it to believe in God than to believe that his witness is true which he has borne concerning his Son?[1] Do you see that faith in Christ is always included in the Scriptures? You who believe in God, says Christ, believe in me; just as he that sees me sees God.[2] See, then, and believe, and do not marvel if I insist upon this faith. I have expressly said, and I now say, that Paul always preached this faith; and if he sometimes speaks of faith indefinitely, he presently adds the limitation, *in Christ*, so that this faith means faith in Christ. Again, B2a that he preached this faith before he wrote, is proved from the Acts; both from his preaching and from the command about preaching which he received from Christ. For the whole foundation of the apostleship of Paul is laid in these words of Christ: *I send thee unto the Gentiles, that thou mayest open the eyes* of the blind, *that they may be turned from darkness to light and from the power of Satan unto God, that they may receive remission of sins and an inheritance among them that are sanctified by the faith which is toward me.*[3] Do you see this faith by which the saints are justified? This faith, which is in Jesus Christ, Paul never forgot, but he always expressly preaches it in the Acts. For *straightway in the synagogues he proclaimed him, that he was the Son of God*; and again, *affirming that this was the Christ.*[4] *And this,* he says, *is the Christ, whom I proclaim unto you.*[5] *And every Sabbath he reasoned, and persuaded, and testified to the Jews that Jesus was the Christ.*[6] He preached the same faith to Felix the governor.[7] That he was sent to proclaim this faith, according to the commandment given to him, he writes to the Romans, the Corinthians, and the Galatians. I would have you consider what kind of faith the people gained from this preaching, and see at all events that it is not proclaimed in our time. I should

---

[1] I. John v, 9.   [2] John xiv, 1, 9.   [3] Acts xxvi, 17, 18 (Pagn.).
[4] Acts ix, 20, 22.   [5] Acts xvii, 3 (Vulg.).
[6] Acts xviii, 4, 5.   [7] Acts xxiv, 10–21.

desire, at least, that men were used to believe and to confess that Jesus Christ is the Son of God; for, since these are the confessions of Scripture, they can not beget an evil custom. Indeed, light its very self would follow the custom. Not only in Paul, but in Peter, who is wont to feed his sheep very plainly, we have a threefold confession to this effect, namely, that this is the Son of God.[1] His preaching also in the Acts is very clear. Likewise in John you will find several times that Jesus is the Christ, and Jesus is the Son of God, as I have said at the end of Book III.[2] Moreover, with regard to this matter there is the clear confession of John the Baptist, of Martha, of the Centurion, of Nathanael, of the Eunuch, etc. Would that my soul might die in their simplicity and faith, and not in the subtleties of any of our teachers. Moreover, clearest of all is the double witness of the voice from heaven, that this is the beloved Son of God, witnessing both at the Jordan and on the mount. And this witness is for our sakes quoted many times by the Evangelists, even as Peter also quotes it. I say nothing here of the words of Christ, which always teach us that it is the work of God, and eternal life, if we believe that he is the Son of God. Indeed, nowhere in the Scriptures will you find a word about believing where it is not commanded to believe this.

11. *Pet.* I marvel that hitherto the schools have not believed that this Jesus is the Christ, and the Son of God.

Mich. Really they have not any one Son, but two half ones; one from the Father alone, the other from the mother alone. And in admitting this proposition they do not believe that the man Christ is indicated by the Scriptures, but the second being. Yet some now feel bound to say that they believe that this man is the Son of God, not because he is born of God, but as it were in a figure, because another Son is made man like this one,[3] even as bread is said to be the body of Christ through an impanation [4] which some have devised. Others by no means attribute a kind of sonship to the man, but admit that Jesus is the Christ and

---

[1] John vi, 69; Matt. xvi, 16; II. Pet. i, 17.
[2] De Trin., Book III, paragraph 20.   [3] *Huic hominitus.*
[4] The doctrine that after consecration the bread and wine are united into one Substance with the body and blood of Christ.

the Son of God, in order that he may furnish the foundation for the second being. This is taught in the schools, for through the *communicatio idiomatum* the second being, which they call the Son, is called man. But that the man himself, or, as they call him, the human nature, should be called the Son of God, they would consider a great crime; because they would prove from this that there are two sons or, as some pretend, two kinds of sonship, a natural and an adoptive. But why are we lingering in reciting these trifles and inventions of men? Proceed to the other things, if you have anything else to say.

12. *Pet.* How do you understand that we were created after the image of Christ, of old and of late?

Mich. Paul explains this in Romans and Colossians. For in the former he says that we have become conformed to the image of Christ,[1] which is to be understood of the image of the new man, which follows the type of the old, even as the forming of the new man is prefigured in the forming of the old, on both sides in imitation of Christ our head, that we may by all means be conformed to his image. For we are renewed and born again after the image of Christ, just as we were created after his image.[2] For when Paul there calls Christ the creator of the new man, he is alluding to the creator of the old Adam, as also in the passage cited from Romans he infers from that image that Christ is the firstborn among the elect, even as he was formerly the firstborn among other creatures. Christ comes to his own, and not to others', and those that had his sign on them, and were his, he reconciles to himself, and again makes them like himself, and renews them, that we may follow his image again, being born again through baptism, as new creatures in newness of life,[3] even as we shall follow that image again in the final resurrection.[4] These mysteries are great, by which you are abundantly taught always to regard Christ Jesus himself, and now in the new man to follow his image, which you followed in the old. For those Chimaeras are of no profit unto edification; but only the cross and the image of our head, Jesus Christ, who

---

[1] Rom. viii, 29.
[2] Col. iii, 10.
[3] Rom. vi, 4.
[4] Phil. iii, 10; I. Cor. xv, 49.

completes and fills the old creation as well as the new with unspeakable fulness.

13. *Pet.* Did we not follow the image of Adam in the old man?

Mich. You are right; but you are touching upon another aspect of the mysteries, which is also fulfilled through Christ. I am speaking of the bare creation of man; you are speaking of the carnal fault which followed afterwards. Was not Adam himself created after the image of Elohim Christ? For the prototype is not Adam but Christ; but Adam is the father of the sin, in which we have followed his image. And Christ, setting us free from that, has restored to us the former image after which we were created.

BOOK II

Synopsis

1. Christ is not a creature, but the Creator, begotten of God's Substance as the Word, in fleshly form. 2. The early Fathers admitted this, but held that there was a disposition of God's Substance as Creator, by the ineffable mystery of the incarnation, in which man is mingled with God. 3. This does not involve a confusion of Natures, for this term does not apply to God. 4. Without the incarnation, the divinity of Christ can not be maintained. 5. Christ thus shares both God's nature and man's. 6. Christ's resurrection means that he finally laid aside the flesh again, and became equal to God in glory. 7. Christ is in every respect an infinite being, dwelling in the highest heaven with God. 8. He enters us when we eat the Lord's Supper, joining us in the spirit. 9. The Father does nothing save through Christ, who forgives sins, and is to be worshiped. 10. By his resurrection Christ was glorified, both by his nature and as the gift of God. 11. Christ is of the same Substance and power as the Father. 12. The Holy Spirit, sent by Christ, is of divine Substance, but has a different office from Christ. 13. The Holy Spirit exhibits and impresses on us the mind and character of Christ. 14. The ineffable God sent his Word and Spirit to make his presence and power known in the world. 15. The dove was only a symbol of the Holy Spirit.

BOOK THE SECOND

PETRUCIUS. MICHAEL.

1. They say that this man of yours is a creature, and a finite one; hence we ought not to worship him, because it is commanded: *Thou shalt worship the Lord thy God, and him only shalt thou serve;*[1] and, *I will not give mine honor to another.*[2]

Mich. They are entirely mistaken. On the contrary, this Christ of mine, so to speak, is the one who gave this command that we worship him alone. Through him God made their own

---
[1] Matt. iv, 10.   [2] Isa. xlii, 8; xlviii, 11.

wisdom foolish, which persuades them that he is not to be worshiped, although he often permitted himself to be worshiped. With great blasphemy they despise him as a creature. On the contrary, I shall easily persuade you that he is the creator, if with firm faith you hold the whole order of the dispensation of Christ's kingdom, namely, the Word with God, and its going forth into the world through the incarnation, and its return to the Father through the resurrection. In the first place, according to the dispensation under which he was himself the Word with God, there is no question of a creature, for God himself was that Word. Moreover, Christ came forth into the world not after the manner of creatures, but being conceived by the Holy Spirit, being brought forth not out of nothing, but out of the very *hypostasis* of God, and being born of God's Substance through the Substance of the Word incarnate and made flesh. Oh, if you could understand the ineffable way by which the flesh came forth from God! Reflect upon this, for *no word is impossible with God.*[1] Bear in mind that one can not be called a son who has not come forth from the Substance of his parent. Here you should ponder the old difference between being created and being begotten, which the philosophers have twisted for us into another being. Take counsel of Isaiah, who will plainly tell you how he was begotten and came forth from God. For he shone as a lamp that is kindled from the brightness of God; hence he is called a λάμπας, and the ἀπαύγασμα[2] of his glory. Again, the words of Christ themselves powerfully affect me when I consider that it is no light saying that Christ came forth from God,[3] as he also says, *I came out from the Father.*[4] And that the more, because in both places he is making a comparison, saying that he has come forth from God in the same way in which he returns to God again. Therefore it was a coming forth of the Substance. Moreover, he goes on to say, *I came out from the Father, and am come into the world.*[4] Weigh the words, *came out*, and *come*. Read for yourself the words of Christ, which are of greater power than I could explain. Therefore the stone

---

[1] Luke i, 37 (Vulg.).
[2] *Lampas, apaugasma*; lamp, effulgence. cf. Isa. lxii, 1; Heb. i, 3.
[3] John xiii, 3.   [4] John xvi, 28.

which came forth from the mountain [1] was not created out of nothing, but came out of the Substance of God. It is so because even from the very fact that God speaks and says, *Let there be light*, he does not create the light or the Word, but through the omnipotence of God brings forth from himself both the light and the Logos; so once more, when he causes the light and the Logos to be flesh, the flesh is not created out of nothing, but is brought forth from God, and becomes flesh, and exists in that *hypostasis* which was the Logos and the light, because the Logos ἐγένετο,[2] that is, became, and had existence as flesh. Again, unless Christ had this Substance of the light and of Deity, he would not shine naturally, nor could it be said, *This is the true light*,[3] and, *I am the light of the world*.[4] Again, unless his Substance were truly that Substance which was the Word, he would be said to be really a new God. Again, he would not be before all things, nor would all things exist through him, did he not exist in Substance. Again, God could not be seen in this flesh in the way in which he was seen face to face in the person of the Word, nor would it be said that there is in this flesh the substantial character of God, and a bodily divinity. Again, when Christ said that the Father was in him, you should not understand that it was through the union of God with the flesh, but because the Father is in the Son in Substance; else Christ would not have proved by this saying that in seeing him we see the Father. In fine, this body of the Word is the body of Christ's flesh, and God's Substance became the Substance of his flesh, because that Word became this flesh; and the Substance of the Word was such that after the incarnation it could be touched by John, the flesh being touched whose body and Substance are the same.

2. In this sense the earlier writers, from whom the truth had not yet been taken, admitted the bodily Substance of the Word. Moreover, although I admit that this was the Substance of the Word, yet I do not for all that deny that there was a *disposition*;

---

[1] Dan. ii, 45.
[2] *Egeneto*, became.
[3] John i, 9.
[4] John viii, 12; ix, 5.

for Irenaeus and Tertullian so call it.¹ There was a *disposition* of Substance and of Essence, surpassing all man's comprehension; for the accidentals of God are more essential than our quiddities.² Indeed, there was no other Substance of God than that Word which was his true Essence, and the cause of all things that are. God in himself can be limited by no manner of body or Substance, but in himself he created these things when he was about to create the world, that there might be an Essence, giving being to other things; and this is the creation of the name *tetragrammaton*.³ And not only through the Substance of the Word and of Christ, but through any other accidental *disposition*, however great, which he disposed in himself, even if it were as a grain of mustard seed, God could create infinite worlds, and through it give them being, and body, and life, and light. I say that God in himself created the name *tetragrammaton*, and the Substance of the Word; even as also some of the ancients admitted, in a good sense, that Christ was created; with whom I also have admitted this, that I might make the minds of the weak turn away from that magical fancy, even as for the same reason I have treated of certain other things more rudely than I should like. Yet to one that rightly understands, there is in this no detraction from the glory of Christ, for indeed the dispensation of this mystery is ineffable, so that words of men do not suffice to declare it. Great and ineffable is the mystery, that that flesh is the same as our own, and that by its own Nature it has a divine Substance; that it was conceived in the womb of a virgin, and born from the Substance of God; that it was brought forth after the likeness of us, coming forth from God even from everlasting; that Christ was made from a woman, born of Mary, and was at the same time born and begotten of the Substance of God; and as no one can

B5b

---

¹ Irenaeus, adv. Haer. I, vi, 1; Tertullian, adv. Praxean, ii, iii (MPG. vii, 503; MPL. ii, 156–159; ANF. i, 324; iii, 598 f.; ANCL. v, 25; xv, 335–339). cf. note to Book I, paragraph 41.

² i. e., what is merely incidental in God is more important than what is essential in us.

³ The group of four consonants (JHVH) representing the ineffable divine name in the Hebrew texts.

declare his generation,¹ so *no one knoweth who the Son is, save the Father*.² Just as it is ineffable that God should have a Son, and
B6a that the Son of God should be born of a woman, so there is an ineffable mystery in his one flesh, that he should have something in common with a father and a mother, and participation in the Substance of each; not according to parts of different sorts, but in accordance with himself, and whatever has a share with him, with God, and with man. And it must needs be so if you admit that it was born of God and man, even as you too have whatever you have at once from a father and a mother. And you ought to notice this resemblance, if you truly believe that this is the Son of God, who was born of Mary. One sole hallucination the philosophers had, which deprived them of this knowledge. They say that the Substance of God can not be mingled with the Substance of man. Oh, pitiable madness! What else is the mystery of the incarnation but a mingling of man with God? What is it that the older writers call man mingled with God? They do not see in what an assish way they treat the mystery which took place in the womb of the Virgin. Unless I were of this persuasion about the flesh of Christ, I should have no hope in him. For even with us it is to come to pass that we are made sharers of the Substance of God, even in the flesh, just as even now in the spirit we have become partakers of the divine nature.³ They do not see how they destroy the mystery of Christ's redemption, so that we as members can not follow the example of our head, which nevertheless we shall follow, as the Apostle teaches.⁴ Nevertheless, as the Apostle confesses,⁵ our comprehension can not lay hold of this glory of the resurrection.

B6b 3. Besides, the philosophers say that this is a confusion of Natures, because the Nature of God is here confused with the Nature of man. It is to be deplored that we are so imbued with philosophical habits of speaking that we are rendered blind in examining the divine mysteries, and wish to seem wiser than God himself. In the first place, this is to be noted: that the

¹ Acts viii, 33. ² Luke x, 22. ³ II. Pet. i, 4.
⁴ Phil. iii, 10, 21; I. Cor. xv, 49; I. John iii, 2, 3.
⁵ Phil. iii, 13; I. John iii, 2.

term, Nature, is improperly applied to God;[1] for that which is inborn in any being from birth, and is characteristic, is called his Nature. Hence one ought to declare that this flesh of Christ, since it is born of God, has a divine Nature, even until death. But God in himself has no Nature nor origin such as his Son has. No kind of Nature was appropriate to God, but something else ineffable. But that those things which are God's should, as it were, be given to some creature by his natural origin and birth, and be in him, ought to cause in us no blasphemy, but admiration of the works of God. I would that if there are to be any adversaries they might fear to offend Christ in this way, but might better consider how great a thing it is for this man to have come forth from God, how great a thing it is to be the Son of God, how great a thing it is for the Word of God to be flesh. Let them consider who can be a true mediator, unless he be partaker of God and man. Let them consider that our salvation is not placed in Chimaeras, but in the flesh and blood of Jesus Christ, and in the passion of him by whose wound and stripes we are healed.

4. Therefore without doubt a great mystery lies hidden in the knowledge of Christ's flesh, and those who do not admit that Christ's flesh is of one Substance with God prattle in vain of their defending the divinity of Christ; for they defend Chimaeras, and not Christ. Indeed, the Antichrist could not have done more to destroy the divinity of Christ than they themselves do, who ascribe to the man Christ none of those things which belong to divinity. But you, if you are to convince your understanding, and confess the divinity of Christ's flesh, ought without doubt to believe that God could have brought forth from his own Substance not only Christ's flesh, but (to speak foolishly) a stone, and have saved us by means of it. But it was fitting that to men a man be given as Savior, expressly on account of his spirit. We therefore glorify the Nature of Christ, and of his flesh, and of his body, exalted unto God; nor is there in this any confusion or plurality of beings, but one sole being,

---

[1] The argument here rests upon the etymology of the Latin words used, and is of course apparent only in the Latin: *natura*, nature; *innatus*, inborn; *nativitate*, birth; *naturalis*, natural; all related to *nascor*, to be born.

one *hypostasis* or one Substance, one thing formed of heavenly seed planted in the earth and coalescing into one Substance. Concerning this sprouting of heaven's rain and earth's soil into one shoot, many things are contained in the law and the prophets: that this is the form, the sprout, and the tender plant, which has sprouted from the dew of heaven and the fruit of the earth, Isaiah admirably declares.[1] This same thing is the sprout wonderfully bursting forth from the transplanted marrow of the lofty cedar.[2] Clearly also in Jeremiah.[3] This very sprout is the man Christ himself.[4] Yet as to this sprout the philosophers never knew which of those Natures is spoken of; indeed, with them, without the one Christ there is true Babylon and confusion. For they so distinguish the plurality of Natures or beings in the one Christ that they confuse them again with their own *alloeosis*,[5] making their notions about one being pass over into the other, and by their abominable fictions abandoning the true Christ, and by their impious equivocations corrupting the simplest Scriptures; although in Holy Writ there is no passage which expresses such a separation and aggregation of beings, or indeed gives any hint of such a being. But human philosophy, ignorant of the works of God, forces us to it. Moreover, in accordance with my purpose, I would have you revere this mystery with fear and trembling, so that you may acknowledge your weakness in this alone. For if you can not know in yourself in what way it happens that whatever you have you have at once from your father and your mother, how much more will you be unable to discern in the Son of God that whose generation is unknown even to angels. At the instigation of the wicked Adversary, with the design invented by some one concerning a confusion of Natures, we have been deprived of knowledge of Christ; for in that way there will be confusion in every generation, if you call a mixture of seeds confusion. And consequently this very confusion will prove for me that this is a true generation in which man is mingled with God, and the seed of the latter with the seed of the former. Again, the Natures of things that can be mingled are said to be confused, when neither thing re-

---

[1] Isa. iv, 2; xiv, 8; liii, 2; iv, 2.   [2] Ezek. xvii, 22, 23.
[3] Jer. xxiii, 5; xxxiii, 15.   [4] Zech. vi, 12.   [5] Gr., change, alteration.

mains but they pass over into a third Nature. But the Nature of God remains in Christ, and the Nature of man remains in the one Substance.

Christ is not a creature, but a partaker with creatures.

5. From this it appears that Christ has participation in God and man, so that he can not be absolutely called a creature, but one fairly partaking with creatures, as the Apostle particularly teaches.[1] Nowhere will you find Christ more clearly expressed than in the Epistle to the Hebrews, if you read it often and without caviling. Christ himself who sanctifies, and we who are sanctified, are from the same mold; hence he calls us brothers in the same place, and you should constantly notice this. For indeed it became him, if he as captain of our salvation was to make us sons, that he too, as well as we, should become partaker of flesh and blood, which you should note again in the same passage. But there is this difference, that he is himself partaker of flesh and blood, whose flesh and blood are nevertheless the flesh of God and the blood of God.[2] Again, unless he were partaker with creatures, he could not be said to have become a truly mortal man, though nevertheless his incarnation made him truly mortal. For, *though he was a Son, yet in the days of his flesh*,[3] etc. Moreover, he is indicated as a partaker with creatures in the fact that he is called the firstborn of them.[4] And as a firstborn son, begotten of the bowels and Substance of his father, is called the power and beginning of his father's strength; so Jesus the Son of God, shining out from the bowels and Substance of the Father, is his power, and might, and the beginning of God's creatures.

6. This dispensation of the incarnation was followed by another admirable one in the resurrection, in which the existence of the creature, which he acquired through his incarnation, was laid aside just as if it were an accidental thing. There is nothing now in Christ which is animal. Christ has been wholly perfected and glorified by his resurrection, so that he has returned to the original state of the Word, and exists as God, and is in God, as before. This appears in the figure of the rod, which was taken back into the hand of Moses in the same condition in

---

[1] Heb. ii, 14
[2] Acts xx, 28 (Vulg.).
[3] Heb. v, 7, 8.
[4] Col. i, 15.

which it was before it turned into flesh.¹ The return from man to God took place in the same way as the proceeding from the Word into flesh took place before. And to this Christ himself clearly bears witness, for he says that the Son of man is to ascend where he was before.² Hence he is now in God in the same place and in the same way as before. Likewise he says that just as he came out from the Father, so he returns again to the Father.³ Again, if he had not been brought to this perfect equality in this way, his prayer would have been made in vain, where he prays that he may be glorified again with the same glory which he had had with God before the world was.⁴ And thus we can urge this argument upon our adversaries; for according to them the divine nature receives no glory, hence the human nature became equal with God, and it had glory with God before the world was made. The Christ himself is now by his resurrection raised to so great glory that he would not now say, *The Father is greater than I*. But when he was upon earth he said, *I go unto the Father: for the Father is greater than I*;⁵ that is, With him is another glory which I shall obtain when I have gone to him. But now that the glory of the Father has been obtained, this causal glory ceases. And neither is he less, nor the Father greater. Nor is there any other power of God than the Son himself, whom Paul thus calls the power of God.⁶

C1a 7. He therefore whom God begot from his own Substance as his only Son, who has all the power of God, whose are all things that God has, is not a finite being; nay, is in every way infinite, both in power and in worth and in duration. Nor is he limited by the size of a certain place, but with his fulness fills the world below and that above.⁷ And he it is that had said that he fills heaven and earth.⁸ Indeed, the former was a figure of the latter, and Christ in filling all things fills also this prophecy with all manner of fulness. *He walketh upon the wings of the winds*;⁹ *he rideth through the wilderness*;¹⁰ *he sitteth upon the circle of the earth, and meteth out heaven with his span, as well as the waters of*

---

¹ Ex. iv, 2–4.   ² John vi, 62.   ³ John xvi, 28.
⁴ John xvii, 5.   ⁵ John xiv, 28.   ⁶ I. Cor. i, 24.
⁷ Eph. iv, 9, 10.   ⁸ Jer. xxiii, 24.   ⁹ Ps. civ, 3.   ¹⁰ Ps. lxviii, 7.

the sea with his hand.[1] Christ is just as near us now as when he once said, *I am a God at hand.*[2] Just as truly now as of old, *Heaven is his throne, and the earth the footstool of his feet.*[3] Indeed, the things that now are were represented by those, and are fulfilled in him. Christ is not therefore inclosed in any particular place, as though in a perpetual prison, as some suppose. Indeed, his place is not to be sought among the atoms,[4] nor among the stars, but in the third heaven, as Paul's revelation teaches.[5] Nor did Christ remain in any particular part of the heaven, but together with the Father he dwells above all the heavens in the same light unapproachable; else were he not at the right hand of the Father. They have a carnal mind who, arguing from his sitting at the right hand of the Father, snatch Christ away from us; for this fact would prove rather that he is not at the right hand of the Father. But they fancy, perhaps, that Christ is a living man, and that the right hand of the Father is some fixed place, or at all events they suppose that the flesh of Christ is situated in heaven, simply that it may be something to look at. But we say that Christ is in that heaven to which the angels do not attain. He is in the third heaven where, and whence, he fills all things; not ovens and drains, but things spiritual and fit for his habitation, whether they be in heaven or on earth. For in the new heaven the spiritual body exists independent of any extended body just as it does independent of any place. Thence his Spirit comes also to us, as if to a new sphere; not by moving nearer in space, because Christ is no more absent from us in space than God is, nor is God elsewhere than in Christ. There must needs be one place, even as they are one. And God himself is not in drains, and stones, and other things, as the vulgar imagine. Nor do the Scriptures speak otherwise of God's place than of Christ's. Nor does God through his Spirit communicate himself to us otherwise than does Christ; for this Spirit is the Spirit of Christ, and Christ is there, and acts by the breath of his mouth. Nor are some right in trying to prove that Christ is absent in a local sense, for the reason that his Spirit is present. Indeed, the contrary is proved; for as there

C1b

---

[1] Isa. xl, 22, 12.   [2] Phil. iv, 5; Jer. xxiii, 23.   [3] Isa. lxvi, 1 (Vulg.).
[4] *Elementa.*   [5] II. Cor. xii, 2.

can be no Spirit of God without God, so there can be no Spirit of Christ without Christ. Nevertheless the flesh and the Spirit of Christ are said to be two gifts, through two dispensations, according to one of which he is in us continually by his Spirit, which he said would abide in us forever.[1] In another way, or by means of another dispensation, Christ is in us when of himself he comes to us and manifests himself to those who love him, and makes his abode in them.[2]

C2a 8. Again, he enters into us when he truly offers his body to us to be eaten in the holy supper. Nor does he afterwards depart from us in a local sense, nor is there in this any movement from place to place; but only, through a certain dispensation, a joining of him to us, which is in the spirit alone; and the body of Christ is mystically eaten in the mystical bread. But since the true use of the Lord's Supper has been buried in oblivion, and Christ is not yet known, the taste of this eating seems insipid. And, what is the more to be deplored, no one will acknowledge his own error; for it is certain, as I shall show elsewhere,[3] that there is none who has arrived at the truth of the Lord's Supper. For some amuse themselves with irrelevant figures of speech and take offense at the flesh of Christ, while others profanely turn it into bread, etc. But what we have to say here is in opposition to the earlier writers, since they are the weaker; and having glorified the power of Christ, and his position, they understand him in a physical sense. This, at least, I would that they might know: that Christ distinctly said, and that without regard to the giving of the Holy Spirit, that he was to come, and to make his abode among us.[4] Something else, therefore, is here intended. There is some other result of the coming and of the eating of Christ, besides the giving of the Holy Spirit. Again, he does not know that Christ is the head of the Church who keeps him from being joined to his own members, for he is joined to us through the real presence of his own very body, in so much that we are said to be members of his flesh and of his bones. The body of Christ and the body of the Church are one flesh, just as the flesh of a man and the flesh of

---

[1] John xiv, 16.   [2] John xiv, 21–23.
[3] Not fulfilled.   [4] John xiv, 23.

his wife are one flesh, in which fact Paul exclaims that there is a great mystery.¹

9. As a result of this, the blasphemy concerning a finite Christ is rendered clear, and will be rendered clearer; and as to Christ, you will know how great he is if you firmly believe that the greatest blasphemy is that of those who say that God is, or acts, somewhere out of Christ. For, as I have said, all the Scriptures that make mention in the law of the place where God is, speak of Christ himself, and are full of him; and as to God, those know not where he is who are ignorant of Christ. All these things will Christ supply to you;² for the conclusion as to where God is, as well as that with regard to our seeing him, follows from these words: *Believest thou not that the Father is in me?* and, *The Father abiding in me doeth his works.*³ Which can not be proved true if the Father does other works apart from him. As the Father did all things through him, so he now does all things through him; and without him there is nothing, either in heaven or on earth. Moreover, you will understand that Christ is not finite, if you know that his power is now as great as it ever was, because he it is that then existed, not only in power and person, but also in Substance. He it is that said, *My glory will I not give to another, surely not to graven images,*⁴ but it shall remain in me, even if it is manifested in the flesh. He it is that said that he alone blots out sins, for Christ fulfilled this. But those that deny that he is to be worshiped will for the same legal reason deny that he can blot out sins. And thus the Pharisees are born for us again, treating Christ with dishonor and saying, *Who can forgive sins, but God alone?*⁵ For these slanderers do not ascribe this to the man Christ; but, with a zeal like that of the Pharisees, while deeming that they are defending the glory of God they blaspheme against his Son, although no sins can be forgiven but by him. Christ is the very one who said, *To me every knee shall bow,* as Paul explained.⁶ But these slanderers do not believe that he is to be judge, because they will not bow the knee to worship him. You now see well enough the evil things they have said about a finite being,

---

¹ Eph. v, 32.   ² John xiv, 26.   ³ John xiv, 10.
⁴ Isa. xlii, 8.   ⁵ Luke v, 21.   ⁶ Rom. xiv, 11.

about a creature, and about not worshiping Christ. We, to repeat, worship him as the Apostles and many others did; indeed, all the angels worship him.[1] Nor should I eat his flesh unless I worshiped it; but they neither worship nor eat him. We worship him who received the glory, and created all things.[2] We worship him who is living, and was dead, and is now alive forevermore.[3] We say that this man is to be honored with all the honor with which the Father is honored; indeed, the Father can not be honored save through him.[4]

10. *Pet.* How did he receive glory in his resurrection, if all glory was his by nature?

Mich. It is not something by nature because the Son presently possesses all things that are the Father's; but by nature all inheritance and glory of the Father are due to the Son. And this glory, by a divine dispensation, Christ did not fully obtain until he was perfected through death.

Pet. You had said elsewhere that Christ was God through grace, not through nature; but do you now ascribe all things to him by nature?

Mich. As I gave the first elements to babes, so I also said,
C3b *in accordance with his nature*, and, *by nature*, in the manner of this philosophical age, which has nothing in common with the Scriptures; for the philosophers will have nothing exist through grace, nor do they say that the will of God is the cause of the generation of the Son, but that it merely happened by nature that one of the beings then produced the other, and now produces it daily. Wishing to oppose this dream, I have maintained by all the Scriptures that his exaltation and glorification are the free and voluntary gift of the Father, denying their magical Natures and Generations. Nor do I now retract what I said of grace, but add to it, since it belongs to the glory of Christ that all things should be meet for him by nature, by reason of his filiation. Nor, according to the truth of Scripture, is it a contradiction to say that he was begotten and chosen by the grace and will of God, and along with this that by nature all the inheritance and glory of the Father is due to him. For

---

[1] Heb. i, 6.   [2] Rev. iv, 9,   [3] Rev. i, 18.   [4] John v, 23.

it is a rule of nature: if son, then heir. And he is Son by nature, as I have said, because he was ineffably begotten of the Substance of the Father. Not born of another, and afterwards adopted, but born of God, and born a Son by an original begetting. If you also knew that the word nature is to be taken for the natural property itself of a being, just as whatever belongs to it from birth is called natural, you will easily distinguish and discern two Natures in Christ, and all his properties. For Christ received his Substance from God and man, and whatever is appropriate to him in accordance with the nature of the flesh, that is, in accordance with his partaking of man, and in accordance with that property which he received from the seed of man; even as Paul says, that he was *born of the seed of David according to the flesh*.[1] For although the flesh of Christ is derived from the seed of God and of man, yet by the word *flesh* in this passage we signify his partaking of man. Since therefore Christ by his nature is partaker of God and man, he must needs have double properties, and divers considerations, and some stated as of God, and others of the flesh.

C4a

11. I mean here to infer that we are not inventing a new Son in order to abolish the inequality of the Arians, but are saying that this man is the Son, and of the same Substance with the Father, and that in his one Substance there is one power. We never have anything in the world from God save Christ, nor shall we ever have anything else until the judgment day, when Christ presents us before God the Father. Although you might take a unique name which would be suitable to the only invisible God, even as he is called the only Father; yet a common name which expresses glory or power in respect to us is quite suitable to the Son as well as to the Father, indeed, is applied to the Father by the Son. The name *tetragrammaton* is his own, although I have said that the Prophets in their prophecies, which proclaim in express words about the future that he will be a man upon earth, do not apply this name to him. For this is not so because it does not befit him, but they are then using other names, in order more clearly to express the dispensation by which he was to be a mortal man upon earth.

[1] Rom. i, 3.

12. *Pet.* Explain to me better what is your view about the Holy Spirit, and why Christ says that another than himself and than the Father is to be sent.

Mich. Christ is always urging this upon us, that we may understand that what is made by the Father is made by him. He first gave honor to the Father, saying that the Spirit was to be sent by the Father. Afterwards he included himself, saying, *Whom the Father will send in my name.* Again he said more strongly, *Whom I shall send unto you* from the Father.[1] I said that his saying *another* referred to an angel, because the deeds of Christ, along with an inner mystery, have an outward token, and so the sending was represented by the ministry of an angel. Yet according to the inner truth of the mystery it is evident that there is another otherness,[2] even an otherness of protection now in the Spirit other than there then was in his visible presence; and from all these things Christ took occasion for his saying. This otherness is known from this: for as Christ has a certain difference from God, so also does his Spirit, whose distinction arises from the distinction of Christ; because the Spirit is the Spirit of Christ, and as the Word became flesh, so the Spirit of the Word became the Spirit of the flesh of Christ. In the Holy Spirit, as also in Christ, there is a divine Substance; and at once with this a certain assimilation of the creature or the human spirit. Yet blind philosophy does not accept this mystery. Not only in the flesh and Spirit of Christ, but in the Word which was God himself, there was a certain dispensation of the creature, or man. And who can admit that the Word was created by God, although it was not something created apart from God? Nor can the Holy Spirit be said to be created, except in so far as you admit that God created a new *disposition* in himself. And as the Word received a partaking of the flesh, becoming flesh in Substance, so his Spirit acquired a certain substantial semblance of the human spirit. Whence the difference, which existed between God's Word and his Spirit, was once not so real or substantial as it now is. And, to speak more clearly, I say that the Holy Spirit is now a Person, while in the law it

---

[1] John xiv, 26; xv, 26.   [2] *Alietas.*

was not thus a Person. I call it a Person because it is a divine *hypostasis*, or Substance, breathed by nature into Christ alone, and thence flowing out through Christ into us. Properly speaking, then, we do not say that there is a Person, or a face, in the Spirit, although in that breathing there was always a divine Substance, according to the dispensation of the God who breathed it. Moreover, just as Christ, along with the dispensation of the incarnation, said that the Father was greater, so he said that the Spirit was to be sent by him, because Christ was not yet glorified, so that he might show that the Spirit was gloriously to proceed from himself. Indeed, the Spirit of the sons of God, glorifying the man and making him heavenly, did not exist before the resurrection of Christ. Therefore he made it different from himself, saying, There will be another than I; indeed, I shall be another; the foretaste of glory in him will be far other than you can now perceive in me. Therefore he said, *He shall glorify me.*[1]

13. Here you have it that this Holy Spirit is the mind of Christ, through which we so keep the very mind of Christ that we live with Christ's very life; nay, that it is no longer we that live, but Christ liveth in us.[2] Moreover, the Spirit so proceeds from the inmost Christ that the Holy Spirit is called a kind of image of the Son, because in a certain measure he exhibits the character of Christ. And Christ in saying, *He shall take of mine,*[3] points out that the natural property of himself will be in the Holy Spirit. Hence from the fact that this is the Spirit of the Son, Paul proves to the Galatians by powerful reasons that we are made sons through him.[4] For he stamps upon us the character and sonship of the Son of God, so that, as brothers of Christ, we cry, Abba, Father! Because it was never given to any one under the law, nor before the resurrection of Christ, that he should be a brother of Christ, or that he should be joint-heir to his kingdom; for this Spirit did not yet exist, nor did its power, nor the power of the kingdom of Christ. Moreover, it is the Spirit of Christ, as it were his servant, that always stirs us up to knowledge of Christ, and always renews

Christ, after his resurrection, calls us brethren. Matt. xxviii, 10; John xx, 17.

---

[1] John xvi, 14.   [2] Gal. ii, 20.   [3] John xvi, 14.   [4] Gal. iv, 6.

us after his image; and it is through him that Christ is formed in us, and by him that we are transformed into the image of Christ, and through him that we are made to eat and drink Christ's flesh and his blood.

14. Finally, I would have a certain meditation recommended to you. If you could separate God entirely from his creatures, you would easily understand how he sent his Word, as it were to a new region; how Christ went forth from God and came into the world; how his Spirit proceeds from him to us. For just as God in himself is incomprehensible, so he is separated from the Substance of all his creatures. He was in another heaven, whence his Word was sent, and his Spirit was sent. And so when we say, God, we are considering him separately, apart from every creature, and ineffable. But when we say, the Word, we are considering his presence made known in this world. And when we say, the Spirit, we are considering his power breathing in the world. But now the Substance of the Word is the Substance of the flesh of Christ, and the Substance of the Spirit of God is the Substance of the Spirit of Christ. And they now exist in the same dignity and office as ever; and the Spirit of the Word has become the Spirit of the flesh of Christ, even as the Word has become flesh; so that in both ways they are the gifts of Christ, who not only redeems us through his flesh and blood, but also makes us alive through his Spirit. From the above consideration, the saying of the Apostle is also understood, when he brings the firstborn into the world.[1] He is brought into this world from another world, and coming forth from God he enters and comes into the world.[2] Nor in the sending of the Word, the Spirit, and Christ, of which I have spoken, was there any movement in space, although the descent of the Holy Spirit was outwardly indicated in a dove, by the symbol of a kind of motion in space. However, the true sending and proceeding from God takes place inwardly.

15. It appears from what has been said that the Holy Spirit is not an angel; but by means of it, as by an outward symbol, we say that the Holy Spirit was seen descending. And we admit that this is the Holy Spirit, in a sort of figure, even as we

[1] Heb. i, 6. [2] Heb. x, 5.

admit that this bread is the body of Christ. For just as through this bread the body of Christ invisibly communicates itself to us, so in another way through the outward symbol of a messenger the Spirit of God is inwardly shed abroad. It is therefore not to be understood that the Holy Spirit acts in us through angels, although we read in the law of many things of this sort being done by angels; which are a shadow of the things to come.

ON THE RIGHTEOUSNESS OF CHRIST'S KINGDOM

Synopsis

CHAPTER I. — On Justification. *1. By a copious citation of texts from Romans, Paul's doctrine of justification is stated: it is conferred on all that believe in Christ; by it we are reconciled to God, and have peace with him, and receive his grace, and shall enjoy his glory, and inherit eternal life. By this justification we become free from sin and death, and become sons of God and joint-heirs with Christ, and are God's elect. 2. Similar teaching is given in Ephesians and other Epistles, and in the words of Christ. 3. This justification was also foretold by the Prophets. 4. All the promises of the law are spiritually fulfilled in those that have believed in Christ. 5. Other promises in the Law and the Prophets are similarly fulfilled in us. In fine, all Christians have been justified by faith in Christ. 6. Justification, purification, and sanctification are here taken as one, being all accomplished through Christ, as formerly through ritual observances. 7. To be saved means in the Gospels to be restored to health of mind as well as of body, and this has already been accomplished in us.*

CHAPTER II. — On Christ's Kingdom. *1. Christ's kingdom is a spiritual one. Its eternal life already abides in us, its future and its present are the same, and it is entered only by the justified. 2. Christ and the Apostles proclaimed the kingdom, and it is open to us if we believe on him. 3. The Gospel is the proclamation of the good news that the kingdom of God is at hand, and it fulfills the promises as Christ fulfilled the ordinances of the old law. 4. This kingdom is for none but the righteous. 5. It is more than a mere name. 6. Immediate justification by faith, and the future reward of good works, are not the same thing. 7. Servitude of the will does not follow from the free grace of God.*

CHAPTER III. — A Comparison of the Law and the Gospel. *1. The difference between law and Gospel is that between works and faith, flesh and spirit, Moses and Christ, shadow and truth, death and mercy. Christ's grace justifies and gives the kingdom to us who have been predestined to receive it. 2. Through the Gospel we first offer true spiritual worship; we have spiritual forgiveness and the law of Christ written in our hearts, bringing us life and freedom and enduring glory; and thus we are transformed into the likeness of Christ. 3. The righteousness of the law was carnal; that of the Gospel is spiritual; likewise its rewards and punishments. 4. The justifications of the law consist in doing what God commands, whereby his favor is won; but Christ has justified us by faith (though works of the law were also good, as many examples show) and ensures us forgiveness and eternal life. 5. Eternal life is given us on the sole condition of faith in Christ. 6. The Psalms and the Prophets teach that the righteousness of the law was one of works. 7. This was superficial, not being of the heart. 8. So neither can men be justified by merely keeping the laws and rules of the monks, which renew the old system that God had wished to do away. 9. The flesh hinders us from obedience to the law. 10. The law provided no true justification, but left all men in sin. 11. Under it men could be justified only by deeds, which must not be omitted, even by those that have faith.*

CHAPTER IV. — On Love. *1. Love fulfills the law, and all excellence is ascribed to it. 2. The law could not make us free from the death of Adam, but faith in Christ has done this and procured us other blessings, whose fulness we could not understand without the gift of the Holy Spirit. 3. Yet love holds the highest place. Faith must be followed up by works of love, which ensure the readier forgiveness and increase the reward of glory. 4. Outward acts spring from the inward spirit. Good deeds react on the character, but active effort is required. 5. Faith precedes love, and is the foundation of salvation; but love is greater and has a wider range, is more difficult to exercize, and more permanent, and is directed to both man and God. 6. It is through love that faith leads to eternal life. Love follows faith and perfects it. 7. Faith opens the way to all good things, 8. but it must find its complement in love, which is a voluntary act, and spreads more widely; and important as faith is, yet love has its own reward. 9. Epilogue.*

ON THE RIGHTEOUSNESS OF CHRIST'S KINGDOM

Compared with the Righteousness of the Law; and on Love

C6b   The present tract I shall divide into four chapters. In the first I shall enlarge upon the views of Paul which he brought forward concerning justification. In the second I shall say something of Christ's kingdom. In the third I shall compare the Law with the Gospel. In the fourth I shall tell of the ways of love. Christ grant that this may tend to the glory of God and to knowledge of the truth.

Chapter I. On Justification

1. Paul, whenever alluding to justification by the law, declares that we have been justified by the grace of Christ, because we have believed in Christ Jesus. This he everywhere teaches, notably in Romans, where he treats both of death, which entered through Adam, and of unrighteousness, which entered through the law; that he may show the great grace of Christ who justifies us, who has set us free from this death, and from unrighteousness, and from all our sins, by reconciling us to God as an act of grace. In the first place, in the third chapter, Jews and Gentiles being shut up under sin, he goes on to say: *But now a righteousness of God hath been manifested,* and is conferred *through faith in Jesus Christ unto all, even upon all them* C7a *that believe.*[1] And afterwards he says again that we are *justified through the redemption of Jesus Christ, whom God set forth as a reconciler through faith*; and that the righteousness of God is shown in him, because of the remission of past sins.[2] Therefore we have now been justified, who have been reconciled, and whose former sins have been remitted since the time when we believed and gave our names to Christ. This appears the more for this reason, because, adding limitations, he says that this grace is conferred now, and in the present time, namely, at the

---

[1] Rom. iii, 21, 22 (Vulg.).   [2] Rom. iii, 24, 25.

time of the coming of Christ; for among Jews and pagans it was not so. From the fourth chapter also we have it that we have been justified after the likeness of Abraham; and even as it was imputed unto him because he believed, so it has been reckoned unto us for righteousness, because we have believed that he is our Messiah. And even as Abraham, for that one act of faith, became the friend of God, so we, for the one faith in Jesus Christ, have been reconciled to God, and have become his friends, who were his enemies, and from children of wrath have become children of God. Moreover, there is nothing clearer than what he says in the fifth chapter, for he draws his conclusion as though it were already sufficiently proved that we have been justified. For he says, *Being therefore justified by faith, we have peace with God.*[1] Notice the words, *justified,* and, *have peace.* We already have, and have obtained, this peace, by the grace of justification which has been conferred upon us. Moreover, he says that we have been brought over, or *have had our access by faith into this grace wherein we stand, and* in this grace we *rejoice in hope of the glory of God.*[2] Notice the words ἐσχήκαμεν and ἐστήκαμεν.[3] Of this grace in which we have stood since the time when we knew Christ, Peter makes mention in the fifth chapter of his first epistle; and Paul, in the eighth of Romans and the eleventh of Second Corinthians.[4] This grace brings with itself the fact that we rejoice in hope of the glory of God, because we know that this glory which we have obtained leads to another glory. This is itself an inheritance panting for another inheritance. Elsewhere he says that we have been *made heirs according to the hope of eternal life;*[5] for the glory of this inheritance is a glory of the Spirit, and a foretaste of that which is to come.[6] And this glory which we have already obtained arouses in us a stronger hope, and makes us sure that we already have a foretaste of it in the glory of the Spirit that is given us. That we are already heirs of this inheritance, and have become pos-

C7b

---

[1] Rom. v, 1.   [2] Rom. v, 2.
[3] *Eschekamen, estekamen;* have had, stand.
[4] The passages here incorrectly cited are perhaps I. Pet. v, 12; Rom. v, 2; II. Cor. viii, 6, 7.
[5] Tit. iii, 7.   [6] Heb. vi, 4, 5.

sessors of it through the Spirit, is proved in Ephesians and Titus.¹ Paul proves this by reasoning: *If a son, then an heir.*² For we are sons, and joint-heirs with Christ, who have received the spirit υἱοθεσίας.³ Moreover, in the same passage Paul says that we have now been reconciled, and have now received the reconciliation.⁴ Again, he says that the grace and the gift of God has abounded unto the many, justifying them from their many trespasses; and that through Christ many are made righteous who *receive the abundance of grace and of the gift of righteousness.*⁵ In the sixth chapter there is a noteworthy saying: *He that hath died is justified from sin.*⁶ Therefore none can have died through baptism with Christ who has not been justified. In the same passage he also says that being made free from sin we become servants of righteousness.⁷ In the eighth chapter he draws an inference, as much as to say: If, then, we have been thus justified, there is now no condemnation among them that have been ingrafted in Christ Jesus. He says furthermore that *the law of the Spirit of life made us free from the law of sin and of death.* Again he says that what the law could not accomplish, God has accomplished through Christ, that the ordinance of the law might be fulfilled in us.⁸ Note how, in alluding to the righteousness of the law, he teaches that the completing of the justifications of the law has been fulfilled in us, even as I shall show below that the other things expressed by the law have also been fulfilled in us. Again, he says that through this justification we live in the Spirit, and are sons of God, and joint-heirs with Christ.⁹ Again, God called, justified, and glorified us, as *conformed to the image of his Son*; and from this he concludes that we are God's elect.¹⁰ Again, *Christ is the fulfillment of the law unto justification to every one that believeth;*¹¹ and in these words he shows that the justifications of the law have been fulfilled through Christ in them that believe. Again,

---

¹ Eph. i, 18; Tit. iii, 7.   ² Gal. iv, 7.
³ *Huiothesias*, of adoption.   ⁴ Rom. v, 10, 11.
⁵ Rom. v, 15–17.   ⁶ Rom. vi, 7.   ⁷ Rom. vi, 18.
⁸ Rom. viii, 1–4. Servetus here (following the Vulgate) adopts the translation *justificatio* for δικαίωμα, ordinance, thus associating it with *justitia*, righteousness, as in the argument following.
⁹ Rom. viii, 10, 17.   ¹⁰ Rom. viii, 30, 29, 33.   ¹¹ Rom. x, 4.

the kingdom of Christ, in which we are, is righteousness;[1] and Christ has received us to the glory of God.[2] Also in the first epistle to the Corinthians he teaches very clearly that we have been justified, saying, *Ye were justified, ye were washed, ye were sanctified*,[3] etc. And God reconciled us unto himself through Jesus Christ, not reckoning unto us our trespasses, that we might become the righteousness of God through him.[4] Again, *We believed on Christ Jesus that we might be justified by faith in Christ*.[5] Notice the verb ἐπιστεύσαμεν,[6] that is, we believed, that we might be made just. He also declares that this justification means the remission of sins, saying: *If, while we seek to be justified, we are found sinners*,[7] etc. And once more, he proves that the righteousness of Christ is in him, because having died unto the law he lives unto Christ, having been crucified with him.[8] And in order to show that we have been justified, he concludes that we are sons of God from the fact that we have believed in Christ Jesus.[9]

2. Moreover, in another epistle, that to the Ephesians, God has caused us to be dear, and has bestowed upon us the riches of his grace through Christ, through whom we have our redemption and forgiveness of our trespasses, and through whom we have received our inheritance, and after we believed were sealed with the Holy Spirit, which is an earnest of our inheritance, unto the redemption of this possession, that the glory of the inheritance of Christ may now be rich in us.[10] And he says, He *made us alive together with him, and made us to sit in the heavenly places*, and all this he freely gave us without works of our own. Indeed, we became *his workmanship, created in Christ*, that henceforth we may do well.[11] Likewise, *the new man after God hath been created in righteousness*;[12] therefore he that is a new creature is already justified. Also, having, he says, a righteousness of mine own, even that which is of faith in Jesus

---

[1] Rom. xiv, 17.
[2] Rom. xv, 7.
[3] I. Cor. vi, 11.
[4] II. Cor. v, 18, 19, 21.
[5] Gal. ii, 16.
[6] *Episteusamen*, believed.
[7] Gal. ii, 17.
[8] Gal. ii, 19, 20.
[9] Gal. iii, 26.
[10] Eph. i, 7–14.
[11] Eph. ii, 5–10.
[12] Eph. iv, 24.

Christ.¹ And, He *made us meet to be partakers of the inheritance of the saints in light, he delivered us out of the power of darkness, he translated us into the kingdom of* Jesus Christ *his beloved Son, through whom we have the forgiveness of our sins.*² Again he says, *We were in time past alienated, yet now hath he reconciled us,* that he might make us holy and just.³ Moreover, we were dead, but now he has made us alive, and we have now put off the body of our sins, and have risen together with him.⁴ Moreover, *He saved us, and called us with his holy calling,* and by thus calling sanctified and justified us through Christ, through D1a whom he brought life to light.⁵ And, *He gave himself for us that he might purify us;* and, *He saved us that, being justified by his grace, we might be made heirs.*⁶ We are therefore justified, as well as saved, and have been made heirs; and all this because we have believed, even as it says, οἱ πεπιστευκότες,⁷ that is, they who have believed. This inheritance itself is a rest, into which οἱ πιστεύσαντες,⁷ that is, we who have believed, have been brought. Through this faith we have received the inheritance of the promise.⁸ *We have been sanctified through the offering of the body of Jesus Christ made once for all. By one offering he hath perfected them that are sanctified.*⁹ He took away our sins when he justified us, and thenceforth he is said to be at peace about our iniquities.¹⁰ Therefore when our iniquity was removed, righteousness was imputed. Moreover, *Ye have purified your souls in your obedience to the truth.*¹¹ And the same Peter says, Cleansing by faith the hearts of them that believe.¹² And Christ *called us out of darkness into his marvelous light, ... and bore our sins, that we, having died unto sins, may live unto righteousness, by whose stripes we are healed.*¹³ Again, *We have obtained a precious faith through righteousness, and have been called through glory and truth,*¹⁴ and have obtained exceeding great gifts.¹⁵ Finally, we

---

¹ Phil. iii, 9. Servetus has omitted the negative of the original.
² Col. i, 12–14.   ³ Col. i, 21, 22.   ⁴ Col. ii, 11–13.
⁵ II. Tim. i, 9, 10.   ⁶ Tit. ii, 14; iii, 5, 7.
⁷ *Hoi pepisteukotes, hoi pisteusantes;* they who have believed, we who have believed; Tit. iii, 8, Heb. iv, 3.
⁸ Heb. vi, 12.   ⁹ Heb. x, 10, 14.   ¹⁰ Heb. viii, 12.
¹¹ I. Pet. i, 22.   ¹² Acts xv, 9.   ¹³ I. Pet. ii, 9, 24.
¹⁴ Servetus has apparently read here *veritatem,* truth, instead of the correct *virtutem,* virtue.   ¹⁵ II. Pet. i, 1, 3, 4.

have the words of Christ: *He that believeth hath eternal life, and hath passed from death to life.*[1] And, *Already are ye clean,*[2] so that as branches planted in Christ himself ye may bear more abundant fruit.

3. From the Prophets also it appears that we are saved, set free, and redeemed, indeed that we are all righteous, as it says at the end of Isaiah: *Thy people also shall be all righteous.*[3] They are all *trees of righteousness.*[4] The reason presently follows on both sides; for they are righteous because they are the seed of the planting of Christ.[5] They are all clothed in the garments of salvation and in the robe of righteousness with joy.[6] To the same end God visited Zacharias and wrought redemption among his people, that we being delivered from our enemies may serve him in holiness and righteousness.[7] And those that have been set free and ransomed by the Lord will walk in Zion with joy and gladness,[8] and, they shall be called the holy people, the redeemed of the Lord.[9]

D1b

4. In confirmation of what has been said above, we can draw one general corollary: that all the promises of the law are fulfilled in us, who have believed in Christ. I am speaking in a spiritual sense; for literally speaking they received their promises, and obtained the land of Canaan, and were satisfied with both milk and honey. In the first place, Abraham is promised the blessing of seed, multiplying, and an inheritance; and all these Christ has conferred upon us through faith. For we are the seed of the blessing, having obtained rest of spirit, and a heavenly inheritance of the grace of God, through faith in Christ.[10] We who have believed have been brought into his rest.[11] Again, it was promised that the righteous should live by faith; and it has been fulfilled, for he who has believed in Christ lives, being justified, and he lives with a heavenly life through the life-giving Spirit. There are other promises: as that God would take away our sins, and ungodliness from Jacob, would

[1] John v, 24. [2] John xv, 3. [3] Isa. lx, 21.
[4] Isa. lxi, 3. [5] Isa. lx, 21. [6] Isa. lxi, 10.
[7] Luke i, 67–75. [8] Isa. xxxv, 10. [9] Isa. lxii, 12.
[10] Rom. iv, 11–13; ix, 8; Gal. iii, 7, 9; Heb. vi, 12.
[11] Heb. iv, 3.

D2a put his law in our hearts, and himself would dwell in us, and be at peace with us, and that we should be his people.[1] And all these things have been fulfilled, although by the harshness of the times they may not have seemed fulfilled hitherto. Again, that all flesh should see the salvation of God;[2] that every one that looked upon the serpent should be healed;[3] that God would give us the true bread from heaven;[4] that we should be taught of God;[5] that the Spirit of God should be poured forth upon men.[6] Likewise the other promises concerning the calling of the Gentiles[7] were fulfilled.

5. There are in the Law and the Prophets other promises after the likeness of those mentioned, all fulfilled in us, even as the other figures of the Law and of prophecy, which had regard to his own person, have also been fulfilled in the person of Christ. From this you may infer as to our theme that all the righteousness of the law has been fulfilled through Christ in us who have believed in Christ, who alone is the completing and fulfillment of the law. The sum of this chapter is, that all Christians have been justified, and that to be justified is for an unrighteous man to be made righteous, which is done only by faith in Christ.

6. Notice this in passing: that we take being justified, and purified, and sanctified, for the same thing; although in the view of the law the matter is different. For the one Christ is the completing of the whole law. He alone is the goal of all the things that are in the law. The various acts of the law meet to
D2b one intent in the one Christ. By the law men were said to be purified by certain observances, by the sprinkling of blood, by washing, by shaving, and by remaining without the camp, etc. Likewise by the observing of other ceremonies, by offerings, and touchings, and ointments, they were said to be sanctified. But justifications were something more general; for all the commandments of the law were justifications, so that one observing them was justified. Thus Paul always speaks of justification as

---

[1] For all these, see Rom. xi, 26, 27; II. Cor. vi, 16; Heb. viii, 10; I. Pet. ii, 10.
[2] Luke iii, 6.   [3] John iii, 14, 15.   [4] John vi, 32.
[5] John vi, 45.   [6] Acts ii, 17.
[7] Rom. ix, 24; xv, 9; Acts xiii, 46; xv, 17.

of a rather notable word, so as to comprehend all works of the law, that is, whatever is commanded in the law. But according to Christ, all these are one. The sole faith in Christ both purifies, and justifies, and sanctifies, although in these there are different shades of meaning, and various mysteries of Christ are expressed by various figures of the law. For we also, as well as they, have been purified by blood;[1] but we obtain this through faith in Christ. Likewise they were sanctified by ointments and offerings, but we by the anointing of the Holy Spirit, and by the offering of Christ once for all. Moreover, they were justified by the commands of the whole law, and by observances; but we are justified by keeping the law of Christ, which is entirely a law of faith.

7. From this is made manifest what it means to save, and how faith has saved us. To save means, in the Gospels, to make whole, or to make well one who was sick. They are saved who are called to the kingdom of Christ. To save is to restore to a state of health, when sins have been forgiven. And so in the Gospel you will often find, *Thy faith hath saved thee*, or, *hath made thee whole*. For Christ cured men of diseases of the mind as well as of the body, by forgiving sins. The prophecy of the angel contains just this: *He shall save his people from their sins.*[2] Therefore he saved, who took away sins. Likewise, *I will save you, and ye shall be a blessing, after you have been a curse*;[3] and, *Israel has been saved in the Lord with an everlasting salvation.*[4] Finally, the whole law has regard to this way of saving, when those placed in peril pray, *Save me, O Lord, and make me whole.*[5] But the words of Christ alone, if you carefully notice them, teach very plainly just what salvation is, always expressing that they are saved, by a verb in the past tense. Even as Paul also says, *He saved us*,[6] *Who saved us*,[7] and, *Ye have been saved*;[8] and truly saved, because set free from death and hell, and not only delivered from them, but at the same time with this translated to heaven, having also obtained the gift of the Spirit, even

---

[1] Heb. ix, 14.   [2] Matt. i, 21.   [3] Zech. viii, 13.
[4] Isa. xlv, 17.   [5] Ps. lxxi, 2, 3 (Vulg.).   [6] Tit. iii, 5.
[7] II. Tim. i, 9.   [8] Eph. ii, 8.

eternal life, through faith in Christ alone, by the mere grace of Christ, without works of our own.

CHAPTER II. ON CHRIST'S KINGDOM

1. A conclusive reason why we say that we are already saved and glorified is derived from our knowledge of Christ's kingdom, which Scripture, not without reason, calls the kingdom of God, and the kingdom of heaven. For it was announced to us as to this kingdom, that it is a kingdom of the spirit, where Christ reigns among his saints, with sparks of the eternal glory kindled in their hearts, so that the Apostle says that they have already *tasted the powers of the age to come*,[1] and have already become *partakers of the glory that shall be revealed.*[2] We already have this eternal life abiding in us, because we are now living in the Spirit with the eternal life with which we are to live in the flesh. He that does not feel this in himself is not yet reborn of Christ, but is still living a pagan life. Christ's kingdom that is and will be are one and the same; and all the prophecies which refer to the glory of the resurrection are even now fulfilled in them that are justified, through the glory of the Spirit that has been given them. Whence, not without reason, Christ called the righteousness of his kingdom justification by faith, saying: *Seek ye first the kingdom of God and its righteousness,*[3] which is the same as if you said, Believe first on the Son of God. For through this faith we shall be justified, and this righteousness is the righteousness of the heavenly kingdom, which will make you partakers of Christ's kingdom. Christ was raised for our justification,[4] because even as Christ's kingdom was established from that time on, so justification took effect from that time on, that those may rise justified who are to enter that kingdom. God could indeed justify man without the heavenly gift of his Spirit by which we ascend to heaven; but this heaven can not be ascended into save by the justified, since the kingdom itself is righteousness.[5] Nor can this heavenly kingdom be obtained but by those that have risen with Christ.[6] Hence Paul joins with Christ's resurrection

---

[1] Heb. vi, 5. [2] I. Pet. v, 1; Eph. i, 18. [3] Matt. vi, 33.
[4] Rom. iv, 25. [5] Rom. xiv, 17.
[6] Rom. vi, 4, 8; Col. ii, 12; iii, 1; John iii, 13, 15.

the fact that we sit with him in the heavenly places.¹ For through the power of Christ's resurrection it has been given to the justified to sit in Christ's kingdom, and to reign as joint-heirs with Christ, and as his brethren. Regarding this kingdom we have the text, *Even as my Father appointed unto me a kingdom, so I appoint unto you a kingdom, that ye may eat and drink at my table in my kingdom.*² But alack and alas! that Satan has snatched away from us both the table and the kingdom, or at least has suppressed them for a time, on account of the abomination standing in the holy place.³ In the same chapter Christ also says that he shall not eat until the kingdom of God is fulfilled, nor drink until the kingdom of God comes;⁴ that is, until after his resurrection. Likewise he said in another place that his disciples should not taste of death till they saw the kingdom of God come with power;⁵ and that they should not have gone through all the cities of Israel till the Son of man were already come.⁶

2. Concerning this kingdom we also have the prophecy of John, which is soon to be fulfilled: *Thou madest us unto our God kings and priests, and we shall reign upon the earth.*⁷ From this is explained what is frequently read in the Gospel: that Christ and the Apostles preached the kingdom of God, and that they were preaching the gospel of the kingdom, and the kingdom of heaven, and were speaking of the kingdom of God, as did Christ and Paul.⁸ For behold, I am proclaiming to you the kingdom of God, and the kingdom of heaven; I am proclaiming to you that Christ lives and reigns; I am proclaiming to you that such a one is our king, and reigning in heaven; that if you believe on him you shall be justified, and made partakers of his kingdom. Would that our preachers had preached Christ's kingdom in this sense; for if they had held to the correct meaning of the Gospel, and of faith in Christ, they would not have invented for us so much imaginary nonsense about the promises. Always when one proclaims the heavenly gifts of Christ conferred upon us through his coming and his Spirit, such a one is said to pro-

---

¹ Eph. ii, 6.   ² Luke xxii, 29, 30.   ³ Matt. xxiv, 15.
⁴ Luke xxii, 16, 18.   ⁵ Mark ix, 1.   ⁶ Matt. x, 23.
⁷ Rev. v, 10.   ⁸ Mark i, 14; Acts xxviii, 23, 31.

claim the kingdom of God brought to us. He preaches that the kingdom of God has come who proclaims that Christ has been raised, and lives and reigns with great power in heaven, and that heavenly gifts are conferred on us through him. Nor does he know that Christ has come, who does not know that gifts have come with him. Christ expressed it also by outward deeds, by healing the sick, expelling demons, and giving eyes and clearness of sight to those affected with blindness, from which he concludes that the kingdom of God is come upon us.[1]

3. In whatever way others limit the Gospel by the promises, I say that the Gospel is the word of Christ, and of John the Baptist, and of the Apostles and all the disciples: *The kingdom of God is at hand, the kingdom of heaven is at hand.*[2] Pray notice the emphasis on these words, and why Christ commanded that they be preached so often. I call the Gospel the announcement of the grace of God, or the proclamation of the kingdom of God, when one proclaims that these have come, even as the four Evangelists, and sometimes other apostles, notably Paul, proclaim and declare it. The Greeks also called news, and the heralding of good deeds, εὐαγγέλια.[3] That this is the true Gospel, Isaiah is witness, saying: *How beautiful are the feet of him that bringeth good tidings of peace, that bringeth good tidings of good, that publisheth salvation, and saith unto Zion, Thy God reigneth,*[4] that is, Christ. In the same chapter he also sings and gives praise, because the Lord hath redeemed Zion, and hath comforted his people.[5] In the same way the angel brings good tidings of great joy, because he is born who shall save us.[6] We do not call the Gospel a promise, but we say that the promises are fulfilled through the Gospel, as has been shown. All the promises, as Peter says, have been granted unto us.[7] So much has the word promise pleased them that they define faith also by this same word; and for this they may bring forward a text of Paul: The inheritance is given as a result of faith, *to the end that the promise may be sure.*[8] But where Paul speaks of the

---

[1] Matt. xii, 28; Luke xi, 20.
[2] Matt. iii, 1; iv, 17; x, 7; Luke x, 9.
[3] *Euangelia*, evangel, good news.
[4] Isa. lii, 7.   [5] Isa. lii, 9.   [6] Luke ii, 10, 11.
[7] II. Pet. i, 4.   [8] Rom. iv, 16.

promises made to Abraham, he also speaks of our faith in Christ, through which the promise is fulfilled, even as he also says elsewhere that the promise to Abraham is given to those that believe, as a result of their faith in Christ.[1] Faith in Christ makes the promises sure, when he makes true, and puts into effect, that which was promised to the fathers. For the promise is made sure and established when that is fulfilled which was promised. Even as also the law is established and fulfilled through faith, because faith in Christ renders stable and true that which the law wished to be done, as I shall say more clearly in a tract on circumcision and on the sabbath.[2] For faith in Christ has fulfilled both the sabbath and circumcision, even as also the purifications, justifications, and sanctifications of the law are fulfilled by this faith, as I have said. Moreover, this faith in Christ, and his righteousness, and all the promises founded upon it, and forgiveness of sins, a gentile can obtain, D5b even though he had never heard of these promises. And the promise made to Abraham, which Paul cites as a proof from example,[3] as well as the other promises made in the Scriptures, forms no part of justification. Forgiveness of sins is given on condition of faith in Christ, not of faith in the promises, as the words of Peter make clear.[4] But they wrest the words, and wrongly interpret the chief article of faith. Therefore we limit neither the Gospel, nor the faith which springs from the Gospel, by the words of the promise. We do not call our Gospel a promise, but we say that the Gospel itself was promised.[5] It was promised when the promise was made that this blessing of God, and forgiveness of sins, would be through Christ, and we, together with Peter and Paul, proclaim that this has come.[6] And this is truly to preach the Gospel, as Philip did.[7]

4. This is itself the Gospel of the kingdom of God, because that kingdom, along with the blessing of God and the forgiveness of sins, is conferred upon them that are justified, through the gift of the Spirit. To this kingdom are called none but the

---

[1] Gal. iii, 22.

[2] These tracts were not published, but there is a chapter on Circumcision in the author's *Christianismi Restitutio*.

[3] Rom. iv, 13. [4] Acts x, 43. [5] Rom. i, 2.
[6] Acts iii, 25; xiii, 38. [7] Acts viii, 35.

righteous, those, that is to say, whom Christ justifies by calling them, even as Paul says: *Whom he called, he justified.* And upon this justification there presently follows the kingdom of heaven; for even as God justifies by calling, so he glorifies by justifying, even as Paul says again: *Whom he justified, them he also glorified.*[1] Therefore we that have believed are already justified and glorified. The heavenly city Jerusalem is within us, witnesses the Apostle;[2] else we are no Christians, and the kingdom of God is not in us. It is thus a great thing to reign with Christ, so that we are all kings, and priests. And we truly do reign, because we have been delivered out of the power of darkness, being translated into the heavenly kingdom of Jesus Christ.[3] God has called us into his own kingdom and glory.[4] We have been called into the fellowship of Jesus Christ the Son of God.[5] And we have already become partakers of the glory to come, through the earnest of his Spirit, that the glory of the inheritance of Christ may be great among his saints.[6]

5. Some, however, since they do not perceive what these gifts of Christ and his glory and kingdom are, suppose only that they are merely things in name, even as the sophists settle the whole matter of Christ by certain qualities imparted to him. They have not tasted the power of the resurrection of Christ, nor his birth from above, that they may know what it is to sit with Christ in the heavenly places; human animals, since there is no Spirit in them, they can do nothing but speculate upon qualities. But the anointing teaches something else in those that are reborn and have risen with Christ, who also sit in the kingdom of God as joint-heirs and brethren of Christ.

6. From all this I would have you notice that it is one thing to be justified by faith and to be now in the kingdom of heaven, and it is another thing to hope for a reward of good works in the world to come. This I shall show more at large below, for Scripture also speaks distinctly of these two. Moreover, the gentiles have not obtained this righteousness by faith in Christ. Likewise the righteousness of the law, as I shall show below, was not a result of faith but of good works, approved by the witness

---

[1] Rom. viii, 30. [2] Heb. xii, 22. [3] Col. i, 13.
[4] I. Thes. ii, 12. [5] I. Cor. i, 9. [6] Eph. i, 14.

of conscience alone. They will all have their reward, inasmuch as Christ is to judge them according to what they have done.¹

7. From what has been said above you will also notice the great fallacy of those that reason about the servitude of the will;² and we can easily show here that their proofs are lame in the other foot. For, as I shall presently say, the kingdom of the Jews was a kingdom of the flesh, likewise also the kingdom of the gentiles, which was ours; but Christ's kingdom is a kingdom of the spirit. And the change from flesh to spirit, which is the entrance to Christ's kingdom through knowledge of him and faith in him, since it is bound to be made through the heavenly birth, and we are human animals, is nowise placed in human powers, but must entirely take place when the Father draws, and enlightens, and of his mere grace calls and justifies whom he will; because it is not of him that runneth, nor of him that willeth, but of God that hath mercy.³ But to prove from this the servitude of the will is as if you said, I can not fly, therefore I have no free will. Indeed, that the height of the grace of Christ may be known, there must be some powers in us, feeble though they be in comparison with what Christ has given. And this is the true grace, when with the gift you compare the things which it was impossible for our own powers to acquire. Yet what glory will it be, or what skill will it take, for you to lift this stone? But this error about the servitude of the will, even though it involve profound thought, we shall, please God, explode in another place.⁴ Suffice it now to have said what relates to knowledge of Christ's kingdom, and its excellence. For you must know that there is a certain time, and only one, when Christ calls and draws you, and when from being unrighteous you are made righteous, and when forgiveness of sins, and the kingdom of heaven, and eternal life, are bestowed upon you; for before this you were a sinner, and a child of wrath, and under the dominion of Satan. Moreover, this is the time when you apprehend Christ by faith, and are given the Holy Spirit, by which you are caught up into the heavenly places, and are born from above. You ought to distinguish the times when you were

---

[1] Rom. ii, 14–16.
[2] *Servum arbitrium.*
[3] Rom. ix, 16.
[4] This intention was not carried out.

under Adam, and when under Christ, and how you have borne the body of sin, from which you are now unclothed; for every man, before he is drawn by Christ, is a pagan.

Chapter III. A Comparison of the Law and the Gospel

1. In the law it was the righteousness of works; in the Gospel, the righteousness of faith. In the law, the righteousness of the flesh; in the Gospel, the righteousness of the Spirit. But in order to show this the more clearly, I shall state some distinctions between the law and the Gospel. The greatest difference, and a manifold one, is one on which John touches, saying: The law came through Moses; grace, through Christ.[1] The shadow came through Moses; the truth, through Christ. But what is the law like, and what is grace like? The law of Moses is a law of death, and the strength of sin; but the grace of Christ is pure mercy. And it says χάρις,[2] that is, favor freely given, or a kind of goodwill of one conferring kindnesses, and giving many gifts, and befriending and directing us in every respect. It is grace that makes us free from sin, justifies us freely, pours out the Holy Spirit upon us, bestows the kingdom of heaven on us, etc. Under the law there was never any one in the kingdom of heaven, for the kingdom of God had not yet come, which came to us when Christ came. There was never in them the spirit of υἱοθεσίας,[3] but they had the carnal filiation of sons; but to us was given the Spirit whereby we cry, Abba, Father! This proof is clear from Paul to the Galatians, and the coming of Christ has wrought this; for God sent his Son, that we might receive the adoption of sons.[4] Hence we say that we were delivered from bondage to the law through the coming of Christ. None of them was ever elect, or predestined by that election which God predestined concerning us, namely, that we should receive the adoption of sons, and be brethren of Christ.[5] Yet there are some who interpret predestination in these passages incorrectly, and wrest the meaning of Paul into another than he intended.

---

[1] John i, 17.   [2] *Charis*, grace.   [3] *Huiothesias*, of adoption.
[4] Gal. iv, 4, 5.   [5] Eph. i, 5; Rom. viii, 15.

They are ignorant of the mysteries of Christ's kingdom, and they wrongly make the Jews elect and sharers in this predestination equally with us. They do not well understand what it is that was there predestined, or what the grace is which, given before the world was, we have now acquired. It is certainly the kingdom of God which, according to the dispensation of the fulness of the times, God appointed from the foundation of the world, to be given to all nations, through faith, at the appearance of Christ. Which mystery of predestination, like all the law and all the promises, has now been fulfilled, as Paul proves in the mystery of the calling of the Gentiles, and in the accepted adoption of sons. Christ also says that the time was fulfilled according to the dispensation of this predestination, and hence that the kingdom of God had now drawn near them.[1] Indeed, according to the word of Christ, not one jot, nor one tittle, has passed away until all things have now been done.

2. Again, besides what has been said above, there is the difference that God of old time spoke through the Prophets, but now through his Son.[2] Now he is seen, and before he was not seen. Now the Father is for the first time truly worshiped, for before there was only the shadow of true worship, as I have said in the Dialogues.[3] Worship was formerly carnal and earthly, in groves, high places, images, and tabernacles of wood and houses of stone. But now God is spiritually worshiped in the living Christ alone. Again, he now destroys all sins, to which we were kept exposed by the law. Indeed, in the law no other forgiveness of sins was known than a carnal and earthly one. They did not ask to have their sins forgiven under pretext of eternal damnation, but besought, as from a king, that their transgression be pardoned, lest the anger of the Lord swallow them up, and the carnal vengeance of the law overtake them, as we read that it often overtook rebels and transgressors; though of the punishment of eternal damnation there is no mention. For this carnal expiation, sacrifices were appointed in Leviticus, and the shedding of blood for sin and for transgression, in which there was no true forgiveness of sins, as the Apostle teaches.[4] The Lord never gave them rest of conscience,

---

[1] Mark i, 15. [2] Heb. i, 1, 2. [3] Dial. I, 5. [4] Heb. ix, 9, 10; x, 1, 4.

but under this shadow they always had their hearts veiled. Moreover, the manifestation of Christ brings with itself a great glory of brightness, and of light, and of revelation, as well as rest; and a great part of Christian happiness lies in this, if it has been given to one to be able thoroughly to look into it. Moreover, Paul notices a manifold difference between us and them. First, that the law of Moses was written on tables of stone; while the law of Christ is, according to Jeremiah, a law of the heart,[1] that is, a law of faith, by reason of which, in the very fact that we know Christ, we are all made θεοδιδάκτοι,[2] because, if the Father draw us, we learn Christ. This law need not be written in the outward way, and even had the Apostles written nothing (if knowledge of Christ had nevertheless continued in us), this new law of Christ could have stood, written with an inward ink, which is the power of the Spirit of the living God, who impresses the law on the tables of the heart. Moreover, the Apostle says that that ministration was one of death, by reason of transgression; but this ministration of life is bound by no decrees. Again, that ministration was one of bondage; but this, one of freedom. That ministration was of the letter; this ministration is of the Spirit. Moreover, he compares the glory of the face of Moses with the glory of our spirits; for that glory was on the surface, and in the face, which endured for a time; that is, when the face of Moses shone from the intercourse which he had with God.[3] But ours is a glory of the Spirit, and more complete and enduring, even as the face of Christ, transfigured on the mount, now continually shines forth in heaven; and with it we have a perpetual intercourse, even as Moses had a temporal one. Moreover, the glory there was veiled, while ours is unveiled. And in confirmation of all these things Paul significantly cites that the Lord is the Spirit. Hence the true ministries must be spiritual ministries, even as in the same way Christ proves that the true worship must be in spirit.[4] Again, it follows from the same antecedent that true ministries must be free; for, *Where the Spirit of the Lord is, there is liberty.*[5] From which it is clear enough that this Spirit and glory of his was not

---

[1] Jer. xxxi, 33.   [2] *Theodidaktoi*, taught of God.
[3] II. Cor. iii, 7–11; Ex. xxxiv, 29, 30.   [4] John iv, 24.   [5] II. Cor. iii, 17.

in them, else Paul's proof would have been null. We, therefore, with unveiled face behold and manifest the glory of the Lord,[1] that is, the face of Christ, in the illuminated mirror of the Spirit in ourselves; because our illuminated spirit is itself the mirror in which this glory shines forth. And by the Spirit we are transformed into the same image, that is, into the likeness of the glory of the Lord. For our spirit is transformed through its brightness in like manner as the face of Moses, and as the face of Christ, was transformed. And we are transformed from glory to glory,[1] from the glory of the face to the glory of the Spirit, from glory veiled to glory unveiled, from glory temporal to glory perpetual. You see clearly that any of us, even the least, who is in Christ's kingdom, is greater than Moses, David, and all the others. Moreover, that we surpass them all is gathered all the more from the argument of Christ; for the kingdom of God came to us after John the Baptist, and he that is but little in the kingdom of God is greater than John himself,[2] who was greater than they all. Therefore we, who are greater than John the Baptist, are greater than they all, who were less than he.

E1b

3. Another noteworthy difference, and one which bears on our purpose, is that in the law it was a righteousness of the flesh; while we have a righteousness of the Spirit. All, even the most holy, who were under the law, were carnal. Although the Holy Spirit spoke prophecies through them, although they foresaw the future, yet in their deeds they savored of nothing but the carnal. All were born under a shadow, and their carnal things were a shadow of spiritual ones, as is rendered manifest from the history of David. Paul also proves that they were carnal: *Behold*, he says, *Israel after the flesh.*[3] And most clearly when he says, *What then shall we say that Abraham, our forefather according to the flesh, hath found?*[4] Notice the expression, *according to the flesh*; for the type of spiritual things shines forth from the things that were done in him according to the flesh. Again, notice the carnal priesthood of Aaron, and the carnal commandment.[5] The justifications of the law are justifications

---

[1] II. Cor. iii, 18. [2] Matt. xi, 11.
[3] I. Cor. x, 18. [4] Rom. iv, 1. [5] Heb. vii, 11, 16.

ON THE RIGHTEOUSNESS OF CHRIST'S KINGDOM 243

of the flesh.¹ The law was given to a carnal people, for the spiritual man is not under the law. Again, the rewards which the law promised were all carnal to them, nor are they wont to ask any but carnal ones from God. Likewise the penalties and curses of the law were all carnal and earthy, as appears from Leviticus and Deuteronomy.² Yet some say that the Israelites in Egypt were spiritual, and equal to us in the Lord's Supper; E2a because Paul says that they ate and drank the same spiritual food and drink,³ and so they ate the flesh of Christ, even as also we, since we have eaten nothing but figures of speech. But the history will not suffer us to be deceived, if we do not confound the letter with the spirit. Doubtless they cared more for the flesh-pots of Egypt, and to eat leeks and onions, cucumbers and melons. Christ also makes an infinite difference between those that ate manna and us who eat the flesh of Christ.⁴ Nor is it for you to say that some were spiritual; for Paul speaks of them all, and says that all ate the spiritual food, and drank the spiritual drink. It was spiritual, therefore, on account of a mystery spiritually foreshadowed, both in the bread and in the rock.⁵ Also Christ feared a carnal people, which now feeds on spiritual food, even as they as well as we were saved by the same, although some in one way, and others in another. All the things that happened to them, as Paul says, were by way of a figure;⁶ and in this way there is said to be a certain spiritual identity, corresponding to a consideration of the mystery. It serves as an example if you say that the same spiritual Christ was seen by them in the brazen serpent, just as the same one also was eaten by them in the manna. Moreover, the same one was spiritually slain in Abel from the beginning of the world.⁷ For if you draw an allegory out of the history, whatever is in the law E2b will upon this consideration be called spiritual, even as the son Isaac is called a son after the Spirit,⁸ because he allegorically signified the spiritual Christ. For in himself he was carnal; but Spirit here meant something else, as in the drink and food of the

¹ Heb. ix, 13; Phil. iii, 9.
² Lev. xxvi, 14–39; Deut. xxviii, 15–68.
³ I. Cor. x, 4.   ⁴ John vi, 31–35.   ⁵ Ex. xvii, 6; Num. xx, 11.
⁶ I. Cor. x, 11.   ⁷ Rev. xiii, 8.   ⁸ Gal. iv, 29.

Israelites so we, spiritually considering, say that there is an identity, just as Paul did. They therefore fall into no mean error who confuse the Testaments by making comparisons of this sort; and they lessen the grace of the coming of Christ by making the Jews equal to us. They have not the spirit of Paul so as to know how great are those things which have been given us by Christ.[1] Indeed, if they pay attention, they are treating the Spirit of grace with despite.[2] They have their hearts veiled lest the light and glory of the Gospel shine upon them, so that they wish still to live under the shadow of the law. The fathers *never obtained the true promise, because God had provided some better thing concerning us, that apart from us they should not be made perfect.*[3] Although Abraham saw the day of Christ in the birth of a son that had been promised, namely, Isaac, yet notwithstanding this he was carnal, and asked God for carnal things, and his righteousness was carnal, prefiguring one that was spiritual.[4] These things do not make out that he was less loved of God, because God appointed thus before the time; and however God wills, it is the justification of life, and life itself, to comply with his will. In this faith he lived upon the earth, upon which we now live in heaven, that through him we may apprehend the exceeding grace of Christ toward us.

4. We have said that in the law there was a righteousness of works; which is proved by this alone, that to the Jews was given the law of works, and that works of the law are called justifications. But the reason why they are called justifications is this: that since God is righteous, he can establish nothing except in righteousness; that his judgments, laws, and statutes, and commandments, not only may be just in themselves, but may also make righteous him that follows them. So those statutes are rightly called justifications.[5] They are also often called justifications in Psalm cxix, according to the Vulgate and the Greek translation, and to this manner of speaking the Apostles adhere. And of necessity he walks in accordance with righteousness who does what God commands to be done. Hence it is that, when

E3a

---

[1] I. Cor. ii, 9.   [2] Heb. x, 29.   [3] Heb. xi, 39, 40.   [4] Rom. iv, 2–4.
[5] Luke i, 6; Rom. ii, 26 (Pagn.). Eng. tr., ordinances; cf. note on Rom. vii, 1–4, chapter I, paragraph 1.

the law of works had been given them, it was permitted to them to seek righteousness through works. And God always promises them his favor, if they keep his law, and ceremonies, and judgments. And therefore they are wont to recount their benefits before God, that he may grant their prayers.[1] That this is permitted by the law is expressly held in Deuteronomy xxvi, 5–10. David also often boasts that he has kept the commandments and justifications of the Lord. Yet for us it would be great folly to do this, and ignorance of the benefits of Christ, through whose exceeding favor we have become debtors and servants, so that, whatever we do, we ought to say, *We are unprofitable servants; we have done that which it was our duty to do.*[2] For Christ went before us, claiming us for himself as slaves, that we might be freedmen. So great are the gifts conferred upon us through Christ, apart from works of our own, that it is a great shame if you strive to satisfy him by works, or think that you deserve such things for your works. Christ goes before all our works, himself alone blotting out our sins on his own account.[3] And the force of our justification lies in this: that Christ has betrothed us to himself in righteousness.[4] He has justified us by bearing our iniquities.[5] He has established us in righteousness upon a foundation of rock,[6] that is, upon a justifying faith in Christ, which is the rock. And yet it is not because we work as debtors that we work to no profit; nor will Christ leave such works without reward as vain, but he will give recompense, as we shall say below.[7] Moreover, the righteousness of the law is approved, and it is necessary to confess that works of the law were of profit; else God would have played a rude people false in commanding that things be done in so many ways, and in promising his favor to those that observed them. It would be an empty name to call them justifications of the law, if in works of the law there were no righteousness. Indeed, unless this meant something, Paul's argument would be worthless, and he would have been raising a point about what was not in question.

---

[1] This appears in Neh. ii, 8, 18; Ezra v, 5; Hezekiah's song in Isa. xxxviii, 9–20; II. Kings xx, 2, 3.
[2] Luke xvii, 10.   [3] Isa. xlv, xlviii.   [4] Hos. ii, 19.
[5] Isa. liii, 11.   [6] Isa. liv, 14.   [7] Paragraph 11.

Therefore this ought to be taken for granted, that regard for justification through the law lay in deeds. The words of the law are numberless, and they can be scorned by none, wherein the Lord admonishes them a thousand times to do what is just and right. But what is doing what is just but the righteousness and justification of the law? Likewise, what is doing judgment and justice, of which one reads here and there in the law, but the righteousness and justification of the law? What is it that Moses commands to give as a pledge, that you may keep your righteousness in the sight of God?[1] Who can deny that Zacharias and Elizabeth are called just because they walked in all the justifications of the law?[2] Consider only this, why they are called justifications. Why did Christ say, To fulfil all righteousness?[3] Why does he call it righteousness, if there was no righteousness in deeds? Likewise he says, John came in the way of righteousness,[4] that is, observing the law. We can also show from single events that the righteousness of the law consisted in deeds; for Phinehas was justified by piercing through the fornicators; yet it was a righteousness of the flesh, so that it was the covenant of a priesthood to him and to his seed.[5] The deed of the Rechabites was of profit to a like carnal righteousness; and that this deed was righteousness the Divine righteousness declares, which presently gave them recompense, as it did to Phinehas.[6] Yet in this deed of the Rechabites some pretend to find a kind of faith, in which they had dreamed of forgiveness of sins, as though the witness of their consciences were not then sufficient, which prescribes that they should be obedient to their parents, as the answer of the Rechabites itself very clearly proves. Again, in addition to what has been said before, it is said of many kings that they did what was right in the sight of the Lord; for what else is this but righteousness? And you may say in general that every deed of this sort which you find in the law, as James makes clear,[7] is righteousness. Just as the deed of Rahab in receiving the spies was righteousness, so the fast of

---

[1] Deut. xxiv, 6, 10, 12, 17.
[2] Luke i, 6.
[3] Matt. iii. 15.
[4] Matt. xxi, 32.
[5] Num. xxxv, 7, 8; Ps. cvi, 30.
[6] Jer. xxxv, 1-10, 18, 19.
[7] James ii, 21-25.

the Ninevites was righteousness, entertaining the angels was righteousness, Daniel's abstinence from wine and polluted food was righteousness, etc.[1] Also the alms which Daniel prescribed to Nebuchadnezzar [2] were righteousness; indeed, the Hebrew text expressly calls them acts of righteousness. Nor is it any objection if you say that they all had faith also; for we are explaining the force of the law, whose righteousness was not of faith but, besides deeds, had regard to the commandment, and was a righteousness of the commandment. Although they all had faith, yet it was necessary for them to perform all those statutes in order to be justified; but for us, on the contrary. Nor was there ordained for them a certain faith, by which alone they might be justified; but for us, on the contrary, because Christ has been proclaimed to us, who has preached the justifying article of faith. We have no works of the law by necessity of salvation, for only the preaching of Christ and faith in him gives us those things which works of the law ought to have given, and far more; for only by faith in Jesus Christ is eternal life given us, and through his grace alone are our sins taken away. Yet the sophists here object, and do not wish Christ to be so liberal, but limit his grace in a certain way, so that they overturn the foundation of our salvation. But we do not concern ourselves about their nonsense, for it would be a ridiculous thing to say that Christ is the Savior of the world, and that through him the sins of the world are taken away, because he has given us a certain quality which they call the first grace. Alas for them! that with their fictions, and their envelopes of qualities, they have rejected Christ and his passion by robbing him of his gifts. For through the grace of Jesus Christ there was no quality given to us which needed their impostures with regard to salvation, but the whole gift was given, which is eternal life.[3]

5. Hear, I pray, and understand, all of you that suppose you are Christians. See whether in the days of an age there has been shown such grace that eternal life is given you on this sole

---

[1] Josh ii, 1–14; vi, 22, 23; Jonah iii, 5–10; Gen. xviii, 1–8; Dan. i, 8–16.
[2] Dan. iv, 24 (Vulg.), (27, Eng. tr.).
[3] Rom. vi, 23.

condition, that you believe that this Jesus is the Christ, the Son of God, the Savior of the world.[1] Consider whether this grace is a quality. You see wherein you surpass Jews or Gentiles; for they that live well have also some hope of their own salvation. But with you it is not so, if you have learned Christ. Yet it is as certain that you will have to be saved in this faith as it is that he is a Savior who saves freely. Again, I beg you, observe this conclusion, because this is the sum of Christian doctrine, without which I have always said, and shall say, that you are not Christians, but a kind of pagans, who echo nothing but Christ's name.

6. Again, in addition to what has been said, it is proved from the Psalms of David and other prophets that the righteousness of the law was a righteousness of works, as for example: *He that worketh righteousness*; *My righteousness, the cleanness of my hands*; *The ordinances of the Lord are righteous, and in keeping them there is great reward*; *The eyes of the Lord are upon the righteous, that depart from evil and do good*; and he calls him righteous that worketh righteousness; and, *Blessed are they that do righteousness at all times*; and, *He hath dispersed, he hath given to the needy, and his righteousness endureth forever*.[2] And so of many other places where mention is made of doing righteousness. And the word righteousness is connected with works, as you have it at very great length in Psalm cxix. Moreover, in other Psalms David finds fault with the righteousness of the Lord, desiring Christ, when he sees that the righteousness of our works is insufficient. Likewise in Isaiah you will find that righteousness is the result of deeds.[3] And most clearly of all you have it in Ezekiel xviii, where he is discussing the subject of justification, showing that to do well, and to perform the commands and judgments of God, is to do righteousness. Just this the whole law teaches, if you read the Pentateuch. From these things it appears that Scripture does not call only Levitical ceremonies justifications of the law and works of the law, as some wicked interpreters of Paul hold; but all the things that the law com-

---

[1] John iii, 36; v, 24; vi, 40, 47.
[2] Ps. xv, 2; xviii, 20; xix, 9, 11; xxxiv, 15, 14; cvi, 3; cxii, 9; I. John iii, 7.
[3] Isa. iii, 10; v, 7; xxvi, 2; xxxii, 17; lviii, 6–8; lxiv, 5.

mands to be done are works of the law, which is said of other works more particularly than of ceremonies, as appears from Ezekiel xviii, Psalm xv, and Isaiah lviii and lix. For Paul has regard to works of the law in which the righteousness of the law consisted, when he speaks of justification; and, excluding all else, he wishes us to be justified by faith in Christ. But they understand neither the law nor Christ. Their adversaries also understand neither; for they do such violence to Paul that they will not credit deeds of the law with righteousness. But we shall presently prove from Paul himself, of whom they boast, that according to the law righteousness and justification consisted in deeds. This he evidently takes for granted in Romans ii, where he even calls works of the law righteousness and justifications, and then sets forth his argument in the following manner.

7. By this kind of works of the law and justifications many seemed to be righteous in the sight of men, who yet were sinful in the sight of God. Accordingly Christ said to the hypocrites and Pharisees, *Ye justify yourselves in the sight of men; but God knoweth your hearts.*[1] And from these and like words of Christ is to be gathered the argument of Paul, so that we learn to weigh the words of Christ, and understand that Paul, as a true disciple, follows the steps of his Master. For, like Christ, Paul said in the first place that men are not rightly justified in the sight of God by works of the law, although it often seems so in the sight of men.[2] Again, and in the second place, Paul imitates Christ in another way in the same passage; for just as Christ argues with the Jews about breaking the law,[3] so Paul said that men are not justified by the law on account of transgression; for to what he had said he added the cause, and reason, and limitation, saying that they could not have been justified through the law, because through the law came knowledge of sin. In the same way he says in the same passage that there is none righteous, but that they have all turned aside.[4] This reason, and the hindrance of transgression of the law, he confirms, saying that they could not have been justified, for the reason

[1] Luke xvi, 15.
[2] Rom. iii, 20.
[3] John vii, 19–23.
[4] Rom. iii, 20, 9, 12.

that every one is cursed who has not continued in all the things that are written.¹

8. From this reasoning we can infer that men can not be justified under the monastic laws, just as they could not be even under the law of God, but are cursed. For it is a most pernicious thing to accept the decrees of the Pope, and the monastic laws, as if they necessarily bound us to salvation, and to put oneself under oath to keep them. In the first place, because their need of salvation would prove that Christ's salvation is defective if it does not suffice without them. In the second place, because the freedom from the bond of the law made through Christ is there brought back into bondage to the law. In the third place, because the laws make us guilty of transgression; for by the law guilt is increased by transgression.² God wished to do away with the divine laws by this kind of transgression;³ and we, building up again the things which we had destroyed, make ourselves transgressors.⁴ Indeed, what is worse, we build up human laws in place of divine. The laws of Moses, even if they were Divine, even had they the power of justifying, have been done away; but we endure human laws, which neither save nor justify, but lead to more sinning. Let the law of our members suffice us for sinning, that there may be no need of other laws to multiply sins. I can not wonder enough (to come back to my subject), when I hear that from the vows and the Nazariteship of the law they force upon us similar vows; for if this is true it follows that they are still under the law. We shall show elsewhere that there is for Christians one vow, in which all vows of the law are fulfilled, and that all the Nazariteships of the law are fulfilled in all Christians in a single act through Christ. For just as all the offerings of the law are summed up in a single act of offering in the passion of Jesus Christ, so by that single act of his passion we are all sanctified, made Nazarites, and consecrated to God, through the great sacrament in baptism, in which the sufferings of Christ are represented in our bodies, and in which we have died with Christ, and have been buried together with him, and have risen with him, having become lords of heavenly things, so that

---

¹ Gal. iii, 10.   ² Rom. v, 20.   ³ Jer. xxxi, 31–34.   ⁴ Gal. ii, 18.

nothing from those earthly ceremonies and decrees pertains to us.¹ God will sometime give them understanding, that they may understand the mysteries of Christ and the power of faith in him, which alone will make their consciences free from these miserable superstitions and bands. Then they will bitterly weep at so many relapses of Christianity into Judaism, all for the most part born of not knowing how to distinguish between the law and the Gospel. I should like you to know and to turn over often in your mind that the acts of the law in no wise refer to us literally, but through a great and spiritual mystery, fulfilled in us through Christ, as [my tract on] circumcision ² will show. But the monks suppose that they must judaize quite as literally, deceived, perhaps, by the fact that the Apostles sometimes imitated the law, as appears from the vow and the shaving of the head in the Acts.³ In the same way the example of John the Baptist deceived them, because they did not notice that he was under the law, and had not been born again by the baptism of Christ. Of this we shall say more when the monks have ears to hear, and when they have gone through the epistle to the Colossians. I have wished only to have these things said, that they may learn to compare the law with the Gospel, and to distinguish Christ from Moses.

^{margin:} The vows and sabbaths of the law concern us no more than circumcision.

9. Let us now return to the argument of Paul which, to complete his proof, expressly made mention of the flesh, saying, *By the works of the law shall no flesh be justified in the sight of God*;⁴ where he clearly shows that it was no fault of the law that we were not justified through it, but that of our own flesh. For the law of God is spiritual, and has in itself the power of justifying by the sole fact that it was the will of God; but the flesh lusteth against the Spirit. And this rebellion of the flesh which causes transgression Paul follows out and expresses in the same epistle ⁵ as the greatest hindrance to justification under the law. Whence, on account of the weakness of our flesh, he concludes that we need another way of being justified; and this proof you will

E7b

---

¹ Col. ii, 12; iii, 1.
² This tract was not published as here contemplated, though a chapter on this subject is contained in the author's *Christianismi Restitutio* of a later period.
³ Acts xviii, 18; xxi, 24.   ⁴ Rom. iii, 20.   ⁵ Rom. vii, 18–viii, 8.

gather from David in Psalm liii. The law could not furnish justification, not because it had in itself no power of justifying; but it was by reason of our infirmity that we could not obtain it, as it says in the beginning of chapter viii.[1] And he does not say that the righteousness of the law was void, but that he that has done these things shall live thereby, according to the word of the Lord.[2] And it is proved that there is life in the deeds of the law.[3] And the living which the law promised was not founded upon some article of faith, but upon deeds; as Paul says, that the law is not of faith, but that they should live through their deeds.[4]

10. From what has been said above it appears, in the first place, that there was in the law no justification of the spirit, nor was there any true justification, just as there was also no true forgiveness of sins, although for a time it was given them for salvation, that they might live under the shadow. It appears in the second place that it was not easy to acquire justification such as was under the law; indeed, for the flesh it was impossible, since, if God enters into judgment with us, there is no man living who has obtained righteousness by keeping all the commandments of the law.[5] Hence, in order to show the righteousness of Christ, all men are shut up under sin, that the righteousness of Christ, justifying them freely, might dawn upon them.[6]

11. That the justification of the law has regard to deeds, we have said[7] would also have to be proved from Paul himself. Paul proves this, moreover, in Romans; for, when about to come to the righteousness of Christ, he first examines the righteousness of the law, and compares it with the Gentiles, so that at length, when both have been condemned, he may proclaim that the grace of Christ has been conferred through faith. He clearly teaches that the righteousness of the law is of deeds; indeed, he notices all the justifications of the law as pure deeds. Yet by the fact that he says that the doers of the law will have

---

[1] Rom. viii, 3.
[2] Rom. x, 5; Lev. xviii, 5.
[3] Deut. iv, 1; v, 33; Ezra ix, 12; Ezek. xx, 11, 13, 20.
[4] Gal. iii, 12.
[5] Ps. cxliii, 2.
[6] Rom. xi, 32; Gal. iii, 22.
[7] Paragraph 4.

ON THE RIGHTEOUSNESS OF CHRIST'S KINGDOM 253

to be justified, the monks are deceived, and many others with them, who will not admit to us that Christ alone can justify us through faith, because Paul says that works of the law justify. They do not see that Paul is aiming his discourse at the Jews, and is explaining the state of the law; otherwise they would also prove that we ought to be circumcized because Paul says that circumcision profiteth.[1] I have already said that for an ordinary being they ascribe great titles to Christ, as that he is said to save us, and to take away our sins, and to give us eternal life. The Lutherans also, who do not enough distinguish the law from the Gospel, explain: Doers of the law will be justified, that is, will be declared righteous. Let this mockery and this ignorance of the mind of Paul pass, if it can, with them; but what would they say to the passage in Galatians where Paul says that in the law there is no righteousness of faith, but a righteousness of deeds?[2] What justifying faith, I inquire, do they imagine here? But let us leave them with their opponents, both walking in their own darkness, and let us follow out the views of Paul. *The doers of the law*, he says, *will be made righteous*,[3] and, *Those will be justified who have observed the righteousness of the law*.[4] And, *Circumcision profiteth if thou observed the law;* and, *They know the righteousness of God*, namely, *that they that practise such things;* and, Those that do evil things obey unrighteousness; *To those that work good shall be glory, honor, and peace; God will render to every man according to his works*, that is, *to those who persevere in well-doing, eternal life*. Indeed, he says that by good deeds glory, honor, and immortality are sought. Again, that these good deeds or evil deeds, since their rule is defined by the law of nature, will profit or injure both Jew and Greek.[5] Moreover, it belongs to the law of nature to do that which is according to conscience, and is good in the common opinion of all men, so that you will not do to another what you do not wish for yourself. It follows from this as a consequence that these good works, since they are naturally good, profit both Jew and Greek, and will be of some profit even to us who have been justified. Hence Paul charges that

---

[1] Rom. ii, 25. [2] Gal. iii, 12. [3] Rom. ii, 13.
[4] Rom. x, 5. [5] Rom. ii, 25; i, 32; ii, 6–10.

they who have believed God take the lead in good works, that he might purify unto himself a people for his own possession, zealous of good works.[1] From this you may gather that we have been purified, consecrated to Christ, and justified without works; but that this justification leads again to this, that we should give ourselves all to good works, and walk in them.[2] Notice, and you will see, how great a mistake it is to make out that good works, commended in so many ways, are unprofitable.

Chapter IV. On Love

1. It now remains for us to speak of love, and for the highest praise of it we might be content with this one saying of Paul: The greatest of all is love.[3] But let us speak of it more fully, that no one may praise it to us by its title alone; for it can not be called greatest without having very great properties.

This is to be noted first: that the title of perfection is always ascribed to love, thus: *Love is the fulfilling of the law.*[4] And in this word the whole law is briefly comprised, even as Christ also said that the whole law consists in love;[5] for he that loves does not steal, does not kill, etc. Again, other good works, which Paul in the same passage calls the armor of light,[6] are born of love; and by these we also put on Christ, as Paul witnesses in the same passage.[7] This is the wedding garment which any one must always have on who has entered the marriage feast through faith in Christ.[8] This is the oil which those must always have in their lamps who through faith have lighted the lamps in the kingdom of heaven.[9] This is the fiery law in the right hand of God;[10] for unless thy heart be inflamed with this fire there will be in thy right hand no power of doing anything well. Moreover, Paul calls it the excellent way of love,[11] and in the whole chapter following he proclaims it greater than all things else. Love edifies, love abides, love is long-suffering, is kind, beareth and endureth all things, etc. Moreover, Scripture

---

[1] Tit. iii, 8; ii, 14. [2] Eph. ii, 10; Heb. x, 24.
[3] I. Cor. xiii, 13. [4] *Perfectio legis*, Rom. xiii, 10.
[5] Matt. xxii, 40. [6] Rom. xiii, 12 [7] Rom. xiii, 14.
[8] Matt. xxii, 11. [9] Matt. xxv, 4. [10] Deut. xxxiii, 2. [11] I. Cor. xii, 31.

ON THE RIGHTEOUSNESS OF CHRIST'S KINGDOM 255

never ascribes such effects either to faith or to other virtues.
F1b Besides, he teaches in one word the fulfilling of the law in love.[1] And, If, with your roots laid in love, you are strong to know the love of Christ which passeth knowledge, you will be filled unto all the fulness of God.[2] And, The body of Christ makes in us the increase through love.[3] Again, above all things he commends *love, which is the bond of perfectness.*[4] And, *The end of the charge is love out of a pure heart;*[5] and James calls it the royal law,[6] which is fulfilled by love. And Peter earnestly charges them above all things to have love, which covereth a multitude of sins.[7] Finally, John concludes that there are two commands of Christ: first, *that we should believe in the name of Jesus Christ the Son of God;* second, that we should love one another,[8] for, He that hath not love hath not God; for God is love.[9]

2. But that you may the more fully understand the meaning of faith and love, notice in the first place the death of Adam, in which you were involved, knowledge of whose death you ought to have that you might the more fully understand the meaning of justification; for it was for this reason that Paul in his epistle to the Romans brought this death into his treatise on justification.[10] Knowledge of this matter would be in the highest degree necessary, but yet it is wrongly understood by our age, as I shall show in a treatise on original sin.[11] In the second place, notice that the justifications of the law were unable to make you free from this death; indeed, sin abounded on account of the transgression.[12] In the third place, notice that you, through the righteousness of faith in Christ, not only have been made free from the death of Adam, and from the unrighteousness of the
F2a law, but also have obtained other excellent gifts of the Spirit, and the heavenly kingdom, and eternal life. Moreover, that you may duly enjoy this grace through faith in Christ, you ought first of all to hear Christ, and to devote yourself wholly to him by penitence, denying yourself, and reposing all the con-

[1] Gal. v, 14.   [2] Eph. iii, 17–19.   [3] Eph. iv, 16.
[4] Col. iii, 14.   [5] I. Tim. i, 5.   [6] James ii, 8.
[7] I. Pet. iv, 8.   [8] I. John iii, 23.   [9] I. John iv, 8.
[10] Rom. v, 12.   [11] Never written.   [12] Rom. v, 20.

fidence of your life in the fact that he has paid the price of your redemption with his own blood, and that by his mercy and grace alone, without any merits of your own, your sins have been pardoned and your life restored; for before this you were dead in Adam. This sense of life ought first to be acquired in you, and when you have smelt this delight of grace you will know that the kingdom of God has come, so that you have been justified. For only faith in Christ quickens, justifies, saves, and redeems. It quickens from death, it justifies from sin, it saves from weakness and damnation, it redeems from captivity. Adam made us captives, and Christ redeemed us from that captivity through faith alone. Adam killed us, and Christ made us alive through faith alone. Adam made us sinners, and Christ justified us from sin through faith alone. Adam cast us down into hell, and Christ raised us into heaven through faith alone. Likewise the law held us as slaves under the yoke, and Christ made us free. The law accuses us, and Christ is propitious to us. By the law sin is increased on account of transgression; but Christ has both destroyed the sin and taken away the occasion of transgression. Finally, Christ, through faith alone, has freed us from all the curse of Adam, and of the law, and of death; and along with this has given us heavenly gifts, and eternal life, through his grace alone, without works of our own. I always say that without the gift of the Holy Spirit, and without knowledge of Adam and the law, no one can understand what a redemption has been made through Christ; nor without these is any one able to know that he has been justified, and that he has become a citizen of the heavenly Jerusalem, all of which things faith in Christ has conferred by justifying us. And not only was grace conferred, when we believed, but only through faith in Christ is every righteous man kept in this grace, who lives by faith; and through this faith alone eternal life has been fully given, and we are kept always in sure hope of this faith only by our faith in Christ.

3. But all this deprives neither love nor works of their reward. Notwithstanding these, nay, with their aid, works of love have consideration with respect to the glory to be revealed in the world to come. Indeed, in building up the body of Christ

ON THE RIGHTEOUSNESS OF CHRIST'S KINGDOM 257

in us love has the highest efficiency; for just as we through the loving offices of one member to another are more and more built up into one body, so the body of Christ more and more maketh increase in us through the same love.[1] Nor is this effect of love merely temporal, but it avails for treasuring up a reward of eternal glory. The words of Christ in this matter are so plain that one must wonder at those who will not acknowledge this fruit and reward of love and good works. We would follow the usage of Scripture, especially the teaching of the words of Christ, saying in the first place that to those that believe on the Son of God eternal life is freely given, both apart from any F3a work, and by his grace alone.[2] In the second place, we say that in that life we treasure up the reward of glory through love and through all good works.[3] Indeed, giving a cup of cold water has its reward.[4] We ought therefore to beware of those who would make us so idle as to neglect this regard for reward; for very great destruction of souls lies hidden under this outward show of piety. Indeed, he is no Christian who does not with all his might obtain and treasure up this reward for himself. And we shall be most unprofitable servants if, when a talent is given us, we gain no other talents. But we gain the other talents on the foundation of faith, through works of love, through prayers, and alms, and fasting, etc. Nor can any one accuse us, because their consciences will always be uncertain of their own salvation, and they will never be without fear, if salvation comes through works of our own, for we never work as much as we ought. For we say that salvation is made sure only by faith in Christ; and only through faith in Christ is access to eternal life open to us; nor is there now the fear which there was under the law, about keeping the commandments.[5] Faith in Christ procures peace for our consciences, nor is there any fear in those that do not reject the grace that is offered through Christ. So certain and devoid of fear should be our trust in Christ the Savior, that whoever is not certainly persuaded by faith in Christ that he shall have eternal life is in danger of damnation. F3b Nor can one otherwise believe that he is a Savior who has freely

[1] Eph. iv, 16.
[2] John iii, 16; vi, 40; xvii, 3.
[3] Matt. v, 12; vi, 20; xxv, 34–36.
[4] Matt. x, 42.
[5] Heb. ii, 15.

taken away our sins. Moreover, it is no contradiction that to us that have been given eternal life through grace and faith the reward of glory is increased by works of love; but Christ wished to leave us this that we might trade in the meantime, even as he gave command that we must do, else we live in the world in vain. If the meaning of love were known to all, some would not marvel that Christ said that many sins were forgiven to the woman because she loved much.[1] For, although this is a property of faith, even as Christ also said in the same connection that her faith had saved her, yet he that loves Christ is more than he that believes. And when love is added to faith, or some good work, sins are much more emphatically forgiven, and the reward of glory is prepared for him that loves more than for him that does not so love of his own accord; and it could even then be said, Because thou hast done this, thy sins are forgiven, as James argues from Genesis xxii.[2] For God bears such witness to good works that the angel says that the alms and prayers of Cornelius have gone up in the sight of God.[3] For the grace of God does not detract from works, inasmuch as it has been given without works; nor would Christ have our works be of none effect on account of the gifts that he has freely given us, for in the sight of God account is to be taken of them either for good or for evil, else were God an unjust judge, punishing for evil deeds and giving no reward for good ones. This reasoning by contrast our adversaries do not perceive, or they do not believe that any one will suffer punishment for his evil deeds, nor believe that each one is to be judged according to his deeds.

Judgment will be in proportion not to faith but to deeds, for faith alone is the prerogative of salvation.

4. It would not be expedient here to inquire further into the causes of works, but rather to express them by deeds, because after all many seem to me to philosophize wrongly. Moreover, I wish to bring forward my own philosophy. I judge that there is a proper and spontaneous cause of works, even apart from any faith and love whatsoever. There is a movement of the Spirit which breaks out freely into works, apart from any willing or inward quality; for the outward act is governed by the movement of the heart alone which sends its spirits to the mem- F4a

---

[1] Luke vii, 47.   [2] James ii, 21; cf. Gen. xxii, 9, 10, 12, 16–18.
[3] Acts x, 31.

bers. And this movement, or spontaneous pursuit, is superior to any action of the will. Moreover, Holy Scripture has a wise regard for works, and distinctly commends them, and makes separate commands about not stealing and not coveting the things of another, because there is here a new sin. Those also that have reasoned more wisely have learned by experience that a happier state results from works agreeable to virtue, and that by these the character is made good, and that by these a good habit is produced, and that the inward character is tested by difficult acts, and that good works bring with themselves a good action of the heart. Beside all the desires and habits of the Stoics, and beside all the Platonic ideas of perfect actions, one ought to add a new effort in working, for I wish and know many things, but do few. Once more, beyond all that has been said before, Aristotle knows that the labor itself remains; and he rightly makes it as the ultimate end beyond the others, which also presupposes the others, lest careless men boast to us of their happiness. For indeed it appears that according to the rule of Christ we may know them by their fruits;[1] because they do not offer that which they say ought forcibly to arise from their faith, but they produce idle men, who are content with the mere fact that they say they have a good conscience with God, so that also with that excuse they permit themselves certain vices without fear of punishment. There are also others doubly idle, who do nothing good, who say that they have wills that are in bondage, and can do nothing unless grace be given them, for whose presence they would look in every act, else every good work would be a sin. But they are wretched, and are driven out of their normal minds; for the grace of God, after it has once been conferred, never deserts one who abides in faith in Christ. They manifestly speak falsely, and imply a contradiction, when they boast of having faith, and say they can do nothing, for *all things are possible to him that believeth,*[2] and *I can do all things through him that strengtheneth me,*[3] etc.

5. It will perhaps seem odious to compare faith and love with each other, since indeed, as they say, any comparison is odious. Yet Paul made a comparison between them, showing that for

---

[1] Matt. vii, 20. [2] Mark ix, 23. [3] Phil. iv, 13.

certain reasons love is called the greatest. Also, although faith and love have inseparable brotherhood, yet they can be compared with each other, so that we may show what is proper to each; for there are various treatments of these virtues in the Scriptures. No one in this matter can deny that faith is first, and hence it is said that it works through love,[1] because a man, though dead, is made alive through faith, and receives strength to work, the Spirit making that faith alive, and the love being born through which faith has its efficiency. Faith is the greater, because through it we have the grace of Christ, and with this grace nothing can be compared. Faith is the greater because it is the *hypostasis*, or foundation, of eternal salvation. Yet because the excellence of faith does not belong to faith but to the grace of God, it will be no contradiction if we say again that love is the greatest. Although the prime and permanent foundation ought to be in faith, yet if you come down to special acts you will find that love is the greater, because the breadth of love is far greater, and the exercizes of love are more, and its acts are difficult, having great recompense of reward. A difficult virtue is poverty, which arises from love. Let this be the first reason why I call love the greatest; because those things which are demanded of us, being given through faith in Christ by the grace of justification, lie especially in love and will bear greatest fruit. A second reason for its being different, and greater, is that love does not fail as faith does.[2] Love naturally harmonizes with the kingdom to come, where there will be nothing but love. A third reason of difference is that faith is shown toward God; but love, toward God and one's neighbor, that is, toward the head and the members. For the body of Christ is built up in us through love, through the services of one member toward another. But perhaps you call faith every act which has regard to God, always concealing love under that name. You do not fully know Christ so as to love him; for if you acknowledge him as head, you will love him and all his members, and since you are a member you will love the other members equally with yourself, since without the others you can not be a member.

---

[1] Gal. v, 6. [2] I. Cor. xiii, 8.

Other reasons for which love is declared to be greater Paul states in I. Corinthians xiii, drawing them from its very many very great and unique qualities. Certain other properties also of the excellence of love I shall state in what follows. For the present, keep this subject in mind.

6. Faith is the door, love is the perfecting. Or, to say it in another way, faith is the door of Christ's kingdom, eternal life is the end aimed at, love is the whole way between. This order is proved from the deeds of Christ, from whom, as from a true master, you will learn all truth. For he, when about to preach the kingdom of God, always called us by faith; but afterwards, on his last day, he gave the command of love, wonderfully recommending its power.[1] Christ is then in us when we love him with affection; then he reveals himself to us and makes his abode in us.[2] Faith was established in the first place for new beginners, that afterwards they may love Christ more and more, and even their faith may be strengthened. And so Christ at first instructed his pupils in faith, by promises and miracles. Nor was Peter's love required from the beginning, because it was not yet in him although he had already believed. But afterwards love was found in him, that is, in the perfected man. Then was his faith made perfect, for it is made perfect through love. Then he might truly have said, I will lay down my life for thee. Nay more (so great is the difficulty of true love), Peter's love was thrice demanded, that no one may believe that he truly loves unless he has been several times tested; for Christ then asked, *Lovest thou me? Lovest thou me more than these?*[3] and, *Leave all, and follow me.*[4] You see here two proofs showing that love is last: the last command of Christ, and the last love of Peter. Do you see how Scripture rightly calls faith the door, and attributes to love the qualities of perfection? This is another reason especially arguing the perfection of love, that it requires greater knowledge of Christ to love him than to believe him. For, like Peter, you love him later, namely, when you have long accompanied with him. Love and affection for

---
[1] John xiii, 34, 35; xiv, 21, 23, 24; xv, 9, 10, 12, 13.
[2] John xiv, 23.   [3] John xxi, 15–17.
[4] Matt. xix, 27; Mark x, 28; Luke v, 11.

Christ then grow when the excellence and goodness of the thing have been experienced. Also, in addition to what has been said before, one may find traces of the teaching of Christ in his faithful disciple Paul; for just as Christ kept the order of faith and love in his teaching, so Paul, keeping this order in his epistles, always begins them with faith, and finally closes them in love. Which first appears in the epistle to the Romans, where he wishes them, after having made progress in faith, to be made perfect in love, and turns to love.[1] He does the same thing in I. Corinthians xiii, and in other epistles.[2]

7. From this order we discover how faith leads to love, and opens the way for works of love, and works through love. Because through faith the hindrance of sin is taken away, which prevented from acting righteously. Through faith we receive the sense of the life in which we live unto Christ. Through faith a door is opened without entering which one can not labor in the Lord's field. Through faith, beside all these things, the Spirit is given, enlightening us, and inflaming us with love, so that we then overflow on all sides with good works. Through faith the Lord our God circumcizes our hearts, that we may afterwards truly love him.[3] Through faith the tree is made good, that it may bear good fruit. And yet other things without number, all of which only faith in Christ confers upon us.

F6b

8. Yet some suddenly turn all these marks of faith around into love, and say that they all cling to Christ with true faith, and depend wholly upon him. But we reply that this can be done neither through faith without love, nor through love without faith. Indeed, they are rather effects of love, and arise immediately out of affection. For if I love something intensely, I am wholly attached to it, and depend on it, and it leads me whither it will. For it is a property of love to open your compassions to one whom you love, and for all your will to be fixed on him, and that all that is his be pleasing to you. You do not see Christ, who shows himself to you such that you may love him as a friend and brother, and your propitiator in all things, who so loves you that he is glad to have undergone death for

---

[1] Rom. xiii, 8–10. [2] II. Cor. vi, 6; Gal. v, 6, 13, 22; Eph. iv, 2, 15, 16.
[3] Deut. xxx, 6.

you. Christ is the precious pearl which, when the Gospel is preached, you find through faith; and then leaving all you follow him, and love him more than father, and mother, and wife, and riches. Do you see how you always begin with faith, and are made perfect in love? You begin with faith, that then you may love Christ, and cling to him, as you have said; for he that loves Christ is in him as the branch in the vine. The state of love is a kind of new kingdom, and, as Paul says, a kind of excellent way. There your heart grown soft spreads you out wholly for the service of others, so that for any reason whatever concerning one of these little ones you go, and return, and wholly wear yourself out, and are not alarmed by any difficulty. There we know the body of Christ, where we prove the working of the edification of the members through the offices of love. Out of love Paul was willing to spend and be spent for our advantage,[1] and out of loving affection to impart his own soul.[2] Nor is believing such an act of the will as loving is; and it was through miracles that Christ first induced men to believe. Force of reasoning and miracle often compel us to believe, because what is recognized as truth must needs be believed; but nothing can be loved thus under compulsion, nor by one who pursues it with hate. And from this I gather another reason why I say that love is greatest, and attribute excellence to it more than to faith: because it is more spontaneous, and brings the whole will of man in its train. This it is that keeps and fills and perfects us in the compassion of Jesus Christ. Faith, moreover, if you simply and purely consider its character and nature, does not spread itself abroad so widely as love. And faith in Christ affects us in another way, the way of the things connected with it; that is, because through it Christ makes us alive, and gives us the Spirit which makes it alive. Christ considers this faith acceptable, and through it justifies us freely, and forgives us other things which he could also have forgiven through some other act; because it is not the nature of faith but the grace of Christ that accomplishes our justification. Christ justifies them that believe of his mercy alone, and not for the excellency of their faith. But although Luther was able to attain such a height of faith

[1] II. Cor. xii, 15.   [2] I. Thes. ii, 8.

that he never feared when placed in any danger, and overcame all the powers of hell and death and Satan, and by virtue of this ruled over the powers of earth and heaven with such effect that he made the angels of heaven descend to minister to him when abandoned in any solitude (which I doubt not can be done, for hell can not prevail against them that believe, even as it also could not against Christ, so long as they have become partakers of Christ's kingdom and his power; and they themselves also will do all that Christ did, if they have faith in him), still it will never follow from this that acts of love and good works do not have their own reward in whatever way he thinks they ought to proceed from such faith.

9. These are the things that occur to me with regard to the present article, in which I do not in all points agree, nor disagree, with either the one party or the other. All seem to me to have some truth and some error, and every one perceives the other's error and no one sees his own. May God in his mercy cause us to realize our mistakes, and that without clinging to them. Yet it would be easy to decide all points if all were permitted to speak quietly in the church, so that all might be eager to prophesy, and (because the spirits of the former prophets were made subject to the prophets that followed) that when they spoke, if anything were revealed to them, the former ones might keep silence in accordance with the command of Paul. But our party are now struggling for honor. May the Lord destroy all tyrants of the Church. Amen.

THE END

www.ingramcontent.com/pod-product-compliance
Lightning Source LLC
Chambersburg PA
CBHW070234230426
43664CB00014B/2303